THE ROME-BERLIN AXIS

ELIZABETH WISKEMANN

THE
ROME–BERLIN
AXIS

A STUDY OF THE RELATIONS
BETWEEN HITLER AND
MUSSOLINI

COLLINS
ST JAMES'S PLACE, LONDON
1966

First published in 1949 by the Oxford University Press

TO BILL DEAKIN—A TRIBUTE

CONTENTS

CONTENTS

ILLUSTRATIONS

FOREWORD

Some eighteen years ago I plunged rashly into print on the subject of the Rome-Berlin Axis: I was anxious, not quite mistakenly, to write something while the smell of the period was still in my nostrils. This led to certain crudities as well as a few errors in my text. At that time a proportionately greater amount of direct Italian evidence was available to me, but now I have been able to balance this by the use of more German sources. A good deal more material is now accessible and the perspective is longer. The plot of the drama emerges as very much what one had originally supposed, but the décor needs to be modified: above all the bibliography requires extension.

I am anxious to emphasize that a study within these dimensions of a relationship of this kind—the preliminaries from 1922 to 1934 and the intensification from the time of the first meeting to the end—makes no claim to compete with detailed work on the scale of Mr. Deakin's *The Brutal Friendship*. I have only tried to marry a reasonably scholarly approach with a survey of the twenty-three years of this strange relationship.

I am aware of the risk I have run in attempting to make statements about the thoughts of two hysterics such as Nietzsche and Hitler, and even in relating them. Both these men could suddenly deny their apparently most passionate convictions with even greater passion. At one moment Hitler was proud to resume the mission of Attila, at another he raved against the Mongolian barbarism of the Russians. The anti-Mongol outcry was required by the public at home and abroad, while he himself was proud to be a great destroyer. I am convinced that Nietzsche would have been horrified by the result, but he none the less helped to provide, perhaps indirect through the pamphleteers of Vienna, an idiom to express the emotions of Hitler.

The " Axis " liaison, and the " Steel " Pact into which it

later solidified, appropriately symbolized an age which was hailed in those days as the Age of the Engineer rather than that of the Common Man. In other languages the words considered equivalent to " Axis " mean very much the same as " axle." Webster, however, defines the word as meaning " a straight line, real or imaginary, passing through a body, and on which the body revolves or may be supposed to revolve." In September 1923 Mussolini in a foreword to a book about the Weimar Republic by an Italian journalist declared that there could be no doubt that the axis of European history ran through Berlin.[1] The first to have used the word in its Rome-Berlin context seems to have been the Hungarian Premier, Gömbös. On 20th June 1934, immediately after the first meeting between Mussolini and Hitler, in addressing the Magyar Upper House he expressed himself as follows : " I have repeatedly said, for the first time twelve years ago, that Berlin and Rome form the two ends of an axis which, if it should find itself in a state of equilibrium, could provide a basis for a peaceful evolution of European affairs."[2] Schuschnigg more aptly quoted Goethe's couplet :

> Der Achse wird mancher Stoss versetzt,
> Sie rührt sich nicht und brich zuletzt.[3]

Elizabeth Wiskemann

[1] The book was called *Germania Repubblicana*, its author R. Suster.

[2] The text of this sentence, as published in the *Pester Lloyd*, ran as follows : " Ich habe schon wiederholt gesagt, zum ersten Male vor zwölf Jahren, dass Berlin und Rom die beiden Enden der Achse bilden, die, wenn sie sich im Gleichgewicht befindet, allein die Basis einer ruhigen europäischen Politik bilden könnte." (*ruhig* combines restful with quiet in meaning, and *Politik* in this context means more than policy).

[3] " The Axis is exposed to many a knock; it does not stir but breaks in the end."

NOTE ON SOURCES

In 1947 the Foreign Office Library allowed me to consult the original text of all documents quoted at the trial of the major War Criminals at Nuremberg and to go through a number of official Italian documents which had come into Allied possession through the defeat of Italy. Since then many volumes of British, German, Italian and, since 1965, two volumes of French Foreign Office documents have been published. As far as possible I have altered less convenient references in favour of references to these.

As an active student of international affairs since shortly before Hitler came to power I lived fairly close to a certain amount of what I have tried to describe in Germany, Austria and Italy, as also in Czechoslovakia and the Balkans. In this way I met a great many of the ordinary people concerned and a few of the extraordinary ones.

During most of the subsequent war I was at work in Switzerland, and in one way or another, chiefly because former friends and acquaintances managed to convey fairly accurate information to me, I was able to keep in some kind of contact with the Axis world. I shall always be grateful to Albrecht Bernstorff for the trouble he took and the danger he faced.

After the end of the war I talked over different portions of the history of the Axis with various people who had been personally concerned : these included Monsieur Lipski, Monsieur François-Poncet and Dr. von Schuschnigg (see index of persons). The former Italian Ambassadors, Cerruti and Guariglia, were helpful to me, as was also Marquis Antinori who had for many years been Italian Press Attaché in Berlin. Count Magistrati kindly allowed me to read through the manuscript of his book which now appears in my bibliography.

A word should perhaps be said about the Ciano Papers in *L'Europa verso la catastrofe* which help to fill the gap still existing in the published Italian Foreign Office Documents. The Papers were written with more courtesy and caution than were Ciano's diaries because such Minutes were liable to be handed round among the rulers of the countries friendly to Fascist Italy : thus it has to be borne in mind that Ciano knew that Hitler and Ribbentrop might read them. On the other hand the same book contains papers like Ciano's Memorandum of May 1938 on Albania; this was intended solely for the eyes of the Duce. It is unfortunate that the notes to this and similar publications are full of inaccuracies. I should add that I read diaries like those of Ciano and Hassell in the original language and made my own translations before a translation into English had been published; I have usually retained my own version.

Much valuable work has been done by various research centres since the first edition of this book. In particular the publications of the *Institut für Zeitgeschichte* founded in Munich in 1950 have been highly illuminating; I have drawn attention to several of them in my bibliography.

My gratitude remains to those who helped me to compile the first version of my history of the Rome-Berlin Axis. For help over its revision I should like specially to thank Mr. Brian Melland of the Cabinet Office, Mr. Wheatley of the Foreign Office Library and the staff of the Wiener Library at the Institute for the Study of Contemporary History. Mr. F. W. Deakin has given me both advice and encouragement.

Chapter I

PUPILS OF NIETZSCHE

The Dark Ages began when the savage vigour of the Germans broke up the system of Mediterranean civilization which the Romans had established; a tradition of conflict between Italy and Germany lingered on ever after through the centuries. To transform this antithesis into the synthesis of the Holy Roman Empire was something dreamt of rather than achieved. The Italians resisted what to them were the encroachments of the German Emperors and were fortified in doing so by the Church of Rome. While the Imperial forces periodically overran Italy, trying to satisfy the Emperors' nostalgic desire to discover the secret of civilization, Germany relapsed into centrifugal chaos.

Some common background the German and Italian peoples had in the unstable coalition of forces expressed in the Empire; both came to owe a partial allegiance to the Habsburg dynasty which at last imposed the stability of hereditary succession upon a considerable portion of Europe. In the nineteenth century the nationalists both in Italy and Germany were at one in their struggles to escape from this Habsburg domination; Prussian victories against Austria in 1866 and 1870 served the Italians well, for they were able to add Venetia and Rome to the Kingdom of Italy without military successes of their own. While the Bismarckian Germany which emerged in 1871 was a federal state ruled by an irresponsible monarch, Victor Emmanuel II had become the constitutional ruler of a unitary state which was over-centralized through the extension of the Piedmontese prefectorial system to the whole of Italy.

Between 1882 and 1914, thanks primarily to German instigation, Germany and Italy established a Triple Alliance with the very House of Habsburg against which both had been in revolt; at first this alliance was directed chiefly against France, but later more and more against the Slavs of eastern Europe. It is important that at that time Italy stipulated that she could only participate in the alliance provided that it should never bring her into action against Great Britain; in those days the rulers of Italy had no illusions about Mediterranean strategy. Apart from this Italian requirement, which was formally included in the Triplice treaties, the Alliance became an exceedingly uneasy one after 1900; anti-Austrian combined with pro-French feeling in Italy to bring about a Franco-Italian *rapprochement* to which the Germans reacted with blustering annoyance. In those days a very different Austria lay between Rome and Berlin, and the Italian, rather than the German, Government was on bad terms with the Vatican, the steadfast friend of Vienna. There is something fascinatingly familiar, however, in the description given by the French Ambassador of William II's visit to Rome in May 1903, when, staying at the Quirinal though he was, he honoured the Pope with an IMPERIAL demonstration, and German pilgrims acclaimed the new Charlemagne.

"Jamais on ne vit autour d'un souverain," wrote M. Barrère,[1] "plus de panaches, de casques, de maréchaux, de Ministres bottés (le comte de Bülow a été constamment en bottes), de princes, de cuirassiers gigantesques, de voitures dorées (amenées de Berlin), de chevaux caparaçonnés . . . Les Italiens n'aiment pas qu'on prenne chez eux des allures de Charlemagne. Il leur déplait que l'on exhibe dans leurs rues des soldats étrangers choisis parmi les plus gigantesques." ". . . d'autre part," he had noted earlier, "1,500 agents de police en bourgeois, mêlés savamment à la foule sur la place du Quirinal, ont procuré à son arrivée une bruyante ovation." Little King Victor Emmanuel, young and pro-French in those days, was exquisitely annoyed. But in one thing the Italians had their way: on this occasion Austria-Hungary, the absent partner, was not mentioned in the official toasts at the Quirinal.

The Habsburg Empire had been shaken to its foundations in the "year of revolutions" in 1848. In the struggle to maintain its hold upon the now conscious nationalities which had sprung up like armed men from dragon's teeth, the dynasty, after the defeats of 1866 and the severance of

[1] M. Barrère to M. Delcassé, 10th June 1903.

Austria's political link with the rest of Germany, made the Compromise of 1867 with Budapest; from this time the Empire became Austria-Hungary, with the river Leitha as the frontier between the two autonomous areas of Austria and Hungary. In Austria the warring nationalities subjected to the Emperor Francis Joseph included large and, in some districts, aggressive German groups, and a relatively small Italian population in the Trentino (South Tyrol), Trieste, and Dalmatia. In Hungary he had German subjects sprinkled in a number of scattered settlements, and Italian subjects in Fiume, which was Hungary's only port.

In addition to the anti-Austrian tradition in Italy which was primarily associated with the Risorgimento, there were all kinds of troubles between the Austrian authorities and their Italian subjects at the beginning of the twentieth century. The Italians in Austria had been clamouring for an Italian University in Trieste; instead, in May 1903, the Austrian Government allowed some Italian courses at the University of Innsbruck, the capital of the Crownland of Tyrol, which in those days embraced the Trentino right down to Riva on Lake Garda.

" Cette concession," wrote the French Ambassador in Vienna, " a été l'origine d'un antagonisme chaque jour croissant entre étudiants allemands et italiens et d'une surexcitation qui a fait récemment explosion à l'inauguration du cours du professeur Lorenzoni, dont les auditeurs ont été fortement molestés, à coup de bâton, en signe de protestation par leurs camarades allemands. Les maîtres de ces derniers, loin de les calmer, se sont associés au mouvement : la presse les a encouragés et les autorités ont fait preuve d'une indifférence et d'une mollesse qui ont pu être interprétées comme un acquiescement ou tout au moins comme une neutralité bienveillante."[2]

No sooner did this news reach Italy than anti-Austrian demonstrations took place at nearly all the Italian universities. To round off this picture of Italo-Austrian relations one finds a little later in the same year that Italians are intriguing at Fiume in favour of the further separation of the Hungarian portion of the Dual Monarchy from the Austrian half;

[2] Marquis de Reverseaux to M. Delcassé, 28 May 1903.

the Italians hoped that a change of this kind would weaken Austria to the extent of ceding the territory tacitly claimed by Italy.[3]

At the beginning of 1902 when it was known that some kind of Franco-Italian agreement had been made, the German Chancellor, Prince Bülow, adopted an attitude of optimistic condescension and indulged in the much-quoted comment that in a happy marriage the husband should not take umbrage if his wife has an innocent dance with someone else. By the spring of 1904, however, when Italy invited President Loubet to visit Rome officially, William II and Bülow could no longer contain themselves. In March the German Emperor ordered Victor Emmanuel to his yacht, the *Hohenzollern,* which he anchored off Naples, and insisted that the King of Italy should make warm public references to the Triple Alliance—it was hinted very broadly that refusal to comply would constitute a breach with Germany. The Germans even tried to pledge Victor Emmanuel to sing the praises of the Triplice in the presence of Loubet. William II's high-handedness was less successful than Hitler's. The Italians were exceedingly angry at this crude attempt to force them to quarrel with the French and ceased from that time to conceal their preference for the other European camp. By this time France and Britain had come to terms.

Many other factors were working in the same direction. At the beginning of the twentieth century Italy, a good deal later than Germany and long after Britain, was becoming industrialized on the basis of a rapidly expanding population and no essential raw materials; above all, her national life came to depend upon coal which she did not possess, and which, until 1914, she imported almost entirely from Britain. It is impossible not to associate her growing tendency after 1900 to align herself with the at first embryonic Entente with her growing dependence upon British coal. Free-trading Britain was altogether more helpful than protectionist Germany. At this time, also, Italy had more interest in the disintegration of the Turkish Empire in the Balkans and

[3] M. Revelli, French consul in Fiume, to M. Delcassé, 13 September 1903.

North Africa than in opposing Slav aspirations, and, when Britain and France arranged to succeed Turkey in Egypt and Morocco, Italy's parallel interest was recognised in Tripolitania.

Italy's war for the conquest of what she preferred to call Libya and the controversy around her intervention in the war which broke out in 1914 gave prominence to a young Italian Socialist—scarcely twenty-eight years old in 1911 when the Libyan war began—whose name was Benito Mussolini. In order to embarrass the middle-class moderates of the Italian Socialist Party and thereby gain personal prominence and power, this young man agitated furiously against Socialist support of the Italian Government in the North African war; he was rewarded the next year (1912) with the expulsion from the Party of the men like Bonomi whom he opposed, and he himself was sent to Milan as editor of the chief party newspaper, the *Avanti*. Two years after this Mussolini agreed with Bonomi and his friends in favour of joining the Allies, while the Socialist Party decided for a pacifist policy and Mussolini's expulsion. For other motives might and did lead Italians to wish to fight for the Allies after August 1914, but it would seem that Mussolini's pro-French ardour was inspired—apart from the help which the French Embassy and the French Socialists seem to have given to his new interventionist newspaper, the *Popolo d'Italia*—by vanity and opportunism and by his natural preference for activity rather than neutrality.

Benito Mussolini came from the Romagna with its anticlerical and its eternally revolutionary tradition. His father was a blacksmith, his mother a schoolmistress, both probably of peasant origin. The father had been a Mazzinian at one moment and an anarchist at the next and was several times in prison, and the son showed little but turbulence and self-assertion in his youth; he reacted strongly to the shocking way in which he was handled at the Salesian Fathers' college at Faenza for two unhappy years.[4] He became an elementary-school teacher later, really for lack of anything

[4] See his early autobiography, *La mia vita* by Benito Mussolini, 1947.

better to do, at Gualteri in Emilia. In 1902, in order to avoid military service in Italy, the nineteen-year-old youth rushed off penniless to Switzerland and picked up odd jobs wherever he could. It was there that his schoolboy Socialism was accentuated, not thanks to much genuine political conviction or benevolent aim, but, as it would appear, in petulant rebellion against the Swiss police, with whom he was often in trouble. He had been sentenced in Italy for desertion, but in 1904 an amnesty made it possible for him to return. In the last years of the nineteenth century Marxist Socialism had become a great force in Italy, and after 1903, when Giolitti became Prime Minister, until Italy joined in the First World War, the Socialist leaders often worked with him; they thus acquired considerable influence upon the government of the country. In this way the Party became too 'respectable' for its revolutionary wing which was powerfully affected by syndicalism in France, that is to say, by the political doctrines of Georges Sorel which conquered the French trade unions at Amiens in 1906. Though his best-known book, *Réflexions sur la Violence,* was only published in 1908, Sorel had been politically active since the early nineties.

In Switzerland Mussolini had not only picked up a fair amount of French and German, he had also made a very modest début as a revolutionary journalist and a popular orator of theatrical appeal; it was as such that his chief exertions were made after his return to Italy. All his life he remained essentially a journalist with a telling turn of phrase and a tendency to jargon. In Switzerland he first imbibed the doctrines of the anti-democratic prophets of the end of the last century. Pareto was still lecturing at the University of Lausanne for the brief period when Mussolini studied there. Though the Marxist character of his political education has been emphasized, Mussolini showed more interest in Kropotkin and Kautsky than in either Marx or Lenin.[5] It may be surmised, indeed, that his Marxism came to him through the crooked channel of Sorel who was just

[5] He said afterwards that he did not know whether he had met Lenin in Zürich; he had several Russian Socialist friends in French Switzerland, including Angelica Balabanoff.

coming into vogue among the rebels of the Socialist Party
in Italy at the time of Mussolini's return.

In this period Mussolini seems to have begun his reading
of Nietzsche, who, with his " nothing true, everything
allowed," provided a happy hunting-ground for ambitious
misfits. Here again Mussolini had been prepared by Sorel,
and in so far as the superman meant anything to him other
than a glorification of himself, for many years it stood for
the glorified proletarian. In 1908 the wise old Jew, Claudio
Treves, then editor of the *Avanti,* gave a lecture at Forlì
on Nietzsche, in which he defined the superman as a piece
of adolescent symbolism. This outraged young Mussolini
who burst into a series of articles, in a local weekly called
Il Pensiero Romagnolo, in defence of the philosophy of
force. This was the beginning of a personal vendetta which
lasted for some years but then turned in Mussolini's favour,
for it was Treves whom he had ousted from the *Avanti*
when he took over its direction in 1912. Meanwhile Mussolini had spent seven months in 1909 in Trent, until the
Austrian authorities expelled him; he worked there partly in
conjunction with the admirable Cesare Battisti whom the
Austrians executed as a traitor in the subsequent war.

The man who more than any other swept Italy into the
war in the " radiant May " of 1915 was the poet D'Annunzio.
It was he in his latest role of Nationalist, and not Mussolini
nor the moderate pro-French Left, who exerted the decisive influence. In the long run, however, both this victory
of D'Annunzio, which was won against traditional parlia-
mentarism, and D'Annunzio's Regency after the war at
Fiume, served Mussolini very well. Under the poet's régime
marvellous experiments in political stage-production were
carried out; the black shirts of D'Annunzio's self-consciously
fiery *Arditi,* together with all kinds of exciting badges and
emblems, Roman salutes, and the intoning of political ritual,
first became familiar here. Thus the Nazis, too, were to owe
a tremendous debt to the Italian poet. It was at Fiume
that a Statute was framed in which the first blending of
a modern syndicalism and medieval corporativism seems
to have been realized. Indeed, it is not on account of the
excitement of the time that D'Annunzio's occupation of

Fiume is historically important, but rather on account of
what he thereby bequeathed to Mussolini and to Hitler and
Goebbels.

Mussolini, it has been seen, lived by " incessant agitation "[6]
to gain notoriety and power by any available means, but
provided he were powerful he had no definite aim for
which his power should be used. When he was expelled from
the official Socialist Party he founded working-men *Fasci* of
Revolutionary Action to agitate for intervention; it should
be noted, however, that the word *Fasci* only meant bunches
or groups and was at that time in current use among people on
the Left. After the war the Socialists were stimulated by
the Russian Revolution and the Nationalists by D'Annunzio,
and Mussolini found himself in the shade : he had served
in the Army until discharged in 1917 when he returned to
his office at the *Popolo d'Italia.* It was in Milan on 23rd
March 1919, in the Piazza San Sepolcro building which
became the seat of the *Fascio*, that his nascent Fascist Party
formulated a violently revolutionary programme directed
against everything, Church, Monarchy, and Senate all in
one. This programme was dropped very soon, but the Piazza
San Sepolcro retained a symbolic importance for the Fascists,
and Milan remained a city with which Mussolini felt an
intimate emotional link. It was after the failure of the
metal-workers' occupation of the Milanese factories in September 1920 that Mussolini felt that things were swinging
to the Right, and that, in order to gain more power, he
must seek new allies and new syntheses. Within two years
his Fascists had merged with D'Annunzio's *Arditi;* both of
them preached violence and easily recruited crowds of *dés-
orienté* post-war young men. The success of the Communists in
Russia made it expedient, if one would not be for them,
to be fiercely against them on passionately nationalistic grounds.
As for the rest, it was easy to tell his working-class supporters that the corporate ideas of the Nationalist leader,
Rocco, and his followers were the same thing as syndicalism;
the atheist Mussolini could even whisper to the pious that
all this derived from Pope Leo XIII's Encyclical of 1891.

[6] Cf. C. J. S. Sprigge, The Development of Modern Italy 1943.

And to secure the support of the middle classes, hatred of whom was perhaps the least unstable emotion in Mussolini's make-up, he abandoned his enthusiastic Romagnol republicanism one month before the Fascist ' March on Rome '; it was an essential move in order to conciliate the Army as well as the King who would have the last word.[7]

About the technique of Mussolini's coup d'état in October 1922 a Fascist " myth " was deliberately created by the Fascist journalist, like Malaparte. More sober judges consider that a little energy and conviction on the part of the Army and police, instead of a good deal of connivance, would have to put a quick end to the Fascists' seizure of key points after which they marched into Rome. In 1931 Malaparte published a book[8] in which he tried to perpetuate the story that Mussolini had exactly imitated Trotsky's technique of 1917. Perhaps Malaparte wished to exploit Giolitti's remark that he had learnt from Mussolini that a government should defend itself against the tactics, not the programme, of a revolution; undoubtedly Mussolini had a certain technical equipment, while, as for a programme, he was the first to admit that he had none. In 1922 he became head of a coalition Government in which the Fascists and Nationalists had the whip hand, and he mouthed vague phrases about the Myths of the Nation; it was not until 1925 that he established a Fascist régime through the suppression of all other parties, and really Fascist legislation began with the *Carta del Lavoro* in 1927. All this time he eschewed a formulation of Fascism (which has been seen to mean nothing as a word but groupism), declaring it to be Pure Act in process. It was astonishing that a man with more than the usual Italian pleasure in political journalism should have shown such reticence. The condition of his health cannot be neglected by anyone attempting to analyse Mussolini's character. It was notorious that he had taken insufficient steps against a syphilitic infection in his journalistic youth : this may help to account for his instability

---

[7] Victor Emmanuel had met Mussolini as a sick soldier in hospital during the war.

[8] C. Malaparte, *Technique of a Coup d'Etat* (1931). He also misinterpreted Hitler.

and megalomaniac tendencies. In addition he developed a
duodenal ulcer in 1925, which gave him considerable trouble
for the following two years, but was then in abeyance until
1937 : an ulcer of this kind is often associated with chronic
vacillation. Mussolini was, indeed, a man of indecision and of
scepticism who was influenced now from this side, now
from that, by personal motives, by vanity, or a desire for
revenge. As the years passed he compromised with both
Monarchy and Church, and he always preserved the pre-
Fascist Senate. He quoted Nietzsche on the morality of
violence and Sorel on the importance of the political myth,
but he had no clear conception of his own aims or methods.
He set up a Fascist Grand Council, which was to occasion
his downfall, and he relied on Fascist education to shift the
bases of power with the passage of time. Later Mussolini
established a Chamber of Corporations in the place of the
Chamber of political deputies. This was a lame attempt to
practise syndicalism, but whereas the Syndicalist movement
was anarchist in origin and sought to replace the State by
a Trade Union Congress, the Fascist corporations were
constructed as the bastions of a dictatorial state.

There was one political innovation of first-rate importance
which Mussolini introduced into Italy. The Syndicalists had
wished to abolish politics and parties along with the State.
And yet Sorel and other believers in élites were responsible
for that totalitarian contradiction in terms, the idea of the
One-Party State. If the latter was first realized by the Russian
Communists (creating an essential distinction between Communism and other forms of Socialism), Mussolini followed
them in 1925 when he made himself Head of the State and
appointed the extremist, Roberto Farinacci, Secretary of
the Fascist Party.

" At this time," wrote Adolf Hitler of the year 1923,
" I confess frankly, I conceived the deepest admiration for
the great man south of the Alps, who in passionate love for
his people refused to make terms with the internal enemies
of Italy, but sought their destruction by all ways and means.
What will place Mussolini among the great of the earth
is his determination not to share Italy with Marxism, but

rather in condemning internationalism to destruction, to save his country from it " (=Marxism?).[9]

In Germany this man, nearly six years younger than Mussolini, had already become so oddly prominent that in the spring of 1922 a man like Pechel, editor of a serious review, the *Deutsche Rundschau,* felt it right to lunch with him in Munich and then to invite him to speak at the exceedingly nationalistic *Juni-Klub* in Berlin, where Moeller van den Bruck and Hitler met for the only time.[10] How many superficial resemblances have been discovered between Adolf Hitler and Benito Mussolini, their petit-bourgeois nearly peasant origin, their " Bohemian " poses, their fight against liberalism and democracy! But perhaps no two people intimately connected by history were ever more different; and perhaps the essence of the difference between them is that Hitler was obsessed by a set of fixed ideas which after 1924 at the latest never changed and which he committed to paper some eight years before he became master of Germany, while it was not until ten years after he had come to power that Mussolini was willing to sponsor a celebrated article on the doctrine of Fascism in the *Enciclopedia Italiana* in 1932.

Hitler could never have been what he was had he not been Austrian. The historical phenomenon of Adolf Hitler can be explained, and can only be explained, when one remembers that the year 1848 had heralded a frenzy of German nationalism within the Habsburg Empire; as industrialism developed and the Slav birth-rate rose, the Germans of Austria-Hungary, most of whom we traditionally call Austrians, became a proportionately decreasing racial group; as they came to realize this, those of them who did not, like the aristocracy or the active Catholics or Socialists or the isolated Liberals among them, feel some generalized human allegiance, became fiercely

[9] *Mein Kampf* (Verlag Franz Eher, Munich, 1933) part ii, chapter 15.

[10] Rudolf Pechel, *Deutscher Widerstand* 1947. Moeller was the author of an excessively obscure outburst of nationalism whose title, *Das Dritte Reich,* was adopted with a flourish by the Nazis to signify the régime which they aspired to establish. He, however, wrote in good faith. (The Holy Roman Empire was the first Reich and the Hohenzollern Empire the second.)

nationalistic. This meant that, since democracy robbed them of the dominance they claimed by virtue of their German blood, they became its enemies and embraced cults of some élite; since the Slavs were growing numerically and in Slav consciousness, many German-Austrians became violently anti-Slav. And, since on principle they hated under-dogs and intelligence, they developed an anti-Semitic creed which fitted in with their contempt for Christianity whose founder was a Jew.

Adolf Hitler, the son of a small customs official, was born in Upper Austria, on the Bavarian frontier, but very near Bohemia which was the German-Slav battleground *par excellence*. He spent his schooldays in Linz, which he always regarded as his home. Hitler inherited the views of a fairly small but active group of the Austrian middle and lower-middle class[11] influential in the *Grenzländer* where the Germans touched upon the Slavs, i.e. in Bohemia, Silesia, Styria, and Carinthia. These views were familiar, however, to the general Austrian public; they coloured the opinions of very different groups with what often seems to us a rather silly chauvinism; for no evident reason they were exceedingly popular in Linz and were preached by the teachers at Adolf Hitler's school, and indeed at many Austrian schools and at the universities.

The nationalistic[12] Austrians regarded the division between Austria and Germany in 1866 as a crime, and it was an essential part of their creed to wish to undo the wickedness of Bismarck and of Francis Joseph, and " restore " German unity. The subsequent successes of Bismarck earned him their forgiveness, and their agitation took the shape of working for the incorporation of Austria, with or without its other nationalities, in the Hohenzollern Empire which German patriots declared to have become the true successor to the Holy Roman Empire. It is necessary to remember all this in order to understand what happened between 1933 and 1938 and the behaviour of the Austrians at the time of the *Anschluss*. It is necessary to remember it also in order to

[11] Cf. Papen's dispatch, Vienna to Berlin 27 July 1935, in which he refers to this (D. G. F. P. Series c. vol. IV, no. 232.)
[12] In German the adjective is plain *national*.

explain Hitler's praise of Ribbentrop in later days as greater than Bismarck. When Schuschnigg went to the Berghof in 1938 he noted the portrait of Bismarck by Lenbach in a prominent position,[13] and Gafencu in 1939 found Ribbentrop at work with a similar portrait on the wall at his back.[14]

The leader of the *national* extremists or *Alldeutsche* in Austria was for many years a certain Georg von Schönerer, who distinguished himself as the ringleader in a famous incident in 1888. William I, first Emperor of Bismarck's new Germany, lay dying, and inadvertently an Austrian paper in Jewish hands, the *Neues Wiener Tagblatt,* pre-announced his death. Schönerer arose in wrath to chastise the staff of the *Tagblatt*; with a group of his followers he perpetrated a nasty piece of 'beating-up.' The incident was prophetic of hundreds of the kind in Germany between 1933 and the 'final' liquidation of the Jews of Europe by Hitler; the only difference lay in the fact that Schönerer was tried and punished while his imitators half a century later were promoted and praised.

Adolf Hitler was born one year after the Schönerer affair. In his childhood Pan-German[15] societies spread from Austria into William II's Germany; Hitler was eight at the time of the Eger riots when the Austrian Pan-Germans demonstratively crossed into Hohenzollern territory in order to flout the Austrian police. From the time of the Austrian annexation of Bosnia until the murder at Sarajevo, nationalistic intransigence, especially among the Germans of Austria, became something like red-hot; Hitler was nineteen when Bosnia was annexed and twenty-five when the Great War began.

The Prussians, who became the scapegoats of Pan-German admiration because of their efficiency, were far less given to ecstatic racial dreams. (There was to be scarcely one Prussian among the Nazi leaders, who were predominantly

[13] K. von Schuschnigg, *Ein Requiem in Rot-Weiss-Rot,* 1946, p. 45.
[14] G. Gafencu, *Derniers Jours de l'Europe,* 1946.
[15] There were nuances between *Grossdeutsch* and *Alldeutsch* and *Pangermanisch,* but the latter name was least used though we use Pan-German as the translation of *Alldeutsch.*

Bavarians or *Auslandsdeutsche*.) The Prussians had their own Slav neighbours certainly, but the Poles were opposed to Pan-Slavism and the Polish question did not draw the Prussians into polemics such as the Bohemian question created around Prague, which was known in *Alldeutsch* terms as the Western Moscow long before the days of Dr. Beneš. There was, of course, much foolish Pan-Slav talk in Austria-Hungary and in Russia from 1848 onwards, in reply to the Pan-Germans. It should also be noted that whereas there were enough Jews in positions of privilege or hardship to create a Jewish question in Austria-Hungary where race-consciousness was stimulated by racial diversity, in Prussia the most hysterical anti-Semite would have found it hard to prove a real case against the Jews before 1914; it was only after the First World War that immigration created something of a Jewish problem in Republican Germany, and particularly in Berlin.

The case of sheltered Bavaria, which had neither a Slav nor a Jewish problem, is particularly strange; it is difficult to find any adequate explanation for the rabid nationalism generated there. From the time of the foundation of the *Alldeutscher Verband* in the Reich, Munich, generally regarded by foreigners as an artistic centre only, was also the unofficial headquarters of the Reich Pan-Germans. This was perhaps no contradiction since Futurists sometimes indulged in the wildest chauvinism, especially in Italy. Further Ludwig II of Bavaria had been the patron of Wagner with all his Germanic mysticism, and this tradition lingered on in twentieth-century Munich. On 24th January 1906 Mr. Reginald Tower, British consul-general in Munich, addressed to Sir Edward Grey[16] the best extant account of Pan-German activity in the Germany of that day and of its designs upon the subjects of the Emperor Francis Joseph. It was in Munich, he reported, that the publisher, Lehmann, brought out most Pan-German periodicals and pamphlets. Bismarck's federalism had left the Wittelsbachs on the Bavarian throne, and the Pan-German Bavarians were, it seems, as hostile as their Austrian confrères to the dynastic and Catholic

16 F.O. 371/76, no. 14. Lehmann's activities continued into the war period and beyond.

influences around them. Above all they were anti-clerical.

From Linz Hitler went to Vienna to try his fortune as a painter. The research of Dr. Jetzinger[17] has exposed the falsity of the myth Hitler created in his speeches and writings about his youth. It is now clear that when Hitler's mother died in 1907 he was left very comfortably off; it would appear that he got into financial difficulties in Vienna only because he was idle and extravagant, always wanting the best seats when he went to the opera. In consequence he came to spend squalid days of privation among the heterogeneous riff-raff of the least German town of German Austria. Unlike Mussolini he spurned the " proletariat " and its Marxism, which was as bad as Christianity in his eyes, for it, too, was the faith of the down-trodden and the weak. In Vienna perhaps, certainly later in Munich, Hitler picked up, with a smattering of Nietzsche, the opposite religion of the strong. It is difficult to make precise statements about Hitler's reading—he himself always avoided doing so; at any rate he probably absorbed Wagnerian and Nietzschean emotions together with a flavouring of Schopenhauer, from the half-lunatic pamphlets which circulated in pre-1914 Vienna, some by a man called Adolf Lang. To Hitler, Nietzsche's superman, in so far as it meant more than a glorification of himself, meant the heroic German who should know no Habsburg law[18] in loosing his *Furchtbarkeit*[19] against Slav and Jew. The impact of Nietzsche upon Hitler was in a sense all the more direct because, while the mind of the one was brilliant and of the other banal, both suffered from obvious paranoia.

In 1913 Hitler was able to transfer himself from cosmopolitan Vienna to Pan-German headquarters at Munich, which became as important to him as Milan to Mussolini. Mussolini, as it happened, was established in the offices of the *Avanti* in Milan a year earlier. Hitler was able to live in Munich by painting fancy postcards and designing posters until 1914. The outbreak of war, the Pan-Germans felt, was the answer

[17] Franz Jetzinger. *Hitlers Jugend*, 1956.

[18] There was an elaborate, though not always effectual, system of legislation to protect the nationalities in Habsburg Austria.

[19] Cf. Nietzsche, *Der Wille zur Mach*: "Zur Grösse gehört die Furchtbarkeit: man lasse sich nichts vormachen."

to their prayers. "To me," Hitler wrote in *Mein Kampf,* "those hours (at the beginning of August 1914) seemed like salvation after the resentments of my youth. Even to-day I am not ashamed to say that I sank on my knees in wild enthusiasm and thanked Heaven with a full heart that I had been fortunate enough to live at such a time."[20] It was consistent with the Austrian Pan-German point of view that Hitler joined up in Bavaria, and not in the "k-und-k"[21] army which owed allegiance to the Habsburgs, in his eyes the corrupters of all true Germans because the protectors of Slavs and Jews. The Hohenzollerns, on the other hand, he conceived as the heirs to the medieval German Knights who had planted German colonies in Slav lands to the east of the Holy Roman Empire. To be the imitator of the Knights upon a titanic scale was to be one of Adolf Hitler's major aspirations. And so he went off to do his bit towards the setting-up of a German *Mitteleuropa,* to drive back the Slavs, and to colonize the collapsing empire of the Tsars. Already German ambition had combined the hope of extending the Habsburg Empire in the Balkans with that of expanding German influence over the Baltic Sea.[22]

The defeat of the Central Powers marked a decisive stage in Hitler's evolution. No doubt it appealed to his fantastic megalomania to feel that he, the Saviour of the Germans, must now start from the beginning to catch up with history and then change its whole direction. In 1918 he claimed to have spent several months in hospital owing to a temporary blindness, and there he says that he reflected upon the mistakes which had been made both by the Pan-Germans and by the Central Powers for whom they had fought. Both had failed in propaganda.

It had long been obvious that Schönerer and his lieutenants and successors had failed to create a mass movement, and it was to rectify this that a German Working-men's Party

[20] 1933 edition, p. 177.

[21] *kaiserliche-und-königliche.* Hitler probably went to Munich to avoid military service in Austria; he was afterwards let off by the Austrians on account of bad health.

[22] See Fritz Fischer. *Griff nach der Weltmacht,* 1961. Hitler, of course, only served in the west.

had been founded in Austria so early as 1904.[23] It was only, however, in Bohemia and Austrian Silesia that any Austrian working-men could be persuaded to join so chauvinist a party, for elsewhere they voted fairly solidly Social Democrat;[23a] the German Working-men's Party sent no more than three deputies to the Austrian Parliament in the elections of 1911, the second voting after Austria had introduced something very like universal suffrage for males over twenty-four. The Working-men's Party was led by Hans Knirsch, deputy for the mixed German-Czech mining town of Dux or Duchcov; in May 1918 he expanded the Party's name to be German National-Socialist Working-men's Party (*Deutsche National-sozialistische Arbeiter Partei* or D.N.S.A.P.). It continued to exist within the new Czechoslovak and Austrian Republics after the peace treaties. Hitler seems to have had no con-nexion with Knirsch in the Habsburg days, perhaps simply for geographical reasons; in Vienna at that time the only politic-ian he found praiseworthy was the Christian-Social mayor, Lueger, who was anti-Semitic in an arbitrary way, and who was, above everything, an orator with popular appeal.

As he lay in that hospital in 1918, Hitler tells us, he perceived the possibilities of propaganda along the lines of Northcliffe and the successful British leaflets which had demoralized the Germans. Instead, however, of retaining some relation to fact, as British propaganda had, Hitler's proganda would be totally unscrupulous : the bigger the lie the better. He recovered his sight and went back to Munich to become a political agent of the Reichswehr—a certain Captain Karl Mayr[24] discovered him—on whose account he attended all kinds of political meetings. Having once joined in a public discussion he revealed a phenomenal ability to inflame mass opinion when he spoke.[25] In 1920 he was co-opted on to the committee of a Working-men's

[23] They shared some of their ideas with the very nationalistic German Agrarian Party as well as with the German Radicals and the remains of the *Schönererianer* from whom the German Radicals were descended.

[23a] Socialism in Austria was, however, surprizingly *national*.

[24] E. Deuerlein—*Der Hitler Putsch* (1962), p. 29.

[25] Cf. Gafencu (op. cit.) who felt him as the embodiment of the German masses.

Party recently founded by Drexler, a Munich metal-worker.
Hitler renamed it National-Socialist German Working-Men's
Party (N.S.D.A.P.): in August he and Drexler met representatives from the Austrian and Czechoslovak D.N.S.A.P. at
a Pan-German Congress at Salzburg. From this time the
other parties looked to his.

Later Hitler developed a theory that by the age of thirty
a man, or at any rate a Hitler, should have formed his
final opinions. Hitler was thirty on April 20th, 1919. It was
at about this time that Mayr singled him out, partly for his
anti-Semitism. Already on 1st August, 1920, that is to
say before the Salzburg Congress, Hitler advocated an Italian
alliance against France,[26] an extraordinary thing for a young
Austrian to recommend at such a time : this was before
there were any Fascist deputies in the Italian Chamber.
(There is no evidence that Hitler looked to Britain until
the Ruhr crisis betrayed the difference of opinion between
Paris and London.) In 1922 he seems to have become
more practical about his pro-Italian policy. He discovered[27]
that Mussolini felt very strongly about the so-called *italianità*
of the South Tyrol. Very shortly after Mussolini had become
Prime Minister of Italy the Duce made special enquiries
about Bavarian separatism. The wildest ideas were current
in Munich and there was much talk of breaking with
Berlin and absorbing some of Austria, certainly the Tyrol
to the Brenner or beyond. Mussolini charged an Italian
member of the Inter-Allied Delegation at Bad Ems with
a mission to Bavaria. On 17th November, 1922, this man,
Adolfo Tedaldi, reported that Hittler, as he called him, had
recently stated to a group of the Bavarian People's Party
that it must be made clear to the Italians that the South
Tyrolese question did not exist for " us," the Germans.
Hitler, Tedaldi said, was a young man " more Latin than

[26] W. W. Pese—*Hitler und Italien* 1920-26. *Vierteljahrshefte
für Zeitgeschichte,* 1955.
[27] Probably through Lüdecke, whom Hitler apparently sent to
Italy to investigate both in 1922 just before the 'March on Rome'
and in the autumn of 1923. See K. Lüdecke—I knew Hitler (1938).
Also E. Deuerlein op. cit., specially pp. 544-7.

German in voice and gesture:"[28] the Italian said nothing of Hitler's views on Italy's anti-Semitic mission which he had aired in the previous August. By this time, indeed perhaps before the end of 1919, Hitler must have read " The Protocols of the Elders of Zion " which finally convinced him of a Jewish world-conspiracy against the ' better ' races.

In the middle of October 1923 he found time to give an interview to an Italian paper in which he spoke scornfully of the hundred and eighty thousand South Tyrolese.[29] This was three weeks before the notorious November *Putsch,* an attempted insurrection against Stresemann's Government which had called off passive resistance to the French in the Ruhr. It was on 9th November that Hitler, together with General Ludendorff and a motley collection of followers— it included Streicher, Göring, and Gregor Strasser—improvised their ' March on Berlin ' in Munich. Hitler declared Ludendorff to be Reich Minister of War and prepared himself to take on the modest post of *Reichskanzler.* The actual head of the Army, General von Seeckt, who was given special powers by President Ebert, considered it too early to turn against the democratic Republic—he had been piqued by the insubordination of some of the Reichswehr officers in Bavaria. Hence, although Seeckt despised Stresemann, the Bavarian police were instructed by officers loyal to Seeckt to shoot at Hitler's followers, and there were sixteen casualties. The *Putsch,* which seemed almost comic at the time, for instance to the Italian Consul in Munich,[29a] led to Hitler's trial and imprisonment. The trial gave him a new and particular platform for publicity, and ended in a sentence of five years' imprisonment in a fortress, Landsberg on the Lech; there he lived in comfort, with a number of Nazi comrades, from April 1924 until the end of the year, when he was pardoned and released. This period of retirement gave birth to *Mein Kampf,* which was published

[28] D.D.I., series 7, vol. I, no. 131.

[29] In Tedaldi's report they were referred to as two hundred thousand.

[29a] D.D.I. Series 7, vol. II, no. 474.

in two parts in the next year or so, the Koran of the National Socialists. "There is no right but might" was the basic burden of its message.

Endless disputes soon arose as to whether Hitler stood on the Right or on the Left—opposed to social change or in favour of it—but they were irrelevant because such issues did not concern him. Fundamentally he aimed at social injustice, and social change was only of interest to him in so far as it furthered his other objectives or did the reverse. He believed that the Germans should be established as a ruling caste within which, as within the medieval Orders, authoritative command was to prevail; the rest of humanity was to be at their disposal in varying degrees of slavery. In this way he combined his Pan-German heritage with those doctrines of Nietzsche which he had chosen to imbibe. His ruling caste or *élite* was sometimes expanded to cover a hypothetical German "race," but tended to contract from signifying the German Nazi Party in command of a One-Party German State to signifying at times the Nazi Storm Troopers (S.A.) and finally the Nazi *Schutz Staffeln* or S.S. He knew that his aim could only be achieved by the total destruction of the moral values accepted in Europe hitherto and would therefore almost certainly require war on a grand scale; the German occupation of Europe between 1940 and 1944 was to a great extent its realization. He defined his objectives with insolent sincerity in *Mein Kampf,* but they were something so alien to Western minds that, like the warnings of several of his countrymen,[30] they mostly fell upon stone-deaf ears. The West was also utterly misled by Hitler's cries for freedom since it did not know that to the Pan-German mind German freedom meant power to dominate.[31]

"National Socialism is not an ideology but a technique of domination," wrote Heiden, and the pre-announcement of the methods Hitler intended to use was as little credited as that of his objectives. Adolf Hitler's genius, if such it may

[30] Especially Heiden (op. cit.) and Rauschning (op. cit.).

[31] Prof. Dahlmann in April 1848 wrote: "Through power to freedom, this is Germany's predestined path"; he was among the more enlightened German leaders of the day.

Mussolini's arrival in Germany, September 1937

Victor Emmanuel and guest

The rally on the Maifeld at which Mussolini's notes got soaked

be counted, lay in the idea of the economy of force which
he developed after the failure of his *Putsch* in 1923. After
this he perceived that so long (and only so long) as the world
did not wake up to his method he could eke out and
increase the force at his disposal by the unexpected completeness of his falsity. In the negation of right as hitherto
accepted new weapons of might could be forged, the better
while old acceptances lingered. Further, any temporary compromise was permissible solely in order to concentrate upon
one objective at a time. It is easy to illustrate these doctrines
of Hitler's. A useful definition is to be found in the
address he delivered to the German industrialists[32] just before
the elections of March 1933, where he erroneously stated
that he had thought in this way since 1918. He insisted
that one should never use force so long as one is gaining
strength in other ways (this is, of course, very close to
the famous Clausewitz formulation); for this reason he
suggested that if the elections of 5th March did not turn
out as he required he would then use other than the apparently
constitutional means (i.e. the ruthlessly intimidating propaganda) which had served him well enough so far. When
the struggle for power within Germany had been crowned
with success, he continued, exactly the same methods would
be used to gain external power. There would be plenty
of ' conciliatory offers ' to the world, but Hitler's principles
included *die Ablehnung der Völkerversöhnung*,[33] and Germany would rearm when he was ready to do so, not when
Geneva agreed.

The success of Hitler's technique depended partly upon the
fact that the Germans, and at least as much the German
Austrians, were familiar with no-right-but-might ideas which
had been pronounced in Germany for many years. The
English-speaking peoples were morally restrained by what
others called their hypocrisy, while the Latin nations—and
this is true of Fascist Italy—might bring forth individuals
who idolized force, but were constantly inhibited from the
logical consequences in action by a persistent legalism which
one can but attribute to the influence of ancient Rome.

[32] On 20th Feb. 1933.
[33] = " the rejection of international reconciliation."

Hitler's success, however, depended still more upon his psychotic make-up. If he was inhumanly cold and logical and clear-sighted in the pursuit of his ends, at the same time and quite separately he lived in a state of paranoiac adolescence. The more one studies *Mein Kampf* or his letters or speeches, together with his behaviour and actions, the more one feels that he really believed in a world of Wagnerian heroes and monsters. He himself was something between Wotan and Siegfried fighting a mystic fight against Loki, the Jew, who was at the same time like the terrible serpent of the Sagas which encircled the earth. His superstition and his pride in his sleep-walker's certainty were a part of this fairy-story; the same is probably true of the tears in his eyes[34] whenever he thought of Mussolini's sympathy at the time of the Anschluss, when in fact he had—as we shall see—persistently weakened Mussolini and strengthened himself until the moment was ripe. Naturally people could not believe that this emotional absurdity, with its seeming hesitations, was a phenomenon of political logicality. There was, fortunately for him and unfortunately for the world, something sincere about the ridiculous scenes which puzzled a brother Austrian and a *Freikorps* adventurer like Prince Starhemberg[35] almost as much as they perplexed the Latins or the British. For this reason even in Germany until 1933 a considerable section of the public simply smiled at this man's unexaggerated threats; for this reason a larger proportion of opinion in the world did the same until 1939. But for this reason also, the sincerity of his own ridiculous hysteria, he could mesmerize mass meetings and seduce in the mass a number of individuals who privately discussed him with scepticism. We shall never know whether this man could have intoxicated non-German crowds in the same fashion; many Germans have strong hysterical tendencies which bound them to him in a particular way. It is interesting that Hitler deliberately praised hysteria : " the greatest transformations in this world would have been unthink-

[34] Cf. Ciano Diary (Rizzoli, Milan, 1946), 20th Nov. 1940, and below.

[35] See *Between Hitler and Mussolini*, by Prince Starhemberg (Hodder & Stoughton, 1942), pp. 84-5.

able," he wrote, " if the impulse behind them had been only the bourgeois virtues of order and tranquillity instead of fanatical, yes hysterical, passions."[36]

According to his own inaccurate account Adolf Hitler had decided in 1918 that he would need Britain and Italy as his allies in order to crush France and establish his German caste hegemony : if they should object to his plan when they had recognized it they could, having been used, be destroyed. With his relations with Britain this book is not directly concerned, but only with his relations with Italy, with the extraordinary manner in which he advanced inexorably towards the subjugation of Italy independently of his romantic hero-worship for the Duce, and yet—perhaps unconsciously—using this sentimental devotion, which was based on false premises, in order to complete his political mastery.

It was the intellectual fashion in Germany to attribute the collapse of the Roman Empire to an excess of racial inter-breeding, and to despise the Italians as its hybrid descendants. This view had been formulated with éclat by Houston Stewart Chamberlain, a renegade Englishman who married one of Wagner's daughters : his main work which he called *The Foundations of the Nineteenth Century* was published in 1899 and was greatly admired by the Kaiser. To racialists like his Balt friend Alfred Rosenberg, to whom Hitler entrusted the direction of his chief party newspaper, the *Völkischer Beobachter*, Italians were only fit to be low-grade slaves to the Germanic ruling caste : Mussolini himself might be regarded as a scion of nothing nobler than that Latin proletariat which, according to Rosenberg, had risen against its Germanic overlords to perpetrate the deplorable revolution of 1789.

Hitler did honour to Chamberlain as a *völkische Schrift-steller;*[37] he was proud to have met the old man at Bayreuth in 1923. But he discovered a theory independent of race which conveniently justified the policy towards Italy upon which he had determined, and he rarely allowed the Nazi press to abuse the Italians. In Munich in the first years follow-

[36] *Mein Kampf* (1933 edition), p. 475.
[37] See reference in *Mein Kampf*.

ing the war Professor Karl Haushofer was busy working out his new science of *Geopolitik,* which claimed geographical expediency as the basis of policy, and divided the world into the ' expansion areas ' of such powers as it pleased. Haushofer, who had been a general in Japan, was the advocate of a German-Italian-Japanese alliance; he held that, since Japan had expansion-space in the Pacific and Italy in the Mediterranean, neither need collide with a resurgent and expanding Germany. Through his young Nazi protégé and assistant, Rudolf Hess, who was imprisoned at Landsberg with Hitler, Haushofer was brought into touch with the Führer; indeed he frequently visited the prisoners. Hitler first preached *Ostexpansion* in the first volume of *Mein Kampf,* no doubt as the result of Haushofer's visits.

Hitler was the only German or Austrian of whom one ever hears who felt no bitterness against Italy for the *Verrat* of 1914-15. On the contrary, judging the Italians by himself, he declared in *Mein Kampf* that they were right to ally themselves with Austria-Hungary only to prepare war against her, while the Germans had been fools enough to bind themselves to the festering Habsburg corpse. Now he had a new basis for a partnership with Italy's Great Man. In accordance with the theories of *Geopolitik* Mussolini was to use the Mediterranean—without the Adriatic—as his expansion-space, leaving old Austria-Hungary, in terms of which Hitler always thought, and Russia, to the Führer.

The Duce became his model and he imagined the Fascist revolution to have been what he desired for Germany; in the ten years between 1933 and 1943 he was to cultivate the notion of the identity of " our two revolutions." Disobedient facts were unable to deter him, and he conveniently ignored Mussolini's corporations which he had no wish to emulate. Though Rosenberg was publicly to lament the absence of anti-Semitism in Fascist Italy, in *Mein Kampf* Hitler described Mussolini's struggle against " the Jewish world-hydra " as " perhaps fundamentally subconscious (though I personally do not believe that it is)." With the enthusiasm of the Pan-German Austrian Hitler wrote in an open letter in 1931 : " Prussianism is a moral, not a geographical, conception. Mussolini is a Prussian." He meant that Mussolini was a man of violence, the only superman who had begun to drive out the religion of the weak with that of the strong. He used Prussian in this sense, although Nietzsche had despised the North Germans as submissive and contemptible people.

Very shortly after this declaration of Hitler's about Mussolini, the Duce's play about the Hundred Days, the *Campo di Maggio*,[38] was performed at Weimar; this was due to the fact that the Nazis were strong in Thuringia where one of them, Frick, was already a Minister. Hitler and Hess arrived quite unexpectedly for Mussolini's play. On the following day Hitler, laden with flowers for Nietzsche's aged sister, visited the *Nietzsche Archiv*; alone[39] before the bust of the master he seemed to fall into a pious trance. Inspired by the Duce's piece about Napoleon played in the town of Nietzsche's death where republican Germany had dared to draft a democratic constitution, did he vow to be the most ferocious superman of all?

[38] Mussolini gave his name to several plays in conjunction with a certain Forzano.

[39] A friend of mine, unseen by Hitler (he supposes), by chance enjoyed this memorable scene. He also witnessed the enthusiastic reception of Hitler by Nietzsche's sister, Elisabeth Förster. This was early in 1932.

Chapter II

THE QUARREL OVER AUSTRIA

In Habsburg Austria the Crownland of Tyrol extended to Lake Garda and included a considerable Italian population; it was one of the grievances of Italian patriots that this was so. After the fall of the Habsburgs, against whom both Mussolini and Hitler had stormed, the grievance was inverted to become a German one. By the Peace of St. Germain in 1919 the southern portion of Tyrol was transferred to Italy; for strategic reasons the new frontier was drawn at the Brenner Pass, so that over two hundred thousand German Austrians were included in Italy. This created the problem of the South Tyrol (or the Alto Adige as the Italians preferred to call it) and the greatest stumbling-block in the way of an Italian-German alliance; no real solution of the question was ever reached between Mussolini and Hitler. The rights and wrongs of the matter can be studied elsewhere. There is no doubt that the Austrians who lived south of the Brenner were badly treated by the Italian authorities as soon as these became the organs of an over-centralizing Fascism; this was the first and best-ventilated minority scandal of the time and caused international indignation.[1]

To Hitler, who was determined both to ally with Italy and to absorb Austria into Germany, it was essential to keep clear of an Italian-Austrian controversy around the chief area where Italians and Germans impinged upon one another. It has been seen that Mussolini was highly susceptible in the matter, and Hitler knew that, in order to win Austria, he would be wise to suspend his own susceptibilities as an Austrian : on no account must he suggest that his Reich might one day descend into the valley of the Adige. His attitude towards South Tyrol could now be explained as geo-political. He was ready, he announced, to divide Europe with Mussolini at the Brenner, the frontier indicated by geography—

[1] The Italians were not bound by any treaty obligations with regard to their minorities.

a few "unredeemed" Germans to the south of it could be ignored. In *Mein Kampf*,[2] indeed, he declared any agitation on behalf of the Austrians of the South Tyrol to be part of the Jewish-Legitimist conspiracy aimed at the prevention of a German-Italian *rapprochement* by those who had reason to fear an alliance between Berlin and Rome. Propagandist agitation on behalf of a minority, he added significantly, is in any case hypocrisy, for it only makes difficulties for those it professes to champion; the one way in which oppressed peoples can really be helped is by making oneself strong enough to help them by force. (When the Czechs remembered this statement later on they were reproved by the West and left in the lurch.) Hitler's approach to the South Tyrolese question was unpopular in Germany, and in 1927 the Nazi Party programme still refused " to renounce any German, whether of the Sudeten German districts, South Tyrol, Poland, that League-of-Nations colony Austria, or of any of the Successor States." In 1931, however, Alsace-Lorraine replaced the South Tyrol on the list: the courting of Italy had begun officially.

The five or six years following Hitler's release from the fortress of Landsberg on the Lech at Christmas 1924 were fairly uneventful from the point of view of his Italian aspirations. Italy became a Locarno Power but failed to achieve the application of the Locarno guarantee to the Brenner frontier. In February 1926 Mussolini crossed rhetorical swords with Stresemann over the South Tyrol, but after that the Duce's growing tendency to lead dissatisfaction with the European *status quo* made his relations with the Weimar régime relatively good. He had little interest, therefore, in contact with a revolutionary German Party which appeared, until the elections of 1930, to be losing ground, and when Brüning came to Rome in 1931 it is said that two Nazis who shouted "Down with the Jews' Chancellor!" were arrested and imprisoned.[3] About the middle of the 'twenties Hitler announced to a party comrade that Mussolini had invited

[2] As in a pamphlet published in February, 1926, *Die Südtiroler Frage und das deutsche Bündnisproblem.*

[3] A. François-Poncet, *Souvenirs d'une ambassade à Berlin,* 1946, p. 24.

him to Italy, but that he could not sacrifice his Party's prestige by going without at least three motor-cars which he could not yet afford. The truth is that at about the same time he had applied to the Italian Embassy in Berlin for a signed photograph of Mussolini; the request was forwarded to Rome, but elicited nothing but unqualified refusal. And yet Hitler had gone to unheard-of lengths in 1928. By this time the Fascists were known to have treated the South Tyrolese abominably. In August of that year Hitler met Tolomei, the villain of the story of South Tyrolese persecution by the Italians, and declared to him that he regarded the Brenner frontier as final.[4]

The Italian Embassy in Berlin was visited during the twenties rather by Sudeten German Nazis like Knirsch than by direct followers of Hitler; in this period the Croat Ustaše[5] were among its constant visitors. The practical foundations of a Fascist-Nazi alliance were laid by Göring who, after Hitler's *Putsch* of November 1923, fled abroad and spent about a year of his four years' exile in Italy. He endorsed the Hitler point of view about the South Tyrol and he easily made friends in Italian Air Force circles. And then for a flashy social figure and a collector of *objets d'art* all sorts of things were possible, for instance, his friendship with the Prince of Hesse, who was also a friend of the Prince of Piedmont. Philip of Hesse had Fascist connexions, Nazi inclinations, and a doubtful reputation; he lived a life typical of Berlin at that time, with no visible means of support, sharing a flat with a reputedly perverse Russian prince. In spite of this and of Hesse's unusual hideousness, Prince Umberto's sister, poor Princess Mafalda, fell deeply in love with him. The situation was sufficiently painful for the diplomats to be disturbed, but the Italian Embassy in Berlin remained discreetly silent. When the German Embassy in Rome, however, felt it necessary to warn the Quirinal,

---

[4] L. Salvatorelli & G. Mira. *Stories del Periodo Fascista*, 1964, p. 725.

A month or so earlier Hitler said the same in his *Zweites Buch* which was never published till many years after his death.

[5] See below, chapter III.

King Victor Emmanuel was irritated by the interference, and in September 1925 the Prince of Hesse, the "winged messenger" of the Axis to be, became the son-in-law of the King of Italy. Another confidant of Hitler's with an interest in Italy was his solicitor, Hans Frank, whom we now connect too exclusively with Poland. Frank was given legal work for the Nazi Party soon after its foundation; he, too, had fled to Italy in November 1923 and often went back there; he claimed to speak Italian fluently though Anfuso[6] says that his Italian was absurd. But the most popular of all the Nazi envoys to Italy was probably the more presentable Ritter von Epp; he, too, travelled south from Bavaria frequently.

Göring returned to the Fatherland in 1927, and in the elections of 1928 became a deputy; from now on he acted as Hitler's foreign affairs expert, but he had no dealings with the Italian Embassy until later. There is no evidence of any concrete connexion between Mussolini and the Nazis at the time of Hitler's speech to the Nazi Party on 24th May 1930, when he said, rather as if he had been Chancellor for years, "I have been striving for many years for a relationship with Italy." At the time when he began to finance Starhemberg's Austrian *Heimwehr* (or Home Guards), it is unlikely that Mussolini had ever given money to the German Nazis.

Hitler had continued to imitate Mussolini's technique. According to Heiden he first used the "Roman salute" as his Party marched past him in Weimar in July 1926. Meanwhile Goebbels was working out bigger and better D'Annunzio-of-Fiume methods. The present writer experienced an unforgettable mass meeting (there were about 10,000 persons in the audience) at the *Sportpalast* in Berlin soon after the election of Sept. 1930 (when the Nazis made great gains) in a period when Nazi uniforms were forbidden in Prussia. Goebbels himself was the speaker and he gloried in the frightful fate which would soon overtake the "traitors of Versailles"; the almost voluptuous delight of the public

[6] F. Anfuso. *Da Palazzo Venezia al Lago di Garda* (1957), p. 16.

was stimulated by Nazi youths in white shirts and top boots who at suitable moments intoned Nazi slogans or rolled what looked like barrels round the galleries to sound like the rolling of drums. Collapsing banks and a sensational increase of unemployment in Germany gave the year 1931 a catastrophic flavour which delighted the Nazis, and in August 1932 Papen and all those who blindly imagined they could harness the Nazis to their own chariot urged Hindenburg to take Hitler into the Government. Summoned to Hindenberg's presence Hitler doggedly insisted he must have the powers Mussolini had had in 1922, but the President listened sceptically and refused.

By this time Mussolini had become interested and flattered. He had now written in the *Enciclopedia Italiana* that Fascism was the conquering creed of the twentieth century, and he looked forward with interest to the day when Germany might become his satellite. Until now he had felt uncertain about Hitler whom Malaparte[7] designated unrevolutionary and pro-bourgeois (this was to be Hitler's final judgement on Mussolini in 1943). German diplomats, men like Neurath, and Hassell who succeeded Neurath as German Ambassador to Rome in 1932, hinted that Hitler was foolish rather than dangerous. In 1930, Hitler, with his extraordinary assurance, had suggested to Starhemberg that he should make contact with Mussolini, whereupon the Duce made the most of the opportunity to cross-question Starhemberg about Hitler. "Will Hitler come to power in Germany? Is he any good? . . . At any rate he is a strong man. A great demagogue. But isn't he mad? . . . He has certainly done a great deal, but his racial theories are nonsense. . . ."[8] "Race, it is an emotion, not a reality; 95 per cent. of it is emotion" Mussolini had written. It was the nation which he was eager to apostrophize, "not a race, nor a geographically

[7] Op. cit.

[8] See Starhemberg, *Between Hitler and Mussolini*, referred to above. This book was written many years later and after the loss of valuable notes. Although its author might be dismissed as an inaccurate type, his testimony is mostly borne out by the available evidence and by subsequent developments.

determined region, but as a community historically per-petuating itself, which is the will to existence and to power. . . ." There was no room for anti-Semitism nor for *Geopolitik* here.

The Nazi-Nationalist demonstration of Harzburg in October 1931 did most to impress Mussolini in favour of Hitler, for it seemed to him to be a wise acceptance of his own example. Shortly after the Harzburg meeting Göring was received by the then Italian Ambassador in Berlin, Orsini-Baroni; he held forth upon the great strength of the Nazi movement, but the Ambassador, who had always diagnosed it as a minor disorder, was unimpressed. It was only when Cerruti succeeded Orsini-Baroni in August 1932 that the Italian Embassy began to take National Socialism seriously.

Mussolini, it has been seen, had drawn his own conclusions and he interested himself eagerly in the plethora of elections which overtook Germany in the year 1932. He, or at any rate his more pro-German Press Chief, Polverelli, went so far as to think that Hitler would beat Hindenburg in the Presidential election in April, and he expected the much-talked-of 51 per cent. Nazi vote, which was never obtained, at the Reichstag elections which followed. All through 1932 Mussolini looked for a march on Berlin, but when the Nazis lost two million votes in November that year and did not promptly organize a *coup,* he decided that they had lost their chance for some time.

It was a disagreeable autumn for Hitler. When the *Fondazione Volta* invited Rosenberg to Rome to lecture on the philosophy of National Socialism he was introduced to Mussolini; but the Duce thought poorly of this Nordic doctrinaire and altogether he made a bad impression. To-wards the end of the year Gregor Strasser, who had the reputation (outside Nazi circles) of being the most serious Nazi leader, began to negotiate with General von Schleicher, the Army politician who was now Chancellor of the Reich. Mussolini thereupon accepted the journalistic talk of the day and decided that Strasser, not Hitler, was the horse to back, for Mussolini had no idea of how relentless Hitler would always be. He himself was ever in a state of vacilla-

tion between his good judgement of a situation and all
kinds of chimerical temptations. Hitler often hesitated—
to hear his voices, as it were—before making practical
decisions, and he invented the most contradictory lies to
achieve his purposes, but he never vacillated. At the end
of 1932 he dismissed Gregor Strasser from his position in
the Party. Strasser was one of the few Nazi leaders who
had shown some independence towards Hitler and an un-
fanatical readiness to compromise; for this he paid with
his life on 30th June 1934. (According to Spengler, who
knew Gregor Strasser fairly well, Strasser was the only
Nazi who bore a certain physical resemblance to Mussolini.)
For the present Hitler remained lavish in declarations that
he regarded Mussolini as the head of his own movement
without whom he could never have succeeded. Not until
the spring of 1933 did he experience his first disillusionment with the Duce; he was forced to admit then that
Mussolini was no staunch anti-Semite.

Towards the end of January 1933 it became clear that
Hindenburg was again being worked upon by Papen to
admit Hitler to the Government. Mussolini began to telephone feverishly to his Embassy in Berlin to learn particulars
about this unexpected success, and on 30th January, that
fateful day, he was informed that his *soi-disant* disciple was
Chancellor of Germany; there is evidence,[9] even, that Hitler
and Göring wished Mussolini to approve the list of the
new Nazi-Nationalist Cabinet.[10] At all events the Italian
Ambassador, Cerruti, became what his French colleague François-Poncet called the Lord Protector of the Reich, and for
the next three years, before the Axis was forged, in a sense
Mussolini was the most powerful man in Europe.

The glorification of Cerruti lasted for about two months.
Although he was able to transmit Mussolini's offer on 1st
April that Italian representatives abroad should deny all
' propagandist ' news about persecution of Jews in Germany,
he was also obliged to read a long telegram from the Duce
to the Führer in which the former insisted that Hitler's anti-

[9] According to Renzetti, of the Italian Chamber of Commerce
in Berlin, who was a friend of Göring.
[10] It contained only three Nazi Ministers, Hitler, Göring, and Frick.

Semitic policy was a dangerous mistake which discredited the dictatorships.[11] This occasioned one of those formidable tirades for which the Führer was to become famous. " I have the most absolute respect for the personality and the political action of Mussolini," Hitler shouted, " only in one thing I cannot admit him to be right and that is with regard to the Jewish question in Germany, for he cannot know anything about it."

Already another issue, linked with the Jewish question to form the measure of Hitler's hatred of the Habsburgs, had become critical between the new Germany and Italy. In the first paragraph of *Mein Kampf* we find, exactly as his background would lead us to expect, that the reunion of Germany with Austria was for Hitler " eine mit allen Mitteln durchzuführende Lebensaufgabe,"[12] and indeed the Nazis regarded Austria as automatically Nazified along with the Reich on 30th January 1933. While Hitler could talk pure racialism with such frantic conviction that the world —or most of it—believed so late as September 1938 that he wanted " no Czechs at all," it has been seen that his aim of world domination by a German ruling caste was sometimes better served by *Geopolitik*. To him the annexation of Austria always meant the *Mitteleuropa* policy of the Central Powers during the First World War, absolute German control of the whole Danubian basin. His longed-for alliance with Italy postulated the expulsion of Italian influence from here and Italy's consolation in the Mediterranean area. It is characteristic of Hitler that he did not bear the Duce malice over Austria. He proceeded with his strangely logical and methodical duplicity to drive Mussolini out of Danubia into the Mediterranean, and at the same time to preserve his sentimental enthusiasm for the Duce's " genius." What was even more characteristic was that Hitler's Danubia included the Adriatic. He may have sympathized with Italian

[11] On 30 March 1933 Mussolini's *chef de Cabinet*, Aloisi, noted in his diary that the Duce had said to him that one should never conflict with the Jews or the Church. See Aloisi, *Journal* (1957) p. 105.

[12] = (only approximately) " the task of a lifetime to be carried out with all possible means."

anti-Habsburg nationalism, but only within the limits of German expediency. Far from caring about its emotional importance to the Italians, he blamed the Habsburgs for not having germanized Trieste and the Adriatic coast. He was, in fact, heir to those Pan-Germans of the Reich who were closely associated with the German Navy League and whom Mr. Tower described in 1906[13] as, "unreasonable as it may seem," pressing for Trieste as a future outlet for the Hohenzollern fleet. There is an interesting dispatch from the French Consul in Trieste a few years earlier[14] referring to the buying up—at a loss—of the *Südbahn*, which controlled Trieste, by Reich Germans to whom he refers as " le groupement de forces qui voudrait faire de cette place . . . une sorte d'annexe commerciale de l'Allemagne, en attendant une autre annexion." (At the end of this dispatch there are " détails sur la présence de Gabriele D'Annunzio à Trieste.") Between the two great wars it was convenient to tantalize the Yugoslavs with the thought of their Trst, but, as soon as the Second World War made it possible in 1943, Hitler annexed Trieste and the whole *Küstenland* region—as well as the South Tyrol—to Nazi Germany, with complete indifference to the reactions of Mussolini.

"The Fascist State," Mussolini had written in the *Enciclopedia,* " is a will to power and to government. In it the tradition of Rome is an idea that has force. . . ." For Mussolini longed to revive the glories of Imperial Rome. This ambition fitted ill with Hitler's geopolitical programme, for it drew the Duce's gaze as far north as the Danube into a region which Hitler regarded as his *par excellence*. Indeed Mussolini took a very active interest in central Europe; it was as its defender against Nazi Germany that Hitler made him great, only to dethrone him mercilessly when the time should come. When Mussolini and Starhemberg first met in July 1930 the Duce declared with visible concern that an Anschluss with Germany must never be permitted; already he announced Austria to be " the bastion of Mediterranean civilization " while " Prussia means barbarism. . . ." Shortly after this it seems that Mussolini encouraged Star-

[13] See dispatch quoted in chapter 1.
[14] M. de Laigue to M. Delcassé, 26th May 1902.

hemberg to refuse a Nazi offer of collaboration brought from
Hitler by Gregor Strasser; and already in the Austrian
elections in November 1930 the Heimwehr received Italian
money in order to fight the Austrian Nazis. In June 1932
when they met again, still six months before Hitler took
over authority in Germany, Mussolini insisted to Starhemberg
that the incorporation of Austria in Germany would mean
a constant threat to Italy and that her fight between 1915
and 1918 for the Adriatic would have been in vain. " Trieste
will cease to be Italian. Italy can never permit that." At
this point Starhemberg told Mussolini what he knew directly
from Hitler to be the Führer's intentions with regard to
Trieste. " Yes," said Mussolini excitedly, " Pan-Germanism
is stretching its tentacles towards the Adriatic. Italy has
as little use for Pan-Germanism as for Pan-Slavism. That
is why Austria is so important. If Austria ceases to exist,
there can be no more order in Central Europe. Great dangers
will then threaten Italy."

Early in 1933, not long after Hitler had become German
Chancellor, Mussolini spoke to Starhemberg[15] of the Danubian
Basin as " our European hinterland. That is why we seek
a firm position there. Without it we shall be forced to
play the insignificant role of a peninsula on the edge of
Europe. We might even be pushed to Africa," and Italy cease
to be a Great Power. There is no time to be lost, the
Duce added, for Hitler will start rearming immediately.
Starhemberg for his part spoke of the desirability of a
Danubian federation led by Austria, to which Mussolini
replied with the suggestion of some sort of conglomeration
between Austria, Hungary, and, to Starhemberg's astonish-
ment, Croatia, with Italian economic influence as its background. Italy and Hungary had been on particularly friendly
terms since Bethlen's visit to Rome in April 1927, and
the practical results of this third visit of Starhemberg to the
Duce[16] were the Rome Protocols of March 1934. According
to these Italy, Austria, and Hungary made each other what
economic concessions they were able. The increase of the

[15] op. cit. All this can, of course, only be an approximate indication of the words Mussolini used.
[16] Mussolini continued to finance the Heimwehr.

export of Austrian timber to Italy comprised, in Dr. Schuschnigg's view for instance, the most useful help from abroad
which Austria received between 1933 and the Anschluss.[17]
At the same time Italy hoped to find a solution of her own
raw materials problem in central and south-eastern Europe.[18]

After the elections in Germany on 5th March 1933, the
Nazis evicted the legitimate authorities in Bavaria, and
on 18th March the Munich wireless station greeted the
" oppressed Party comrades in Austria who thanks to the
unintelligible folly of their Government are being compelled
to endure the worst terrorization . . . Austria is now the
last portion of Germany in which anyone still dares to
oppress *das deutsche nationale Wollen*," and the speaker
" in all friendship " warned the Austrian Government not to
cause the Nazis in the Reich to take over the protection of
the freedom of German *Volksgenossen* in Austria. The man
who broadcast this declaration of war was the Italophile Hans
Frank, Reich Commissar for Justice and newly appointed
Minister for Justice in Bavaria. In May he was invited to
Vienna by the Austrian Nazis to help them celebrate the
two hundred and fiftieth anniversary of Sobieski's victory over
the Turks. Cerruti appealed to Göring to prevent this
journey and Göring responded very affably; he himself
was just back from Rome where he had promised that the
Austrian question should not be brought up. After Cerruti's
appeal, however, he overslept until it was too late to take
any action. So Frank travelled triumphantly around Austria
as Hitler's deputy, until finally the Austrian police turned
him out.

It is not intended here to recite the whole history of
Austria from this point until her extinction in 1938. But
certainly until 1936 Austria was the crux of the relations
between the two dictators, and it will be necessary to recapitu-
late the essential characteristics of the Austrian situation.
On the one hand, the post-war Republic of Austria had

[17] Dr. Rost van Tonningen, the financial representative of the
League of Nations in Vienna, who afterwards became a leader
of the Dutch Nazis, agreed with this.

[18] At the time of the signature of the Rome Protocols Mussolini
agreed to the private teaching of German in the South Tyrol.

to contend with the problem of adjusting the economic life of a former part of a big free-trading area to that of a small area surrounded by tariff barriers and with an enormous capital city. The adjustment was bound to be painful, but it was far from the impossibility of which Nazi propaganda spoke : the new Austria was proportionately richer in raw materials than either Switzerland or Italy.

On the other hand, the Austrian Republic was politically afflicted by its division into three blocks, Clerical, Socialist, and Nationalist, none of which could arrive at a parliamentary majority alone. In the days of the Weimar Republic the Austrian Socialists as well as the Nationalists were in favour of union with Germany; the majority, perhaps, of the Clerical Christian-Socials preferred a separate Catholic Austria. With Hitler master of the Reich the lines of division were modified but above all they were sharpened. The Socialists became the uncompromising enemies of the Anschluss, but, luckily for Hitler, Mussolini's rancour against Socialists in general (which demonstrated the proverbial ardour of the convert) was exaggerated in the case of the Viennese ' Reds ' by the attention they had drawn at the beginning of January 1933 to the smuggling of arms from Italy to Hungary across Austria, the so-called Hirtenberg affair.

The hostility of the Christian-Social Party and the Austrian clergy to Hitler was weakened by their dislike, too, of the Socialists, and by the " national "—this word in Austria, it has been seen, always meant pro-German, *Grossdeutsch*— inclinations natural to the Sudeten German Archbishop of Vienna, Cardinal Innitzer. The Concordat between the Papacy and the Reich negotiated by Papen in July 1933, though it proved to be abortive, had a similar effect.

As for the Nationalists, they were divided into extremists, some of whom had had their Nazi Party before Hitler's and now had their S.A. in imitation, and the Heimwehr led by Prince Starhemberg which had busied itself chiefly with opposing the Austrian Socialists. Starhemberg had himself been with the Nazi freebooter, Sepp Dietrich, in the German *Freikorps,* and had later worked with the notorious Pabst to steal weapons from Italy; he was intimately aware of the Pan-German tradition of the Austrian lower middle class from which Hitler sprang. It is interesting not only that Hitler suggested his first visit to Mussolini, but that Hitler's idol then inspired Starhemberg with the idea of using the Heimwehr to defend the independence of Austria against Hitler. It was a *tour de force* that this was done for a few years; in spite of the hatred of Italy in Austria and the knowledge that Starhemberg depended on Mussolini, only the Styrian section of the Heimwehr openly seceded to the Nazis.

It was a *tour de force* in particular because Hitler, with Frank's broadcast and the appointment of Habicht, the Inspector of the Austrian Nazis,[19] as German Press Attaché in Vienna , had let loose the Nazi terror, with all its ' refinements,' over Austria. It is a dreadful fact of which Hitler was well aware that no one who has not experienced the workings of Nazi sadism (exactly how much it owed to Hitler's own inventiveness it is not possible to say) is able to believe in them. It would be unconvincing here to make a list of all the subtle and unsubtle methods which were used, followed always by an inimitable evasiveness. Thus the responsibility of the Reich Government for these things could never be proved—this Nazi speaker's national ardour had run away with him, that crime had been perpetrated by a Jewish or Communist *agent provocateur*. What it may be worth while to notice is that Mussolini never fully understood, for he and his Fascists were too haphazard and naïve. They knew about brutal police methods and gangsters with bottles of castor oil, they knew about marvellous lies in the Press, but they could never have arrived at the Nazi conception of the concentration camp or the German system of gassing the Jews.[20]

The intense Italo-German friction over Austria in the summer of 1933 was partially obscured by the Four-Power Pact in June. When Cerruti saw Hitler about this the Führer at first seemed likely to be truculent. But Neurath and Blomberg[21] were there, and, while Neurath remained silent, Blomberg insisted that ten years of peace were worth having;

---

[19] Recently transferred from Wiesbaden where he was *Gauleiter*.
[20] See E. Kogon, *Der S.S. Staat*, 1946 and chapter XVII below.
[21] Minister of War.

however little he thought this, it suited Hitler to concur for
the moment. This seeming success of Mussolini's was un-
done when Germany roughly left the League of Nations
in October. The Duce was annoyed at her unruliness towards
him, the more because it still suited him to have the
German card in his hand at Geneva. Not long after this, at
the beginning of 1934, one of Hitler's few criticisms of
Fascism before the Second World War is recorded. To
Rauschning's surprise he now stated that Fascism had not
understood " the real meaning of the great upheaval of
our era. . . . Ultimately we National Socialists stand alone,
as the only ones who know the secret of these gigantic
changes, and therefore as those chosen to set their seal
on the coming age."[22]

There was one mistake in the Austrian game for which
Mussolini's responsibility has become clear. On 1st July
1933 he wrote to Dollfuss, the Austrian Chancellor, that " If
instead the Social-Democratic Party is treated with consideration . . . the much greater and more concrete danger exists
that thereby the anti-Marxist weapon will be delivered into
the hands of the Nazis."[23] In August Dollfuss visited Mussolini at Riccione where the Austrian was urged towards
more evident dictatorship. After something of a pause Suvich,
the Duce's right-hand at the Palazzo Chigi, made a demonstrative appearance in Vienna in January 1934; a fortnight later
civil war broke out between the Dollfuss régime, which
professed to be defending the integrity of Austria against
Hitler, and the Austrian Social Democrats, the most sincere
believers, now, in that integrity. The instigation of the
conflict may be attributed to Fey in whom Suvich had
expressed his confidence to Dollfuss.[24] The crushing of the
' Austro-Marxists ' helped no one but Hitler, and the German
press gleefully exploited the opportunity to insist upon the

[22] R. Rauschning, *Hitler Speaks*, (1939). Cf. Hitler and Goebbels
on Mussolini in September 1943; see chap. XIX below.

[23] See Mussolini to Dollfuss 1 July 1933 in State Archives, Vienna,
Liasse Italien, Fasz. 477, published in *The Tragedy of Austria*, by
Julius Braunthal, Gollancz, 1948.

[24] Ibid. Suvich to Dollfuss, January 1934. At the time Fey was
Vice-Chancellor with special security powers.

reactionary wickedness of a Government which shot its
workers down. When on 1st May Dollfuss launched his new
corporate constitution the winds were adverse from the
start. However much Hitler nursed the notion of Mussolini
as his mentor, his official and his clandestine Press neglected
no opportunity of stirring up every anti-Italian emotion in
the Austrian breast against this servile imitation of the Fascist
corporate State; the Dollfuss experiment was also damned
in Nazi eyes as inspired by the Encyclical of 1891 and thus
by the Vatican.

At this point Hitler must have realized that the deterioration of his relations with Mussolini was almost complete. He
believed profoundly in the importance of personally addressing
masses or individuals, though his approach was so imper-
sonal that he made little distinction between the two. " I
know that one can win people over much more readily with
the spoken than the written word," he had said in the foreword to *Mein Kampf.* One day Röhm, at lunch at Neurath's,
began to ventilate the idea of a meeting between the Leaders
to clear up all misunderstandings. Mussolini reacted cautiously
and instructed Cerruti that he would only agree if a clearly
defined programme were settled beforehand. Cerruti took
the initial steps, then went on a few days' leave to Italy.
What was his surprise to meet there by chance the irrepressible
Papen, who informed him that the meeting was arranged
—" It will all go off beautifully,"[25] he announced with his
cheerful smile.

So Adolf Hitler, preceded by a band of S.S. toughs like
Sepp Dietrich to watch over him, set out upon his first
journey abroad, for the first of a strange series of meetings
with the genius beyond the Alps. It developed into one of
those ridiculous occasions which deceived the world into
not taking him seriously. Mussolini came to meet him in
superlatively military costume while Hitler arrived in a rain-
coat (concealing a black jacket and striped trousers) and
patent-leather shoes, holding a grey felt hat with which he
fidgeted incessantly. No one had ever noticed him with
a civilian hat before, and one French journalist described him

[25] Papen had by chance met Mussolini at the Opera in Rome
on 28th March. See D.G.F.P. series c. vol. II no. 368.

as looking like "un petit plombier tenant un fâcheux instrument devant son ventre." It was by Neurath's advice that Hitler had descended to civilian clothes on this occasion and it is likely that his resentment against Neurath was permanent.

The discussions had been fixed to open on 14th June at the beautiful Villa Pisani at Stra near Padua where Mussolini took up residence on the previous day. The Villa had long been out of use and much time had been devoted to making it habitable. Disrespectful mosquitoes, however, teased the dictators to such an extent during their first meeting that on 15th June Mussolini moved to Venice where Hitler was staying in the Grand Hotel; Mussolini, gossip added, had felt himself disturbed by the ghost of Napoleon who had inevitably slept at Stra. Thus the second Great Men's tête-à-tête took place at the Alberoni golf-course in Venice on 15th June. According to the German Foreign Office documents[26] Hitler did the talking on 14th June, demanding that Nazis should be taken into the Austrian Government and elections be held in Austria; on 15th June Mussolini spoke most of the time but of other things—there is no evidence as to his reaction to Hitler's Austrian demands except that Hitler told Rosenberg that he agreed to them.[27] As the two men really were alone, no one will ever know all that was said; Neurath, who was one of the German party which had come to Venice for the occasion, told his friends that the two roared at one another like bulls. Hitler certainly held forth, mainly it is thought about the affinity between Fascism and National Socialism and about the cruel persecution of his brother patriots in Austria. (As if by magic the Nazi terrorist bomb outrages there had stopped on 14th June.) It seems that Suvich, who was vastly amused, told Starhemberg a month later that Hitler had declaimed to Mussolini about the superiority of the Nordic race. One thing applies to all the Duce-Führer tête-à-têtes. While Hitler spoke no word of any language but German, "the Duce," as Schuschnigg said, "was accustomed to speak

[26] D.G.F.P. series C. vol. III, no. 5. No Italian Foreign Office documents are available.

[27] *Das politische Tagebuch Alfred Rosenbergs* (1956), p. 28.

German—it was hard, very slow and carefully articulated; one was aware that it involved an effort which he enjoyed."[28] Paul Schmidt, the German Foreign Office interpreter, was present at Venice on this occasion, but he does not seem to have been called upon. Yet if Mussolini denied the necessity with implied indignation it is unlikely that he followed with precision the floods of slightly Bavarianized Austrian which poured from Hitler. Later the Duce's receptivity depended upon his state of health, and undoubtedly declined with the passage of the years. Thus Schmidt's role as the medium between Mussolini and Hitler gradually increased in importance.[29] This, however, modified but could not clarify the relationship between the dictators, not merely because a third personality was placed between them, but also because Schmidt knew no Italian and translated Hitler's German into French; even so Schmidt was sometimes inaccurate.[30] Mussolini for his part could undoubtedly express himself better in French than in German, but his linguistic vanity left him at a disadvantage with which Hitler was never troubled. The basic relationship of these two men was mirrored in this situation, the psychological importance of which will be clear to anyone who has grappled with circumstances of this kind. One should add that the lesser German and Italian lights usually spoke to one another either in English or in French. Fascist diplomacy, moreover, was notoriously careless about its linguistic and legal technique; in Fascist Italy's dealings with Nazi Germany the interpreters and legal experts were always provided by the Germans.

There is an apocryphal story that at this first meeting Mussolini quoted to Hitler the Tarquin story about cutting down the flowers that grow too high.[31] Certainly he felt him to be intractable. For their part the Nazi visitors wrote off Mussolini as dully traditional, though Hitler's dual personality made it possible for his fixational attitude to continue

[28] Schuschnigg, op. cit. p. 220.

[29] See an interview with Paul Schmidt's wife in the *Journal de Genève,* 29th October, 1945.

[30] This fact was noticed by Sumner Welles and I have found traces of it. No interpreter, obviously, can be expected to be infallible.

[31] Cf. François-Poncet, op. cit., p. 183.

at the same time. It is difficult to know how much he was even aware of the hostility of the Venetian crowds which acclaimed only with "*Duce, Duce,*" while Starace[32] tried to explain to Hitler that *Duce* meant *Führer.* On his return to Germany Hitler described the homage of the Italians to Mussolini, and his Caesar-like pose, with great admiration to Rosenberg.[33]

The Stra and Venice meeting was the prelude to two notoriously horrible events: the massacre of 30th June in Germany and the murder of Dollfuss on 25th July in Vienna. There is no clear evidence of whether Hitler thought he had convinced Mussolini in any way and had thus acquired *carte blanche* for his crimes: certainly he did not care, for he had decided to liquidate Röhm and the S.A. before he went to Italy. To the news of 30th June there was no open Italian reaction. Those Italians, Fascist or otherwise, who knew what had happened were horrified by this example of German savagery; the frigidity, which had been intensifying all the year, of the Italian Embassy in Berlin towards the Nazi régime sank to freezing-point. With the murder of Dollfuss on 25th July the Italian Press was let loose, retrospectively too. The Germans were denounced as a nation of *pederasti* and *assassini,* and if Hitler had lectured him on Nordic nobility Mussolini himself hit back in the *Popolo d'Italia;* if these theories of racial purity were correct, he declared, the Lapps would have to be honoured as the highest type of humanity.

The events leading up to the murder of Dollfuss were some of the most complicated in the rivalry between the S.S. and the S.A. and other Austrian and German factions, but they do not call for analysis here. It is not uninteresting that after the meetings of Venice the Nazis in Austria told one another that Hitler had dictated terms to Mussolini there, that Dollfuss would shortly be ousted in favour of Rintelen, and the Italian Legation in Vienna change its attitude.[34] Rintelen, the uncrowned king of Styria as he was called, had been *Landeshauptmann* there for many years; in August

[32] At that time Secretary of the Fascist Party.
[33] Rosenberg, op. cit.
[34] This I experienced in Vienna myself at the time.

1933 he was politely exiled by Dollfuss, who had sent him
as Austrian Minister—of all places—to Rome. He was
closely associated with the *Alpine Montan* Company, which
owned the excellent iron-mines of Styria and which was flourishing now upon the requirements of German rearmament.
From the point of view of *Wehrwirtschaft* it was the Styrian
Erzberg which made Austria important to Germany. More
than half the *Alpine Montan* shares were already owned by
Thyssen and the German Steel Trust, and Nazi pressure on
the employees of the *Alpine Montan* was very strong. On
23rd July Rintelen arrived in Vienna and on the 25th, when
the Nazi rebels seized the wireless station, they broadcast
his appointment as Austrian Chancellor. He would have done
Hitler's job as well as Glaise-Horstenau or Seyss-Inquart. But
Rintelen was defeated by Morreale.

The Italian Minister in Vienna in this period was Gabriele
Preziosi, but the most important person at the Italian Legation was Eugenio Morreale, a vigorous and competent person[35]
with the elastic title of Press Attaché. His activities, in
other words, were various. He did in fact stimulate ' cultural '
relations between Austria and Italy and, considering the
unpopularity of the Italians in Austria, did so with astonishing success; all possible use was made of the ' common
Latin heritage' as contrasted with the Reich which, except
for the left bank of the Rhine, had remained beyond the
limes. But Morreale was also very well informed politically
and he did jobs like handing over the money which Mussolini had promised Starhemberg to pay to the Heimwehr.
On 25th July Preziosi, like his French and British colleagues,
was on leave, and it was Morreale who kept both Rome
and the Austrian Vice-Chancellor, Prince Starhemberg (who
was on holiday on the Lido), informed about Austrian
developments; at 7 p.m. he was obliged to telephone to
Riccione, where Dollfuss's family was staying with Mussolini,
that Dollfuss himself had bled to death. In Austria Morreale
persuaded his Heimwehr friends to mobilize and occupy
various key-points. This made it possible to reserve the
Viennese telephone for Austrian official use and for the use
of the Italian, French, and British Legations, while the

[35] To everyone's surprise he became a neo-Fascist in 1943.

German Legation was cut off; Rome rang up every half-hour all the afternoon and evening. It was a time when, in view of an Anschluss possibility, any unheroic Austrian thought twice before compromising himself with Hitler's enemies, and it has been suggested[36] that Morreale was instrumental in causing the publication of an anti-Nazi Ministers' statement from which it was impossible to retreat. Rintelen was arrested at once, and later, in March 1935, condemned to a life-sentence.

Mussolini was genuinely enraged against Hitler by now. He ordered the Alpini to the Brenner and sent Starhemberg, as acting Austrian Chancellor, a very strong telegram. Cerruti and the Nunzio were the first two diplomats to deliver their condolences to the Austrian Minister in Berlin. A little later when the Duce visited an Austrian boys' camp at Ostia he stormed against the Führer, telling Starhemberg that Hitler was Dollfuss's murderer, " a horrible sexual degenerate, a dangerous fool." The climax of his anti-German campaign was reached at Bari on 6th September, when, speaking from a tank at the inauguration of the fifth *Fiera del Levante,* he said : " Thirty centuries of history allow us to regard with supreme indulgence certain doctrines taught beyond the Alps by the descendants of people who were wholly illiterate in the days when Caesar, Virgil and Augustus flourished in Rome."

The Duce was not content with journalism and speeches, nor yet with his mobilization on the Brenner or the pleasures of being acclaimed as the saviour of civilization. At the height of his fury against Hitler he decided upon the conquest of Abyssinia. It was in August 1934 that he spoke to Schuschnigg of a conflict over Abyssinia as inevitable,[37] and before the end of the year he had discussed the necessity with his military chiefs and some of his diplomats. He told them that because of Hitler Italy could not afford to wait. He calculated that a year would be required to subdue Abyssinia, and then

[36] By U. Grazzi, Italian Chargé d'Affairs in Vienna in 1934, in articles published in *Politica Estera* in Nov. and Dec. 1945, under the pseudonym " Muzio Gertbraz."

[37] Schuschnigg, op. cit. p. 220. Mussolini had thought earlier of attacking Abyssinia, but without making a final decision.

the Italian Army must be back at the Brenner in full force—
Germany, he added to Cerruti with considerable acumen,
would not be ready for war until 1938. He did not foresee
difficulties from the West if he could come to an agreement
with France. It was thus to a large extent as an anti-German
action that he contemplated the subjection of Ethiopia.
" If one poses the question what political constellation at
the turn of the year 1934-35 determined the initiation of
Italy's policy against Abyssinia," Hassell wrote on 6th February 1936, " the answer must be that it was the German-
Italian conflict over Austria."[38] Little wonder that Hitler
believed in the particular favour of destiny when action
planned against him was to be the key to his extraordinary
success between 1936 and 1940.

[38] D.G.F.P. series c. vol. IV, no. 545.

Chapter III

GERMANY AND THE ATTACK
UPON ABYSSINIA

Diplomats who worked for many years with Mussolini believe that he always yearned after an alliance with France, about which, in his completely different way, he had some of Hitler's feelings about Britain. After the murder of Dollfuss, while he obviously enjoyed the prestige he was winning as the protector of Europe and the champion of civilized values, he several times threw out the hint that Italy could not always be the only Power to mobilize against Hitler. The 25th July 1934 had in fact brought about a small-scale *rapprochement* between Italy and the Western Powers in Vienna, where the three Chargés d'Affaires (in the absence of their Ministers, who were away on holiday) spent the days and nights from 25th July to 28th July together. The Little Entente representatives, incidentally, did much the same, watching the three Chargés of the Great Powers nervously.

In Fascist eyes Czechoslovakia, Yugoslavia and Roumania were nothing but the lackeys of France. The relations between Fascist Italy and the Powers joined in the Little Entente were also conditioned in a general way by Mussolini's revisionism and encouragement to Hungary, and more specifically by the anger which his support of Croat separatism engendered at Belgrade. The leading *Ustaša* or Croat terrorist, Ante Pavelić, who also had connexions with the I.M.R.O., the Macedonian terrorist organization, had left Yugoslavia in 1929 and spent the intervening years in Italy and Hungary, and occasionally in Austria and Germany. The Croats were traditionally the most *kaisertreu* of the former Austrian Slavs, and their quarrel with the Serbs fortified the fierce Serb hatred of the Habsburg dynasty. This united Czechs and Serbs and made the Little Entente fanatically hostile to the possibilities of any kind of Habsburg restoration. For years these feelings gave the arch-hater of the Habsburgs, Adolf Hitler, a useful weapon in dealing with his future victims of the Little Entente, not

excepting Dr. Beneš. Göring's visit to Yugoslavia earlier in
1934 had strengthened the Serbs in the belief that the
Anschluss might be the best veto on a restoration, at which,
as the Nazis always insinuated, Dollfuss and the Clericals—
both Austrian and Italian—were aiming. At the same time,
of course, the Nazis flirted with Croats and Macedonians—
disruptive elements might be useful anywhere. Rosenberg,
who was, roughly speaking, Hitler's agent for the disruption
of Russia, though he never stooped to the racial depths of
Latin questions, patronized all kinds of Slavs, including a
group in Berlin called the " Croatia-Presse."

At the time of Dollfuss's murder it seemed as if war might
be provoked, not directly between Italy and Germany but
rather between Italy and Yugoslavia. The Yugoslavs were
frightened of the Italians on their weak northern frontier,
and on the other hand it was, perhaps, only a *démenti* of
news that Yugoslav troops had entered Austria which prevented the Alpini from crossing the Brenner. Many Austrian
Nazis subsequently took refuge in Maribor (Marburg), in
Slovenia. On 9th October the Adriatic air became heavier
still with the murder at Marseilles of Alexander of Yugoslavia together with the French Foreign Minister, Barthou,
by a Macedonian terrorist. Now Mussolini at that time had
little interest in the perpetration of this crime, which might
have been engineered at the last moment by no higher
authority than the I.M.R.O. and the *Ustaše*; certainly it
served no one's purpose except that of the Germans. Though
the terrorist Göring assured the Yugoslav journalists at Belgrade on 17th October that the Reich countenanced no terrorists, on 27th October he admitted to François-Poncet,[1] as
did Neurath on the 24th, that Rosenberg had been " careless."
Clues implicated Pavelić and his fellow-conspirator, Kvaternik,
who were arrested in Turin on 18th October, and it was
subsequently discovered that Pavelić had left Berlin for Milan
very suddenly on the eve of the murder. François-Poncet
himself experienced the difficulties made by the Germans,
when, after many warm offers from them, a representative
of the Sûreté Nationale came to Berlin to investigate.

[1] See François-Poncet, op. cit.

Meanwhile Mussolini refused the extradition of Pavelić and Kvaternik, and it was tacitly agreed that Yugoslavia should vent her anger against Hungary as the protector of assassins. It took several months for the rage of Yugoslavia to subside.

Barthou had been intending to proceed to Rome, and Mussolini had already prepared to welcome him in his speech in Milan on 6th October, when he warned Germany that she should not " estrange herself from Europe's historical evolution,"[2] and spoke with enthusiasm of his hope of an understanding with France. It was finally with Laval in January 1935 that a Franco-Italian agreement was signed. After the noisy speeches of many years, Italy showed herself astonishingly yielding in the matters of territorial readjustments in Africa and the status of Italians in Tunisia; a few faintly practical steps for the international defence of Austria were planned. In February an Italo-Austrian Cultural Agreement was signed, and shortly afterwards the Italian *Capo* himself contributed a rather trite article to the *Popolo d'Italia* on the " Historic Mission of Austria," which he defined more or less as that of a clearing-house for Italian artists. He laid great emphasis upon the Catholicism of Austria, and concluded with the importance of Austria's community of language with Germany and of religion with Italy. The German return to conscription on 16th March did nothing to lessen Mussolini's expressions of wrath against northern barbarism and led to a fresh Franco-Italian encounter, to which the British were invited, at Stresa in April. Both at Rome in January and at Stresa in April Mussolini showed the technical incompetence as a negotiator of a man who was little but an orator and a journalist. He lacked the legal training of higher Italian functionaries, and where Hitler deliberately generated clouds of confusion by his interminable speeches, Mussolini, even before his young son-in-law, Count Ciano, took charge of the Palazzo Chigi, created confusion through sheer amateurishness. Others who were concerned with the Franco-Italian agreement consider that Laval was well aware that Mussolini was being generous in the hope of gaining liberty of action in Ethiopia, but Laval imagined that there

[2] = estraniarsi del corso della storia europea.

would be no breach of the peace—the Italians would proceed as the French had in Morocco a generation earlier; Laval was certainly speaking the truth when he afterwards insisted that he had never agreed in any form to an open attack on Ethiopia. At Stresa there was a tremendous gathering of diplomats and journalists. A succulent lunch at the Isola dei Pescatori brought together the respective specialists on Ethiopia, including the Foreign Office representative, Mr. Maurice Peterson, and while the greatest cordiality reigned and agreement about obvious Ethiopian technicalities was expressed, the possibility of *action* in Ethiopia was never mentioned. The result was that Mussolini became convinced that both France and Britain were willing for him to annex Ethiopia as it might please him, in return for his services against Germany. Ciano echoed the Duce's phrases about civilized man and northern barbarism when, as Minister of Propaganda, he opened the exhibition of Italian painting in Paris. And if Britain were still in doubt it was Ciano who received Lord Tyrrell at his country-house in August, and, when asked what Italy really wanted, replied without hesitation, "But we want Ethiopia."[3]

At French instigation an Italian-Yugoslav *détente* had been initiated when a new Italian Minister arrived in Belgrade in March. This gave substance to the project of an Italian-led south-eastern Europe, and when in May 1935 the Franco-Russian and Czech-Russian treaties were signed the solidarity of the Continent against Hitler seemed complete. Great Britain's White Paper early in March had drawn attention to certain obvious dangers in National Socialism, but at Stresa Sir John Simon was cool about Austrian integrity. Suddenly the solidarity of Europe was shaken in June by the —as it seemed to the Continent—inexplicable defection of Britain, and the Anglo-German naval treaty created a breach in the wall of Germany's isolation.[4]

---

[3] Ciano recounted this incident to his brother-in-law, Count M. Magistrati, from whom I learnt it. Of course Ciano may have been boasting.

[4] Cf. Papen's Dispatch from Vienna to Berlin, 27 July 1935, quoted below.

Thus during the first half of 1935 the relations between Mussolini and Hitler were as bad as they could be. It is interesting that on 1st March 1935, when Hitler appeared in the Saar after the plebiscite in January and received Aloisi, he thanked him as if the Saar Territory were a gift from Mussolini. Although Aloisi was the Duce's *Chef de Cabinet* he had appeared in the Saar only as chairman of the Committee of Three of the Council of the League of Nations, the Committee which had been charged with preparing and carrying out the plebiscite.[5] The Polish Ambassador, Lipski, was something of an *homme de confiance* to the German régime, since the German-Polish Agreement of 1934 had brought Hitler this one strange friendship; he had a talk with Göring at the Schorfheide at the end of April 1935, when Göring complained bitterly that Mussolini was working against Germany in every possible field.[6] At the beginning of May Lipski saw Göring again; the latter was still angry. He grumbled that, as they had told Mussolini at the time, Germany had only come into the Four-Power Pact to please the Duce and this was Germany's reward. . . . Like nearly all Göring's frank confidences, this was untrue; it has been seen that Germany had joined the Pact of June 1933 because her Minister of War had wished to do so.

After the assassination of Dollfuss, the Austrian Government and State had been patched together somehow and even attained a certain appearance of solidarity for the next couple of years. The Clericals, through the President of the Austrian State, Miklas, insisted upon Schuschnigg as successor to Dollfuss, with Starhemberg still as Vice-Chancellor; since Schuschnigg was far less flexible than Dollfuss, the new Clerical-Heimwehr coalition was difficult from the start, and since Schuschnigg was known in principle to desire a Habsburg restoration, it gave, as one or two clear-sighted individuals at once perceived, marvellous opportunities to Franz von Papen. This political harlequin has been seen to have been instrumental in bringing Hitler into power in

[5] Aloisi, *Journal* (1957) p. 257.
[6] Information supplied by Monsieur Lipski, as below.

Germany, and then into the presence of his chosen Master at Venice on 14th June. Three days later Papen delivered his famous Marburg speech written for him by the unfortunate Edgar Jung in anything but a Nazi spirit. Everyone thought for a moment that Germany was returning to her senses, only to learn that Jung had been among those murdered by Hitler's orders on 30th June, while Papen, after one of his habitual thriller-escapes, blandly accepted the murder of his personal secretary and other of his close associates : what was more, he also accepted the post of Hitler's special envoy to Vienna on the day after the murder of Dollfuss. The Italians were not amused and insisted that Miklas should delay the *agrément* at least until after the funeral of Dollfuss on 29th July.

Until the autumn of 1935 a certain stability was maintained in Austria. Schuschnigg had quickly found occasion to visit the Duce to establish personal contact. His stiff ascetic personality and his Tyrolese associations did not please Mussolini; the Duce, however, arranged to keep in direct touch with him through Senator Salata, a Triestino who was director of the Italian Institute in Vienna, and who had intervened, against the wishes of the Italian Legation there, to bring about the Duce's acquiescence in Papen's special mission. For his dealings with Starhemberg Mussolini still used Morreale, who was on the worst of terms with Salata.

For the moment Austria profited economically from the political situation. During the summer of 1935 there were enough other tourists to make up for the Germans who had for two years been kept north of the frontier by the 1,000-mark tax demanded by the Reich Government from those of them who wished to cross it. The Rome Protocols served Austria well, various exports to Italy increasing,[7] and the expansion of Italy's Danubian horizon created a strong Italian interest in the Danube Shipping Company. Above all, Italian preparations for an attack on Ethiopia kept the Hirtenberg arms factory in Austria fully employed.

For a year Papen made no progress. On 27th July[8] he,

[7] See figures in, for example, the *Annuario Statistico Italiano*.
[8] D.G.F.P. series c. vol. IV, no. 232.

Hitler addressing the Maifeld rally

At the war memorial in Berlin

or some more intelligent member of his staff, wrote an important dispatch to Berlin which deserves a good deal of quotation. It begins by referring to the general hostility to Germany caused by the Austrian question. Every German effort in a south-eastern direction will run up against this opposition, especially since Italy regards the Danube basin as her *Expansionsgebiet*. As between Germany and Austria Papen absolutely condemns the Habicht type of open terrorism which had culminated in the Dollfuss crime. Austria is now based upon militant Catholicism and a Heimwehr which is " enthusiastically favourable to Mussolini." " The dream of resurrecting the Holy Roman Empire around Vienna becomes more grotesque the more this idea of the Austrian imperialist romantics is exploited by Mussolini in order to advance his conception of a new *imperium romanum* at the expense of the German nation." We must, continues Papen, create a mission of the united Germans to triumph over the idea of an Austrian mission, and we must insist that our mission, if opposed to political Catholicism, in no way undermines the fundamental Christianity of Germany. It was Papen who had negotiated Hitler's Concordat with the Vatican in July 1933—that first external concession to Hitler, as Pechel[9] emphasizes—and it was mainly on account of his Catholic connexions that Hitler had sent him to Vienna. Mussolini was only too well aware, as he said to Starhemberg,[10] that Papen, with his astonishing ability to make everyone feel he was their particular friend, was more dangerous than Habicht.

All this time, far from finding the champions of the Austrians in South Tyrol mere drivellers, Adolf Hitler found them all too useful. In vain did Mussolini and Dollfuss or Schuschnigg try to emphasize that the Italian authorities were being more conciliatory on account of the Rome-Vienna friendship; the young Tyrolese, whether of Innsbruck or Bolzano, were convinced that Hitler had dictated terms at Venice or at some point later. The Bavarian press was allowed to be extremely violent about Italian oppression, which had been drastic; but without any particular justification the wicked Latins were attacked in the winter of 1934-5 for

[9] Pechel, op. cit.   [10] Starhemberg, op. cit.

suppressing noble Nordic Christmas-trees. It was easy to whip up feeling against Italy in Germany, and of course in Austria and South Tyrol, and at the end of April 1935 the *Münchner Neueste Nachrichten*—the leading newspaper of Munich—was banned in Italy.

The German press was also clearly hostile to Italy in the matter of her East African policy, and an Ufa film called *Abessinien von Heute,* which was markedly friendly to the Negus and his rule, was shown all over Germany during this spring (1935). In June there was a passing, if prophetic, rumour of an Italian-German deal, Italy to drop Austria and Germany to back her over Abyssinia, but the Germans' pose, and indeed their only hope just then after the Naval Agreement, was to be Britain's friend and as such opposed to Italy. This was in fact the policy of the German Foreign Office and the Naval Staff, as also of the Reichswehr, which despised the Italian Army and expected a fresh Italian fiasco in Abyssinia. The Nazi Party felt confused between its contempt for racial inferiors and the defenders of Austrian " separatism," and its hatred of the League of Nations and the *status quo.* In northern Germany hatred of Italy on account of the so-called treachery of 1915 and the South Tyrol was a little less intense than in the south; especially at this time the feeling about Danzig was stronger and therefore perhaps also the feeling against Geneva. Until it was clear that Mussolini's Abyssinian policy would bring him into conflict with the League, this policy enjoyed no sympathy in Germany.[11]

In Hitler's mind, however, no breach with Mussolini occurred, and there were one or two individuals whose interests urged them to encourage this belief. Baron Braun von Stumm held an important position in the Press Department of the German Foreign Office; his second wife was a highly neurotic Italian woman, Giuseppina Antinori. Probably before the end of 1934 she and Ciano's sister, who was Countess Magistrati,[12] met Hitler secretly without the

[11] The Germans felt a strong interest in Abyssinian economic development, but this did not identify their interests with those of Italy in spite of the *Società Mineraria italo-tedesca* in Abyssinia.

[12] Ciano was still Minister of Propaganda at this time.

knowledge of Cerruti, to try to counteract anti-Italian pressures. The Braun von Stumm household was in every sense an Italo-German meeting-ground;[13] it was here, for instance, that Professor Manacorda of Florence University was often received. He was both ultra-Fascist and ultra-Catholic, and on his journeys to Germany (which began in 1936) he gave himself the airs of an important intermediary between the Vatican, Italy, and Germany. But, though he occasionally saw the Pope and the Duce and the Führer, it is unlikely that he affected the trend of their relations perceptibly.

At the beginning of August 1935, on account of the Danzig-League of Nations crisis, Lipski visited Hitler at Berchtesgaden. With a certain regret the Führer remarked that his path had diverged from that of Mussolini on account of Austria. Mussolini had failed to understand the situation, and he was now taking a grave risk in provoking the other Powers over Abyssinia. But, added Hitler, though the Duce was hostile to Germany he would regard a defeat of Mussolini as a disaster, because it would constitute too great a blow to their common Fascist-Nazi ideology. It was always the same thing. Hitler knew. Anyone who did not accept his view did not understand. And Mussolini never really knew—until perhaps on the shores of Garda in 1944—that Hitler had cast him for his partner in his own Satanic revolution.

At all events it was clear to Lipski that Hitler was already determined, whatever Neurath and the German Foreign Office might wish, to prevent the humiliation of Mussolini. And, as always seemed to happen in that fatal decade, events so played into Hitler's hands that when he spoke in March 1936 of his *schlafwandlerische Sicherheit*[14] it was difficult not to be impressed. Already by the end of June 1935, without evidence (beyond Schacht's general policy) of any German scheming to bring it about, Italy had become the leading buyer of German coal. By now Cerruti was scarcely on speaking-terms with the Wilhelmstrasse and still less with Hitler. Mussolini decided to move Cerruti to Paris and to bring

[13] See L. Simoni, *Berlino—Ambasciata d'Italia* 1934-43, 1946, pp. 27-9.

[14] The self-assurance of a sleep-walker.

Attolico, his Ambassador in Moscow, to Berlin.[15] Attolico, the man who four years later kept Italy out of the war, was so anxious in August 1935 to start his mission well that he would not wait till Hitler's return to Berlin in September in order to present his credentials. It was arranged that Hitler should come from Berchtesgaden to Berlin at the end of August for this purpose, and in consequence Attolico was bound to go to the Nazi Party Congress in September 1935, although in 1934 no Italian diplomat had attended it. This was not, of course, without the approval of the Duce, who had shown signs of anxiety about his relations with Germany since June; at this time a breakdown in the League negotiations over the Abyssinian controversy was becoming apparent.

In October Mussolini attacked Ethiopia, which he could probably have had without firing a shot. It is interesting that several leading Fascists told Starhemberg that they were opposed to the venture.[16] But Mussolini's was a journalistic determination to fight at all costs as a demonstration of force, because purely political action might be too 'decadent' to impress that self-same Hitler who never wasted superfluous force upon the acquisition of power. The outbreak of war in Abyssinia was followed by a superficial strengthening of the Duce's position in Austria. While Schuschnigg remained Chancellor, Starhemberg on 17th October got rid of Fey, who had been undermining the Heimwehr in Hitler's interest, and took over the Ministry of the Interior for himself; at the same time he put at the head of the Austrian Ministry of Finance Draxler, hitherto legal adviser to Starhemberg's friend, the arms manufacturer Mandl, who, according to Papen, inspired Starhemberg with all his own Jewish *ressentiment* against Hitler. Mandl was the owner of Hirtenberg and of arms factories in Italy, and as unpleasant as arms manufacturers are traditionally said to be. It was a most valuable asset to the Nazi cause that Austrian policy could now be interpreted as subordinate to Herr Mandl's desire for

---

[15] Attolico spoke no German and never succeeded in learning much; he and Ribbentrop always conversed in English.

[16] Starhemberg, op. cit.

profit. " How far Italian pressure affected Starhemberg . . .
cannot be exactly gauged. But I learn on good authority
that Mussolini urgently demanded a strengthening of the
authority of the Austrian Government "; Papen had also
heard that Starhemberg was convinced that Italy's venture
would succeed.[17] The German Minister in Vienna was quick
enough to sense that the Austrian Italophiles had overreached
themselves. The unpopularity of Italy was now reinforced in
Austria by dislike of being identified with Mussolini's defiance
of Geneva and by anxiety as to the defence of Austria if
the Italian Army were busy in East Africa. People complained
that Austria had been led into a cul-de-sac; she now depended
einzig und allein upon the victory of Mussolini.[17]

A week or so later it was the talk of Vienna that Herr
von Papen's car had been left several times, gaily and indiscreetly flying its swastika flag (which was forbidden in
Austria), outside the office of the Clerical and semi-official
newspaper, the *Reichspost*. It was here that together with its
editor, Dr. Funder, he now began to plan the Press Agreement
of the following July. Funder seems to have been perfectly
genuine; it is all the more surprising that he should have
been willing to discuss with Papen at this time not only
an agreement about the press, but also the question of the
Austrian Nazis who had become Austrian Legionaries in
the Reich and were being trained for a *coup*. He actually
told Papen, if the latter may be believed, that he favoured
a secret agreement because there were so many people both
within Austria and without who were interested in preventing an Austro-German agreement.[18] In May the acceptance
by Mussolini of the Press Agreement which emerged later
on may be regarded as the occasion of the birth of the Axis
friendship; it was made possible by Mussolini's weakness, and

[17] Papen to Berlin, 18 Oct. 1935. D.G.F.P. series c. vol. IV, no.
363.
[18] Papen to Berlin, 26 Nov. 1935. D.G.F.P. series c. vol. IV, no.
428. For the agreement and its text see chapter IV. See also F.
Funder, *Als Oesterreich den Sturm Bestand*, 1957. Funder says he
worked also with Glaise-Horstenau over this and kept Schuschnigg
informed.

because he was weak it was certain to spell the end of Austrian independence.

When Mussolini visited Berlin in September 1937 he spoke of the autumn of 1935 as the period of the birth of the Axis, but all this time the atmosphere around the Italian Embassy in Berlin was, Attolico notwithstanding, extremely cool. The Reich Government forbade the export of arms to either belligerent, so Attolico concentrated his energy on procuring coal and other raw materials from Germany, but even over supplies such as these the Germans were not encouraging. In October German exporters were warned to be cautious towards Italy in view of the large accumulation of lira balances awaiting transfer, and at the beginning of November the Reich declared an embargo upon the export of oils, fats, textiles, potatoes, iron, and steel, but not coal. On 7th November, soon after the League Sanctions decision, when Austria and Hungary voted with Italy, the *Deutsches Nachbrichten Büro* issued the following statement :

" The German standpoint with reference to Germany's neutrality is well known and has in no way altered. Should an abnormal increase of exports of raw materials or foodstuffs become apparent, which threatens Germany's own economic interests, the German Government will prevent it by appropriate measures."

If Neurath in conversation with foreign diplomats showed a slightly pro-Italian inclination, the line he followed was that, between Italy and the League, Germany was absolutely neutral. In Papen's already quoted dispatch of July he had written :

" It might be possible that through the menace to British imperial interests the Abyssinian adventure would help to bring nearer the realization of the New Order. It remains more probable, however, that a compromise will be made at the Negus's expense—at the cost perhaps also of a notable blood-letting of Italy."

Indeed, the possibility of this compromise tormented Hitler and his Nazi colleagues during the last months of 1935;[19]

[19] It was at this period that Ribbentrop began his advances to Japan.

were it to be realized, Hitler feared for the programme of his life. On 9th December it seemed that the blow had fallen, for on that day the Hoare-Laval Agreement of 7th December was revealed in the French press. Consternation reigned in Berlin at the renewed possibility of complete German isolated, and the German press suddenly became the champion of the League of Nations against this " plot." Lipski was treated to a lecture in this vein when he visited Neurath about a week later. Two days after this he saw Hitler, who was greatly excited and asked him over and over again what on earth the British were doing. He then indulged in a long apology for Germany's exports to Italy. He was not, he insisted, profiting from the situation, but he had to consider a serious problem of unemployment in his coal-mines : the French might accuse him of having placed an embargo upon the export of arms to the belligerents because he wished to stack up all possible armaments for himself, but this was unjust, for the deliveries in question would have been too trifling to affect the Reich. After speaking of other things Hitler reverted feverishly to the Hoare-Laval plan.

Mussolini might have been ready under protest to accept the Franco-British proposition, and the French, who knew that if the Abyssinian war were not stopped Hitler would re-militarize the Rhineland and thereby emasculate the Treaty of Versailles, hoped to preserve the Stresa front and the isolation of Germany. The French believed, however, that the British (contrary to the popular legend) were less politically practical than themselves; some of them also knew of the instinctive anti-Latin and pro-German character of British public opinion, which confused the commonplace opportunism of Mussolini with the fearful logic of Hitler. It was therefore planned in Paris[20] to spring the news on Baldwin, who would have difficulty in repudiating his own Foreign Secretary. The remarkable and admirable reaction of

[20] It was said that Pertinax and Madame Tabouis learnt of the Hoare-Laval plan from Herriot, but Laval afterwards told Cerruti that Herriot did not know, and that he (Laval) suspected a Quai d'Orsay official; naturally he himself disclaimed all responsibility for betraying Hoare to the press.

the British against the Hoare-Laval plan was all the greater, the Stresa front was dissolved, and Hitler unshackled, let loose to advance step by step, from the militarization of the Rhineland to the invasion of Poland.

Chapter IV

"THIS BERLIN—ROME LINE IS NOT
A DIAPHRAGM BUT RATHER
AN AXIS"

The first half of 1936 was a period of uneasy pregnancy. It gave evidence, which only subsequently became public, of the fundamental incompatibility between Italy and Germany, but also of the inexorable persistence of Hitler which throve upon the weakness of Mussolini. In his Austrian policy the Duce was for Hitler the arch-divider of Germany, and other influences in Germany were hostile to Italy as treacherous and weak; slowly but steadily Hitler nevertheless advanced towards a written Italo-German alliance. Mussolini, as both Schuschnigg and Starhemberg testify, was better informed, more open-minded, more receptive than Hitler, yet his vacillation and his Italian touchiness played into Hitler's hands every time. Mussolini, it has been seen, knew very well what Papen was up to in Vienna; he made it clear that he fully understood the danger of a rearmed Germany; Starhemberg's testimony on these points derives chiefly from the spring of 1936, but there is plenty of material to confirm it. Yet the moment the Duce had flung himself into military ventures he became childishly sensitive to every slur upon Italy's military reputation, and he reacted particularly to German implications which were often coupled with references to Italy's attack upon her former allies in 1915: perhaps because of his own fiery interventionism in those days any reference to Italian turncoats touched him to the quick.

It has often been supposed that Abyssinia, the Rhineland, and Spain formed a chain of Nazi-Fascist connivance. This is not true—how untrue in the case of Ethiopia has already been seen. But from the moment of the failure of the Hoare-Laval Plan Ethiopia became a trump card for Hitler,

because it had split the Stresa front and freed him from
" encirclement."

On 6th January 1936, when the Italians were still in
grave difficulties in Abyssinia, it was in fact Mussolini who
made an astonishing offer through Hassell; he appears to
have said, " If Austria, as a formally quite independent state,
were thus in practice to become a German satellite, he would
have no objection."[1] At this point the German reaction,
even that of Hitler, seems to have been one of deep
suspicion, the more since the reports coming in on the internal
situation in Italy were gloomy.[2] Whether Italy had really
turned her back on a Stresa policy, as Mussolini again
assured Hassell on 28th January,[3] could be judged by the
advice she gave the Austrian Government. This, however,
was still obscure, only emphasizing the need for agreement
with Germany in general terms with regard to Central
Europe.[4]

By the middle of February it must have become clear
to Hitler that Abyssinian resistance was breaking and that
the Italian Army might soon be free for other tasks. By
12th February[5] the *Führer* had decided to anticipate his remilitarization of the Rhineland which he told Hassell on
14th February he had planned for the spring of 1937.
No doubt partly in order to test the sincerity of Mussolini's
advances Hitler suggested that the Duce should take the
lead in the matter;[6] it seems that Hitler was also trying
through the pro-German Fascist, Dino Alfieri, to use the
situation to undermine the anti-German influence of Suvich
at the Italian Foreign Office.[7] When Hassell saw Mussolini on
22nd February, the latter, although he referred to his Austrian
offer of 6th January with some prevarication, was careful

[1] D.G.F.P. series C. vol. IV, no. 485. Attolico claimed to have
inspired this offer.

[2] D.G.F.P. series C. vol. IV, nos. 497, 506.

[3] D.G.F.P. series C. vol. IV, no. 525.

[4] D.G.F.P. series C. vol. IV, no. 544.

[5] See Hossbach *Zwischen Wehrmacht und Hitler*, p. 97.

[6] D.G.F.P. series C. vol. IV, no. 564. Italy, like Britain, was a
guarantor of Locarno.

[7] D.G.F.P. series C. vol. IV, no. 574.

not to commit himself over the Rhineland.[8] Hitler nevertheless decided that the Western Powers and the League were
weak enough, and Mussolini sufficiently vacillating, for the
remilitarization of the Rhineland to be risked on 7th March.
He decided further that it might subsequently be worth
while to return to Geneva to exploit the difficulties of the
League for his own ends; for this purpose the Germans
began the demand for a new, up-to-date Locarno, in spite
of their habitual insistence upon bilateral pacts at the expense
of collective agreements. On the economic side, although
Hitler had piously deplored sanctions as disordering to international trade,[9] Germany could not merely hope to achieve
Italy's dependence by becoming the source of her coal,[10] but
had also a splendid opportunity to make use of Italy's impoverishment. Actually her imports of some categories of
goods from Germany had been reduced because she could not
pay for them; in the new situation the gain for Germany lay
in the fact that the Reich could now supply Italy's Danubian
markets on Dr. Schacht's terms, and, in this material way,
oust Italy from Central Europe, from which the geo-politicians
had always intended to expel her.

On the whole Mussolini understood as well as the French
and better than the British the ominous significance of
Hitler's Rhineland *coup* and the prestige it would give to
the Führer; there is plentiful evidence of this besides

[8] D.G.F.P. series C. vol, IV, no. 579. While the Palazzo Chigi
was stating that Italy regarded the Locarno Pact as unaffected by
the Franco-Russian Treaty, the *Popolo d'Italia* had expressed the
opposite view already on 26 January. It is worth noting that
Aloisi, Mussolini's *chef de cabinet,* recorded in his Diary on 19
February that the Duce was complaining of Hassell, even at this
point wishing to demand his recall.

[9] François-Poncet, op. cit., p. 247.

[10] During 1935 and 1936 Italy imported a much smaller quantity
of general commodities from Germany and less in value. See
Annuario Statistico Italiano 1937. The tables overleaf show the
changes in the sources of her coal supplies in the thirty years from
1909. After 1920 she was able to develop her production of
electric power very greatly, so that she became less absolutely
dependent upon imported coal. The South Tyrol was the scene
of important hydro-electrical development.

Italian Imports of Coal 1909-38.

(Figures in metric tons: ooo's omitted)

Year	Total imports	From Great Britain	%	From Germany	%
1909	9,304	8,841	94.9	169	1.8
1910	9,339	8,428	90.2	494	5.3
1911	9,596	8,767	91.3	443	4.6
1912	10,057	8,637	85.9	890	8.8
1913	10,834	9,397	86.8	968	8.9
1920	5,620	3,035	54.0	987	17.6
1921	7,470	...	...	...	...
1922	9,135	5,774	63.2	2,735	29.7
1923	9,166	6,506	71.0	1,597	17.6
1924	11,170	5,896	52.8	4,358	39.0
1925	10,517	6,734	64.0	2,735	23.9
1926	12,258	3,826	31.2	4,522	36.9
1927	14,059	6,421	45.7	4,598	32.6
1928	12,697	6,439	50.7	4,439	35.0
1929	14,603	7,111	48.7	5,534	37.9
1930	12,902	7,072	54.8	4,008	31.1
1931	11,094	5,834	52.6	3,220	29.1
1932	8,778	5,249	59.8	3,120	35.5
1933	9,562	4,747	49.6	2,201	23.0
1934	12,734	4.614	36.3	4,538	35.7
1935	14,590	3,498	24.0	7,461	51.1
1936	9,265	96	1.0	5,917	63.9
1937	12,927	1,999	15.5	7,628	59.0
1938	12,032	2,290	19.0	7,003	58.2

1909-26—Coal.   1927-38—Coal and coke.

Sources

1909-25. League of Nations International Economic Conference, May 1927.

1927-31. League of Nations Economic Committee, *The Coal Problem,* May 1932.

1932-8. *Annuario Statistico Italiano.*

For Year 1938.

U.S. Tariff Commission: *Italian Commercial Policy and Foreign Trade,* 1922-1940. Following figures are given of Italian imports of coal from principal countries:

Germany	58.5 per cent.
Great Britain	21.3 ,,
Poland and Danzig	12.3 ,,

Starhemberg's account of his angry twisting and untwisting of the paper-clips which lay on his table.[11] It was clear to the Duce that however often Hitler spoke of peace, it was war that he prepared. Among Mussolini's weaknesses, however, was a certain blindness in the question of Czechoslovakia which was to cost him dear. He could not forgive the Czechs three interrelated things: their democratic convictions, their opposition to Hungarian revisionism, and their support of the Austrian Social Democrats who had been allowed to transfer their headquarters to Brno in Moravia. For these reasons Mussolini failed to grasp that in Hitler's mind the liquidation of Austria and Czechoslovakia were two aspects of the same undertaking. Hitler was far too old-style Austrian to think otherwise, and he made it clear enough later on that this was so. It was therefore absurd of Mussolini or any other statesman at the time to suppose that one could bolster up Austria without backing up the Czechs; only too late and too rarely does the Duce seem to have understood this.

Now the strategic importance of the remilitarization of the Rhineland lay in the fact that it would make any military co-operation between France and the Czechoslovak Republic infinitely more difficult than it would have been before; it emasculated at one stroke the Franco-Czech and the Franco-Russian alliances. It was this new strategic situation which Mussolini half-realized, but which he did not seriously face. The watch on the Brenner had become more solitary, but there was a margin of several months before the new Rhenish fortifications would be ready, and serious policy should have used this breathing-space; it appears that the Italians on the Austrian frontier were strongly reinforced.

The Duce was, of course, annoyed that Hitler's Rhineland move pushed him back into the League just when he had meant to sweep out of it, but he swallowed his pride over this, and tried to enjoy a fresh phase of Hitler as the international bad boy instead of himself. Relations between Italy and Germany had not ostensibly improved in the spring of 1936. It is difficult to gauge the point of Neurath's remarks to Bullitt on 18th May because Neurath was nearly

[11] Starhemberg, op. cit., p. 192.

as false as his Nazi colleagues, and, further, the Party did not always confide in him. But there is no particular reason to doubt his sincerity in saying to his American visitor that " the demonstrations of friendship between Germany and Italy were mere demonstrations without basis in reality. He went on to say that at the present time he could see no way to reconcile the conflicting interests of Germany and Italy in Austria." For the moment Germany would not encourage the Austrian Nazis because " until the German fortifications had been constructed on the French border, an involvement of Germany in war with Italy might lead to a French attack on Germany ".[12] Thus the German Foreign Minister had apparently been expecting Mussolini to follow his original plan and to patch things up with France and Britain now that Badoglio had occupied Addis Ababa on 5th May. But after the French elections of 26th April and 3rd May Léon Blum and the *Front Populaire* were about to take over the government of France and with them Mussolini would never come to terms; he had further revealed a new susceptibility; he had conquered an empire, as he claimed, for his king, and in future he would be willing to exchange the substance of other strength for the shadow of the recognition of Victor Emmanuel as Emperor of Abyssinia.

In the middle of May Mussolini telegraphed to Attolico that he was to inform Hitler that the Italian Government was gravely concerned to observe that Spain was inclining more and more to the left. The Germans appeared to take very little interest. When Italian intervention in Spain began seriously towards the end of July they were delighted. At one time they had hoped the Abyssinian war would have kept Italy busy for more than one winter, but this was an excellent substitute. Mussolini planned to occupy himself in Spain no longer than he had in East Africa and then to return again to watch on the Brenner. There is every reason to think, however, that the Germans' much more modest activities in Spain, apart from their aspect as useful manœuvres, were intended to keep the Spanish war going

[12] U.S. Document I. 150: Memorandum of Bullitt-Neurath Conversation, in *Nuremberg Trial Proceedings*, 1946, Pt. i, p. 233.

indefinitely. Hitler made it particularly clear at the now notorious Conference at the Reichskanzlei on 5th November 1937 that in Spain he had Italy exactly where he wanted her, and there is no reason to suppose that he had been slow to realize this. Meanwhile he could dangle before the Duce the probability of a German recognition of Italy's new imperial quality in exchange for Italy's surrender over Austria.

In his talks with Starhemberg in the spring of 1936 Mussolini is wavering again. He sees clearly that Germany is treacherous and stronger by two years' rearmament. He cannot continue to stand at the Brenner alone. What does it matter about the Mediterranean—" our sea or the French sea or the English sea, whichever you like "? (Hitler could never have spoken like that.) Or did it matter? Was it fear of a ' Red ' French-Spanish combination precisely there which changed his mind? Was it the influence of the Ciano ' set ' or some German hint about his Empire? Or was it some report from Vienna? For according to Zernatto,[13] who was very well informed, it was Mussolini himself who a few weeks later, i.e. early in May, suggested to Schuschnigg through Salata that it would be wise to sacrifice Starhemberg in order to placate Hitler; in view of his links with the Heimwehr leader, this was an act of personal resignation : Schuschnigg records that at the same time Mussolini asked that Starhemberg as his personal friend should not be victimized in any way. So on 13th May 1936 Papen triumphed through the agency of Salata, and a new Schuschnigg Cabinet was formed without Starhemberg. At almost exactly the same time Mussolini had agreed to the secret Austro-German Press agreement. Did Neurath really not know?

The testimony of Schuschnigg in all this affair is valuable and interesting; its historic worth rests upon this man's obvious sincerity, but must be qualified by his strange inflexibility and particularly by his natural *naïveté*, the weakness for which, as he himself recognizes, he was chastized for seven horrible years in the Hotel Metropol in Vienna and

[13] G. Zernatto, *Die Wahrheit über Oesterreich* (Longmans, 1938). The author was the Secretary-General of Schuschnigg's Patriotic Front.

in the concentration camp of Oranienburg. And, if his
book *Ein Requiem in Rot-Weiss-Rot*, was written largely on
the basis of notes made at the time of the events it records,
the setting was added after that long and cruel imprisonment.
If Mussolini was slow to feel sympathy for Schuschnigg, the
Austrian Chancellor thoroughly enjoyed the Duce's society; he
noticed his extraordinarily close contact with the press, but
mistook this Italian journalist for a really cultivated man.
From Schuschnigg we hear how Mussolini loved not only to
show off his German but also to quote his Nietzsche.

The conversations between Mussolini and Schuschnigg in
these years 1934, 1935, and 1936 show that both men knew
pretty well how things really stood—Mussolini, for instance,
says (in August 1934) " After all, you know how plebiscites
are managed in the Reich," and Schuschnigg knows that
Italy without the Stresa front may at any time make terms
with Germany at Austria's expense. On 5th June 1936,
though Mussolini repeats the formula which had resulted
from Badoglio's visit to France in September 1935 about
the invulnerability of the Maginot Line, Schuschnigg describes
him as in the throes of a final decision against France—
it was the day after Blum had formed his cabinet. The
now current formula of an easier situation for Austria if
Italy and Germany were friends[14] was attractive and—on
the face of things—not altogether false.

There was a hollowness about the Italo-Austrian relationship which was half admitted between Schuschnigg and
Mussolini the first time they met.[15] In Austrian eyes the
Italians were still the despised hawkers of toy cats, *Katzel-
macher*. They might man the Brenner, but this was bluff
because they could never cross it. Not only was the Austro-
German frontier all but impossible to hold, not only would
Italian troops in Austria bring in the Yugoslavs and perhaps
the Czechs, but they would make all Austria pro-German
and the regular Austrian Army would desert in large batches

[14] See L. Jedlicka. *Ein Heer im Schatten der Parteien* 1955,
pp. 140-141.
[15] In 1940 Ciano rather carelessly talked to Sumner Welles as
if a full admission had been made, cf. Schuschnigg, op. cit., p. 251,
and Sumner Welles, *A Time for Decision* (Harpers, 1944), p. 81.

to Hitler. A few cultural interchanges between academic personages were all very well, but attempts at athletic fraternization were a disaster every time. The scuffle at Mürzzuschlag because the Italian cyclists' tyres were punctured by the nails laid for them along the road was one of many such incidents. A climax was reached in March 1937 when the Nazis in Vienna turned up *en masse* to beat up a visiting Italian football team. The Germans themselves saw to it that Mussolini was supplied with a garbled version of this story.

The eternal South Tyrolese question was a major element in the whole situation. Mussolini was right enough when he said to Schuschnigg in 1935 that demonstrators in Bolzano with their white stockings and *Heil-Hitlers* were just the same Nazis as those against whom Schuschnigg was forced to take action in Austria. Such concessions as the Italian Government made at this time were drowned by the outcry, discreetly stimulated by the various Pan-German organizations such as the *Verein des Deutschtum im Ausland* based on Stuttgart, over the calling-up of young men from the Alto Adige to fight in Abyssinia : if a few troublesome ones were removed in this way, there is insufficient evidence for the presumption that the Italian authorities called up more recruits here than in the other provinces of Italy.[16] But Austrian and South German solidarity with the South Tyrolese against Italy in the first half of 1936 was a convenient instrument, among all his others, with which Hitler could bring Mussolini to heel.

It was three weeks after the eviction of Starhemberg from the Austrian Cabinet, when Schuschnigg visited Mussolini at his Romagnol country-house at Rocca delle Caminate, near Forlì. With Starhemberg out of the way, Papen's intrigue with Funder could materialize, and on 5th June Schuschnigg put the project of a Press truce between Vienna and Berlin before the Duce, who, repeating yet again that he never would nor could weaken in maintaining the complete independence of Austria, approved. On 11th July, therefore, the fateful

[16] It is said that Tolomei suggested that South Tyrolese peasants should be settled in Abyssinia. See C. Latour *Süd-Tirol und die Achse Berlin-Rome* 1938-45, 1962, p. 21.

Austro-German Agreement was published in the form of three clauses : (1) Germany recognized Austria's full sovereignty; (2) Germany and Austria each undertook to mind their own business, i.e. not to interfere in anything concerning the internal political structure of the other State. The third clause ran : " The policy of the Austrian Federal Government, both in general and towards the German Reich in particular, shall always be based on principles which correspond to the fact that Austria has acknowledged herself to be a German State. This will not affect the Rome Protocols of 1934 and the supplementary agreements of 1936, or the position of Austria in relation to Italy and Hungary as her partners in these protocols."[17] It was added that a series of measures to relieve tension was envisaged, but the character of these measures, the most interesting part of the agreement, was only revealed later, piecemeal; as if in deference to Dr. Funder's anxieties, no official reference was made on 11th July to the question of the Press.

With their eyes open to Hitler's treachery, well aware that he would never leave a separate Austria in peace, both Mussolini and Schuschnigg allowed themselves to be fascinated by the Führer's spells. His victims always retained their lucidity more easily when faced with problems not immediately their own; Starhemberg has shown that this was true of the Duce, and when Mussolini made his first agreement with Hitler in the autumn of this year Fuchs[18] quotes Schuschnigg as saying " Hitler will reap what Mussolini has sown."

The July Agreement made the Anschluss a foregone conclusion, the more as the nature of the measures ' to relieve tension ' was revealed.[19] It was soon announced that an amnesty would be extended to a considerable number of Austrian Nazis serving various sentences. The five German newspapers which were allowed into Austria were ample to feed every racial passion, while the five poor little Austrian papers which got into Germany were swamped; Schuschnigg

[17] D.G.F.P. series D, vol. I, no. 153.

[18] Martin Fuchs, *A Pact with Hitler*, (Gollanz, 1939).

[19] The secret so-called Gentlemen's Agreement has been published in D.G.F.P. series D. vol. I as no. 152.

hoped they would bring comfort to a few faithful German Catholics who were probably victimized if they dared to buy them. The 1,000 marks tax on Germans travelling to Austria was, as Papen had long advocated, removed in August 1936, so that German tourists might practise all their arts of penetration. Meanwhile the most intransigent Austrian Nazis were still receiving military training as " Legionaries " in Germany and many of them became guards at the concentration camp at Dachau. In return for all this what did Schuschnigg—and Mussolini—get? Germany, whose word both of them knew to be valueless, had recognized Austria's sovereignty; this Schuschnigg felt—and still felt after the war—was internationally worth while, although at the same time he promised that the policy of Austria would always in principle be that of a German State; in other words Hitler would have grounds for protest against Austria's un-German policy every time Schuschnigg might wish to consult Mussolini.[20] Worst of all, though Mussolini and Schuschnigg had specifically agreed at Rocca delle Caminate that on no account must even isolated Nazis be allowed to enter the Austrian Cabinet (on the model of Hitler, Göring, and Frick in Germany on 30th January 1933), the Austro-German Agreement immediately brought two crypto-Nazis into Schuschnigg's Government; one of them was General Glaise-Horstenau, who became a Minister without portfolio, and the other Guido Schmidt, who was promoted to be head of the Austrian Foreign Office under Schuschnigg as its nominal chief. These two treacherous personages had in fact been instrumental—together with Papen and Funder and Salata—in bringing the Agreement about, and both told Schuschnigg how difficult it had been for Glaise-Horstenau, who had dealt with Hitler on the subject, to persuade the Führer to agree. Glaise, whose obsequious manner to any casual visitor like the present writer was almost grotesque, had persuaded Schuschnigg that he was a faithful Catholic, but it was not very difficult for an untrained nose to smell that he was a Pan-German of the older Austrian generation. He had, moreover, worked

[20] See below, p. 94.

with the German General Staff in the War of 1914-1918; of this he had afterwards written a military history which was particularly offensive about Italy. It gives the measure of Mussolini's surrender to Hitler that he should have seemed to acquiesce in the elevation of Glaise-Horstenau, who in November received the key position of Austrian Home Minister; for it was harder for the Duce to swallow humiliation, personal or relative to the Italians' poor military reputation, which he was determined to reverse, than to abandon political power. The July Agreement synchronized almost exactly with the lifting by the League of Nations of sanctions against Italy. This might have ended Mussolini's dependence on Germany; on the contrary, soon after this he removed Preziosi and Morreale, and nominated the Austrian-born Salata as Italian Minister in Vienna. For the July Agreement had very nearly synchronized also with the news on 17th July of an anti-Republican military revolt in Spanish Morocco.

After the anxieties of 1935, in 1936 a warm sun seemed to be ripening Hitler's long-delayed fruit. All through 1936 he was—according to his plan—systematically gaining power (which could be translated into terms of force) without using force openly. Meanwhile his courtship of Italy appeared as clumsy and treacherous as that of some country-bumpkin in a Ben Jonson or Restoration play, and it must also be recorded that Italy's responses were not much more adroit. Hans Frank paid a visit to Rome in April 1936 to deliver a lecture on National Socialist 'justice,' or in other words, the Nazi rejection of the principles of Roman Law. At a special opera performance in Frank's honour, the Roman orchestra regaled him in return with the old Hohenzollern *Heil Dir im Siegerkranz* (to the tune of 'God Save the King') instead of the Nazi national hymns. In June Mussolini's daughter, Edda Ciano, spent a month in Berlin just when her husband at the tender age of thirty-three had been made Italian Foreign Minister. Adolf Hitler consented to take her in his motor-boat around the network of lakes between Berlin and Potsdam, but as she knew no German and he no Italian their contact was tenuous and illusory. On these and an increasing number of similar occasions no sympathy was felt, only, as one participator said, " a compelling parallel-ism."

At the end of July 1936, the month of Mussolini's formal surrender to Hitler, the Olympic Games were held in Berlin—the last Olympiad before the outbreak of war. Never before had such significance been attached to them. Much German reticence in the previous months had been designed to ensure that the whole world's representatives should join in this festival of heroism—which the Nazis contrasted with democracy—in Germany. Enthusiastic exponents[21] of the demigod qualities of the Germans had long patronized the Greeks of classical times as offshoots of Nordicism, but Hitler's Olympus was a post-Wagnerian Valhalla in which half his divided personality ecstatically believed, and to make the whole world (excepting only the Soviets) witness the triumph of the German Siegfried,[22] with himself acting as Wotan's high priest, was also a matter of serious *realpolitik*. One of his most important methods of gaining power without the use of force was to disseminate a state of ecstasy. There is no doubt that some of the German athletes surpassed themselves through the exaltation with which *der Führer* filled them, and that the foreign visitors were duly impressed by the inspired strength of the ' new ' Germany.[23] " Face à la tribune officielle, où siègent, aux côtés de Hitler et ses lieutenants, le roi de Bulgarie, le Prince de Piémont, la Princesse Marie de Savoie, les princes héritiers de Suède et de Grèce et les fils de Mussolini, les membres du Comité international . . . annoncent l'ouverture des Jeux et reçoivent le serment de l'athlète."[24] The Austrian team was received with German acclamation and when its football contest with the Italians was prolonged into four matches, the demonstra-tions of the German public became more and more anti-Italian; in the end the Italians won. But what one or two

[21] Notably Houston Stewart Chamberlain.

[22] In *Mein Kampf* Hitler often spoke of *der deutscher Siegfried.*

[23] It was, of course, the United States with champions of all races which scored the highest number of events, including several Negro triumphs.

[24] Françoit-Poncet, op. cit., p. 264.

Italian diplomats observed with greater satisfaction was that while the French team appeared to deliver a Nazi salute,[25] the Italian athletes did nothing of the kind.

Schuschnigg attached great importance from the Austrian point of view to the replacement at the Palazzo Chigi of the old official type, Suvich, by the young Fascist Ciano on 9th June 1936 : he seems even to have thought that if Mussolini on 5th June made the theatrical suggestion of paying official visits by air to Vienna and Budapest it was only Ciano who prevented the realization of the plan.[26] Instead the evidence indicates that, while Alfieri, who succeeded Ciano at the Ministry of Propaganda, consistently used such influence as he had in favour of an Italo-German *rapprochement,* Ciano at this time was just the good young Fascist who followed his Duce in see-sawing between grudging admiration first for the graces of France and then for the cynical and successful brutality of Nazi Germany. One can only say that whereas Suvich exerted a certain professional restraint, Ciano delighted in " adventures " such as the Ethiopian war or intervention in Spain or, later on, the seizure of Albania. It had been settled before he became Foreign Minister that the decisive Austro-German Agreement should be made, and when Hasseli returned from Berlin to Rome in the middle of June he immediately intimated Germany's willingness to recognize the Italian East African Empire by way of reward.[27] On the same occasion (18th June) Hassell told Ciano that feeling in Germany had become much more favourable to Italy and was only qualified by the suspicion that Italy was working for a Habsburg restoration. Hassell himself had denied this but the idea persisted : Ciano replied that it was a groundless suspicion. On 29th June Hassell brought Ciano an offer from Hitler to Mussolini to consider the

[25] Monsieur François-Poncet explains that it was an " Olympic " salute.

[26] Schuschnigg, op. cit., p. 246. Suvich, who had been Under-Secretary to Mussolini as Foreign Minister, was actually succeeded by Bastianini, while Ciano was successor to the Duce. See also G. Craig and F. Gilbert. *The Diplomats* 1919-39, 1953.

[27] Ciano Minute, 18 June 1936. (This and other Ciano Minutes referred to are published in *L'Europa verso la catastrofe* (Mondadori Milan, 1948).)

recognition of the Empire without asking for anything in exchange [*sic*] whenever the Duce should consider the time ripe. On 25th July Germany suppressed her Legation in Addis Ababa.

Before the end of the summer an event occurred in Hitler's life which cannot be ignored. Lloyd George was the one British personage for whom we know that Hitler felt respect; the victor in a modern world war, he seems to have been in the running for superman honours. The old Welshman's visit distracted Hitler's attention from Mussolini, for it revived his interest in an alliance with Britain. At that time one could certainly not ally oneself with Britain and Italy at the same time, and Hitler seems not to have mentioned Italy to Lloyd George. He threw himself into fascinating his British guests; Sylvester refers to his " strange dominating mannerism which seemed to grip and compel attention, a curious indescribable something, magnetic, masterful, electrical, compelling, hypnotic. . . ."[28] An agreement with Britain could not be so easily made, but Lloyd George's visit to Berchtesgaden had sinister results which were to be felt later on. For he encouraged Hitler to believe that Nazi Germany was invincible and must never give way, and that the United States could never afford to challenge her power.[29]

In September Hitler's hopes returned to Italy. Through the Prince of Hesse he engineered a secret meeting with Ciano's *chef de Cabinet,* Filippo Anfuso,[30] and Hans Frank appeared in Rome again. This time Frank was charged with an important mission; even the gist of his interview with Mussolini on 23rd September was kept secret and though Ciano recorded it[31] he seems not to have gossiped this time. Frank began by conveying an invitation from Hitler to Mussolini to visit Germany both as Head of the Italian

[28] A. J. Sylvester, *The Real Lloyd George* (Cassell, 1947).

[29] See De Witt C. Poole, "Light on Nazi Foreign Policy," in Foreign Affairs, Oct. 1946. Cf also Hitler's admiration of Lloyd George expressed to Mussolini at the Brenner in June 1941. D.G.F.P. series D, vol. XII, p. 944.

[30] See Anfuso (op. cit. pp. 18-21) who seems to have been unaware of Frank's visit.

[31] Ciano Minute, 23 Sept. 1936.

Government and as Leader of the Other Revolution; in the meantime the Führer hoped that Ciano would come to Germany to make immediate contact. Frank then went on to say that Hitler would only take action in Spain out of loyalty to Mussolini, for he was not concerned with the Mediterranean, which he regarded as Italy's sphere: the Baltic Sea was Germany's Mediterranean. There followed a good deal of talk about the dangers of Bolshevism and the importance of direct relations between the Nazi and Fascist leaders outside the normal channels of diplomacy. Frank assured Mussolini that Germany would be loyal to the Austro-German Agreement, which Mussolini quickly claimed as due to his own inspiration. The Duce declared himself in no hurry to have his new Empire recognized, assuring Frank at the same time that Italy had to all intents and purposes left Geneva. He complained that he could not work with a Popular Front France. Hitler had, of course, been right to make the attempts through Ribbentrop to make friends with the British, but, said Mussolini, it was bound to fail. A little later Frank asked the Master to explain how it was that he had been successful in his dealings with the Catholic Church while Germany, Frank admitted, had not. Religion, replied the Duce, is as elusive as a mist; it is vain, therefore, to struggle against the Churches—he did not now, he added hastily, speak of the Jews because a race is another thing. He had been able to arrange the Lateran Pacts on the basis of "Render unto Caesar . . ." in 1929, and they had in practice spelt the victory of the Fascist State over the Church, which had dutifully supported the war against Ethiopia. When Frank asked him what the function of the party should be within the State, Mussolini replied that it should be a civilian militia at the orders of the State.[32]

For the first time Mussolini had encouraged the fawnings of a Nazi leader like Frank; a month later Ciano set out for Berlin, Munich, and Berchtesgaden. Although he had

[32] In 1929 in the Preamble to the *Statuto* of that year the Fascist Party was defined as a " civil militia " for the service of the nation.

left Rome with some misgivings, he was flattered by a gala performance of *Don Giovanni* in Munich and by a well-organized crowd reception, in which, as it turned out, the Führer had interested himself personally. There is evidence in the German records not only that the Italians had put out feelers before Frank's visit to Mussolini[33] but also that Ciano had made it clear that he wanted a lot of publicity in Germany. By the end of September the Germans were anxious to discuss the Spanish situation, and at Magistrati's instigation Neurath informed Hassell that he would welcome an Italian visit.

Ciano first saw Neurath in Berlin on 21st October, when the German recognition of the Italian Empire was confirmed and the two Foreign Ministers made a *tour d'horizon* of which Ciano's Minute is available. According to Ciano, who does not seem to have been inaccurate in this kind of work, Neurath not only insisted upon the British " encirclement " of Italy but expressed himself in very anti-British terms on Germany's behalf, and he spoke of Ribbentrop's foolish illusions about the possibility of genuine Anglo-German friendship; Ciano felt that his rivalry with Ribbentrop had now made Neurath a real partisan of Rome against London. The German Minister also expressed himself sceptically about any new " Locarno." When Ciano said that Italy would only remain at Geneva provisionally, Neurath said he did not wish to insist upon an Italian break with the League of Nations since Italy could perform " a work of sabotage useful for our common ends " so long as she remained a member.[34] Neurath and Ciano then went through previously

[33] There had been talk of Ciano coming to the Olympic Games, but Neurath was grumpy about Frank's invitations, insisting that only he or the *Führer* could invite the Italian Foreign Minister.

[34] Ciano Minute, 21st Oct. 1936. In the summer the Italians themselves had nearly broken with Geneva (see Ciano letter to the Council of the League read at Geneva on 26th June), while the Germans had almost seemed in earnest about their new Locarno and returning to the League. For German records of the Neurath-Ciano meetings on 21st and 22nd October 1936 see German Ministry filmed archives (available in Foreign Office Library), serial no. 348/201818-31.

agreed formulae on opposition to Communism, a common effort in Spain, and the " independence " of Austria. Since, as the Italians claimed, Austrian independence had now been accepted as axiomatic, the Italians made the best of it by expressing satisfaction over the working of the July Agreement, and Neurath made things easier by referring ironically to the ' totalitarian consolidation ' of Schuschnigg's position.

On 24th October Ciano met Hitler for the first time at the Berghof.[35] The two dominant themes of their conversation were, as Ciano noted, Bolshevism and Britain's encirclement conspiracy. After declaring that " Mussolini is the first statesman of the world with whom no one else had the right even remotely to compare himself," Hitler referred to his own rejection of British blandishments because he realized that Britain intended " to separate our two countries in order to beat them one at a time." This gave Ciano a splendid opportunity to present to Hitler, as the Duce had particularly charged him to do, a circular of Eden's on Germany[36] and a telegram from Sir Eric Phipps, the British Ambassador in Berlin, to the Foreign Office, two documents which had fallen into Grandi's hands and which Mussolini had had translated for the Führer : the telegram was one in which Phipps had referred to the German Government as one of dangerous adventurers. Hitler, Ciano stated, reacted violently. " In the English view," he cried, " there are two countries in the world to-day which are led by adventurers, Germany and Italy. But England, too, was governed by adventurers when she founded her Empire. To-day she is only governed by inept creatures." By raising the anti-Bolshevik standard, Germany and Italy, Hitler said, must now take the offensive against the democracies, though Ciano noted that he spoke as if France no longer counted. There was the usual diatribe about the Mediterranean for Italy and the Baltic for Germany. Germany would be ready for war in three years (i.e. in 1939), said

[35] Ciano Minute, 24th Oct. 1936. No German records have been found of Ciano's encounter with Hitler.

[36] Dated 17th Jan. 1936. Mussolini had referred to this document in his conversation with Hans Frank.

Hitler,[37] but would be still better prepared if she had four or five years' time. Though he was convinced that Britain wished to attack Germany and Italy, together they would soon be strong enough to make her give up this ambition.

The acquisition of new political friends in the anti-Communist campaign was considered. Hitler hoped that Italy would come to terms with Yugoslavia, which Britain wished to make into an anti-Italian base, and he asked that Italy, like Germany, should direct Hungarian revisionism away from Yugoslavia and against Czechoslovakia. Neurath had already spoken to Ciano in this sense when they had discussed economic co-operation in the Danubian basin.

With regard to Japan Hitler only told Ciano that Germany had gone a long way towards an agreement, but Neurath had informed his Italian colleague very fully about this although he himself had been kept in the dark about Ribbentrop's negotiations with Tokyo from the end of 1935 until the middle of 1936; he even told Ciano about the secret clauses of the Anti-Comintern Pact which was signed a month later (25th November 1936); the German Ambassador to Japan seems never to have been fully informed about them.[38] Neurath approved of an Italian recognition of Manchukuo as against a Japanese recognition of the new Italian Empire.

With regard to Spain Hitler pronounced to Ciano the gorgeous lie that Germany had involved herself up to the hilt on the anti-Bolshevik side. It was Italian activity on behalf of Franco which had already reached considerable dimensions.

Ciano's minute on his encounter with Hitler ends with two apt comments. He remarked that " every question was the object of a long exposition by Hitler and that he repeated every formulation several times in different words." He also remarked that Hitler showed uncertainty in his attitude towards Britain; much would still depend on Ribbentrop's activities in London.

The Italo-German " October Protocols " along the lines

[37] In *Mein Kampf* he had said the same thing, i.e. six years from the time that he came to power.

[38] See De Witt C. Poole, op. cit.

of Ciano's conversations were signed at Berchtesgaden but
not published to the world.[39] The results of Ciano's visit to
Germany were only announced in Mussolini's famous speech
in the Piazza del Duomo in Milan on the afternoon of
Sunday, 1st November. After a reference to the July Agreement which had fortified Austria politically, he went on to
say :

" One great country has recently gathered a vast amount
of sympathy among the masses of the Italian people : I speak
of Germany.

" The Berlin conversations have resulted in an understanding
between our two countries over certain problems which
had been particularly acute. But these understandings which
have been sanctioned in fitting and duly signed agreements,
this Berlin-Rome line is not a diaphragm but rather an axis
around which can revolve all those European states with
a will to collaboration and peace.

" Germany, however much encircled and importuned, did
not adhere to the sanctions against us. With the agreement
of 11th July an element of dissension between Berlin
and Rome has disappeared, and let me remind you that
Germany had practically recognized the Empire of Rome
before the Berlin meeting."

It should be added in parenthesis that Germany, not being
a member of the League of Nations, had never been expected
to impose sanctions against Italy.

Hitler had forged the Axis announced by Mussolini,
and Austria was his when he chose to take it. One of the
Führer's most useful agents in Austria, Guido Schmidt, was
responsible for a sinister epilogue to Ciano's October negotiations. Schmidt had been at a Jesuit school in Feldkirch with
Schuschnigg and had gained remarkable influence over him.
He does not seem to have had any great capacity except
for intrigue; Zernatto, who served Schuschnigg and Austria
faithfully and whose judgements are balanced and moderate,

[39] The Protocols included agreement to resist Communist propaganda, to recognize Spain as soon as Franco had taken Madrid,
that Italy should support German colonial demands and so on.
There was nothing unexpected.

describes him as "rather a political juggler than a man who moves forward in a straight line towards his goal."[40] He had a Don-Juanesque way of whispering in everybody's ear "Of course it is only you whom I love, whatever others may tell you," and while he had certainly decided that Hitler's cards would win, it seems that Ciano was right in suspecting in him a vicious delight in intriguing at Geneva.[41] The episode of Schmidt's remarks there to Vansittart at Mussolini's expense in 1937, although discounted as Italian slander by the faithful Schuschnigg,[42] is only too credible.

On 19th November 1936, the day after the Wilhelmstrasse had announced the corollary to the October Protocols, Germany's recognition of Franco,[43] Guido Schmidt, now fully fledged Austrian Foreign Minister, went to Berlin. He dined that same evening with Hans Frank[44] and another fervid Nazi, Bohle, chief of the German *Auslandsorganisation.* The next day he saw Hitler, who welcomed him warmly, and on 21st November he signed a secret procès-verbal with Neurath of which Magistrati in some consternation was able to inform the Palazzo Chigi. The agreement contained declarations in favour of the further stimulation of Austro-German press and cultural and economic exchanges, together with an anti-Communist declaration. From Italy's point of view its second clause contained the sting,[45] for while acknowledging Austria's right to act according to the Rome Protocols it laid down the necessity for preventive Austro-German consultation whenever Vienna might need to act

[40] Op. cit.

[41] Cf. Ciano's account of meeting Schmidt at Vienna in Nov. 1936 in Minute of Conversations at Vienna and Budapest, 9-16 Nov. 1936.

[42] Op. cit.

[43] On 21 Oct. Neurath only spoke of doing this *after* Franco's conquest of Madrid: see Ciano Minute of that date. Italy recognized Franco at the same time.

[44] Guido Schmidt was in Rome from 14 to 17 Sept. 1936, so that one wonders whether he may have helped to prepare for Hans Frank's visit to the Duce.

[45] or so Magistrati thought. Cf. D.G.F.P. series D. vol. I, no. 182.

outside the Rome-Vienna-Budapest triangle. This had only been negatively implied hitherto[46] and virtually annulled the third published clause of the July Agreement by which it had been made acceptable to Italy; it was surely only ineptitude which delayed Italian pressure against Schmidt until 1937, when it was too late. It was characteristically tortuous that before leaving Berlin Guido Schmidt gave an interview to the *Stefani* correspondent in praise of the Rome Protocols; then having opportunely made friends with Göring too, he left Tempelhof for Vienna together with his party in two red aeroplanes lent to him by the head of the Luftwaffe, and marked with huge swastikas so that they looked like two giant Nazi flags. Mussolini and Ciano were placated by the Japanese recognition of Italian Ethiopia[47] which preceded by one week the German-Japanese Anti-Comintern Pact on 25th November 1936. This latter treaty was signed in Berlin on Germany's behalf by Ribbentrop, regardless of the fact that he was German Ambassador in London. After the signature he repeated the geo-political programme to the German press—the world would be defended against Communism, he said, by Japan in the Far East, Germany in central Europe, and by Italy in the Mediterranean. Mussolini and Ciano accepted their allotment contentedly, and concluded a secret agreement with Franco three days later. They did not recognize Manchukuo until their adhesion to the Anti-Comintern Pact a year later; even then their recognition preceded that of Germany, who had a military mission in China until April 1938.

On the last day of 1936 Attolico was already expressing the pious wish to his colleague Magistrati that Italo-German relations might remain fluid, not crystallize dangerously.

[46] See above p. 83.
[47] Announced to Ciano by the Japanese Ambassador in Rome on 18 Nov. 1936.

Chapter V

THE DUCE IN GERMANY

The visits between Nazi leaders and Italian *gerarchi* continued to multiply. Each one tried to cultivate his opposite number. Italian *amour propre* smarted because the Nazis were so tall, but then recovered because they were so ugly. Alfieri as Minister of Propaganda had entertained Goebbels and his wife to a great film exhibition in Venice; in October 1936 Himmler visited the Italian police chief, Bocchini, in Rome; it was when he came back a little later from his return visit to Germany that Bocchini remarked that Himmler was exactly like a laughing hyena in a zoo. But in spite of these people, and Hans Frank, and Neurath at the Foreign Office, it was still Göring who was Hitler's most important *homme de confiance* for his dealings with foreign countries and especially with Italy. He was, as the French Ambassador liked to emphasize, generally accepted as enjoying the authority of Hitler's "Crown Prince." In addition to his connexion with the Italian royal family through the Prince of Hesse, he had a Pan-German Austrian brother-in-law, Dr. Hüber, and through his first wife he had Swedish connexions. Socially he was a cut above most Nazi leaders, and his famous *bonhomie* combined with assurance as a host. His more than childish vanity and Gargantuan demeanour did not startle Germany, and Hitler had no idea that Göring was ridiculous abroad, nor that Mussolini could never take him seriously. Further, Göring was a rascal but certainly no fool; he specialized, like Papen or Henlein, in that particularly German art of intriguing with disarming frankness and total duplicity.

"I say, Chancellor," said this exponent of Italian-German friendship to Schuschnigg on the occasion of Gömbös's funeral in October 1936, "the pair of us really don't need these Italians . . . we'll deliver whatever goods you need. . . .", and he thereupon offered up to six hundred aeroplanes gratis to Austria, and keep and pay for the Austrian pilots in Germany.[1] As Schuschnigg pointed out, Göring was feeling good-tempered just then; during the Abyssinian war Italy had succeeded in gaining a certain footing in the *Alpine-Montan* concern, but by now he had so to speak won it back, ensuring its control through the *Hermann Göring Werke.*

A favourite pastime of Göring as of Neurath was to explain to the British how much the Germans were doing to restrain the Italians; at the same time they frequently warned the Italians of the violent hostility the British felt towards them in spite of all German attempts to explain the Italian point of view. In November 1936, for instance, Göring told Magistrati that the British Government was 100 per cent. hostile to Italy. " By 1941," he said, " Axis naval preparations will be far enough advanced to make the British think twice, but at present you had better be damned careful." After all that the Anglo-Italian ' Gentleman's Agreement' on 2nd January 1937 was annoying, and some ten days later Göring set out, together with Magistrati, upon a visit to Rome. He talked a great deal in the train. Germany would not be ready for three years (i.e. not before January 1940), but Italy and Germany must prepare for a clash with the British. But the object of his journey, he said, was to discuss Austria with the Duce. Of course, he insisted, Hitler had known *nothing* about the plan to murder Dollfuss and he would have shot Habicht at once if Italy's reaction had been less immoderate; and anyway there was not the slightest reason to be afraid of the Germans on one's frontier. Then there was a pause in the conversation and Magistrati went back to his own compartment. Shortly before reaching Rome Göring, however, sent for him to say that the Austrian Question was not really ' actual' after all. " In any case Germany," Göring said, " will indulge in no surprises, and whatever decisions she makes on questions so vital to her as those of Austria, Danzig or Memel will be preceded by understandings with Italy." Magistrati naturally reported all this to Mussolini and Ciano before they saw Göring, and Mus-

[1] See Ciano Minutes, Vienna-Budapest, 9-16 Nov. 1936.

solini protested angrily that it was not that he *feared* the Germans on the Brenner![2]

Göring stayed several days in Rome, then went to Capri, then returned to the capital. On his last day in Italy this time, 23rd January, a long conversation took place between the Duce and Göring, with Ciano and the German interpreter, Paul Schmidt, present.[3] It was interesting for several reasons, one being the fact that Göring was obviously not informed about Hans Frank's interview with Mussolini in the previous September, nor did he know what had passed between Neurath and Ciano in October. When one considers how the 'Ribbentrop-Büro' was conducting a policy of its own, independently of all the others, and that Hitler was likely to disown any of his henchmen whenever he chose, the difficulty of friendship with Nazi Germany is illustrated in yet another way. Mussolini often said different things to different people, but although dictatorship is irresponsible, Ciano at least could be safely accepted as his authentic and fully informed agent.

Thus Göring, unlike Hitler, spoke of limited German action in Spain, and, unlike Neurath, he reproached Italy (and, incidentally, Austria too) for remaining a member of the League of Nations, " for England already a kind of invisible alliance against Italy and Germany." When he came to the point, he blurted out the whole Nazi propaganda campaign against Austria for the next fourteen months. The Austrian régime, he said, was so clerical that it was likely to yield to pressure from the Left [*sic*]. Could not Italy induce Schuschnigg to be more loyal to the Agreement of 11th July?—for if he drove the 'national' ministers out of office there might be an explosion.

Mussolini replied that the relations of Italy with Austria rested upon the principle of respecting Austria's independence " with the respect one owes to her sensibility." Since the Italians were unpopular in Austria he could only act with great caution towards Vienna. The Duce's frankness on

[2] Information supplied to me by Count Magistrati.

[3] See Schmidt Minute, dated " on the journey from Rome to Berlin."

this point suggests that Ciano's account of his visits to Vienna and Budapest in November 1936 had impressed him. For after Italophile ovations in Budapest Ciano was chilled to the bone by his reception in Vienna; the only spontaneity he observed there was when some Nazi enjoyed the excuse for performing a Roman salute which was also Hitler's greeting.[4]

Göring insisted that Austria was in fact being used by sinister international forces to keep Italy and Germany apart. After repeating the assurance that there would be no surprises from Germany, Göring went on to announce that an attempt at a Habsburg restoration in any form could not be tolerated by Hitler and would mean *finis Austriae*. Mussolini offered no objection.

In the Italian view Göring's interview with the Duce had gone badly and Magistrati afterwards warned him that the Italo-German friendship was precarious and depended precisely upon Austria.[5] In the visitors' book in his hotel in Capri Göring had found that someone had scribbled *non svastica in Mediterraneo*. When Göring left Rome, Hesse turned up and was evidently disconcerted.

When Ciano visited Hitler at the Obersalzberg in the previous October Magistrati went with him, and had an opportunity to glance around Hitler's small personal library. There he found a series of photographs of the Nazi movement and a few books on *Deutschtum* and on racial themes in general; although the Führer had always proclaimed that he took no interest in the mere 200,000 Germans of South

[4] See Ciano Minutes, Vienna-Budapest, 9-16th Nov. 1936.

[5] In his affidavit made in 1946 for the Court at Nuremberg, the German interpreter, Paul Schmidt, stated " When Göring visited Rome early in 1937 he declared that the union of Austria and Germany was inevitable and could be expected sooner or later. Mussolini heard these words in German, remained silent and protested only mildly when I translated them into French." Schmidt's testimony was given nine years after the event and he was seriously ill when he gave it; Magistrati's account, which I have used in the text, is based on notes made at the time and is probably more reliable; further, there is nothing to support his interview made on his journey to Berlin which began on the same day. affadavit in Paul Schmidt's own minute of this Mussolini-Göring

Tyrol, Magistrati made the interesting discovery of the works of their leaders, Reut-Nikolussi and Bossi Fedrigotti, on Hitler's scanty shelves. Early in 1937, oddly enough, the German press found it necessary to return to the sufferings of the South Tyrolese, and a German book appeared about the South Tyrolese "martyr," Noldin, who had died after his internment at Lipari. Magistrati called on Göring to discuss this new press campaign on 12 February, when he also brought up the question of Nazi Germany's persecution of the Catholic Church which was well known and much resented in Italy. In March the Pope addressed his message *Mit brennender Sorge* to the German clergy, a message in which he condemned in no uncertain terms the racial theories of the Nazis and their corruption of youth. At about the same time Göring was extraordinarily offensive to Renzetti about the Italian débâcle at Guadalajara, and Mussolini reacted with the snarl that was usual when Italy's military reputation was at stake. Thus the distrust and antipathy between Italy and Germany continued, while Mussolini made the fatal mistake of allowing the Germans to know that they had become indispensable to him; now he was about to show them that they had made him afraid.

Göring's threat about the Habsburgs was the expression of one of Hitler's peculiar susceptibilities and during this winter a clandestine Nazi leaflet was circulating in Austria which might have been drafted by the Führer himself. For this reason it may be worth while to quote its opening sentences. It was headed *Nie wieder Habsburg!*

"In spite of the Pact of 11th July 1936," it ran, "and in spite of growing difficulties in foreign policy, the Habsburg is at work!

"Great danger threatens our homeland, for evil and slimy fingers are grasping at the crown. The dago boy (*der welsche Jüngling*), Otto, and his still more dago and devilish mother are pushing their way back to power. . . .

"*Volksgenossen!* The offspring of the imperial traitors, brought up in hatred of everything German, is to become ruler of this country and leader of its people. . . ."[6]

Mussolini allowed five weeks to pass after Göring's visit.

[6] This came into my hands in Vienna at the time.

Then on 26th February Gayda, the mouthpiece of the Fascist régime, published an article in the *Giornale d'Italia* condemning the idea of a Habsburg restoration in Vienna; afterwards Ciano conveyed a message to the Austrian Cabinet that the article had become necessary in order to demonstrate the solidarity of the Axis to the French, but it was rather a matter of placating Hitler. Towards the end of April the unfortunate Schuschnigg was received in Venice and fêted with Mozart and Schubert played from a garlanded ship among a fleet of gondolas on the Grand Canal. While Schuschnigg was laying a wreath where the Austro-Hungarian sailors who had fallen in the last war were buried on the Isola San Michele, Mussolini in person visited the *Milwaukee,* the Nazi *Kraft durch Freude* ship which was anchored in Venice flying its huge swastika flag for the occasion—it was pointed out that this was the first time the Duce had trodden Nazi ' soil.' Thus Italy's abandonment of Austria, implicit in her policy since the dropping of Starhemberg, was shiftily admitted.

It was on 22nd April that the main political conversation between the Austrian Chancellor and Mussolini and Ciano took place. Mussolini explained that the Franco-British press had been claiming that Italy was faced with the choice: Anschluss or restoration. Hence Gayda's reply. It had also been necessary in order to facilitate his *rapprochement* with Belgrade.[7] Now the West was saying Italy had chosen the Anschluss. " This is false. The alternative does not exist. Neither solution is urgent." First, he needed Germany against Britain. Second, the authoritarian governments as such are drawn together by common enmities though " it is manifest that there are substantial differences between Fascism and National Socialism. We are Catholics, proud of our religion which we revere. We do not admit racialistic theories, least of all in their juridical consequences. Finally we differ over economic plans." But the Axis had become essential. The maintenance of Austrian independence must be synchronized and harmonized with this. And the Duce even echoed Göring's reproaches against Austria's infidelity to

[7] An Italo-Yugoslav Treaty was signed on 25 Mar. 1937.

the July Agreement which Germany had violated from the moment of its signature.

With his usual clumsy sincerity Schuschnigg insisted that he himself remained an unshaken, if academic, supporter of the Habsburgs. He also referred to a common interest between Austria and Czechoslovakia, though no political agreement existed nor was planned between them; he told Mussolini that Hodža, the Czechoslovak Prime Minister, had recently informed him that Prague desired a *rapprochement* with Italy, while if she found herself isolated by the other powers Czechoslovakia would be thrust into the arms of Russia. Two further details in this conversation should not go unrecorded. Apropos the restoration, Mussolini spoke of his own faith in monarchy as an institution while Schuschnigg told him that Neurath, himself a South German, on his recent visit to Vienna had said that Germany opposed the restoration because of the attraction a monarchy in Austria would exert on southern Germany.[8]

In general conversation at Venice Mussolini assured Schuschnigg that if the events of 1934 were repeated—it was obvious that they would not be—he would act in exactly the same way, while Ciano declared that Italy was now protecting Austria no longer militarily but through the Axis, politically, and both of them bandied about their catchword about the Germans being dangerous enemies but difficult friends. At the same time, under Alfieri's direction, Italian journalists disseminated typical Nazi phrases about Austria, and before Schuschnigg was back in Vienna another Gayda article appeared announcing that a Nazi Minister—Glaise and Schmidt only counted as 'national'—would soon join the Austrian Cabinet. According to Zernatto, Ciano had half-sponsored the Austrian Nazi memorandum demanding this when he spoke to Guido Schmidt at Venice, but now he hastened to support Schuschnigg's *démenti* and to disavow Gayda—the point in question, he said, had not been raised. According to Ciano's record as it stands this is true. But when he received Neurath in Rome on 3rd May, Mussolini said that he had advised Schuschnigg " di prendere una rappre-

[8] All this is recorded in Ciano's Minute of 22 Apr. 1937.

sentazione dei partiti nazionali."⁹ Even if this had only
been said on some informal occasion it seems unlikely that
Schuschnigg would have forgotten it so soon. It is always
possible that Mussolini's German was at fault, especially in
dealing with fine distinctions between ' national ' and Nazi
groupings. The Duce also told Neurath that he had forbidden Schuschnigg to approach Prague in any way, since
this would involve Austria in the democratic system and
annul the Rome Protocols. Neurath spoke of Britain's clear
intention to strike first at Italy, then at Germany, or even
at both together. After a brief consideration of " the
internal conditions of Russia and the relations between Germany, Italy, and Japan, the discussion ended."¹⁰

Hitler's steady drive towards his Italian alliance was
making itself powerfully felt, and the idea of an ally, even
Italian or yellow, brought a certain consolation to the
German spirit. The Führer had not forgotten that he
desired a German-Italian-British Triplice, and for this he
had sent Ribbentrop, another Nazi foreign expert, more
dogmatic than Göring, indeed *plus hitlérien qu' Hitler,* as
Ambassador to London. In May the German press began
to suggest that the Axis was pro-British, and when Blomberg returned from George VI's coronation deeply impressed
by Britain, the Germans began to assume the role of
mediators between London and Rome, who were now on
such bad terms that only three British newspapers were
allowed to enter Italy; this was because Britain had invited
the Negus to the coronation. Indeed, the Triple Alliance
upon which he had determined proved to be Hitler's mirage
—since both Germany and Italy felt affronted each time the
other one angled for the favour of Britain; Mussolini was
suspicious now of Sir Nevile Henderson's nomination to
Berlin as a British advance to Germany. About this time
a Palazzo Chigi wit was heard to murmur : " Datemi un
asse e vi farò un' altalena."¹¹

⁹ Roughly = to appoint representatives of the nationalist parties.
¹⁰ Ciano Minute, 3rd May 1937. The trials in Russia gave
satisfaction to the Axis Powers.
¹¹ " Give me an axis and I will make you a see-saw." The word
asse lends itself exactly to this sentence.

All this triangular trouble came to a head absurdly enough when Blomberg accepted the invitation Ciano had sent to him in March; at last he arrived in Italy in June. The Italians were thoroughly nervous about his visit, and apart from the fairly good impression made upon Blomberg by the Navy and Air Force—not by the Army—everything went wrong at the great review at Naples on 7th June. In the pageant of Italian military history Bligny and Argonne made an unfortunate appearance. It was terribly hot and Blomberg perspired a good deal and was concerned to observe the effect of the weather upon the immaculate component parts of his uniform. He entirely discomfited the Italians by asking for a drink of orangeade; there was every kind of wine and vermouth to be had, but it took them three-quarters of an hour to satisfy the Marshal's sober wish. At one point the great soldier was conspicuously unnerved by being piloted by the Duce himself on a short flight. On the boat to Capri afterwards he began to talk with tactless enthusiasm about Britain and finally gave an icy interview to Morgagni, the Stefani representative—" I can't understand these people," sighed the good Fascist, Starace, in disgust.[12]

Mussolini's vanity and confusion of values from his own point of view—his lack of grasp—were revealed in the dispatch which he now ordered Ciano to send to Attolico. Blomberg had said to Morgagni that it was not his affair to make judgements about the military qualities of the Italians. " I shall begin by saying," wrote Ciano, " that no one asked him to pronounce any such judgement. We have proved ourselves on too many battlefields to have need of approval and recommendation even from Marshal Blomberg." Attolico is to exert himself to induce Blomberg to add " because their valour is proven." " This would certainly be useful and would please no one more than the Duce," concluded Ciano. He himself had been further exasperated on the very day of Blomberg's departure by a visit from Hassell announcing that Neurath was accepting an invitation

[12] Starace was Secretary-General of the Fascist Party at this time.

to London. " Von Hassell," he noted on 14th June,[13] " failed
to conceal his satisfaction over the imminent political activity
of his Minister," he himself having always done his utmost
in support of an Anglophile policy.

It was in this same month that Mussolini made up his
mind to accept the invitation which Hans Frank had brought
him, and himself to travel to Germany to visit the Führer.
He was willing to come, he intimated, upon two conditions,
that he should bring no civilian evening clothes and that
it should be possible for him to have contact—and here he
used the German phrase—*mit der grossen Menge* : the great
Tribune wished to show that he could move more than one
people. For a year now he had been trying to deceive himself
and the world into thinking of the Austro-German Agreement as coming within the framework of the Rome-Vienna-
Budapest economic alliance presided over by himself. Of
late Poland and Yugoslavia had become more and more
friendly to Italy as an unprovocative counterpoise to the new
strength of Germany, and Mussolini thought of complement-
ing his visit to Berlin by a conference with Austria, Hungary,
Yugoslavia, and Poland. But the Germans had no intention of encouraging the tendency of the minor states to
cluster around the less alarming dictator, and in the end
Mussolini refused even to receive the Austrian and Hungarian
Ministers in Berlin. The Italian Embassy there noticed that
Guido Schmidt visited Göring between the announcement of
Mussolini's visit and his arrival.

For the visit was announced on 4th September as an
imminent meeting of the Chiefs of the Two Revolutions, and
Mussolini left Rome on 23rd September with the three
Ministers, Ciano, Alfieri, and Starace, and a retinue of about a
hundred people; a new gala Fascist Militia uniform had been
designed for the occasion. At Innsbruck the Duce reviewed
the Austrian *Jäger*. At the German-Austrian frontier he was
met by Hess, Frank, General List, Attolico, and Hassell, all,
of course, in uniform, but it is a little bizarre to find that
Hassell, the would-be anti-Nazi, had preceded Mussolini from

[13] Ciano Minute, 14th June 1937. Later Neurath's visit to London
was cancelled.

Rome dressed in the uniform of the N.S.K.K. (*National-Sozialistische Kraftführer Korps*).[14]

'At Munich, the factory of Hitler's predominantly Bavarian brand of Pan-Germanism, the Führer himself appeared in the military version of the Nazi Party uniform, brown peak cap, brown tunic and shirt with black trousers. Everything was superlatively and gigantically organized at Munich, where it was not the German State but the National Socialist Party which was fêting the sister revolution.

To inaugurate the proceedings Mussolini laid a wreath upon the memorial of the Nazi " martyrs " of the abortive *Putsch* of 1923. After a magnificent lunch-party given by the Party at the Brown House there was an S.S. goose-stepping parade which the impressionable Duce was never to forget. After the Party the Reichswehr had its turn, and displayed its many-sided strength in the manœuvres at Mecklenburg and in Krupp's workshops in Essen; Mussolini was tremendously impressed by the Krupp production figures. At Hanover the mayor presented the Duce with one of the famous Hanoverian breed of horses. This probably gave rise to the story which was afterwards told of the horse Mussolini brought from Italy and then, to his chagrin, could not ride in Germany in deference to Hitler's equestrian incapacity. Hitler wrote off horses as fit for museums but not for the great new mechanical age which his genius bestrode.

Lastly the capital received the state visit of the ruler of Italy. Berlin roared its welcome as best it could from behind the S.S. and police cordons, and the press announced, as it had on and off since 1933, the end of the principles of 1789. Before the climax on the *Maifield* on 28th September, when Mussolini was to have his mass contact by addressing the Berliners in German, Göring gave a lunch-party at Karinhall and took his revenge for many of their meetings in Italy by straining the more sensitive nervous system of the Italian. Göring's young lioness made Mussolini jumpy;

[14] Neurath grumbled at his trial at Nuremberg that Hitler had forced him into S.S. uniform on this occasion; it was, no doubt, in revenge for June 1934. See chapter II above.

what was worse, the Chief of the Luftwaffe kept the unfortunate Head of the Italian Government playing with his toy electric trains until a short time before the great demonstration was due to begin.

A crowd of about 800,000 was gathered. Hitler spoke first and then Mussolini. But of course when it came to public open-air oratory, in spite of the most meticulous rehearsals beforehand, the foreigner's intonation and his gestures made his speech unintelligible. And then, half-way through, there was a tremendous thunderstorm. The loud-speakers behaved as if they were possessed by devils, and Mussolini's carefully prepared notes were soaked by the downpour of rain. Most remarkable of all, German organization suffered a total breakdown and such confusion set in that Mussolini returned alone with his chauffeur; he was soaked to his skin and in a state of collapse. It is worth noting here an indication of his lack of self-confidence: at seven o'clock the next morning he sent for Magistrati to ask whether he had been right to say *Frieden* and not *Friede*. The context had been the sentence " To the whole world, which is anxiously asking what will be the result of the meeting in Berlin—will it be war or peace?—we can both answer, the Führer and I, *with a loud voice*: ' peace '." Magistrati happened to notice that the words in italics had been added to Mussolini's notes in pencil; his texts were always changed about a great deal. It is also worth noting that the Duce's duodenal ulcer had made itself felt again earlier in this same year, though his doctor expressed satisfaction about him to some of the entourage on his arrival in Munich : it was not until the strain of 1942 that the ulcer made Mussolini seriously ill.

This visit of the Duce's was important for a number of reasons. No specific agreements, published or secret, were made, but the Wilhelmstrasse informed all German missions abroad that it had been agreed that (1) an early end to the Spanish Civil War was desired; (2) that if either Germany or Italy should draw nearer to Britain the other should benefit to some extent; (3) that—approximately— Italy should have a free hand in the Mediterranean and Germany in Austria. " Nothing was discussed or agreed upon," it was added, " that Austria could consider dan-

gerous or infringing upon her independence."[15] Mussolini
nevertheless told Schuschnigg that Austria had not been
mentioned so that nothing had changed. Göring told Lipski
that when he showed Mussolini a map with Austria marked
as incorporated in Germany, the Duce had said, "Well,
you are getting on with things, but isn't Czechoslovakia
disagreeably in the way?" There is, of course, no reason
to accept Göring's word, except in so far as Paul Schmidt
confirmed it.[16] According to Mussolini it was agreed that
nothing should be done about Austria "without reciprocal
advance information."[17]

In fact the two dictators themselves scarcely had time
for a tête-à-tête and no preparation had been made for a
discussion between them. Mussolini, however, had three
long conversations in closed cars with the German Foreign
Office Chef de Protocol, Bülow-Schwante, which the latter
recorded. Mussolini told him that in Munich he had agreed
with Hitler to wage an "all-out fight against Bolshevism."
The Spanish war was now in its fourteenth month and the
Conference at Nyon not long over. Mussolini said to
Bülow that Bolshevism would be finished in Europe if it were
defeated in Spain, and boasted of the hundred aeroplanes
and four thousand 'technical troops' he intended to send
there. Apart from this he spoke scornfully of Britain.
Bülow managed to steer him away from both the Catholic
and the Austrian Question.[18]

Apart from any conversation, the impression Nazi Germany made upon Mussolini was probably the most profound
impression of his life. Here was power beyond all his
megalomaniac dreams, and it would be well, he felt in the
glow of the experience, not to hesitate to identify Fascist Italy
with it. "When Fascism has a friend," he had screamed on
the *Maifeld*, "it will march with that friend to the last."
On reaching the Austro-German frontier on his journey south
he invited Hitler to revisit Italy. It appears that this time
in Germany there had been no friction between them, and

[15] D.G.F.P. series D. vol. I, no. I.   [16] See p. 98, note 5.
[17] Or rather, according to Ciano, Mussolini mentioned this to
Ribbentrop on 6th November, 1937.
[18] D.G.F.P. series D, vol. I, no. 2.

Hitler had allowed Mussolini his fair share of applause. Certainly the unstable Mussolini easily revised the judgement he had made in 1934; the personification of so much might and glory who was also one's political partner was not someone to be despised or even disliked. From this time he joined the ranks of those who reacted to the Führer's fascination, a fact of which Ciano was to complain bitterly in the following years.

As for Hitler, long ago he had decided that Mussolini was a genius second only to himself; as time passed he became aware that the Italians did not fit very well into his scheme of things; he convinced himself that only Mussolini could marshal them as he, the Führer, wished. At the *Maifield* he spoke of Mussolini as one of those rare geniuses, not made by history, but makers of it, and from his recurring references at highly secret conferences to Mussolini's genius[19] there is no reason to question his sincerity. It undoubtedly pleased him to have led Germany out of her isolation so obviously, and to speak of 115 million men united in defence of the Nazi and Fascist revolutions. He was incapable of conversation, and his relations with the Duce were the better because declamation had been the order of the day. Most important of all, henceforward he knew in his subconscious way that he had not merely reversed the position of June 1934, but that he had established a personal ascendancy over Mussolini. There was nothing more to wait for profitably, and he was ready, therefore, for offensive action abroad, as he had been within Germany in the spring of 1933. Far from the period of surprises being over, as he had announced in January 1937,[20] it was about to begin in earnest.

[19] e.g. at that at the Reichskanzlei on 5th Nov. 1937, when he spoke of Italy as *geführt durch ein Genie.*
[20] Speech to the Reichstag, 30 Jan. 1937.

Chapter VI

AUSTRIA LOST AND WON

Six weeks after Mussolini had left Germany, on the afternoon of Friday, 5th November 1937, Hitler held a secret four hours' meeting at the Reichskanzlei with Göring, Blomberg, Fritsch, Raeder, and Neurath, a meeting since associated with the adjutant who recorded it, Colonel Hossbach;[1] the Führer, who was always haunted by a consciousness of the Hero's race with death, demanded that the statements he then made " be looked upon in the case of his death as his last will and testament."

The gist of these statements was that Germany required to conquer territory in order not to depend upon imported food, and that the time had come to set about this conquest. " If the Führer is still living, then it will be his irrevocable decision to solve the German space problem not later than 1943-5," but there will probably be earlier opportunities. A preliminary to be tackled at once is the conquest of Austria-cum-Czechoslovakia, the essential nucleus of the Austria of 1914.

Clearly Hitler already hoped to strike at the Austrians and Czechs in 1938, for he believed—indeed he hoped—that the Spanish imbroglio might draw France into war with Italy, leaving him " free " to move.

" . . . From the German point of view," he said, " a one hundred per cent. victory for Franco is not desirable; we are more interested in a continuation of the war and the preservation of the tensions in the Mediterranean. Should Franco be in sole possession of the Spanish peninsula, it would mean the end of Italian intervention and the presence of Italy in the Balearic Isles. As our interests are directed

---

[1] D.G.F.P. D, vol. I, no. 19. It was not verbally recorded, but the Hossbach Minute is considered to give a sufficiently accurate account of what was said. See L. B. Namier, *Diplomatic Prelude* (Macmillan, 1948), p. 213n. What Professor Namier says about Schmundt's, applies equally to Hossbach's, records.

towards continuing the war in Spain it must be the task of our future policy to strengthen[2] Italy in her fight to hold on to the Balearic Isles. However, a stabilization[3] of Italian positions in the Balearic Isles cannot be tolerated either by France or by England and might lead to a war by France and England against Italy. . . .

" The date of our attack on Czechoslovakia and Austria must be made independent of the course of the Italian-French-English war and would not be simultaneous with the beginning of military operations by these three states. He was also not thinking of military agreements with Italy, but he wished to begin operations against Czechoslovakia, ex-ploiting this uniquely favourable opportunity in complete independence. The attack on Czechoslovakia would have to take place with the speed of lightning[4]. . . ."

Earlier Hitler, as usual, spoke of Mussolini as a genius, but his callousness towards Italy as one among the pawns in his game was complete. " No opposition," said Hitler to his military chiefs on 5th November, " to the removal of Czechoslovakia is expected on the part of Italy; on the other hand it is impossible to judge at the moment how her attitude in the Austrian question should be interpreted, for it essentially depends upon whether the Duce is still alive when it comes to the point."

Why was it so important that Germany should not need to import food? Because Hitler's fundamental intention to dominate the world in order to establish his caste system required a war during which much importation would be suspended. The declarations of 5th November, however, show that Hitler had abandoned the idea of a Triple Alliance with Italy and Britain, and was falling back without great enthusiasm upon the geopolitical triangle with Japan in Britain's place; Italy was in fact to be his most useful weapon *against* Britain.

It has been seen that one of Mussolini's worst mistakes lay in his contempt for the Czechs; another fatal error in his

[2] *den Rücken für weiteren Verbleib zu stärken.* By the secret agreement signed on 28 Nov. 1936, Italy had guaranteed Spanish integrity.

[3] *Festsetzen.*   [4] *blitzartig schnell.*

career was his misconception with regard to Britain. This
misconception was perhaps the thing which, thanks to their
ignorance, the two dictators most completely shared; it was
certainly one of the grave miscalculations in Hitler's life :
In 1936 and 1937 it grew into contempt for Britain in the
minds of both Führer and Duce, thanks to the weakness they
thought Britain showed during the Abyssinian and Spanish
wars. Of course there were the old stories of Ireland and
India, but on 5th November Hitler adds to these :

" (1) The weakening of the British position in the Far
East by Japan. (2) The opposition in the Mediterranean by
Italy which . . . is expanding its power position and must
consequently infringe British interests to an increasing extent.
The outcome of the Abyssinian War is a loss of prestige for
Britain which Italy is endeavouring to increase by stirring
up discontent in the Mohammedan World."

The choice between Britain and Japan was an issue between the programme of *Mein Kampf* supported by the anti-
Nazi or less Nazi generals and diplomats, as against the
Nazi leaders, especially the geo-politicians and the S.S. It
is interesting that over this point Ribbentrop and the Party—
or was it the mere chance of circumstances?—defeated Hitler's
original plan. At first the Germans approached the Japanese
in order to break the isolation to which Italy, too, seemed
to have condemned the Nazi Reich, but this very approach will
be seen to have led by degrees from the Anti-Comintern
Pact to the Italo-German military alliance and finally to
the Italo-German-Japanese Tripartite Pact of September 1940.

When the S.S.-Führer Ribbentrop failed to take London
by storm, he reacted violently away from enthusiasm for the
nordicism of his Anglo-Saxon brothers to enthusiasm for the
nordic vitality of the Japanese. Britain, he had soon decided,
was decadent and pluto-bolshevik. Through his acquaintance
with Mrs. Simpson he had in 1936 expected to exert influence
over a reigning monarch and one whom he believed to
be susceptible to Germanic notions.[5] Thanks to a complete
inability to comprehend the constitutional development of

[5] See Ciano Minute of 10 Mar. 1940 and chapter XII below, as also
Erich Kordt, *Wahn und Wirklichkeit* (1947), p. 82.

Britain, the abdication of Edward VIII was interpreted by
the Axis mentality as a sign of decadence instead of
resilience, and Ribbentrop's view was coloured by personal
pique. It has been seen that already in November 1936
he had significantly enough left London to sign the German-
Japanese Anti-Comintern Pact in Berlin, and during 1937,
in spite of the luxurious installations at his residence in
Carlton House Terrace, his restlessness increased. Through
his separate S.S. foreign service he had a staff of personal
representatives who were constantly *en voyage*. One of them,
called Raumer, who was an 'expert' on the Far East,
turned up in Rome in the autumn of 1937 and suddenly
arranged for his master to follow him. Neurath and Hassell
were not unnaturally annoyed, but Ciano knew through
tapped telephone conversations that the Anglophile Hassell
despised and belittled the Italian Foreign Minister; it was,
therefore, Ciano who particularly welcomed Ribbentrop to
Rome towards the end of October 1937, only six years
before the trial of Verona, and Mussolini, too, was bound
to rejoice in again receiving so direct a representative of the
Führer. Within less than a fortnight, and one day after
the Reichskanzlei meeting, Ribbentrop was in Rome again to
sign, on 6th November 1937, the adhesion of Italy to the
Anti-Comintern Pact.[6] On this occasion Mussolini said everything Ribbentrop could have hoped for. Italy, with Sicily
now as her centre of gravity, had become too Mediterranean to care about Austria. He repeated also what he
had been saying since the spring and would repeat in
March 1938, that if the Austrians wanted the Anschluss
he was willing enough for things to take their course.

At the Munich Bürgerbräu celebration on 9th November
Hitler proudly drew a line under Germany's isolation as
a thing of the past. "Three States have come together.
First a European Axis and now a great world-political
triangle. . . . It does not consist of three feeble phantoms,
but of three states that are ready and determined to realize
their rights and vital interests." When Lord Halifax com-

[6] Ribbentrop did not tell the Italians about the secret German-
Japanese clauses whose existence had been mentioned by Neurath
to Ciano.

bined a visit to the hunting exhibition in Berlin with a visit to the Obersalzberg he alluded to the possibility of Germany's return to Geneva as the Germans had themselves suggested in March 1936; this had often been discussed between the Western Powers and Italy, but since July Italy had insisted that Germany should participate in the discussions as an equal. The upshot this time was that Italy at last formally left the League of Nations on 11th December, and within twenty-four hours, as Hitler had promised Attolico, the Deutches Nachrichten-Büro announced that a return of Germany to the League would never be considered again.

At the Reichskanzlei on 5th November Blomberg, and especially Fritsch, " repeatedly pointed out that England and France," to whom Hitler had just referred as Germany's two *Hassgegnern*,[7] " must not appear as our enemies, and they stated that the war with Italy would not bind the French Army to such an extent that it would not be in a position to begin operations on our Western frontier with superior forces." Fritsch, if less emphatically than his Chief of Staff, Beck, represented the conservative caution of the Army as against the Party's *élan*. It was even said[8] that in September, in the presence of Hitler and Göring, Fritsch had remarked to Mussolini that he alone was the *oberste Chef der Wehrmacht,* and if it came to it this would mean that the Air Force, too, must obey him.

Now Hitler had decided upon action, those who responded half-heartedly must be removed. It was a preliminary part of the move against Schuschnigg and Beneš to dismiss Fritsch and Blomberg and the old-school diplomats like Neurath and Hassell. The method of dismissal of the generals was carried out in such typically Nazi fashion that a brief reference should be made to it now that the rumours one heard at the time have turned out to be true. Blomberg was not very popular with the Army; he had been thought to be too servile to Hitler and was nicknamed " the rubber lion " or, after the Nazi propaganda film, *Hitlerjunge Quex.*

[7] This was wrongly translated as ' hateful enemies ' at Nuremberg. It is almost untranslatable, but ' hate-filled ' would be better than ' hateful.'

[8] Cf. Zernatto, op. cit., p. 190.

Himmler deliberately allowed him to marry an ex-prostitute and Hitler and Göring to be witnesses of the ceremony on 12th January 1938 because blackmail potentialities always came in useful to the chief of the Gestapo. When Fritsch protested at the slur on the Army's honour, a homosexual blackmailer who had evidence dating from 1934 against a General Frisch was brought into play, and Fritsch let himself be put aside although a Military Court established his innocence.[9] No new Minister of War was appointed in succession to Blomberg, but on 4th February Hitler became Commander-in-Chief of all the Armed Forces, with Keitel as his *Chef des Oberkommando der Wehrmacht* and Jodl immediately under Keitel.

It might have been thought that Neurath was sufficiently cynical not to get in Hitler's way, but Hitler and Ribbentrop were now determined that Ribbentrop should be Foreign Minister. So Neurath, from whom no protest had come on 5th November, had to make way. As for Hassell, he had expressed too many doubts about the Axis, and, among other things, he was blamed for Blomberg's demeanour at Naples; the Prince of Hesse joined in the chorus against him and hoped to get his job, but in January 1938 Hassell was merely sent on leave, and for three months the German Embassy in Rome remained without a chief. Perhaps it suited Hitler that this should be so throughout the period of the Anschluss. The atmosphere in Germany at the end of January and beginning of February 1938 may be measured by the postponement of Hitler's Reichstag speech, due on 30th January, until 20th February, and by the precipitate flight to Italy of, among others, the German ex-Crown Prince,[10] who was, it is true, notoriously easy to alarm.

For a moment it seemed as if the arch-intriguer, Papen, that genius in being all things to all men, was to be a victim of this purge. He had seemed to be getting on very nicely in Vienna and in Guido Schmidt he had found a partner in treachery. He had always opposed S.A. violence

<hr />

9 See full account quoted by R. Pechel, op. cit.

10 See Zernatto (op. cit.), to whom Austrian frontier authorities reported the arrival of the Crown Prince without luggage or passport.

in Austria such as that which was continually planned by
Captain Leopold, but the star of the S.S. had been in the
ascendant since 1934, and with its representatives Seyss-
Inquart and the " economic expert," Keppler, Papen appeared
to be on the best of terms; he was, moreover, playing
his favourite trick of arranging personal contact, and from
December 1937 was pressing for a Hitler-Schuschnigg interview. Suddenly on 5th February he was rung up by a minor
official in the German Foreign Office and told that he had
been recalled and was to leave Vienna immediately. He went
off not merely crestfallen but scared, but he managed to
see Hitler, persuade him that the interview could be made
into part of the action against Austria, and to return to
Vienna to fetch Schuschnigg only a few days later. It was
characteristic of Hitler, of the romantic adolescent part of
his split personality, that he retained a certain tenderness
for Papen on account of Papen's share in bringing the
German Nazis into power. Hitler knew that he required
for his purposes evil characters who would be faithful only
to his person, and he loved to romanticize all this as his
own Heroic response to fidelity. At Berchtesgaden Schuschnigg heard Hitler say to Papen, " In the decisive hour in
1933 you saved the Reich from the abyss by making 30th
January possible . . . I shall never forget that you did that,
otherwise everything would have rotted into Communism."
    The situation in Austria had deteriorated steadily since
July 1936, if a little more slowly than some people had
feared. Reporting to Berlin on 1st September 1936, Papen
recommended " continued patient, psychological treatment
with slowly intensified pressure, aimed at changing the
régime." The Austro-German Agreement was particularly
corrosive of Schuschnigg's resistance in that, like nearly all
Austrians of his ex-officer category, he was hypersensitive
to any accusation of disloyalty to the *Deutschtum* of the
Austrian State which had now been re-emphasized. Another corrosive factor was as operative here as among the
Sudeten Germans; this was the impression deliberately created
by the Nazis that, though Austria would become part of
Germany, she would retain her autonomy. To the last
Seyss-Inquart feigned to be working only for this, and not

merely large numbers of Austrians, but many foreign politicians, not excluding Mussolini and Ciano, were naïve enough to presume that Austria would be allowed some kind of home rule.

Though the S.S. in Austria as in Germany were steadily gaining in importance, Hitler continued to make use of their rivals of the S.A. In the autumn Schuschnigg was persuaded to allow the formation of what was called the *Siebener Komité* in part from among people associated with the old S.A. plotter, Leopold; its objective was defined as " to pacify and attract ' national ' forces to co-operate with the Patriotic Front," the Austrian Government organization. In other words, Nazi activity became increasingly barefaced, and Nazis insinuated themselves into all sorts of positions in the Ministries, police, and Patriotic Front.

In November 1937, although only seven people had been present at the Reichskanzlei meeting of the 5th, there were numerous indications of the events that were to come. Austria, of course, was constantly accused by the Nazis of breaking her pledges of July 1936. Göring received a group of Austrian industrialists in Berlin and told them that the foreign guns upon which they were counting would never shoot: afterwards he made an ironical apology. In January 1938 a provocative interview published in an obscure Prague newspaper by Tavs, a member of the *Siebener Komité,* caused the Austrian police to search the Committee's office in the Teinfaltstrasse in Vienna. There among all kinds of incriminating material was found a plan signed R. H., the initials of Rudolf Hess, the Führer's Deputy. According to this Seyss-Inquart (who had expressed the gravest disapprobation of the *Siebener Komité* to Schuschnigg) was to be brought into the Government with Glaise-Horstenau and Guido Schmidt; then three months later, that is, after three months of Nazi terrorization, a plebiscite was to be held. There was also provision for the murder of Papen or some other member of the German Legation in Vienna, the crime to be attributed to the Austrian Legitimists. According to the R. H. plan " Italy will not be able to intervene as she will be much too much occupied with other matters. . . . She will certainly do nothing to prevent a change in the Austrian Government if this change is

based on the pretext of the requirements of the Treaty"
(of July 1936). It is interesting that a little earlier Göring
had been playing up the poor Habsburg ghost to Ambassador
Bullitt.[11] "There are schemes," he said, "being pushed now
for a union of Austria, Hungary and Czechoslovakia, either
with or without a Habsburg at the head of the union . . .
for us the conclusion of such an agreement would be an
immediate *casus belli.*" His tongue must have been bulging
out of his cheek, for whatever some Legitimists may have
hoped,[12] there was never the slightest possibility of a Habsburg restoration on this scale. The Hungarians had their
revisionist appetite whetted at just about this time by indications from Berlin that Czechoslovakia was soon to be par-
titioned,[13] and they would not have dreamt of compromising
themselves with the Czechs. Although he suggested that Germany was still holding back on account of Italy, Göring on the
same occasion stated plainly that "Germany would tolerate
no solution of the Austrian Question other than the consolidation of Austria in the German Reich"; "consolidation in"
scarcely sounds like local autonomy.

Towards the end of 1937 and the beginning of 1938 there
was a slight change in Italy's attitude. Mussolini was still
agreeably excited retrospectively by his visit to Germany and
all the more, prospectively, in planning his reception of
Hitler in Italy. Nevertheless, a little more emphasis was
laid upon the independence of Austria, and Ciano was fairly
reassuring to Schuschnigg at their meeting with the Hungarians in Budapest in January, though the Axis was emphasized
again as the base of the Rome-Vienna-Budapest triangle. The
Palazzo Chigi was puzzled and annoyed by the endless
intrigues of Guido Schmidt, and replaced Salata by a new
Italian Minister in Vienna, a man named Ghigi, who was
known to be a man of energy. Ever since the Abyssinian War
there had been talk of an Italian-German economic agree-

[11] Dispatch from Bullitt to Washington, 23 Nov. 1937.
[12] Cf. Otto of Habsburg's offer to Schuschnigg on 17 Feb. 1938:
see below.
[13] Already at Gömbos' funeral a year earlier Göring had remarked
to Kánya that Czechoslovakia would have to be liquidated in two or
three years' time. See Ciano Minutes, 9-16 Nov. 1936.

ment, but nothing had come of it. Ciano now wrote personally to Göring explaining what, for instance, Italy required from Germany for her fleet, but he got no encouragement and felt irritated. This led to renewed consideration of the possibility of a *détente* with Britain, which Neville Chamberlain's mentality was likely to facilitate.

In Berlin the leaders varied between reproaching the British, especially their Press, for showing no comprehension of the needs of 'German unity' and reproaching British Ministers like Halifax for making no objections to the Anschluss in the hope of weakening the Axis. After Halifax's visit in November Hitler spoke in this sense, this time to Renzetti. There was something in it. Chamberlain, it seems, really believed that German action against Austria would goad Italy into resisting it and make her come to terms with Britain. So late as 3rd February Mussolini spoke to Ciano and Magistrati very excitedly as if he were on the verge of war with the British in accordance with Hitler's hopes, but on the 8th Italo-British conversations began in London. From then on until it was too late Mussolini's advice to Schuschnigg was to play for time. The British were the suitors because Mussolini could do more than they to save Austria, and he wished to wait for the better terms he might get if Eden were sacrificed to the blindness of Chamberlain. Ultimately, Schuschnigg was to hope, Hitler might not dare to act if Rome and London had been reconciled; further, his forthcoming visit to Rome had been announced and might act as a brake. The Duce's advice probably contributed to Schuschnigg's acquiescence when his visit to Berchtesgaden was proposed. Eden himself was willing enough to negotiate with Italy if it helped to save Austria, but when he brought up the Austrian Question with Grandi he was told that that subject could not enter into any Anglo-Italian conversation.

The waiting manœuvre was entirely illusory; it gave the Austrian leaders false hopes and diverted their efforts into fatal directions. While Mussolini was waiting for Hitler to drive Eden out of office for him,[14] Chamberlain refused a

[14] Cf. Gayda's article against Eden in the *Berliner Tageblatt* on 4th Jan. 1938.

show of energy on behalf of Austria, as suggested by the
French, in order not to annoy Mussolini. If Hitler, who
had made up his mind, was affected by all this, his determination to act quickly was strengthened : there should
be no Austria left by the time Britain and Italy came to
terms in April. Instead of publishing the material found
in the Teinfaltstrasse and challenging the world as to which
party was breaking the Austro-German Agreement, Schuschnigg kept it to himself and went to Berchtesgaden to be
upbraided for *his* ' treachery.'

Few things are more illuminating in studying Hitler and
his relations with Mussolini than Schuschnigg's account of his
visit to Berchtesgaden on 12th February 1938. An honest
man had fallen among thieves. Schuschnigg travelled with
Guido Schmidt as his companion. At the Salzburg frontier
they were met by Papen, who told them that the Führer
was in the best of moods, but would they mind that quite
by chance several generals had also arrived at the Berghof?
"Who?" Why, only Keitel, Reichenau, and Sperrle, a Luftwaffe general who was back from Spain. When they arrived
they were met by Hitler in his habitual brown and black
uniform accompanied by these three to create a congenial
atmosphere.

Then Schuschnigg was closeted with Hitler. To start with
he was harshly scolded because Austria had not left Geneva;
of course his undertaking to pursue a German policy had
involved this. Austria's whole history was one long betrayal.
Now Hitler is determined to put an end to this story of
treachery. " I have," he declares, " an historic task and
I shall fulfil it because Providence has determined that
I shall. . . . I have had to tread the most difficult path to
which any German was ever condemned, and I have played
a greater part in German history than that to which any
other German was destined. Not through force—I am
supported by the love of my people. . . ."

There were a great many threats. How dare Schuschnigg
fortify the frontier against Germany? Austria could not
hold Hitler up half an hour if he should decide to act.
" I may be in Vienna overnight like a storm in the spring!
Then you will experience something. . . . After the troops

will come the S.A. and the [Austrian] Legion and no one will be able to prevent their revenge, not even I!"

Schuschnigg timidly interpolated that all that might mean war.

"You wish to take the responsibility for that, Mr. Schusch-nigg?"[15] is roared back at him. "Do not believe that anyone in the world can impede my decisions." Italy?—"*mit Italien bin ich im reinen*;[16] there is the closest friendship between us." Then, with grotesque insinuations about the Halifax visit, Schuschnigg is assured that England will not move and that France lost her last chance in March 1936, when she could, if she had acted, have thrown the Germans back sixty kilometres immediately. . . .[17]

"I am not bluffing," said Hitler; "my whole career proves that sufficiently. I have achieved all that I intended and have thus perhaps become the greatest German in history; unlike Mussolini I don't go in for much talking or prenotification; his style is quite another thing. But besides mine, there are other great German names; if I close my eyes to-day everything is planned. We have a Göring, a Hess, a Frick, an Epp, and countless others. I give you the one chance of your life, Mr. Schuschnigg, to add your name to that of Germany's great men."

After two hours of this kind of conversation there was an interval for lunch. At table Hitler talked about the biggest buildings in the world, a bridge in Hamburg, &c., which he would build. Schuschnigg would have liked to smoke after lunch but that was not allowed;[18] already the Byzantine atmosphere weighed heavily upon the visitor from the East.

At 2 p.m. Hitler withdrew. Schuschnigg was kept waiting two hours; he was made aware that, by turns with him, Hitler was discussing Austria with a leading Viennese

[15] *Herr Schuschnigg* was an insulting way of addressing his visitor, In Germany no one who holds an official position is ever addressed as plain "Mr."

[16] Again, like so much of Hitler's German, very difficult to trans-late—perhaps "I have cleared up everything with Italy."

[17] This was indeed exact.

[18] He was a heavy smoker, but Hitler's objection to smoking was played up deliberately. See *Nuremberg Trial Proceedings*, pt. XVI, pp. 191-2.

Nazi called Mühlmann, who had also arrived at the Berghof. Then Schuschnigg and Guido Schmidt were summoned into a small room where they found Ribbentrop and Papen and a ten-point ultimatum. Before Schuschnigg left Vienna Papen had promised him that the Agreement of July 1936 would not be questioned, only its better functioning was to be discussed. Now Papen declared he was completely taken by surprise. The ten points were simply part of the " action " to destroy Austria. It is enough to say that each one spelt the negation of Austrian sovereignty, from the second which demanded that Seyss-Inquart should be given all police powers in Austria to the ninth which abolished all discrimination against National Socialists in the Austrian army.[19]

After a desultory dispute over all this Schuschnigg was brought back into the presence of the Führer. When he stated that he could not commit Austria by signing, there must be three days for Vienna—the Federal President—to accede, Hitler became stormy, at once called for Keitel, and abruptly dismissed Schuschnigg. Outside Guido Schmidt kept up the intensified pressure by remarking to him that they would probably be arrested next. Then came another favourite trick. Schuschnigg was told that " for the first time in his life " Hitler would change his mind and allow him three days. Germany's man of destiny gradually calmed himself and the Berchtesgaden ' Agreement ' was prepared for signature. In the course of further volubility Hitler spoke of Italy again : " Italy in the case of war can be held with a well-trained Air Force and submarine specialists, she only needs 200,000 highly trained men for this. Those she has. That is enough." Hitler also made clear that in his view a German Army of 100,000 could knock out the Italian forces.[20] Here he added, by way of a boast, a threat, and a genuine conviction combined, that he was building up the best Army Germany had ever had ; it would show no sense

[19] D.G.F.P. series D, vol. I, no. 295. In his *Requiem in Rot-Weiss-Rot*, Schuschnigg gave a confused account of this ultimatum, reducing it to seven points.

[20] This is not in Schuschnigg's own account published in *Requiem in Rot-Weiss-Rot,* but he told Zernatto and others of it immediately after his return.

of responsibility to history (this he said twice) not to make use of so magnificent an instrument. The signatures followed. Papen left with Schuschnigg and Guido Schmidt. On the road Papen said, " Yes, that is what the Führer can be like—now you've seen for yourself. But the next time you come it will be much easier. The Führer can be particularly charming." Jodl wrote in his diary on 11th February, " Von Schuschnigg together with Guido Schmidt is again being put under the heaviest political and military pressure." On 13th February he noted the Führer's order " to the effect that military pressure, by shamming military action, should be kept up until 15th February."

Immediately after his return from a Germany which appeared to be mobilizing, Schuschnigg received an extraordinary demand from Otto of Habsburg to be made Austrian Chancellor.[21] This was clear to him, at least, that the smallest hint of legitimism would bring the German Army into Austria at once; indeed, it is difficult to believe that the Archduke's letter was genuine and not the work of an *agent provocateur.*

At the same time Mussolini sent Schuschnigg a message by word of mouth fully approving of his expedition to Berchtesgaden, and repeating that his (Mussolini's) attitude to the Austrian Question and his personal friendship would remain unshaken. This was at the least misleading. On the other hand, Ciano's documents show that the Duce and he were aware of the imminence of the Anschluss and annoyed by Hitler's neglect. When Ciano saw Hesse on 18th February he read a lecture in what the Nazis might have called the English governess fashion. What he said was, briefly, we have behaved in the most correct and considerate way to Hitler, and can but feel displeasure that, contrary to all our reciprocal pledges, he neither consulted nor informed us about Berchtesgaden. " It would be salutary if the German Government would take note of these my observations for the future. I wish to emphasize that we have never failed to inform the Government of the Reich of the smallest particulars relating to questions far less

[21] See M. Fuchs, op. cit., appendix VI.

important to the Germans than is the Austrian problem to Italy."[22] Ciano's claim was true enough. Indeed, the Germans continued to flout their allies and the Italians to behave correctly; even in 1939 and 1940, when it came to Albania and Greece, Italian action was only half-heartedly incorrect. On 20th February, instead of the guarantee of Austrian sovereignty expected in Vienna and asked for by Rome, Hitler made nothing but an empty reference to Austria in his delayed Reichstag speech which was primarily concerned with a furious attack upon Eden : it also announced the German recognition of Manchukuo.

The account of his conversation with Chamberlain and Eden on 19th February sent by Grandi to Ciano is unusually interesting.[23] It is difficult to doubt the facts he provides with regard to Chamberlain's intrigue with him (through another member of the Conservative party) behind Eden's back, for he could have had no motive to invent such a story, and it was obvious that if Chamberlain asked him for ammunition against Eden, as he said, he gladly provided it. With regard to the relations of Italy with Germany and apart from Grandi's refusal to discuss Austria (although Ciano wanted some agreement with London before the Anschluss could take place), the Grandi dispatch raises another interesting point. Chamberlain, quite prepared to accept the answer, asked the Fascist Ambassador whether a bargain had been made by which Italy had given Germany a free hand in Austria in return for German support " in the Mediterranean and in Europe." Grandi replied that this was false though it has been seen that it had been agreed when Mussolini went to Germany.[24] Since the summer of 1936 indeed, Italy had been able to find no way to avoid giving Germany a free hand in Austria. As for Germany's contribution, that we now know was never to have been made; or rather it was to be so small as only to keep Italy engaged in Spain.

[22] Ciano Minute, 18 Feb, 1938.
[23] Also published in *L'Europa verso la catastrofe* (Mondadori, 1948).
[24] See above p. 106.

Thus Eden was forced to resign by his own Prime Minister at the very moment of Hitler's scurrilous attack upon him. While it was clear that the issue between them was Italy, Grandi added to Ciano that Chamberlain would do nothing to resist Germany over Austria and that the British attitude over this would remain one of " indignant resignation." He noted an atmosphere in London comparable with that when the Hoare-Laval plan was announced. But things went the other way now. Eden's resignation left men in office who were willing to accept Guido Schmidt's assurances that Berchtesgaden had witnessed normal negotiations without pressure, and unwilling, therefore, to take any Anglo-French step against Berlin : soon after—it seemed to be part of every Austrian crisis—Paris was without a Government. At last on 24th February, far too late, Schuschnigg made a Thus-far-and-no-farther fighting speech which was well received by the Viennese, but in Styria the Nazis stormed the town hall at Graz and hoisted the swastika.

Of course the Berchtesgaden Agreement was merely a manœuvre for gaining power over Austria without the use of force, without even the bother of an opposed occupation, nothing but a sham mobilization. Graz had begun well and Linz was restive, and Seyss-Inquart encouraged the rest of Austria to follow their example; meanwhile demands exceeding the ' Agreement ' continued to arrive from Berlin. At the end of February Schuschnigg made up his mind to appeal to the Austrians and to the world, and to hold a plebiscite to ask his public whether it desired a free German and Christian Austria. Possibly Kánya, the Hungarian Foreign Minister, who visited Vienna on 3rd March and told him that Hitler was only bluffing, contributed to his decision.

It was clear that Mussolini had written Austria off, if necessary; he would not, that is to say, make a further effort on her behalf. He had sent Salata back to Vienna on a visit, and in consequence journalists nodded their heads, sure that Mussolini had encouraged Schuschnigg to his speech of 24th February. But Salata belonged to the circles which had worked to undermine Austria. At this very juncture it was officially announced that Hitler would pay

a state visit to Rome in the first half of May.[25] Too late
again Schuschnigg sent for his military attaché in Rome,
Colonel Liebitzky, and gave him a full account for Mussolini
of what Hitler had said to him at the Berghof, including
each reference to Italy; at the same time Liebitzky was
to inform the Duce of Schuschnigg's decision to hold a
plebiscite. Mussolini received Liebitzky on 7th March very
promptly and was clearly not indifferent to Hitler's remarks.
But he sent a message back to Schuschnigg to say that the
plebiscite was a mistake because if it turned out a success the
Germans would say the result had been faked, if it were
a fiasco Austria would be finished, and if it were indecisive
it would have been pointless. The fact is that Mussolini
was even more interested in the preparation of Hitler's
reception in Rome than in Hitler's unflattering comments
upon Italy and himself. The obstacle in the way of the
success of Hitler's visit was not the question of Austria,
but the Vatican's irritation with the anti-Catholic policy of
Nazi Germany to which Austria would soon be subjected.
At about the time of Mussolini's conversation with Liebitzky,
Ciano wrote to Berlin to urge from Hitler some conciliatory
gesture towards the Catholic Church, and Magistrati called on
Weizsäcker for a fruitless conversation on the possibility.

It was on 9th March that Schuschnigg announced his
intention to hold a plebiscite on the independence of Austria
on Sunday, 13th March. Though the Nazis had typist spies in
the Viennese offices they did not control, they do not seem to
have got the news more than twenty-four hours before it
was publicly announced. It seems that Berlin was genuinely
taken by surprise—they had not credited Schuschnigg with
so much initiative. It is unlikely that the announcement of
the plebiscite altered Hitler's time-table by very much, but
it gave him the occasion to occupy Austria. He was enraged
by the attempts to put any question to the Austrians other than
"You want to be part of Germany, don't you?" and this
only by the time that the organization of any plebiscite
would be in Nazi hands. And he was certainly apprehensive

[25] At this point the Germans asked Mussolini for a guarantee of
Hitler's safety if he travelled across Austria.

as to the result. No one can tell what would have happened.[26] Styria was already under Nazi control, but in Vienna Schuschnigg had at last approached the Socialists and there was widespread anti-Nazi feeling in the capital. On the other hand, the unseen pressure from the Reich was great, and all cautious Austrians would have felt it safer not to commit themselves. At all events, the plebiscite could not, unless he moved now, provide a 99 per cent. vote in the Führer's favour, which was his idea of what a plebiscite should be.

Hitler, oddly enough, still preferred to seem not perfectly sure about Mussolini. At about midday on Friday, 11th March, Philip of Hesse rang up the Italian Embassy in Berlin to say that he was just leaving with an important and urgent missive for Rome. In the letter which the winged messenger carried that day Hitler wrote to Mussolini:

" In a fateful hour I turn to you, Excellency, to inform you of a decision which the circumstances have seemed to demand and which cannot now be changed. . . .

" In recent months I have seen with growing anxiety how little by little between Austria and Czechoslovakia a relationship has been growing up which we could with difficulty allow in peace-time, but which, in the case of war being imposed upon Germany, would cause the gravest menace to the safety of the Reich.

" In the course of this *rapprochement* (between Austria and Czechoslovakia) the Austrian State has begun to barricade and fortify all the frontiers. The purpose of all this can only be (1) to bring about the Restoration at a given moment, (2) to operate even against Germany if necessary the weight of a mass of at least twenty million people.

" Precisely the close links which bind Germany and Italy have, as was only to be expected, exposed our country to inevitable attacks. . . . The responsibility falls on me to prevent a situation arising in Central Europe which may perhaps, just because of our friendship with Italy, lead to grave complications."

[26] Schuschnigg proposed only to allow those over twenty-four to vote; it was to be like a Nazi plebiscite in that the answer yes was presumed.

Hitler went on to say that Schuschnigg had given him assurances not only that all Austrians should receive equal treatment but also that some military security would be established in order that the Austrian State should not become a Czechoslovak annexe. But Schuschnigg had broken his promise from the first day and with his plebiscite proposal had plunged the country into anarchy; Hitler was bound to step in to re-establish order and tranquillity. He felt responsibility, he wrote, both as Germany's Führer and as Austria's son. The Brenner frontier, Hitler states, like the frontiers of France, he regards as immutable; this he had decided in 1918. He refers to the present hour, in which he gives this evidence of the constancy of his feelings, as critical for Italy. The Führer longs to see Mussolini to tell him all that he feels.[27]

This letter is like a flashlight thrown upon the workings of Hitler's Austrian mind; it is like a flashlight thrown also upon his falsity. It is inconceivable that Schuschnigg could forget such references to Czechoslovakia, which, according to his testimony, was not once mentioned at Berchtesgaden. It is possible that Hitler persuaded himself that he had said these things to Schuschnigg. At all events, when the letter was published in Italy at the week-end, while Hitler's outpourings about the sufferings of the Austrians under Schuschnigg appeared in the papers, everything he had said which related to the Czechoslovak Republic was suppressed,[28] and Göring pledged his word to Prague that the Anschluss meant no kind of threat to the Czechs, the integrity of whose frontiers was assured.

It is clear now that Philip of Hesse's excursion to Rome on 11th March was superfluous, because Mussolini had previously made up his mind, and, as he himself implied in his speech of 16th March, he had done so for the last time not later than Liebitzky's call on 7th March. After seeing Mussolini Hesse telephoned to Hitler from Rome at 10.25 p.m. on 11th March and announced that the Duce had been

[27] D.G.F.P. series D, vol. I, no. 352.

[28] See Göring's instructions to Hesse on 12 Mar. in International Military Tribunal document 2949-PS. (U.S.A. 76). Hitler's letter to Mussolini was not published in Germany.

very friendly about the whole thing. He had told the Austrians that their plebiscite was an impossibility and when they persisted in it Mussolini had said, " in that case he had finished with Austria." Hitler was ecstatic. According to the record of this conversation he said to Hesse four times that he was to tell the Duce he would never forget this.[29] Two and a half years later Ciano noted the tears that came into his eyes at the mere recollection of this occasion. But on the evening of 11th March he made other more important statements to Hesse on the telephone. He was ready, he said, to make quite other agreements with Mussolini now, " Indeed every agreement." " If he should ever be in any great need or danger, he could be certain that I will protect him to the uttermost, whatever may happen, even if the world should rise against him. . . ." In this connexion it may be relevant to quote Jodl's directive to the German armed forces on this same evening : " (1) If Czechoslovakian troops or militia units are encountered in Austria they are to be regarded as hostile. (2) The Italians are everywhere to be treated as friends, especially as Mussolini has declared himself disinterested in the solution of the Austrian question."

Hesse can scarcely have started his flight when in the early afternoon[30] the Austrian Government received a message from Rome to say that the Italian Government had no advice to give; even if this had come through with every priority, it had to be coded and decoded and must have been drafted in Rome several hours earlier. Mussolini himself appears to have disappeared to Rocca delle Caminate, where the Palazzo Chigi found it impossible to reach him ; once he had shown Schuschnigg all the telephonic installations there, adding that he would always be accessible to his Austrian friends. At one moment on that morning of 11th March when Seyss-Inquart and Glaise-Horstenau were threatening him with German invasion unless he immediately resigned in Seyss-Inquart's favour, Schuschnigg tried to put through a call to the Palazzo Venezia, but he himself cancelled it as

[29] This was also repeated in various public speeches made by Hitler in the next four weeks.
[30] See Schuschnigg, op. cit.

Receiving the applause of the crowds at Munich

The supermen in the Hall of German Art

Admiring the Venus of Canova in the Villa Borghese

soon as his visitors had left. Schuschnigg's strangely fatalistic character was an element not to be discounted in this situation, he was so sure that Italy no longer felt concerned: it was perhaps partly this which made the Duce indifferent. Doll-fuss or Starhemberg or anyone with temperament might at least have excited Mussolini, but Schuschnigg knew nothing about bluff; he only joined battle when he should have known it was too late.

Hitler indulged in another of his favourite devices at this time. Demand after demand arrived in Vienna; the plebiscite must be called off, Schuschnigg must go, and so on; each time the thing was conceded, the concession was pronounced to be too late and the next demand was put forward. It was all irrelevant, for the German Army had been ordered to invade and occupy Austria at daybreak on 12th March 1938. Hitler himself rushed to his beloved Linz without the usual police precautions and from there once again, this time in a telegram, he repeated to Mussolini that he would never forget. Mussolini wired back: " My attitude is determined by the friendship between our two countries, which is consecrated in the Axis."

After the Fascist Grand Council meeting on 12th March it was communicated to the press that the Grand Council had taken note of Ciano's statement on Austria; the Austrian Federal Government, he had announced, had not informed the Italian Government of the results of the Berchtesgaden meeting and the action which followed it until they were accomplished facts. The Grand Council also noted that the Italian Government had immediately advised against the Schuschnigg plebiscite proposal, "both as regards method and as regards substance and form." It also took note "with the deepest interest" of the Führer's letter of 11th March to the Duce and declared that this letter would shortly be published—in what a bowdlerized version has already been indicated.

On 16th March Mussolini addressed the Fascist Chamber as follows:

" In the last few days a great event has taken place which has changed the political map of Europe. Austria as a State has ceased to exist, and has become part of Germany. The

R.B.A.   E plebiscite of 10th April will confirm the accomplished fact.

" The tragedy of Austria did not begin yesterday; it began in 1848 when brave little Piedmont dared to defy what was then the Habsburg colossus. . . .

" To those more or less official circles beyond the Alps which ask why we did not intervene to 'save' the independence of Austria, we reply that we had not assumed any obligation of the kind, either direct or indirect, written or verbal.

" The Austrians, I feel bound to state, have always had the comprehensible modesty not to ask for the use of force to defend the independence of Austria, for we should have answered that an independence which needed the help of foreign troops against the majority of the nation no longer deserves the name. . . .

" Italy had an interest in the independence of the Austrian Federal State, but it was obviously based on the assumption that the Austrians, or at least a majority of them, desired independence; but what has happened in the last few days in Austrian territory shows that the people profoundly longed for the Anschluss."

The Duce then insisted rather lamely that when something is inevitable it is better that you should consent to it than let it happen in spite of you or, still worse, against your will. In any case, we Italians know about national revolutions, for just the same thing under the guidance of *il grande autoritario* Cavour happened in Italy between 1859 and 1861. Far be it from Italy to fear eighty million Germans on her frontier. . . .

" . . . why should I not say it? Millions of Germans are listening too. The time has come which may be called the testing of the Axis. The Germans know that the Axis is not merely a diplomatic contrivance which works well in normal times, but that it has proved itself particularly solid at this critical point of the history of the German world of Europe.

" The two nations whose unification has been parallel in time and method, united as they are by an analogous conception of the politics of living, can march forward together to give our tormented continent a new equilibrium.

which shall at last allow the peaceful and faithful co-operation of all peoples."

Italians of all shades of political opinion agree that the Anschluss and Mussolini's reaction to it lost the Duce more popularity than any event after the murder of Matteotti in 1924, when the Fascist régime was profoundly shaken. They were acutely aware of the significance for Italy of what had taken place, and they felt that Mussolini's arguments were either false or discreditable, or both : they had not forgotten that he had eagerly expounded the reverse for many years. And with all the make-believe imaginable Mussolini must have felt uneasy. Even at this moment Hitler had—deliberately or not?—made him feel German contempt for Italy. The whole move had been sprung upon him without consultation, in spite of every pledge that he should be informed in advance. Further, at one moment a promise was given to the Italian Embassy in Berlin that the German Army would halt at Innsbruck in order not to appear on the Brenner. This pledge was completely ignored. And the German officer in command who first formally greeted the Italian troops at the Brenner was the very Nazi Colonel Schoerner who had won his " Pour le Mérite " at the battle of Caporetto. He was to become one of Hitler's favourite commanders in the Second World War.

There is an epilogue to the Anschluss which is not generally known. Though Mussolini had never liked Schuschnigg and though he spoke disdainfully of him in his speech on 16th March, in April the Italian Embassy in Berlin received the following instructions from Ciano: " Please advise the competent authority that it would be in Germany's own interest to avoid the taking of coercive measures against Schuschnigg. If he were permitted to leave Austria this would not only create a generally favourable impression, but would also be regarded with sympathy in Italy where he was always treated with respect and where it would be learnt with satisfaction that he had been free to go abroad."[31] The subject was brought up by Magistrati more than once to Göring. It is a fact to which Schuschnigg himself refers that he was threatened with a staged trial

[31] Material supplied by Count Magistrati.

for the " betrayal of German Blood " which would certainly have led to his execution. This and some of the worst physical tortures to which most Gestapo victims were subjected he was spared, and, although he himself does not seem to be aware of it, the fact may be attributed to Italian intervention.

Chapter VII

THE FUHRER IN ITALY

In an atmosphere of nervous tension in Italy, the Führer's reception had to be prepared.[1] In Berlin, perhaps because of his family connexions with Mussolini, the work fell mostly upon Magistrati. Hitler had boasted to Schuschnigg at Berchtesgaden of his new battleship to be ready in the spring; it was to be called *Tegetthoff* then, in memory of the old Austrian Navy. Now Tegetthoff was the Admiral who had beaten the Italian Navy at Lissa in 1866, the last thing of which the Italians wished to be reminded. After considerable trouble Magistrati succeeded in getting the name changed to that of another Austrian hero, upon whom, since he was of Savoyard origin, the Axis could agree; it was finally the *Prinz Eugen* which was launched by the Regent of Hungary in the following August.[2]

The Anschluss had inevitably stirred up the South Tyrol again. The Nazis of Innsbruck were convinced that the Führer was on the verge of "fetching back" the rest of the Tyrol,[3] rather like a game of nuts in May, and there was a ferment south of the Brenner regardless of the publication of Hitler's pledge to Mussolini on 11th March. It was whispered that when, in his speech to the Reichstag on 18th March, Hitler had spoken of three and a half million Germans who were not yet "freed," this number included the South Tyrolese. On 14th March Magistrati said to Weizsäcker that a decent and final solution of the South Tyrolese question must now be found.[4] On 18th April, however, Ciano wrote to Magistrati asking him to go to Göring and explain that the Italian authorities could no longer tolerate the propaganda and white-stockinged com-

[1] For a time the Italians considered postponing the visit.
[2] Horthy had been an Admiral in the Austro-Hungarian Navy.
[3] Down to the old Riva frontier, they hoped.
[4] D.G.F.P. series D, vol. I, no. 384.

133

motion which was going on and which had actually led to violent incidents. These things soon became known to Italian public opinion, and, Ciano wrote, reawakened the annoyance caused in certain circles " by the sudden German seizure of Austria." In order to strengthen the Axis this situation, he said, must be put straight. Surely some agreement could be brought about similar to that which had been made between Italy and Yugoslavia in the previous year.

Magistrati saw Göring twice about this. The first time Göring prevaricated. The trouble must be due to *agents provocateurs,* &c. On the second occasion the Fat Man assured Magistrati that on 18th March Hitler had referred only to the Sudeten Germans. It would profoundly sadden the Germans, he said, if Hitler's sacred word about the Brenner frontier were not believed in Italy, just at a time when Italy's attitude over Austria had so greatly increased the friendly feeling towards her in Germany. Hitherto, added Göring, with his engaging frankness, our Army people were much opposed to any risk of war on your account, but now they say Germany should back up Italy in the Mediterranean even against Britain—at least they *were* saying that, he added, until your agreement with Britain last week.[5] With regard to South Tyrol difficulties did, he thought, become acute because young men were naturally unwilling to do military service for a country to which they did not feel they belonged. At this point he dropped the first suggestion of a transfer of population such as that which was arranged in 1939—it might be expedient, he suggested, to allow South Tyrolese recruits to opt for German citizenship. At all events this was something which should be discussed between Führer and Duce when the Führer went to Italy.[6]

After the public announcement on 28th February of Hitler's visit to Rome in May, Ciano was put in charge of the festal preparations in Italy. At last, two months later,

[5] The British-Italian Agreement of 16 April 1938 was widely interpreted as an anti-German move on Mussolini's part in reply to the Anschluss. cf. Kordt, op. cit.

[6] It was. See D.G.F.P. series D, vol. I, no. 767.

Ribbentrop managed to appoint a new German Ambassador to Italy; Neurath's son-in-law, von Mackensen, who not long before had had to leave the Budapest Legation on account of his too obvious entanglement with the Hungarian Nazis, was sent ahead to take over the German Embassy and prepare for the Führer in Rome. In Nazi Germany an official jaunt to Italy was always scrambled for, and one reason for the popularity of the Axis in Party circles was the increased scope it provided for journeys of this kind. When Hitler left Berlin for Rome on 2nd May it was with four special trains and a troop of newly uniformed journalists. There was a bevy of Party leaders, Ribbentrop of course, Goebbels and Hess, and Keitel to represent the Wehrmacht, and Himmler to guard his master against the Italian Jews; naturally Hans Frank and Hesse had to come too, and Sepp Dietrich, and there were also Bohle of the *Auslands-organisation* and General Bodenschatz, while Germany was left in charge of Göring. It was announced that the Wilhelm-strasse legal expert, Gaus, would be with the German Foreign Office team, which made people wonder whether an alliance was to be proposed; at the last moment, however, Gaus was ill and remained in Berlin.

To Nazi persecution of the Catholics in Germany had now been added seven weeks' oppression of Catholic Austria; now and then Italian diplomacy had prevented some confiscation of monastic property or whatever it might be, but notwithstanding Professor Manacorda[7] the general tendency was clear and unrelenting. The *Osservatore Romano* maintained an unbroken silence before Hitler's visit, but when the Führer was due Pius XI closed the Vatican Museum and retired to Castel Gandolfo; there on 3rd May, the day of the Holy Cross, he complained to the newly married couples that " the banner of another cross which was not the cross of Christ " should have been raised in Rome that day.

The problem of the Quirinal also presented Mussolini with a good deal of vexation, and the republicanism of his youth stirred uneasily within him. For it was with the King, not with Mussolini, that it was found necessary for the

[7] See above, chapter III.

Führer to stay. Though he was met by both King and Duce at the San Paolo station, it was into the King's horse-carriage that Hitler was obliged to step. He annoyed the King by seating himself first, while his own irritation at finding himself in this museum-piece of a coach, drawn by mere horses, was considerable. He slept in the Quirinal for six nights and no doubt consoled himself with being the guest of a monarch whose name would always be unwelcome to a Habsburg ear. Victor Emmanuel did not conceal his chagrin at having to entertain the ex-corporal, and, if Schlabrendorff's account[8] of Hitler's table manners a few years later is to be believed, it would be difficult not to sympathize with the King who not inappropriately wrote Hitler off as a degenerate psychopath.[9] Hitler was aware that he was not very welcome; indeed, according to the statements[10] Mussolini made later, he was positively neglected in the palace : at one public ceremony it was he who motioned to the Duce to come forward and stand with himself and the King. It has been seen that before this Hitler had felt that Mussolini's was the only authority in Italy upon which he could rely, and after May 1938 his suspicion towards the Italian monarchy definitely increased; some of his Nazis told him that the ladies of the court had made a demonstrative distinction between the Italian Army and the Fascist Militia at the public functions during his stay.

In addition, in spite of Mussolini's enthusiastic preparations, the Roman population—perhaps the most sceptical in the world—received Hitler without any real warmth until after his speech at the Palazzo Venezia banquet on 7th May. This was one of those geo-political perorations with which one was becoming familiar, but it was not without significance. It referred with obvious relish to the Axis *bloc* as containing no longer a mere 115 millions, but rather 120 million souls by now.

" Two millennia," concluded the Führer, " have now passed since Romans and Germans met for the first time in history

8 Offiziere gegen Hitler (1946).
9 Ciano Diary. Entry 7th May 1938.
10 See Mussolini, *Il Tempo del bastone e della carota* (1944).

so far as that history is known to us. Standing here on
this most venerable soil in our human history, I feel the
tragedy of a destiny which formerly failed to draw clear
frontier lines between these two highly gifted, valuable races.
. . . Now to-day . . ., thanks to your historic activity,
Benito Mussolini, the Roman State arises from remote
traditions to new life, and north of you, formed out of
numerous tribes, there has arisen a new Germanic Empire.
Now that we have become immediate neighbours, taught
by the experience of two millennia, we both wish to recognize that natural frontier which Providence and history
have clearly drawn for our two peoples. That frontier will
then render possible the happiness of a permanent co-operation peacefully secured through the definite separation of
the living-spaces (*Lebensräume*) of the two nations, but it
will also serve as a bridge for mutual help and support. It
is my unalterable will and my bequest to the German people
that it shall accordingly regard the frontier of the Alps, raised
by nature between us both, as for ever inviolable. I know
that then, through this delimination, a great and prosperous
future will result both for Rome and Germany.

"Duce, just as you and your people maintained your
friendship with Germany in days of crisis, so I and my
people will show the same friendship towards Italy in times
of difficulty. . . ."

What a riot of dictatorial indulgence! Nothing gratified
Mussolini more completely than to be identified not with a
mere modern Italy but with the far-flung Empire of
Ancient Rome. And that part of Hitler which loved to
believe in heroes and monsters derived the greatest satisfaction
from the make-believe excitement of pretending that fearful dangers had been faced when the German Army marched
into Austria; after 1936 he never moved unless he thought
the risk he was taking was negligible. Meanwhile there were
Italians who noted that Hitler had named, not the Brenner,
but only the Alps *en masse,* by which his frontier delimitation
remained delightfully vague.

The Führer was deluged with every imaginable " sight " in
Rome : historic monuments, military pageants, and peasants
dancing at the Villa Borghese in all the provincial costumes

of Italy. Immediately after his own return from Germany in the autumn before, it had pleased Mussolini to copy the goose-step by the introduction of the *passo romano,* and now he displayed this laborious Italian imitation to his German visitors; there were many sour Italian jokes over this. On Thursday, 5th May, Hitler was rushed off to Naples for the day, where an Italian naval review seemed to make an impression upon him. In the evening there was a gala performance of two acts of *Aïda* at San Carlo; the triumph over the Ethiopians was duly celebrated. Hitler was driven straight to the station from the opera in an open car and was thus revealed in evening dress, wearing, for the only recorded time in his life, a top hat.[11] The usual photographs were taken and showed something so much more ridiculous than the best Chaplin achievements that orders came from on high that not only was nothing to be published but the films were all to be destroyed. Several Italians had a good laugh over this—not so the German Foreign Office official, Bülow-Schwante, who was held responsible and dismissed. On 9th May Hitler left Rome to return to Germany via Florence, where he spent half that day and was received with great enthusiasm. They rushed him round the Uffizi, the Pitti, and Santa Croce and up to the Piazzale Michelangelo, then a reception at the Palazzo Vecchio, dinner at the Palazzo Riccardi (in the Sala Luca Giordano), the theatre, and away. Mussolini[12] said later that, once emancipated from the oppression of the Quirinal, Hitler's mood changed and he pronounced Florence to be the city of his dreams; certainly he spoke ecstatic words about it when he saw the Duce there in October 1940.[13] For Mussolini this visit to Florence was less agreeable. All his life, after all, he had professed ' toughness.' He had resented Italy's reputation as the mere home of Europe's greatest achievements in the plastic arts and had boasted that he had better things to do than to visit picture-galleries; on 9th May, 1938, however, he was forced to enter these museums for the first

11 Hitler carried a top hat at the Garnisonkirche ceremony at Potsdam in Mar. 1933 and on similar occasions, but was not seen to wear it.

12 Op. cit.   13 Ciano Minute, 28 Oct. 1940.

time. Thus, liberated though he was from royal competition, he could not even play the host with assurance in Florence.

It is again difficult to know what passed between Mussolini and Hitler *à deux* during this visit. They were alone for an hour or so in Rome and also briefly in Florence; it seems to be known that Hitler spoke of an alliance to Mussolini in Rome on 4th May and again at Naples on 5th May and at the air display at the airfield of Furbara near Rome on 8th May.[14] This time, although Paul Schmidt came to Rome, the interpreting was mostly done by Hans Thomsen, a German diplomatist then *en poste* in Washington who was brought to Italy solely for this purpose; he was a hard, cynical, snobbish creature, a brilliant linguist who had served in Italy and had kept up his Italian. At Naples on 5th May, on the battleship *Cavour,* Ribbentrop offered to Ciano various drafts of a German-Italian pact of military assistance, secret or to be published, as the Italians chose.[15] Ciano was opposed to the idea for the time-being, partly in order not to make difficulties for Chamberlain after the Anglo-Italian Agreement of 16th April and just before the meeting of the Council of the League of Nations. So he agreed with Mussolini to answer evasively; it was suggested that the Axis friendship made an alliance superfluous.[16] Meanwhile he had produced a counter-draft of an innocuous nature characterized by Weizsäcker as " more like a peace treaty with an opponent than a pact of loyalty to a friend."[17] And yet foreshadowings now appear, with increasing frequency, of what was to become the Steel Pact, and, while the German Foreign Minister felt himself rebuffed, Mussolini had reacted less negatively than Ciano to Ribbentrop's advances.

A French journalist tried to discover that Führer and Duce had wrangled over south-east Europe, but there is no evidence of this. Naturally Hitler's entourage was full of

[14] M. Toscano. *Le Origini Diplomatiche del Patto d'Acciaio* (1956) p. 14. Mussolini's records of his talks with Hitler were made illegible by damp when the Italian archives were later hidden from the Germans.

[15] Ciano *Diario,* 5th May, 1938.

[16] Cf. Kordt, op. cit.

[17] Ernst von Weizsäcker. *Erinnerungen* 1950, p. 158-9.

official optimism; after the *Anschluss,* the Germans in
Czechoslovakia could not be expected to wait long for their
" home-coming " to the Reich (actually it was of their
" autonomy " that one still mostly had the reticence to
speak when abroad), but the Anglo-French conversations
at the end of April need not be regarded as unpropitious.
Instead of the irritation which Göring had shown to Magistrati
with regard to the Anglo-Italian agreement, this was now
interpreted as a device by which—one is almost compelled
to mix metaphors over this—the poor Western democracies
were to be harnessed to the Axis and cajoled into betraying
the Czechs. It seems that Mussolini made it clear that
he was disinterested in the matter of German pressure on
Prague :[18] whether, as Göring had suggested, Hitler spoke
to Mussolini about the South Tyrolese on this occasion is
not recorded, but Ribbentrop did so, again on the *Cavour* on
5th May.[19] While Mussolini offered to allow German schools
and newspapers which never materialized, Ribbentrop offered
to summon South Tyrolese leaders to Germany in order
to induce them to abandon their pro-German agitation.
Later he offered to send a big German delegation headed
by *S.S. Gruppenführer* Kaltenbrunner, South Tyrolese himself, to enrol people in the South Tyrol to visit Hitler
for indoctrination.[20] However, when Mackensen reverted to
this proposition in Rome on 31st May Ciano felt it might add
to the disturbance and vetoed it.[21] In the end only one
South Tyrolese, in Berlin by chance, is known to have been
taken in hand by the *Volksdeutsche Mittelstelle.*[22]

There is no record of any mention of the Jews between
Hitler and Mussolini in Italy in May 1938; it is possible
that the Jewish question was not mentioned between the two.
The persecution of the German Jews had been steadily
developed, and the Anschluss had brought about many outrages against the large Jewish population of Vienna. As for

[18] D.G.F.P. series D, vol. I, no. 762.

[19] D.G.F.P. series D, vol. I, no. 768.

[20] D.G.F.P. series D, vol. I, no. 767, 771.

[21] D.G.F.P. series D, vol. I, no. 775. Ciano Diary 31st May,
1938.

[22] D.G.F.P. series D, vol. I, no. 785.

anti-Semitic measures in Italy, it was in itself difficult to welcome the Nazi leaders without initiating discrimination against the Jews. Before Hitler arrived the Italian police had orders to lock up the Jewish population or send it out of the towns which the Führer would visit. It was said that Goebbels refused to appear at a lunch reception in Rome at which some fellow guests might have been Jewish. Perhaps it simply began in this way.

There was no Jewish problem in Italy. If one out of a hundred of the population was a Jew in pre-Hitler Germany, it was more like one out of a thousand in Italy. The Italian Jews, moreover, had lived in Italy for centuries and were "assimilated." In the country as a whole "race consciousness" was unknown; one had common traditions of language, diet, superstition, or in higher things, but one did not care about a person's breed—the absurdity of such conceptions would have been too grotesque in Naples or in Sicily. In the twenties the German Embassy had started a paper, *Il Tevere,* which was edited by a man called Interlandi, but it had a negligible circulation. When it became anti-Semitic in 1933 it was only regarded as an oddity. An earlier and more spontaneous Italian anti-Semite was a renegade priest called Giovanni Preziosi,[23] who was a friend of the Cremonese ex-railwayman, Farinacci, perhaps the most repulsive and brutal of the Fascist *gerarchi.* Earlier, during the war of 1914-18, Preziosi had been violently anti-German and had led the campaign against the Banca Commerciale Italiana, which had been founded by the Deutsche Bank; the upshot had been the resignation of the President of the Banca Commerciale, who was Toeplitz, a German Jew. Later Preziosi discovered that his anti-German feelings had only been directed against German capitalists who were Jews. He then became editor of an anti-Semitic review called *Vita Italiana.* But neither Interlandi nor Preziosi was of any importance until 1938. The arrival in Italy of Jewish refugees from Germany, and latterly from Austria, had aroused sympathy rather than antipathy for the Jews.

It has been seen that in his Nietzsche-reading youth Mussolini's particular antagonist in the official Socialist Party

[23] Not to be confused with the diplomat, Gabriele Preziosi.

had been Treves, who was a Jew. But unlike Hitler Mussolini had accepted Nietzsche's view that, if Jews tended to be
servile, anti-Semites were the failures who were jealous
of Jewish brains and wealth. Later, as a convert to chauvinism, Mussolini met opposition from Jewish and Masonic
circles, but he still condemned anti-Semitism in an article
in the *Popolo d'Italia* in 1932 as he deplored racialism
in his article on the Doctrine of Fascism in the *Enciclopedia
Italiana* that same year. Since his clash with Hitler in the
spring of 1933 he had not committed himself publicly,
though in private he went a little way to meet the Nazis at
his interview with Hans Frank in September 1936, recoiling
away from them when speaking with Schuschnigg in April
1937.[24] So late as February 1938 the Italian Foreign Office
declared that " a specific Jewish problem does not exist
in Italy " and that the Fascist Government had no intention
of taking any measures against Jews " except such as are
hostile to the régime." It seems, however, to have been in
November 1937 that Mussolini took the decisive step of
boasting to Ribbentrop, without provocation from the German
side, that Italy had begun an anti-Semitic campaign led by
" un uomo abbastanza popolare in Italia, l'On. Farinacci."[25]
It was not until July 1938 that the Duce began publicly to
eat his earlier words with the same apparent relish as
that with which he had swallowed the Anschluss. Three
other motives may have actuated him in the racial offensive
upon which he now embarked. He wished perhaps to induce
a more imperialistic Italian state of mind : anti-Semitism
gratified the Mohammedan world in which he was angling
for popularity : lastly, his régime was in economic difficulty
and the Nazis had shown one that anti-Semitism was profitable. But it would be difficult to believe that Mussolini
would have become an anti-Jewish legislator if it had not
been for the Rome-Berlin Axis. And from the beginning

[24] See the respective Ciano Minutes.
[25] Ciano Minute, 6th Nov. 1937. (Approx.="a pretty popular
figure in Italy.") When he visited Germany six weeks before
this Mussolini said to Bülow-Schwante that he was concerned with
the colour problem in Africa. See D.G.F.P. series D, vol. I, no. 2.

his anti-Semitism was condemned by the Italians as a sign
of his new subordination.

On 1st July 1938 the Italian Government forbade the
public sale of translations of books by foreign Jews. On
14th July a report by several professors was semi-officially
published in favour of an " Aryan-Nordic " racialistic policy
for Italy, and on 25th July Starace, still the Secretary of
the Fascist Party, announced that the principal task of the
Ministry of Popular Culture for 1939 would be to follow up
this report with a further " elaboration and discussion of
Fascist race principles." Farinacci and Gayda were all enthusiasm, and on 5th August Interlandi brought out a new
and sumptuous review, full of anti-Semitism and called
La Difesa della Razza. The rest was to follow in the course
of the autumn. A decree which was published on 1st September declared that all persons whose fathers and mothers
were Jewish, and who had settled in Italy or the Italian
colonies (except Ethiopia) since 1919 must leave the country
within six months under pain of expulsion. On 2nd September
all Jewish teachers and students were excluded from every
school or university in Italy as from that autumn term. In
October and November the anti-Semitic campaign continued,
state or semi-state employment was denied to Jews, mixed
marriages were forbidden, and Jewish property began to
be confiscated. The most immediate sufferers, of course, were
those who had fled from Hitler.

With the one exception of Farinacci, even the Fascist
gerarchi disliked the new anti-Semitic policy because it
seemed to them, as it did to the Italians as a whole, humanly
absurd and—what came to the same thing—only worthy
of Germans. An uneasy foreboding of vassalage was felt.
This reaction did mitigate the practical effects of the new
decrees to some extent. In his speech at Trieste on 18th
September Mussolini himself felt obliged to make exceptions
and to seem generous, though the efficacy of the exceptions
was largely cancelled later on. " Those," he cried, " who
imply that we are mere imitators or, worse still, have
obeyed suggestions, are poor idiots whom we do not know
whether to despise or to pity."

How vociferously had the Axis been declared to be the last hope for the defence of Europe's heritage of civilization! Now Hitler had got so far as to be subjecting some 75 million people to the directly dehumanizing process to which he had pledged himself; at the same time he was causing the arbitrary segregation of human beings into a depressed class in the very home of humanism. And around Germany and Italy the smaller countries hastened anxiously to fall into line, and to cultivate an attitude of at least disdain towards the scapegoat Jews. In what was in fact his de-civilizing action the new Tamburlaine—no Scythian shepherd could have been more remorseless than the son of the Austrian *douanier*—found his Axis partner an invaluable instrument. For since the Italians were not a brutal nation and Fascism had for so long held aloof from the brutalities of the Nazis, the Hungarians, Poles, and the rest felt it wise to fall in with Mussolini in order to keep on the right side of Hitler. Thus if the Duce's policy became servile towards the Führer, how much more was their policy obliged to incline to the wishes of Berlin.

Chapter VIII

MEDIATION AT MUNICH

In the eyes of the world, of the Great Power populations, anti-Semitism in Italy was obscured by the more obviously disturbing problem of the Czechoslovak Republic which was now veritably encircled by the Nazis. Mussolini's series of speeches in Venetia in September 1938, in which he spoke of the Italian Jews, was part of the Axis campaign against the Czechs. It was not for the first time in the history of Bohemia that Czech and Jew had found themselves thrown into alliance against Germanism. The details of the Czech-German situation in the thirties are not directly relevant to the subject of the relations between Hitler and Mussolini,[1] but it is necessary to indicate some of its salient points in a history of the Axis.

The Czechs were a competent, hard-headed, common-sense people who did not expect life to be easy. In 1918 they set up a state in partnership with the far more backward Slovaks from whom they had been separated by a thousand years of history; this state contained also a large German minority and a smaller Hungarian one; lastly, Ruthenia was attached to it, a strip of poor mountainous country with a mixed but mainly Ukrainian population. The extraordinary fact is that in an age of rising nationalistic feeling this state should have been in every way the most satisfactory of the new political entities which emerged from the First World War. The success of the Czechs seems even more remarkable when one considers that they had inherited the most notoriously intransigent Germans of old Austria : the Germans who fringed Bohemia and Austrian Silesia had no rivals in racial fanaticism except in Styria; in Vienna they were mostly spoken of as if they were a little mad.

About three and a quarter millions of these Germans became Czechoslovak citizens in 1919, and from this time

[1] They can be found in my *Czechs and Germans* (1938.)

onwards called themselves (after a mountain range) Sudeten Germans; partly because their numbers gave them strength they were probably the best off minority in the whole of post-Versailles Europe and certainly in a far better position than the Germans, Slovenes, or Croats in Fascist Italy. Of course the Czechs made mistakes. They are an ungracious, inflexible people, and they often indulged in pin-pricking; in view of the arrogance—or worse—with which the Germans had treated them before 1918, it is astonishing that they behaved as well as they did, but pin-pricking often creates more violent repercussions than real oppression, since it leaves its victims so much more able to react.

The Czech leaders, allowing history to override what should have been open questions in their minds, made two grave mistakes. A man like Thomas Masaryk, one of the few great political figures of this century, was so accustomed to the incessant din of Pan-German agitation in old Austria-Hungary that Hitler did not alarm him. I remember his saying in the spring of 1934 that it was foolish to think that there was anything new about Hitler or that Hitler meant war. Alas, there was something entirely new about Hitler. Where Bismarck was *klein-deutsch,* Hitler was the first Pan-German to have all the power of the German Reich behind him. The other mistake the Czechs made in subjection to the anti-Habsburg slogans which they had used as part of their own emancipation campaign within old Austria was to say and to believe that the Anschluss was preferable to a Habsburg restoration. It is true that nothing could have enraged Hitler more completely than a Legitimist success, but the Anschluss—whenever Hitler might bring it about—was bound to spell a strategic death-sentence upon Czechoslovakia.

The truth is that no policy could have saved the Czechs unless (even this is most uncertain) Hitler had believed that he would face a war on two fronts by attacking them; it is clear from the minutes of the conference of 5th November 1937 that he hoped that any danger from Russia need not be considered " in view of Japan's attitude," while he believed " that in all probability England and perhaps also France have already silently written off Czechoslovakia, and that they have got used to the idea that this question would one day be cleaned up by Germany." The Czechs had been the tailors and coachmen of imperial Vienna, where the word " Bohemian " had no artistic allurements but signified very lower-middle-class, or, in other words, socially impossible; Hitler had certainly not forgotten that Hindenburg had originally called him *der böhmische Gefreite*—the Bohemian corporal—which implied this. The Czechoslovak Republic stood for everything Hitler most disliked : it was over-centralized from an administrative point of view, but it was certainly anti-dictatorial and a country where one could vote and write and speak as one chose. What infuriated Hitler most of all was that Czechoslovakia was like old Austria-Hungary on a small scale : it was a *Nationalitätenstaat,* and it was " worse " than Austria-Hungary because it was to a much greater extent under the leadership of Slavs. Hitler could foam at the mouth at the iniquity of such a thing. All the racial groups in Austria-Hungary, he used to declare, were corrupted by intermingling with one another instead of preserving their purity, by thinking of themselves as the subjects of Francis Joseph rather than as members of their race. Above all, this kind of morass dragged the Germans down from the privileged position which was their due on to the same footing as ignoble Slavs and Jews. Whenever Hitler and Rosenberg wanted to work up a case against Russia they accused her, too, of being a nationalities-state which inevitably bastardized its better elements.

Czechoslovakia provoked Hitler further because on the one hand she was a refuge for those who fled from the Nazi terrorization of Germany, and on the other she had important industrial resources with the huge škoda arms-factory at Pilsen, all of which he coveted for the carrying out of his designs. She was traditionally Russophile and Francophile and the driving force behind the anti-revisionism of the Little Entente. Finally, the Czechs were a rationalist people, the last who were likely to be carried away by emotional mysticisms.

Since 1933 the German minority in Czechoslovakia had

been busily used to prepare the destruction of the Republic; the fact that the mainly German-speaking areas had suffered with particular severity from the world depression had facilitated this whole undertaking. Late in 1933 the old D.N.S.A.P. or Nazi Party of Czechoslovakia had ostentatiously dissolved itself, but it was immediately succeeded by a *Sudetendeutsche Heimatfront,* which soon changed its name to the Sudeten German Party (S.d.P.): it was led by Konrad Henlein. From 1933 to 1938 one was denounced as a cynic and a Communist and probably a Jew if one found it difficult to be convinced by the many public announcements of the complete independence of this party from any organization in the Reich and its perfect loyalty to the Czechoslovak State. In the end it became obvious—and in a speech in Vienna in March 1941, Henlein boasted of it—that his party was directed and financed from Berlin. It became obvious, too, that the demands of the Sudeten German Party systematically increased, and that, like so much good Nazi propaganda, they were systematically confused so that it was impossible to accede to them. At one time, though there was no clear language-frontier between Germans and Czechs, Henlein demanded territorial autonomy, at another non-geographically organized personal autonomy for whomever could be claimed as a member of the German group. More and more the Sudeten German leaders insisted, like the Austrian Nazis, that their people must be " free " to profess National Socialist beliefs which spelt the negation of both the Austrian and the Czechoslovak States. More and more Sudeten Germans were terrorized by one method or another into joining the Sudeten German Party. These processes reached a climax with the Anschluss, and two German political groups which had held out until then, the Sudeten German Agrarians and the Catholic Party, immediately offered their allegiance to Henlein. At the same moment Eisenlohr, the German Minister in Prague whom Hitler was planning to assassinate if convenient, tightened up his control of the Henleinists.[2]

Already on 17th March Henlein asked Ribbentrop for

[2] D.G.F.P. series D, vol. II, no. 86.

' an early personal talk '[3] and was secretly received by the Führer on 28th March; the next day Henlein conferred with Ribbentrop, Weizsäcker, Eisenlohr, Professor Haushofer, and S.S. Obergruppenführer Lorenz of the *Volksdeutsche Mittelstelle*.[4] It is worth mentioning that Mackensen was also present on this occasion and thus went off to take over the German Embassy in Rome in April charged with the most detailed information on the Czech-German situation up to that time.

Hitler had condemned Czechoslovakia to destruction, we know, in November 1937, and at the beginning of March 1938, still before the Anschluss, a letter of Ribbentrop's to Keitel refers to military aims against the Czechs which it would be better not to reveal to the Hungarians.[5] On 21st April 1938, six weeks after the Anschluss, Hitler saw Keitel in order to bring the anti-Czech military programme up to date. It may be noted that in considering how the Czechs were to be provoked the new German military chiefs preferred suggestion (3)—" Lightning-swift action as the result of an incident [e.g., assassination of German ambassador in connexion with an anti-German demonstration]."[6] Three days later Konrad Henlein struck a more provocative attitude than he had adopted hitherto at a demonstration at Karlsbad where he made eight demands, claiming a hotchpotch of every kind of autonomy and finally " full liberty for the Germans to demonstrate their adhesion to Germanism and to the ideology of the Germans " (Point 8). A week after this Hitler left Berlin for Rome and was back in Germany on 10th May.

On 18th May the Czechs observed a mobilization of

[3] D.G.F.P. series D, vol. II, no. 89.

[4] D.G.F.P. series D, vol. II, no. 109.

[5] It was at this time that General Ludwig von Beck, the Chief of Staff, who had not been vouchsafed any detailed information whatever, protested against the whole anti-Czech plan; his objections were completely ignored until he protested to Hitler in person in the autumn. He was then told that blind obedience was all that was required of him, and resigned.

[6] *Nuremberg Trial Proceedings*, part i, p. 164. Eisenlohr was a Minister, not an Ambassador.

various S.S. units[7] at certain points on the Bohemian frontier; it was all, as it was no doubt intended to be, a little mysterious, and on 20th May the Czech military leaders[8] insisted upon mobilizing a part of their forces and occupying the Czech frontier fortifications. The Nazi post-Anschluss plans were not quite ready and the Germans could not answer this "intolerable provocation," as Hitler would certainly have preferred, by an immediate attack. It was particularly annoying because on 21st May there had been a perfect frontier incident which had to be wasted. Two Henleinists on motor-cycles had ignored a challenge from a Czech frontier guard and he had shot them dead. The Germans had to be content with a demonstrative funeral on 25th May, with the swastika greatly in evidence and wreaths sent from the Führer personally, at the frontier town of Eger, the heart of Pan-Germanism. Between the incident and the funeral, on 22nd May, Jodl's diary refers to a "fundamental conference between the Führer and K. Henlein."

"The intention of the Führer," wrote Jodl, "not to touch the Czech problem as yet is changed because of the Czech strategic troop concentration of 21st May [*sic*], which occurs without any German threat and without the slightest cause for it. Because of Germany's self-restraint the consequences lead to a loss of prestige for the Führer which he is not willing to suffer a second time. Therefore the new order is issued for Green [attack on Czechoslovakia] on 30th May."

It should be noted, however, that this new order was based on a draft of Keitel's dated 20th May which was probably made before news of the Czech move was received. It was on 28th May that Hitler conferred with his chief advisers on this draft, and on 30th May he signed the conclusions reached after their deliberations. The statement he signed is, not surprisingly, lengthy:

[7] S.S. troops were no doubt used so that Hitler could, as he subsequently did, declare that not a single Reichswehr soldier had been moved: the whole crisis was deliberately confused with normal spring manœuvres.

[8] "On the initiative of President Beneš." See J. W. Wheeler-Bennett, *Munich*, 1948, p. 55.

" It is my unalterable decision to smash Czechoslovakia, by military action in the near future. . . . It is . . . essential to create a situation within the first four days which plainly demonstrates to hostile nations eager to intervene the hopelessness of the Czechoslovakian military situation, and which at the same time will give nations with territorial claims on Czechoslovakia an incentive to intervene immediately against her. In such a case, intervention by Poland and Hungary against Czechoslovakia may be expected, especially if France —owing to the obviously pro-German attitude of Italy— fears, or at least hesitates, to unleash a European war by intervening against Germany."

This time the Führer expected trouble from Russia. All preparations for the destruction of Czechoslovakia were to be ready " as from 1st October at the latest."[9]

What was the state of mind of the Axis Partner by now? The wealth of authentic Ciano material which has become available provides a mirror of the Duce's mind, and there one finds an aggressive serenity on the surface, and beneath it an uneasy awareness of the disproportionate strength of Germany and of her remorselessness, and the same sort of sanguine belief in the possibility of side-tracking Hitler as one found at this time among the Anglo-French appeasers. Mussolini and Ciano, far from accepting their own expulsion from south-eastern Europe by the new super-Habsburg, believed that they could dam up the German flood at the gates of the Balkans. It was this which intensified their interest in Albania and cemented their friendship with the Yugoslav Premier, Stoyadinović.

Just before Hitler's visit to Rome, Ciano had visited Albania, ostensibly for the wedding of King Zog. He was annoyed to find that the King liked to ape all things Viennese, and that the new Queen, though Hungarian, was unfriendly to Italy, while the Führer had provided the most magnificent of all the wedding presents. " We should not forget that the Magyars have very often provided the advance guard of Germanism," and he noticed the tireless activity of the German Minister in Tirana. Finally, he suggested that *un' affermazione italiana,* possibly definitive

[9] D.G.F.P. series D, vol. II, no. 221.

and totalitarian in character, would counterbalance in relation
to the Balkan world the undesirable increase in the prestige
of the Reich brought about by the Anschluss."[10] Thus already
the conquest of Albania was envisaged, and envisaged as
that of Ethiopia had been, as an anti-German move.

Ciano's encounters with the Yugoslavs at this time are
exceedingly interesting. They grumble to him over the
disturbing effects the Anschluss has had upon their German
minorities, and he agrees with them that the German Government is not responsible and must take steps to suppress
this inconvenient exuberance.[11] Now the German settlements
all over old Austria-Hungary were perhaps Hitler's favourite
instrument in the pursuit of his ambitions, and one wonders
whether Ciano and Stoyadinović deliberately shut their eyes
to this unpalatable fact or whether they dared not confess
the truth to one another. Stoyadinović was in other ways a
cold-blooded realist. Already in April, in spite of his
alliance with Czechoslovakia, he contentedly envisaged her
disintegration and the survival of only a much smaller
neutralized Czech State; like Mussolini and Ciano he believed that that would be allowed. He asked of the Hungarians only that they should await their moment and not
take offensive action which would still create a *casus belli*
for him as a member of the moribund Little Entente. It
is perhaps characteristic that when Ciano met Stoyadinović
in Venice on 18th June 1938, while the latter seemed
totally blind to the German menace to Poland, he warned
the Italian that, whatever assurances to the contrary the
Germans might give, they had designs on the Adriatic.[12] In
the middle of July Ciano told Magistrati (who was on a visit
to Rome at the time) that since the Agreement with Britain
was working badly on account of Spain, Italy was being
unwillingly pushed farther towards Germany. Many Italians,
Ciano admitted, would now like Italy to line up with the

[10] Note by Ciano for the Duce, 2 May 1938. (Also published in
L'Europa verso la catastrofe.)

[11] Minute by Ciano on conversation with the Yugoslav Minister in
Italy, 15 Apr. 1938.

[12] Minute by Ciano on conversation with Stoyadinovic, Venice,
18th June 1938.

satisfied nations, but this would be inconsistent with Fascism. "We must consolidate what we have already won." Italy's power of attraction in the Balkans is growing—"some time our position in Albania must be revised. . . . But it will be best not to commit ourselves to anyone."[13]

The Czech question presented itself to Italy as an opportunity not so much for the aggrandizement of Germany but rather for the gratification of dependants like the Poles and the Magyars towards whose claims Hitler was remarkably cold. When the Hungarian Ministers, Imrédy and Kánya, came to Rome in July, Mussolini told them that Italy would support Germany unreservedly, but it was clear that he did not then expect a European crisis over the Czech question. The Magyars did not get the pact with Italy which they would have liked, but Mussolini offered to tell the Yugoslavs that he wished for an increase of Hungary's power, and it was agreed that a statement should be published confirming the validity of the Rome Protocols as between Rome and Budapest although Austria had disappeared.[14]

From the day when Hitler decided on action against Czechoslovakia "as from 1st October" at the latest, he was certain to press more vigorously for a written military alliance with Italy in order to frighten France into inaction. Strangely enough, however, without instructions from Rome and concealing it from Magistrati, Attolico took the initiative in bringing the matter up with Ribbentrop on 31st May, 1938;[15] he also mentioned it to Weizsäcker on 17th June.[16] Two days later Ribbentrop invited Attolico to his house; he treated him to a series of "confidences," which included the announcement that Germany was secretly calling up reservists (to do "labour service") and a reference to the development and invincibility of the Siegfried Line. In a telegram to Attolico dated 27th June Ciano said "All this is very important and interesting" and suggested that

[13] Information supplied by Count Magistrati. The April Agreement with Britain had been invalidated by Mussolini's fierce speech at Genoa on 14 May.

[14] Minute by Ciano, 18th July 1938.

[15] D.G.F.P. series D, vol. I, no. 774.

[16] D.G.F.P. series D, vol. I, no. 781.

he (Ciano) should shortly meet Ribbentrop at Como to discuss it; he also asked Attolico to find out how far negotiations between Germany and Japan had gone. Shortly after this Hesse was sent to Rome to explain to Ciano the advantages of a military alliance between Germany, Italy, and Japan, but the Italians said that they needed more time to reconcile Italian public opinion to the idea.[17]

Attolico's behaviour in the summer of 1938 is difficult to explain. Until July he seemed over-eager to accelerate a written German-Italian pact, acting indiscreetly and on his own initiative. At the same time to Magistrati he seemed always to have been opposed to the idea. By July he seems to have been convinced that the Germans really were mobilizing and to have become alarmed. For he knew that Italy was in no state to do more than bluff. He now knew also that Germany was about to take great risks. On 10th August Reichswehr apprehensions were expressed to the angry Hitler. Jodl complained in his Diary that the General Staff lacked " vigour of soul, because in the end they do not believe in the genius of the Führer. And one does perhaps compare him with Charles XII . . ."; since the conflict between the generals and Hitler " is common talk," even Jodl feared for morale. Already in June the head of the German Intelligence Service, Canaris, who was one of the sceptics, confirmed to the Italian Military Attaché in Berlin that Germany was mobilizing, and Attolico reported this to Rome in the hope of opening Mussolini's eyes.

In July it has been seen, the Hungarian Prime Minister and Foreign Minister visited Rome; on 18th July they saw Mussolini and Ciano. The minute of this meeting, and other indications at this time, suggest that, while Mussolini emphasized his solidarity with Germany, he did not suspect that Hitler had determined upon war against the Czechs in less than two and a half months' time at the latest. On the day of the Duce's conversation with Imrédy and Kánya, Attolico saw Weizsäcker who had succeeded Mackensen as State Secretary at the Wilhelmstrasse. The German minute of this interview records that Attolico took the opportunity

[17] Ciano Diary, 11th July 1938.

to express his personal opinion that France would intervene in a German-Czech conflict. A note in Weizsäcker's handwriting (marked *Mappe Führer*, i.e. for Hitler's special attention) is appended saying that " Attolico added that we had made it unmistakably clear to the Italians what were our intentions regarding Czechoslovakia. He also knew the appointed time well enough so that he could perhaps take a two months' holiday then, which he would not be able to do later on."[18] Attolico, importuned by Rome from now onwards to discover exactly what Hitler's programme was, may have attempted every method, including that of " try-on " assertions, of extracting the information he required. But although the German plan was exactly worked out to the last detail, the least unsatisfactory statement he could get was from Weizsäcker on 3rd August to the effect that he should take his leave before the end of September. A note by Ribbentrop dated 23rd August states that when Attolico had pressed him again a few days before this :

" I replied that in case the Czechs should again provoke Germany, Germany would march. This would be to-morrow, in six months, or perhaps in a year. However I could promise him that the German Government, in case of an increasing gravity of the situation or *as soon as the Führer made his decision,* would notify the Italian Chief of Government as rapidly as possible. In any case the Italian Government would be the first one to receive such a notification."[19]

This, in view of their experience in the past, was wholly unsatisfactory to the Italians who returned to the attack again and again. Though he preferred not to record it, Ribbentrop, urged on by Hitler, continued to press them to make a military alliance with Germany, and it was not unnatural that they were anxious to ascertain the exact implication of this. On 27th August Attolico, according to Ribbentrop's own note, specified that Mussolini asked to be notified of the date upon which the Germans contemplated action in order

[18] D.G.F.P. series D, vol. II, no. 295.

[19] D.G.F.P. series D, vol. II, no. 384. (My italics). This conversation occurred on the *Patria* at Kiel during an official Hungarian visit to Germany.

" to be able to take in due time the necessary measures on the French frontier."[20] It was useless; Ribbentrop would only repeat his formula that the Duce would be the first to be informed, and he grumbled, poor man, that he did not understand what the Italians wanted. "*You* tell us *your* intentions," the obedient Weizsäcker said, helpfully, when Attolico again approached him. The Italian Ambassador, again suggested that the only thing would be for Ciano and Ribbentrop to meet, but Ciano refused this suggestion on 4th September and instructed Attolico to demand from Hitler " exactly how things stand " since he could not, he said, allow the Italian public to think that its rulers " had again been taken by surprise as in the case of the Anschluss." This was exactly four days after Hitler signed Jodl's plan for the staging of the incident necessary to provoke war and one day after a conference between Hitler, Keitel, and Brauchitsch at the Berghof, when the fullest details were elaborated, Hitler for once showing anxiety with regard to danger from the West. Of all this the Italians knew nothing; they were constrained to listen to German public declarations on the wireless for their information. At last on 6th September Hesse arrived in Rome with a long message from Hitler to Mussolini, ranting against the Czechs but repeating that he was " unable to state any definite time because he does not know this himself."[21] To the Magyar leaders who visited Germany between 21st and 26th August the Germans were fairly non-committal, but the Hungarians were at least invited to staff talks on 6th September : Hitler pointed out to them that those who wished to join in the meal must help to cook it.[22] At this point Jodl noted in his diary on 8th September " that Hungary is at least moody and that Italy is reserved." Though the Italians, who might equally be asked to march at any moment, were pressing anxiously for Staff talks, it was not until April 1939 that Keitel managed to find time for them.

[20] D.G.F.P. series D, vol. II, no. 401.

[21] D.G.F.P. series D, vol. II, no. 415. Ciano Diary Sept. 6th and 7th. 1938.

[22] D.G.F.P. series D, vol. II, no. 383

The Nazi Party Congress from 6th to 12th September,[23] at which Hitler praised the action taken " with admirable determination " by Italy against the Jews, inaugurated a tremendous preliminary bombardment which was intended as the overture to war. The Sudeten German leaders, Henlein and Karl Hermann Frank, rushed across the frontier to Germany on 15th September; together with Colonel Köchling, their liaison with the Reichswehr, they were put in charge of the Sudeten German " Free Corps " along the frontiers of Bohemia; the purpose of this corps was defined by Hitler as " Protection of the Sudeten Germans and maintenance of disturbances and clashes,"[24] and from 19th September they were extremely active,[25] violating the boundaries of Czechoslovakia whenever they had a chance to do so. At the same time two S.S. *Totenkopf* battalions were operating *across* the Czechoslovak frontier " on direct orders from Hitler." On 19th September a message was passed to the separatist Slovaks to revolt against the Czechs on the following day. Chamberlain's first visit to Germany (15th to 16th September) had made as much impression as a piece of cotton falling upon steel.

There was a parallel Italian campaign—Mussolini barked while Hitler bit. For the Duce behaved exactly like a dog that barks and wags its tail at the same time, not sure which end of itself it wishes the world to take seriously. On 15th September he published his letter to Runciman in the *Popolo d'Italia* demanding a plebiscite on the Saar model[26] in Czechoslovakia. He meant it half genuinely as a constructive proposal, and he coupled it with a declaration of what the Führer had no doubt said to him in Rome, and was to repeat at the *Sportpalast* on 26th September, that if the Czechs were *offered* to Hitler he would refuse

[23] Ribbentrop invited Ciano to attend this. In fact the two did not meet between May and their meeting at Munich on Sept. 29th, 1938.

[24] See Schmidt file, Document 388-PS, in Nuremberg Trial Proceedings, part ii.

[25] The Reichswehr complained that they were too active.

[26] The League of Nations had held a plebiscite in the Saar territory in Jan. 1935. British, Italian, Swedish, and Dutch troops were sent there to safeguard the public peace. cf. p. 63.

them. Of this the innocent Mussolini appears to have been convinced.

On 17th September the Duce set out upon a ten days' visit to the Venetias, a tour which was inaugurated by the speech at Trieste to which reference has been made. In all these Venetian declamations his theme was : " We hope for a peaceful solution, but we know exactly where we'll stand if it comes to war. Beneš is the man who incited the League of Nations against Italy; now his tyranny over ' eight different races ' must be ended;[27] there must be justice for the Hungarians, the Poles and the Slovaks as well as the Germans." The Italian public was desperately anxious for peace and was, no doubt, thankful to hear from Mussolini at Verona on 26th September (after Chamberlain's second visit to Germany) that, Versailles being extinct, a new Europe could now be born where there would be justice for all peoples and reconciliation between them. From the 22nd to the 24th Mussolini had broken his journey and returned to Rome. There he found a message of gratitude from Hitler and the German people for his " historic " activities, and the ominous news that Hesse, who had been flitting backwards and forwards between Germany and Italy, would shortly bring him a personal message from the Führer.[28] Surely enough the Prince was announced on September 24th. On the following day Ciano met him in Venice and took him to see Mussolini at Schio. According to Ciano, it was at last made clear to the Italians that the destruction of Czechoslovakia would begin not later than October 1st.[29] In one of his last speeches in the north Mussolini referred to the fatal day. This was not, even now, what the Germans had intended, but Hitler made the best of it and followed up Mussolini with his own tirade against Beneš at the *Sportpalast* on 26th September. At 13.00 on 27th September he " ordered the movement of the assault units from their exercise areas to their jumping-off

[27] Cf. his speech at Padua on 24th Sept. 1938; he counted up to seven by inventing a Roumanian minority in Czechoslovakia, and then called it eight.

[28] Ciano Minute of talk with Mackensen, 22nd Sept. 1938.

[29] Ciano *Diario*. 25th Sept. 1938.

points."[30] He did not intend to be defrauded of his war by the ' inept ' rulers of Great Britain and France.

This is not the place to examine the Munich Conference from a general point of view, but only as a part of the history of the Axis to which it bears a particular relationship. Attolico had urged the calling of an international conference, and Göring on 9th September had suggested to Magistrati that Führer and Duce should meet at the Brenner; there had also been feelers from Paris, but the initiative which led directly to the Munich Conference was that of Chamberlain. The Duce returned from Verona with the news that Germany would mobilize at 2 p.m. on 28th September to receive the British request for mediation. The war he had not believed in was upon him and he had not mobilized. He had been playing with fire. Chamberlain gave him the chance not to get burnt, but instead for his features to be lit up by the glow of the flames as they died away. It was probably the greatest good fortune he ever enjoyed.

Attolico was in some ways the hero of the occasion. A telephone message came through from Rome to the Berlin Embassy at 11.5 on 28th September; after Ciano had got the connexion with Attolico, the Duce himself took up the receiver. He began by saying that he stood at the Führer's side in every eventuality, but believing Germany at this moment to have triumphed both morally and materially, he asked the Führer to delay all marching orders for twenty-four hours. A reply was asked for by midday, two hours before Germany was due to mobilize. With the message translated a hatless Attolico rushed out to find his car, but the chauffeur had disappeared. He hailed a taxi and reached the Reichskanzlei, already vibrating with military preparation, just after 11.30 a.m. The French Ambassador was closeted with an excited Hitler when an S.S. officer came in to announce the Italian Ambassador with an urgent message.[31]

---

[30] See Schmundt file in Nuremberg Trial Proceedings, loc. cit.

[31] According to Magistrati, Attolico managed to get his message to Hitler independently of Göring, who tried at Nuremberg to take the credit for its delivery. It is not true that Mussolini telephoned directly to Hitler, as Göring claimed.

Hitler sprang up and left François-Poncet alone for a quarter of an hour. When he came back at about 11.45 he announced that his friend Mussolini had also asked him to hold things up. He paid no more attention to François-Poncet and soon afterwards withdrew. At 12 noon Attolico telephoned the Führer's acquiescence and Mussolini suggested a Four-Power meeting.[32] Hitler offered him Frankfurt or Munich; the Duce chose Munich and within a few hours Paris and London had agreed.

Ciano and his Chef de Cabinet, Anfuso, set out with Mussolini on that same evening of 28th Sept for Munich by train. The next morning Hitler met Mussolini soon after the old German-Austrian frontier at Rosenheim : the Duce mounted the Führer's train. There he found in Hitler's compartment an immense map of Germany's frontiers with France and the Low Countries. Beginning with the statement that he had now completed and perfected the Siegfried Line Hitler held forth nearly all the way to Munich about the perfect opportunity that now presented itself of striking at the " democracies " as he contemptuously called the Western Powers. Czechoslovakia must be destroyed because it immobilized forty German divisions which could otherwise be used against France. Near Munich Mussolini managed to ask what Hitler now demanded of the Czechs. Hitler seemed almost taken aback, but Ribbentrop produced a sheet of paper with what he said were Germany's minimum demands, in return for which she would not be unwilling to come to terms; the German memorandum was handed to the Italians.

When the conference opened at the *Führerbau* in Munich at 12.45 Mussolini chose to sponsor these demands : it is possible that Hitler and Ribbentrop might have declared them " superseded." Daladier and Chamberlain accepted them. They were more or less what had already been agreed at Godesberg, the cession of the Sudeten German territory (as shown on a German map) by the Czechs to Hitler between 1st and 10th October, 1938. Plebiscites under international control were to be held in doubtful territory. When any small difficulty was made, for instance that the Czechs had no:

[32] Without the Czech representative proposed by Chamberlain.

In the Great Hall of the Führerhaus

Ciano (*left*) and Alfieri

agreed or about Czech property, Hitler threatened a European war and Chamberlain and Daladier gave way.[33]

Throughout the Italians were treated as Hitler's favoured friends at Munich. At 9 p.m. a formal invitation to dinner was formally refused by Chamberlain and Daladier, who, however, did not seek each other's company. The Führer took the Italians to dine at his flat in the Heidemannstrasse : according to Anfuso[34] he made spiteful comments about Alexis Léger, the Secretary-General at the French Foreign Office, as a creole. After another three hours of this chaotic conference the Munich Agreement was completed at 1.30 a.m. on 30th September, 1938 : the German proposals put forward by Mussolini were accepted with inessential modifications.

This was one of the strangest episodes in the history of the two dictators. At first Hitler seemed stunned by the fact that the other Nietzschean colossus of the world should have halted him for the moment, for this was what had happened. At the Munich conversations he stood in the shadow of Mussolini, who could put up a creditable show of speaking the four languages of the day though his English was particularly sketchy; Hitler was even more helpless linguistically than Daladier and Chamberlain, whom, nevertheless, he there learnt to despise as vermin. The Italians on this occasion managed to do just as much military swaggering as the Germans, and, if François-Poncet[35] is to be believed, Hitler behaved rather like a doting flapper towards Mussolini, who was delighted to find himself the centre of attraction.

Superficially Munich might be counted as a triumph for Mussolini. The Duce had shown that he did not fear war but he had proved to be the saviour of peace. He returned to Italy perhaps more popular than he had ever been before; the King paid a tribute to his success, for he came from his estate near by at San Rossore to meet him at Florence, on the journey back to Rome. For two

[33] This account is based chiefly upon Anfuso op. cit. pp. 72-74 and Ciano's Diary but also upon Sir Horace Wilson's Note in D.B.F.P. series III, vol. 2, no. 1227 and on Boris Čelovsky—*Das Münchener Abkommen 1938* (1958).

[34] Op. cit.   [35] Op. cit.

R.B.A.   F

years now the Italians had felt themselves slipping down a
slope into the sea of vassalage to Hitler, but now it seemed
that the Duce, alone in the world, could forbid the tide
to rise. The Italian public, like the public in Britain
and France, was only too eager to believe that Hitler
" wanted no Czechs " and that this was Hitler's " last
territorial claim in Europe "; if this were so the period
of crises might be over and peace might be secure. The
British recognition of Victor Emmanuel as Emperor of Ethiopia
on 16th November 1938 crowned the Duce's success at
Munich.

Chapter IX

THE STEEL PACT

It is quite clear now that Adolf Hitler was extremely angry at the temporary interference with his plans at Munich which meant that he had only acquired broad fringes, but not the whole, of Bohemia and Moravia. Oddly but characteristically he did not blame the brother Superman. At a birthday party at his old friends', the publisher Bruckmann and his Roumanian wife, on 14th October, this was made clear. " Mussolini was his reliable friend and would certainly have fought."[1] But it made very little difference. We know that he had decided to seize Austria and all Czechoslovakia for a start, and he was already examining the requirements of breaking " all Czech resistance in Bohemia and Moravia "; a week after the Bruckmanns' tea-party he signed a directive with plans to bring this about.[2]

Meanwhile, the gestures of carrying out the Pact of Munich were half-heartedly gone through. The new Czech and Slovak frontiers had to be fixed, and when adjusted they were to have had a quadruple guarantee. The Munich Agreement, however, had only laid down directions for the new Czech-German frontier, and when Mussolini had expressed the view that his Hungarian[3] and Polish friends must be satisfied before he could guarantee the future Czecho-Slovak State, Hitler was only too pleased. Three Four-Power sub-commissions of the International Commission[4] were set up to trace the new frontiers and arrange the necessary transfer of powers of all kinds; the French and British representatives noted with some interest that

[1] U. von Hassell, *Vom andern Deutschland* (1946), p. 27.

[2] D.G.F.P. series D, vol. IV, no. 81.

[3] The Hungarian Foreign Minister, Count Csáky, had even paid Mussolini an impromptu visit on 29th Sept. at the Prinz-Karl Palais at Munich.

[4] The Czechs were supposed to be represented too, but this stipulation, like that for plebiscites in certain areas, was a dead letter.

their Italian colleagues seemed as surprised as they were
themselves by the shameless dictation of the German members
of the sub-commissions. The Frontier sub-commission, for
instance, was managed as follows: the German members, all
officers or Party people in uniform, sat on one side of a table
with the British, French, and Italians on the other: the
German senior officer, Richthofen, presided. In spite of
a protest from Attolico, the old Austrian census of 1910,
which was undoubtedly unfavourable to the Czechs, was used.
Where a town or village was of ' preponderantly German
character ' it was to be ceded to Germany. But soon the
German members of the Commission announced that ' military
necessity ' obliged them to take several villages with a
Czech majority, and a little later they produced a map of
the frontier as already decided by them, and no one else had
the force to resist them. Just as Italian League of Nations
officials had nearly always found themselves defending the
legalism of the " Geneva institution " against the Nazis in
the Saar before 1935 or in Danzig until 1939, so on these
Munich commissions the Italian attitude was spontaneously
what we have come to call Western.

As for the claims of the Poles and the Hungarians to
a common frontier which would eliminate Ruthenia, the
Poles helped themselves to a good deal more than a tiny
Polish ethnical group could justify, but the Hungarians,
backed though they were by Mussolini, found themselves
halted by Hitler. The Führer was opposed to their claims
for several reasons. It can scarcely be repeated too often
that he thought in pre-1914 Austrian terms, and Hungary
was a rival whom he suspected. He wanted to be sure
that there would be no return to the Dualism of 1867;
Hungary was only to be what, during the later war, he defined
as a *gleichgestellte Hilfsmacht*[5] for Germany—not for Italy,
since he disliked Mussolinian activities in Central Europe.
Further, Hungary's claims were made at the expense of
Slovakia (already under partial German control) and, it has
been seen, of Ruthenia; both of these regions had been
part of pre-1914 Hungary which Hitler on no account
wished to restore. Ruthenia, which the Germans called

5 =" an auxiliary power of equal status."

the Carpatho-Ukraine, opened up other vistas. Indeed, until early in 1939 the Nazis tried the experiment of building it up as a nucleus of Ukrainian nationalism and a German-Ukrainian spearhead pointed at Russia. Hitler's plans included the disruption of Russia through stimulating the nationalism of 40 million Ukrainians, the big majority of whom lived in the most fertile Soviet territory, and who could always, it was supposed, be kept in a state of helotry by the Germans.

Until the end of October, therefore, Ribbentrop sabotaged any sort of arbitration with regard to Hungary's new frontiers. The Italians would have preferred Four-Power action on this issue, too,[6] but feeling it was useless to propose it, they pressed hard for Axis arbitration.[7] Hitler's desire for a written military alliance with Italy was now sufficiently strong for him to wish to humour the Duce over the Magyar-Slovak controversy. On 2nd November, within five days of an ostentatious German surrender on this point, Ciano met Ribbentrop at Vienna and a new frontier was drawn by which Hungary gained the three towns of Kassa, Munkács, and Ungvár, though Ruthenia remained as an all-but-independent federal member of what had become a Czecho-Slovak Confederation. This German-Italian award was signed at the Belvedere, Prince Eugene's magnificent palace built by Hildebrandt. Ciano could not help teasing Ribbentrop about the situation. "My dear Ribbentrop," he said, "you can't, you know, now defend Czechoslovakia with the same enthusiasm as that with which you destroyed her a month ago at Munich."[8] That was the sort of thing Ribbentrop never forgave.

Axis relations continued to the end of the year to be exceedingly tricky. Mussolini had not much appreciated Hitler's signature of Chamberlain's perpetual peace pledge at Munich, though it was obviously meaningless. No sooner had the Duce improved his relations with Britain in order to launch the anti-French campaign announced in Ciano's

[6] The Munich Pact decreed this if the 'respective Governments' had not come to terms at the end of three months.

[7] See Ciano Minute, 28th Oct. 1938.

[8] Information from Count Magistrati.

speech to the Chamber on 30th November than Ribbentrop
left for Paris, where he spent the two days from 6th to
8th December.[9] A declaration was signed on 6th December
guaranteeing the Franco-German frontier; although respect
was paid at the same time to each country's relations with
other Powers, Mussolini resented the timing of the German
Minister's visit.[10] Count Welczeck, the German Ambassador
in Paris, afterwards described Ribbentrop's behaviour in the
French capital as completely pathological; on every occasion
he required that there should be more fuss made about
him than on the occasion of the British royal visit to Paris
in the previous summer. Meanwhile the world, including
Italy, had been horrified by the November pogroms in
Germany, while the Italians themselves, and especially the
Vatican, observed with distress the anti-Semitic laws which
were piling up in Rome.

In addition to his absorption of pre-1914 Austria-Hungary,
which, like pre-1914 Germany, had impinged upon Poland,
it has been seen that Hitler required, before he went farther,
to transform the Anti-Comintern Pact into a military alliance.
During the summer Ribbentrop had constantly tried to encourage the Italians[11] to think in these terms, and at Munich
he had presented Mussolini and Ciano with the draft of a
defensive triple alliance. After Munich Hitler felt that
the Duce was showing too much independence; at this
point it was, however, the Japanese who held things up.
Oshima, the former Military Attaché, now Ambassador in
Berlin, voiced the aggressive and pro-German tone of the

[9] The prelude to this had been François-Poncet's farewell visit to
Hitler on 18th Oct. before he left Germany to become French
Ambassador in Rome. Ciano's speech on 30th Nov. was the
occasion of notorious demonstrations against the French with cries
for Tunis, Nice, and Corsica.

[10] In a report to the Fascist Grand Council on 5 Feb. 1939 he stated
very unconvincingly that he had agreed in October to Ribbentrop's
visit to Paris.

[11] The Italians were not averse to the inclusion of the Japanese,
but Ciano wished, for once, to be prudent; he disliked the form
of the negotiations with the Japanese, through military personnel
and behind the backs of the diplomats. See Mario Toscano, op.
cit.

Japanese Army, but naval and financial circles in Tokyo wished on no account to break with Britain, and they had gained in influence since about the time of Munich. Ribbentrop felt impatient. He knew that Attolico, his eyes opened by what he had experienced in Berlin, had become hostile to a written alliance with Germany. In the days when Ribbentrop was Ambassador to Britain he had sent his agent, Raumer, in the autumn of 1937, to arrange a sudden visit to Rome. Now on Sunday, 23rd October, he suddenly telephoned to Ciano saying he would like to come to Rome on the following Friday or Saturday, the 28th or 29th, as he had a personal mission to the Duce on behalf of the Führer. Only on the 25th, when the thing was arranged, did he tell Attolico that he would be leaving for Italy the next day; even then he feared that Attolico might put a spoke in the wheel and he mentioned nothing but the Hungarian question as the cause of his journey. He did, in fact, preface his alliance offer by giving way over Hungary in his preliminary talk with Ciano.

On 28th October Ribbentrop urged a triple German-Italian-Japanese military alliance upon the Duce and his son-in-law more definitely than ever before. The alliance was necessary, he said, for the inevitable war against the democracies which Hitler expected in three or four years, though of course, he interpolated at one point, the present situation was very favourable for the Axis and *from September 1939*[12] onwards a conflict with the democracies could be faced. Hitherto the Führer had hesitated over the alliance for two reasons, one that it might have weakened Chamberlain and Daladier, and the other that it might have induced an Anglo-American alliance. He had now come to the opposite conclusions: the appeasers were safe and any threat of war would fortify American isolationism.

Mussolini, however, replied that Italian opinion was not ' yet ' ripe. Axis, yes: German military alliance, no. He referred to the Army—the officers, not the rank and file—and his bugbear, the *bourgeoisie,* as hostile, and he added that Germany's quarrel with the Catholic Church created a serious obstacle. Later, when the time had come, the alliance must

[12] My italics.

not be purely defensive " since no one is thinking of attacking the totalitarian states," said the Duce; for our part we Italians know where we are going but we must then have the objectives of our alliance defined.[13] Of course, said Ribbentrop obligingly, the Mediterranean will become an Italian sea. Later he implied that Germany was eager for Italy to have her turn of acquisition soon.

In December a rumoured military agreement between Great Britain and France changed Mussolini's unstable mind, but Attolico carefully failed to find Ribbentrop to tell him so. During Christmas spent at Rocca delle Caminate the Duce's latest decision crystallized, and when he returned to Rome on New Year's Day, 1939, he ordered Ciano to write Ribbentrop a letter accepting the German proposal of 28th October for the transformation of the Anti-Comintern Pact into a military alliance which, it was suggested, the Japanese also seemed ready to sign towards the end of January. The reasons offered to Ribbentrop for Mussolini's decision were exactly the opposite from Hitler's reasons for proposing a military alliance. Ciano gave them as :

(1) " The now certain existence of a military pact between France and Great Britain."

(2) " The prevalence of a warlike attitude in responsible French circles."

(3) " United States military preparation which is intended to supply men and, above all, materials to the Western democracies in case of necessity."[14]

Attolico, who had been in Italy on leave, was charged with this letter to Ribbentrop with which he arrived in Berlin on 4th January. According to Magistrati he was by no means so content as Ciano's diary suggests, and determined, as far as possible, to use his instructions about commercial discussions[15] and the South Tyrolese question as the conditions of any alliance. " It would be a good thing to follow Hitler's project for removing from South Tyrol the

[13] See Ciano Minute of Duce-Ribbentrop-Ciano meeting, 28th Oct. 1938.

[14] Ciano to Ribbentrop, 2nd Jan. 1939.

[15] A commercial agreement was signed in Feb. 1939—see Ciano Diary, 13 Feb. 1939.

Germans who wish to go," Ciano noted in his diary on 2nd January.[16] Ribbentrop immediately produced the drafts of a Tripartite Political Pact and a secret military convention, both of which Attolico dispatched to Ciano on 6th January. When on 18th January Ciano went off for a five days' visit to Yugoslavia, he expected to travel from Belgrade to Berlin to sign a Tripartite Alliance.

Ciano was fascinated by the warmth with which he was received in Yugoslavia compared with the frigidity of the atmosphere when he first went there in 1937. The change was due, he established, to the state of fear and suspicion of Germany in which the Yugoslavs now lived, so that Italy had become a palatable alternative. When Ciano broached the matter of Albania (which lay so close to his heart) to Stoyadinović, the latter hesitated for a moment but then fell in with Ciano's plans, since they would be relatively easy to realize if Germany were agreeable; he added that though he foresaw no German opposition he was convinced that the Nazis would be secretly annoyed by an Italian occupation of Albania.[17]

Unfortunately for the Fascists, Stoyadinović, who was, as he told Ciano, working up to a Fascist system on the Italian model, fell from power a fortnight later. Thereupon Ciano persuaded Mussolini to fix the first week in April for Italian action against Albania. "In the meantime I shall see Ribbentrop and perhaps mention this to him."[18] But the Duce, as usual, vacillated. Again the Japanese were holding things up, but he must at least have his pact with Berlin before seizing Albania. Indeed, at this point he conveniently developed a preference for a dual alliance as less provocative to America and Britain,[19] though the Japanese were making difficulties about an alliance aimed against any country but Russia. Suddenly there was startling news that the Germans themselves had designs upon oil-wells in Albania. Ciano warned Mackensen that Italy considered

[16] See Göring's conversations with Magistrati, above.

[17] See Ciano Minute on Yugoslav journey, 18-23 Jan. 1939.

[18] Ciano Diary, 7 Feb. 1939. He had already made a vague indication in Vienna at the time of the Belvedere Award.

[19] Ibid., 8 Feb. 1939.

Albania as all but part of Italy, and the Germans made haste to deny "baseless" rumours. It was important to them to keep Rome sweet-tempered for the Ides of March, and at last it was agreed that there should very soon be Italo-German Staff talks 'to be announced in the press.'[20]

The moment for the breaking of the last Czech resistance was approaching. This had become obvious to any competent observer in Berlin. It was particularly clear to Attolico because Ribbentrop sedulously avoided him from the beginning of March. On 11th March, at the *Heldenfeier,* Attolico, observing Hitler's hectic face, said to himself that the Führer was certainly on the eve of a *coup.*[21] He telephoned at once to Hesse's residence in Kassel[22] to enquire after the health of Princess Mafalda and thus learnt that Hesse had been called urgently to Berlin. This suggested only too forcibly that the 'winged messenger' was waiting for a 'ritualistic message' for Rome, as Attolico warned the Palazzo Chigi. At last, on 14th March, he was able to see Ribbentrop, who made clear to him that Germany would "incorporate Bohemia (with Moravia), make Slovakia a vassal state, and cede Ruthenia to Hungary."[23] In the night Hacha was bludgeoned into submission and the next morning Hesse set out for Italy, without advising the Italian Embassy this time, and with only a verbal message. Hitler thanked Mussolini for the understanding he had again shown; this last operation had liberated another twenty divisions which could now serve Axis policy elsewhere. But if the Duce were contemplating any large-scale action it would be better to wait another couple of years when a hundred such divisions would be available. Mussolini snapped back that he required no foreign troops for eventual Italian action against France, he only wished to know

[20] See Ciano's telegram to Attolico, 20 Mar. 1939. The staff talks at last materialised at Innsbruck on 5th April.

[21] Cf. M. Donosti, *Mussolini e l'Europa, la politica estera fascista* (Leonardo, Rome, 1945).

[22] The Prince was *Ober-Präsident* of Hessen-Nassau.

[23] Ciano Diary, 14th Mar. 1939. The Anglo-French guarantee of the Munich frontiers was forgotten by everyone except the Czechs or it was said that the attitude of the Slovaks annulled it.

that Germany was disposed to give him raw materials, coal, and arms.

This time Italian opinion was at least as indignant as at the time of the Anschluss; Hassell, indeed, heard from friends in Italy that "feeling against us there is almost the same as in 1934."[24] Ciano said to a colleague that 15th March 1939 was sadder for Italy than the Peace of Campoformio. In his diary he wrote: "The German action destroys not the Czechoslovakia of Versailles but the state established at Munich and Vienna.[25] What weight can one give in future to the other declarations and promises which concern us more directly? It is useless to deny that all this worries and humiliates the Italian people." The remedy he offered was, of course, immediate action against Albania.

Mussolini was in two minds. He knew that Hesse's visits had become grotesque—"every time Hitler takes another state, he sends me a message." But he thought that Germany was now so strong that even if everyone else, including Italy, allied against her, she could only be held, not driven back: it seemed to him therefore that now, more than ever, was the time to ally with the winner (16th March). This was the first important divergence between Mussolini and Ciano. On 19th March the Duce agreed that the German alliance must be dropped—"the very stones would cry out against it,"[26] but on 21st March he admonished the Fascist Grand Council in favour of "una politica di intransigente fedeltà all' Asse." "You are polishing Germany's boots," said Balbo.[27]

Ciano had never seen his Duce in such distress: for Mussolini knew at this moment that he was impaled on the horns of the dilemma which Hitler had created for him. The Balkans were quivering with the shock of the German occupation of Prague, and there was talk of the Croats putting themselves under German protection. "In that case,"

[24] Hassell, op. cit., p. 54.

[25] The Belvedere, or Vienna, Award had itself constituted a breach of the Munich Agreement.

[26] *Si rivolterebbero le pietre.*   [27] Ciano Diary, 21 Mar. 1939.

said Mussolini, " either we must fire the first shot against
Germany or be swept away by a revolution the Fascists themselves will make; no one will tolerate the swastika in the
Adriatic."[28]   Ciano sent for Mackensen and reminded him
that the condition of the Axis was Germany's recognition
of the Mediterranean (including Croatia) as Italy's sphere;
Berlin promptly sent a docile reply, the Mediterranean never
could nor should be German. Mussolini received this
answer, which was contained in a marvellously hypocritical
letter from Ribbentrop to Ciano,[29] with scepticism.

In a moment, however, Mussolini was reacting to the
old turncoat taunts—" We can't be political whores." He was
irritated by the activity of the democracies; he was irritated
by anti-German comments from the King. He must stick
to the German alliance, but its objects must be defined
and the Germans must stick to their own proposals about
the South Tyrol. At this point the twentieth anniversary of
the foundation of the Fasci was celebrated, and Hitler over-
whelmed Mussolini with a personal letter[30] which was so
fulsome that both the German and the Italian Foreign
Office preferred to prevent its publication, though the Duce
himself felt that this " robbed it of much value." The letter
spoke first of the rebuilding of the Roman Empire by
Mussolini. " With the foundation of Fascism a new path
was opened for humanity. . . . Providence has decreed the
fundamental similarity between Nazism and Fascism. . . .
Nothing," wrote Hitler, " can in my eyes bind the German
and Italian people more closely to one another than the
diabolical hatred felt towards us by the rest of the world
which we have never harmed. You felt this when you created
the Empire. We Germans have experienced it in the last
twelve months during which we have simply put an end
to an intolerable situation." These siren notes were too
much for the Duce. On 26th March he made an aggressively
pro-Axis speech : after all, if he gave up the Axis, with which

28 Ibid., 17 Mar. 1939.

29 Ribbentrop to Ciano (Personal), 20 Mar. 1939.

30 D.G.F.P. series D, vol. VI, no. 100. Mackensen, when handing
the letter to Anfuso, asked for it to be kept strictly secret.

he had now identified Fascism, the Fascist régime might be shaken.

It has been seen that, for nearly a year, Ciano had been urging the annexation of Albania to counterpoise the aggressions of Hitler. He now took the childish satisfaction of trying to spring this Italian *coup* upon the German Embassy in Rome in an unconvincing way. On 6th April Mackensen came to him to say that there was talk in every Roman café of an impending attack upon Albania, whereupon Ciano came out with well-worn sentences about the necessary restoration of order; these were duly conveyed to Berlin, though Attolico had informed Ribbentrop on 5th April of the action intended and Ribbentrop had expressed his approval. The Nazis were doubly delighted. It was a justification of their own methods, while at the same time the Albanian move disturbed the relations of London and Paris, as of Belgrade, with Rome, and all in favour of Berlin. When Ciano returned from a flying visit to Tirana he sent secret messages to his Embassies in Paris and London that they were to spread the notion of the anti-German character of the attack upon Albania, but their efforts to do so met with little success. Thus the Albanian action, which Ciano had genuinely planned as a move against German influence, increased Mussolini's fear of isolation and threw him into the arms of Germany. The negative attitude of the Japanese was confirmed on 2nd April,[31] and this destroyed the possibility of avoiding too great dependence upon a single strong ally. It all suited Hitler marvellously. He had ceased to care so much about Japan now when the first flicker of a *rapprochement* between Germany and Russia had caught his eye.[32]

The Italian "Hands off Croatia" move and seizure of Albania were rather as if a cat had proudly caught two mice at the side of a tiger which was chewing the bones of a

[31] See M. Toscano, op. cit.

[32] See Nazi-Soviet Relations (U.S. Department of State, 1948). Since January the Nazis had dropped Ruthenia as a Ukrainian Piedmont, and on 10th March they had had their reward in Stalin's speech to the 18th Congress of the Communist Party of the U.S.S.R.

man. The occupation of Prague had given Germany, more
cheaply but a few months later than Hitler had planned,
Bohemia and Moravia with their powerful industries; it
brought in its wake the subjection of Slovakia and Roumania
by the treaties signed on 23rd March, the Roumanian treaty
safeguarding Germany's oil supplies. At the end of April
the leaders of Hungary, Teleki and Csáky this time, came to
Germany to receive their master's orders; after four and
a half months of the Belvedere Award, they had got their
common frontier with Poland, but in six months' time
Poland herself was to be destroyed. Ribbentrop told them
that if Britain and France should make war against Germany,
Italy and Japan would immediately be at her side, and he
had no doubt that Hungary would join them. The visitors
acquiesced; they also took orders helplessly about the privi-
leges to be granted to the German minority in Hungary.
It is not uninteresting that Ribbentrop repeated to this
audience what he had said to the Duce on his last visit
to Rome, that the number of Axis divisions "must be
counted as double in view of Adolf Hitler and Mussolini
being in command."[33]

Poland was the next direct victim on Hitler's programme.
A month before Munich, that is, on 26th August 1938,
the German Foreign Office had drawn up a secret document
in which, after noting the utility of racialist slogans in
the destruction of Czechoslovakia, it was added that "this
method of approach towards Czechoslovakia is to be recommended because of our relationship with Poland. . . . The
fact is that after the liquidation of the Czech question,
it will be generally assumed that Poland will be the next
in turn. But the later this assumption sinks into international
politics as a firm factor the better."[34] The Nazis need not
have worried; even their friends grasped none of this until
the Ides of March 1939.

Already in October and November 1938 Hitler was
drawing up directives aimed against Poland (and Lithuania),
and it was at this time that Ribbentrop first asked Lipski

[33] D.G.F.P. series D, vol. VI, no. 295.
[34] See *Nuremberg Trial Proceedings*, part ii, p. 134. TC-76—G.B.
31.

for Danzig and an extra-territorial motor road across Pomorze. On 21st March 1939 he returned to the charge, and his arguments were reinforced by Germany's seizure of Memel on 23rd March and by Hitler's denunciation of the German-Polish Treaty (of 1934) in his Reichstag speech on 28th April. At the end of February, when Ciano visited Warsaw, the extensive anti-German demonstrations, made especially by Polish students, were an interesting pendant to the statements in the *Gazeta Polska* about the common interests of Poland and Italy. At the time Ciano felt a little embarrassed, but he was first actually alarmed about Poland when Göring came to Rome in the middle of April for the offer of the Crown of Albania to the King of Italy. The tone in which Göring spoke of the Poles reminded Ciano "too peculiarly" of that in which he had spoken of Austrians and Czechs "at other times."[35] A few days later Attolico reported that he regarded German action against Poland as imminent. "That would be war and we have the right to be informed in time," noted Ciano, and arranged to hasten a meeting with Ribbentrop.[36] This was all the more necessary since the Albanian operation had revealed the military inefficiency of Italy after the long strain of her intervention in Spain. At last the struggle there was drawing to its end, though it was 18th May 1939 before Franco entered Madrid.

While Göring's attitude towards Poland had made Ciano impatient to see Ribbentrop, the German leader's conversations in Rome had put great emphasis upon German-Italian solidarity.[37] A fortnight later the Roumanian Foreign Minister brought a message from Bonnet to Mussolini almost begging Italy to reconcile herself with the West. Gafencu[38] has recorded the state of mind in which he found the Duce on 1st May, evidently tormented by the decision he was in the act of making in favour of a treaty with Hitler. It was three days after this that he gave Ciano his final instructions

[35] Ciano Diary, 16th Apr. 1939.
[36] Ibid., 20th Apr. 1939. On 30 April Ciano wired to Berlin suggesting that Ribbentrop should meet him in north Italy.
[37] See *Nazi Conspiracy and Aggression*, vol. IV, pp. 518-19.
[38] G. Gafencu, op. cit,

for his meeting with Ribbentrop. Three months earlier, in a report to the Fascist Grand Council dated 5th February, Mussolini had declared in favour of negotiating with France (on the basis of the repudiation[39] of the 1935 Franco-Italian Treaty) because Italy could not risk war until 1942. He instructed Ciano now at the beginning of May to make clear that war could not be risked until 1943 for a number of reasons. In the first place Italy needed to pacify Libya, Albania, and, most of all, Ethiopia, where the Italians were in difficulties; later they would be able to recruit large numbers of soldiers there. Further, Italy required time to complete six ships then under construction, while all her artillery needed to be renewed. There were a million Italians in France, the bulk of whom Mussolini wished to repatriate before it came to war. If the Axis Powers waited Japan might have mastered the position in China and therefore be very much more useful. Italy needed time to remove her main industrial centres from the Po valley to the south. Finally, the Duce was counting upon the international exhibition which he had planned to hold in Rome in 1942 to bring in a substantial amount of foreign currency of which he was grievously in need.

In addition, the Duce's instructions reverted to the importance of further preparing Axis opinion, especially by means of a *détente* between Berlin and the Vatican. With regard to Russia it was desirable to prevent her from joining the Western Powers, but nothing more should be attempted; any sort of pact with her would be incomprehensible to the Axis populations and would therefore weaken the Axis structure. Mussolini also complained that the South Tyrolese situation as it stood played into the hands of the enemies of the Axis.[40] Most ironical of all, he stated that the military agreements envisaged must be carefully prepared so that, given the specified circumstances, they would come

[39] Announced on 17th Dec. 1938.

[40] See M. Toscano op. cit., pp. 278-80. One other trifle deserves mention. Usually the Germans lied to the Italians, but in this Memorandum Mussolini stated that he had had no further approaches from France since those of Baudoin (see Ciano Diary), although Gafencu had just brought the message from Bonnet.

almost automatically into effect. He wished, no doubt, to make sure of the Japanese.

The momentous meeting between the Italian and German Foreign Ministers at the week-end of 6th May 1939 was conditioned by Mussolini's susceptibilities towards the city of Milan and towards the French. Milan was the city of the début of Fascism; it was at the Piazza San Sepolcro in Milan that the Fascist Party had presented itself to Italy in 1919. But Milan was the capital of Lombardy where feeling against the Austrians in particular and Germans in general had always been strong. The French press, which had a capacity of getting under Mussolini's skin, declared on 5th May that though he had originally announced its birth in Milan, there had been hostile demonstrations against the Axis there now. At first it had been suggested that Ribbentrop should meet Ciano at some small place on Lake Garda or Lake Como, but Mussolini insisted that Milan be put to the test. Ciano arranged with Parenti, the *Federale,* that special precautions should be taken, but was himself surprised at the warmth—or was it good organization?—of his own and Ribbentrop's reception. At last the Axis could be regarded as " popular."

Ciano found Ribbentrop reasonable and moderate for the first time; in spite of the quips of the Vienna Award days, they got on rather well. While agreeing to an alliance with Germany, Ciano insisted that Italy could not go to war until after 1942 for the reasons Mussolini had enumerated.[41] Ribbentrop said that Hitler must have Danzig and that he would insist on the highway across the Corridor in order to relieve the atmosphere in Germany. Ribbentrop " confirms that it is Germany's intention to let the question mature, ready, however, to react in the sharpest way should the Poles ever change to an offensive policy." After a few months France and England would have lost all interest in Poland.

" Germany, too, is convinced of the necessity of a period of peace of not less than four or five years, though she could, of course, be ready for war much sooner." This is

[41] These reasons were repeated in the Cavallero Memorandum—see below.

what Ciano wrote in his official Minute; though he was lazy there is reason to think that his positive statements were seldom inexact. In the German record Ribbentrop is said to have endorsed the Italian desire to avoid war for the next three years. On 11th April, that is to say twenty-five days earlier, Hitler had signed his Military Directive for the seizure of Danzig and for *Fall Weiss* or the attack upon Poland. Indeed Keitel had signed a directive on 3rd April in the same sense[42] indicating that preparations must be complete not later than 1st September, 1939.[43] Could falsity go much further? In the eyes of Hitler and Ribbentrop, it is true, the attack upon Poland would comprise only a punitive expedition, not war.

After their talk, Ciano gave a dinner for Ribbentrop at the Continental Hotel, and during the evening he telephoned to the Duce to report general agreement along the lines of his instructions. Mussolini reacted with nervous enthusiasm; it is thought that the Anglo-Turkish negotiations mentioned in the House of Commons the day before were preying on his mind. Defiantly he ordered Ciano to publish the news that a written Italo-German alliance had been agreed upon precisely in Milan.

We now know that Ribbentrop had come with quite modest treaty drafts[44] since he was uncertain of Italy's response and Pariani had not been encouraging to Keitel at the Staff talks. By rushing out the statement, before the terms had been agreed, of a written dual alliance Mussolini threw away all the trumps in his hand. Implying that, although the Japanese had been delaying things all the year, it might still be better to wait for them, Ribbentrop did not mention the drafts he had brought with him, but,—cleverly this time—showed reluctance[45] to agree to the dual alliance which these drafts anticipated. In fact he had got exactly what Hitler wanted and far more than the Wilhelmstrasse had contemplated. Before the Führer went farther with his offensive against Poland he required, as he thought, the

42 See D.G.F.P. series D, vol. VI, no. 185.
43 See D.G.F.P. series D, vol. VI, no. 149.
44 See D.G.F.P. series D, vol. VI, nos. 444-449.
45 Ciano Diary, 6-7th May 1939.

Italian Alliance to frighten off Britain and France. As
for the Japanese, though Ribbentrop did press once again
for their inclusion a week later,[46] Litvinoff had fallen[47] and
from now on Germany soft-pedalled on anti-Russian *motifs*.
For some weeks Ribbentrop had been hinting at a *détente*
between Russia and the Axis,[48] and in Milan he continued
to do so; when he left Italy he returned to Berchtesgaden
to join in certain expert discussions on Russia.[49] Neither
Mussolini nor Ciano nor the Italian diplomats in Berlin
took this change in German policy seriously enough; Attolico
had drawn attention to it in a telegram to Ciano on 25th
April, and it has been seen that Ciano had instructions to
protest against it on 6th May, but the protest was completely
ineffectual except in the record.[50]

The extraordinary ineptitude of Fascist diplomacy was
illustrated still more forcibly in the matter of the drafting
of the treaty. Ciano managed to veto 24th May as the
date of the signature since that was always celebrated as
the anniversary of the Italian declaration of war against
Austria-Hungary in 1915. But he left the entire wording
of the new pact to the Germans who by now had a host
of unused drafts to draw upon. The Führer did not
waste the opportunity the Duce had offered him and something quite unprecedented was suggested from Berlin. On
13th May Ciano was startled to receive the text inspired by
Hitler and drafted by Gaus. " I've never seen a pact like
this; it is real dynamite," he noted.[51] Though Mussolini,
it seems, reduced the duration from eternity to ten years, the
main German draft was obediently swallowed by Italy;
it certainly created an automatic liability.[52]

While Attolico was acutely aware of the folly of this,
it is curious that he, like the other Italians concerned, still
attached value to a German signature; they thought that

[46] Ibid., 14th May, 1939.
[47] On 3rd May 1939.
[48] See M. Toscano, op. cit.
[49] The German Ambassador in Moscow, Schulenberg, and his
colleague there, Hilger, had been summoned to advise the Führer.
[50] See D.G.F.P. series D, vol. VI, no. 341.
[51] Ciano Diary, 13 May 1939.
[52] Cf. Ciano's instructions of 4th May 1939, above.

Article II of the new Alliance Pact, which bound the high contracting parties to consult with one another immediately should their common interests " be endangered through international events," would have the advantage of being a safeguard in the future against German " surprises." Article III, however, cancelled out any advantage created by Article II, for it stated that " If it should happen, against the wishes and hopes of the contracting parties, that one of them becomes involved in warlike complications with another Power or with other Powers, the other contracting party will come to its aid as an ally and will support it with all its military forces on land, on sea, and in the air." There was not even the conventional protection that the *casus foederis* required the aggression to have been committed by the enemy. The preamble to the treaty, moreover, was definitely aggressive in tone with regard to the securing of *Lebensraum*—in conjunction, of course, with peace (paragraph 3).

Ciano arrived at the Adlon in Berlin on Sunday, 21st May, to sign the new pact the next day. Ribbentrop, he says,[53] assured him again that Germany required a ' long ' period of peace, at least three years. (The Germans were so insincere and careless about this that the period changed every time.) At a dinner given by Attolico, Ciano invested his German colleague with the Collar of the Annunziata, which made him the cousin of the King of Italy. This brought tears of jealousy into Göring's eyes; he made a great fuss and said he, Göring, deserved the decoration since he had been the true promoter of the German-Italian Alliance.

The treaty was signed with much ceremony on 22nd May by Ribbentrop and Ciano in the presence of Hitler, Göring, Raeder, and Brauchitsch. At one point Mussolini had had the unfortunate idea of naming it the *Patto di Sangue*, but it has gone down to history as the Steel Pact. In the previous October the Duce had said the alliance must not be purely defensive, but this was probably the most frankly " offensive " alliance in modern diplomatic history. Through the mission of Hans Frank leading up

[53] Ciano Diary, 21st May 1939.

to the Axis Protocols (October, 1936), and as the crown
to all Ribbentrop's advances, Hitler had attained his objective. In point of fact by this treaty Mussolini gave him
carte blanche to attack Poland and to plunge into the Second
World War.

A secret protocol was signed at the same time about which
the maddest conjecture has been rife: it was said that
Hitler and Mussolini agreed to give each other support in
the case of either being threatened by internal enemies, a
possibility which Hitler would never have admitted. When
the Allies captured this among all the other documents it
was found to be nothing but a postscript to Article IV of
the treaty. Article IV provided for the establishment of a
permanent commission, subject to the two Foreign Ministers,
for the intensification of military co-operation so that Article
III could be implemented with adequate speed. The secret
protocol provided only for the sending of specialists to
the respective Embassies to develop the press, news, and
propaganda services on behalf of the Axis and to the
detriment of its enemies.

As a matter of fact a good deal of propaganda in favour
of the Steel Pact was required in each of the Axis countries
themselves. Ciano, who was very self-conscious about this
sort of thing, was pleased with the Berlin crowd reactions
to his visit, but Magistrati noted that they were far less
spontaneous than in October 1936. Hassell, who felt a
natural resentment against Ciano, was gratified to learn
from friends, one himself an employer, that "as the Party
had failed to collect enough applauders on the first day
(people being sick to death of these things), the Labour
Front had then been mobilized; at a time of great labour
shortage employers had been implored to send their workmen out, at full rates of pay of course. . . ."[54] Young Pirzio
Biroli,[55] who afterwards married Hassell's younger daughter,

[54] Hassell, op. cit., p. 57. Hassell also quotes the current gossip
about the *Monstrebankett* at Ribbentrop's Dahlem villa on the evening
of the signature of the Alliance and of Ciano's unseemly behaviour.

[55] Son of the General who was afterwards Military Governor
of Montenegro—see Chapter XVIII.

had been staying with the Hassells. He told them " remarkable things "[56] about the irritation in Italy against the régime
and against the Germans. The Italians, he said, were angered
by the presence of Gestapo people and German aeronautic
experts. " The chief cause of the anger of the Italians is, of
course, that Mussolini is simply being dragged along by
us. People are saying *si stava meglio sotto Mussolini*.[57]
They are afraid of war. They only hope Mussolini may
hold Hitler back since he (the Duce) must know how
weak Italy is." Pirzio Biroli gave examples, too, from
his own experience as a reserve officer, of the shocking
state of the Italian Army. All this was before the news
of the signature of the Military Alliance " I have the
honest impression," wrote Ciano on his return to Rome,
" that the pact is more popular in Germany than in Italy."[58]
It should be added that, according to the Italian constitution,
the King's consent, which in this case was neither sought
nor obtained, was required for the signing of treaties. By
his tacit acquiescence Victor Emmanuel lost a magnificent
opportunity of identifying the Monarchy with national fear
and suspicion of the Steel Pact.[59]

Beyond the reaffirmation of the frontier the running sore
of the South Tyrol was not mentioned in the new Treaty,
but yet it may be said that Germany paid for Italian
adhesion by the concessions she at last agreed to make
to the Prefect of Bolzano. It was true that the Anschluss
had aggravated his responsibilities, for good Austrian Nazis
considered that when the Anschluss " liberated " North Tyrol,
ipso facto this should mean the reattachment to it of the
Southern Tyrol, and the Innsbruck Nazis encouraged those
in Bolzano to think that this was imminent. When Magistrati,
to whom the question had been handed over, saw the
Duce in Rome in the middle of April, Mussolini was greatly
annoyed that no progress had been made and told Magistrati

[56] *Wunderdinge.*
[57] =" We were better off under Mussolini."
[58] Ciano Diary, 24th May 1939.
[59] There were rumours that the King had threatened to abdicate
until he received written assurances from Hitler that he would
not invade Poland, but they were not true. See *The Economist*,
" Germany over Italy," 17th June 1939.

to go into the matter with Ribbentrop. At Milan Ribbentrop was conciliatory to Ciano about it and promised to take steps towards the evacuation of at least 10,000 people who had remained Austrian after 1919 and had now become German citizens. At the time the Italian authorities were thoroughly exasperated, among other things by German tourists who motored around the South Tyrol with large Nazi flags as if they were in Germany; at last, to Ciano's dismay,[60] the Italians arrested a Nazi leader in Bolzano called Kaufmann on account of a group march to Merano authorized by a German superior in Rome; Hitler followed this up with what Ciano called the *gesto chic* of offering to punish Kaufmann in Germany.

Hitler, however, was in earnest about transferring the South Tyrolese, and made Himmler, his expert for this kind of thing, responsible. On 30th May 1939 Himmler drew up a memorandum on the subject, toying with the idea of re-settling the South Tyrolese in formerly Czech territory,[61] as Hitler seemed to have suggested at the time of Munich. On 23rd June German and Italian delegations met at the Gestapo headquarters in the Prinz Albrechtstrasse in Berlin to discuss the South Tyrolese question. The German delegation consisted predominantly of S.S. people with Himmler, Heydrich and his friend, the Tyrolese Karl Wolff, who was Himmler's chief of staff; Woermann (a " Ribbentrop man "), Bohle, and Weizsäcker were also members. The Italians were represented by Attolico, Magistrati, the Prefect of Bolzano, the Italian Consul at Innsbruck, and another diplomat or so. Himmler turned out to be very well informed about the South Tyrol, and a plan was fairly quickly prepared on the basis of the indications Göring had thrown out more than a year before. People of German nationality living in the South Tyrol were to be transferred as soon as possible to Germany, while the rest were to opt before the end of the year; if they voted to become German they, too, were to be transferred to the Reich. It is interesting that a rumour was spread by

[60] Ciano Diary, 17th June, 1939.
[61] Conrad Latour. *Südtirol und die Achse Berlin-Rom* 1938-45, (1962) p. 34.

the Germans, and very soon believed all over the world, that the South Tyrolese who opted for Italy would be moved away from their homes to barren districts in southern Italy. Such a thing seems never to have been contemplated by the Italians. The Nazi régime was, not surprisingly, coy about any open reference to the understanding with Italy over the South Tyrol, which was publicly confessed in very sheepish fashion on 4th July. It provided an inhuman example of geopolitics in practice, after all the sacred-soil slogans which Hitler had exploited in the past, and it filled the genuine German patriots of South Tyrol with despair. It is interesting that already on 20th June, three days before the Italo-German commission had tackled the question in Berlin, two South Tyrolese leaders came to Hassell[62] fully informed as to what was in store for them; Lorenz of the *Volksdeutsche Mittelstelle* had told them that he was now forbidden to touch the question of South Tyrol.

In practice the July project[63] was only slowly, painfully, and partially executed. A certain number of *Reichsdeutsch* citizens, nearly all ex-Austrians, were removed during the second half of the year. In December 1939 the German-speaking South Tyrolese were called upon to opt for Italian citizenship or departure to Germany within three years. Out of 266,985 of them, 185,085, or just over two-thirds, voted for the second alternative : of these, 77,772, or less than half, had actually left Italy by 1st September 1943. Some of those who arrived in Germany were settled in Alsace and Lorraine after the defeat of France; some went to Innsbruck and others were left in camps. All along the Italians felt a lack of conviction about the whole business; at just about the time of the signature of the Steel Pact, at a semi-official German dinner, German policy had been expressed as " the restitution of the *ur-deutsch* provinces of Trentino and Trieste,"[64] and this sort of thing was constantly repeated, whatever orders Lorenz might receive. It

[62] Hassell, op. cit. p. 60.

[63] Confirmed in an agreement signed by Ciano and Mackensen on 21st October and published on 21st December 1939.

[64] See *The Economist*, " Germany over Italy," 17th June 1939.

is not irrelevant to note here that Trieste had been gravely
impoverished by the Anschluss, which stopped or diverted
many Austrian exports to and via Italy. On 18th July an
Italo-German Agreement was published by which Germany
received a free zone in Trieste and guaranteed that port a
transit trade of 40 per cent. of Trieste's total trade in 1938.
The Triestini were not very gay about this, for since the
Anschluss Germany had controlled 70 per cent. of their
1938 trade and they felt themselves to be unpleasantly dependent upon Hitler already.

There was an Italian postscript of considerable importance
to the Steel Pact. It is only too characteristic of Mussolini
that its signature left him torn with anxiety. There is no
evidence that Hitler ever looked back in doubt as to the
wisdom of anything he had done. But Mussolini tormented
himself, as well he might. General Cavallero was nominated
vice-president of the mixed commission envisaged in Article
IV of the Alliance Treaty, and on 30th May, the day
before his departure for Berlin, the Duce entrusted him
with a secret memorandum for Hitler which repeated and
developed the instructions Ciano had taken to Milan.[65]
Despite German assurances Mussolini found it necessary to
state again that Italy would not be able to go to war until
after 1942. After repeating the reasons given to Ribbentrop in
Milan, the so-called Cavallero Memorandum re-emphasized
the need to fortify[66] the relations not only between the
Governments but also the peoples of the Axis, for which
purpose a *détente* between National Socialism and the
Catholic Church would be important. And there must be
more fifth-column preparation against the Western Powers;
in this preparation Russia, "introduced into the West by
London," might be useful. Lastly, Mussolini modified his
March outburst about fighting France alone; now he rather
offered that Italy should subscribe more man-power if
Germany could contribute more material. The Axis must
prepare for a long war of attrition, he concluded, and be
ready, therefore, for the swift occupation of Danubia and the

[65] D.D.I. series 8, vol. XII, no. 59.
[66] The Italian word really means " to deepen."

Balkans[67] in order to ensure a supply of raw materials. This was a dangerous suggestion. Hitler was always ready to make long speeches about the Mediterranean for you and the Baltic for me, but it rankled in his Austrian soul that an ousider should, as it were, claim the Habsburg inheritance for "us"; the Danube, rather than the Rhine, was his Germany's river.[68] Always he had more immediate and more precise plans of which Mussolini was unaware.

[67] In Ciano's letter to Ribbentrop on 2nd Jan. 1939, he referred to the importance of drawing Hungary, Yugoslavia, and Roumania into the Axis system on account of their raw materials.

[68] Cf. his interview with Molotov on 13th Nov. 1940, when Hitler stressed this and his claim to former Austrian territories. See *Nazi-Soviet Relations* (Department of State, 1948).

Chapter X

"TO ATTACK POLAND AT THE FIRST SUITABLE OPPORTUNITY"

On Tuesday, 23rd May, the very day after Ciano and Ribbentrop had signed the Steel Pact and while Ciano was still in Berlin, Hitler called together his military chiefs to a secret conference at the Neue Reichskanzlei. There were present Göring,[1] Raeder, Brauchitsch, Keitel, Milch, Halder, Bodenschatz, Warlimont, and six other officers of whom Colonel Schmundt was responsible for the record of the meeting; it is written in his gothic script with a few corrections in another gothic handwriting. " Subject of the meeting : ' Indoctrination on the political situation and future aims '." The major part of the Schmundt minutes were read, in an unsatisfactory English translation, at the Nuremberg Trial on 26th November 1945, and it will only be necessary to refer to the most relevant sentences here. As usual this peroration of the Führer was an odd mixture of clear common sense with blind illusion.

The usual outburst came from Hitler. Germany must be strong in order to acquire living space and must have living space in order to be strong. She cannot afford to wait.

" At present we are in the same state of national exaltation as two other states, Italy and Japan. The national and political unity of the Germans has been achieved. . . . Further success cannot be obtained without the shedding of blood. . . .

" Danzig is not the subject of the dispute at all. It is a question of expanding our living space in the East and of securing our food supplies, of the settlement of the Baltic problem. . . .

[1] At the Nuremberg Trial Göring's presence on this occasion was rather vaguely questioned by Milch: see *Nuremberg Trial Proceedings*, part VIII, pp. 254 and 296.

"In Europa ist keine andere Möglichkeit zu sehen. . . ."[2]
. . . Poland sees danger in a German victory in the West,
and will attempt to rob us of that victory. There is, therefore, no question of sparing Poland, and we are left with
the decision : *to attack Poland at the first suitable opportunity.*[3]

" A repetition of the Czech business is not to be expected.
It will be war this time. The first objective is to isolate
Poland."

There is then considerable confusion because the Führer says
there must be no simultaneous conflict with the Western
Powers, but that there may be.

The central theme of Hitler's discourse was how to defeat
England, in his belief *der Motor, der gegen Deutschland
treibt.*

And àpropos the claim that secrecy is the first essential for
success occurs the following sentence : " Our aim must
also remain hidden from Japan and Italy. The possibility
of an Italian break through the Maginot Line should be
examined. The Führer thinks the break-through feasible."

It is impossible to believe that Hitler had not talked in this
vein to Ribbentrop who had just signed the Steel Pact;
it is equally impossible to imagine the consternation of
Mussolini—whose respect for the Maginot Line was exaggerated—had he known what was being planned for his
ramshackle army. The Italian Embassy in Berlin never had
an inkling of what had taken place at the Neue Reichskanzlei
that day; Attolico's gloomiest moments were not darkened
by this. When Cavallero delivered the Duce's memorandum
to the Führer on 5th June there was no ostensible reaction
beyond a reference vaguely made by Hitler to meeting
Mussolini about all this some time soon at the Brenner;
it was this suggestion which in the end brought Ciano to
Salzburg in August. Cavallero left Berlin for Italy on 10th
June; since the impervious Hitler had in no way protested against the contents of the memorandum, the Italians

[2] Wrongly translated at Nuremberg as " There is no other possibility for Europe." It means that there is no other possibility in
Europe for Germany.

[3] Underlined by Schmundt himself.

in Berlin, as in Rome, took silence to mean assent. Yet
on 22nd June Keitel signed orders for the execution of *Fall
Weiss* and a concealed German mobilization.

On 17th June Goebbels' furious attack upon Poland in
his speech at Danzig combined with other indications to
re-arouse Attolico's fears, and the Italian Ambassador began
to support the idea of another meeting between the Chiefs
themselves.[4] Ciano[5] was still too innocent to believe that
after the Pact with its consultation clause the Germans would
thus conceal their intentions from him, and on the eve
of his departure on a ten days' journey to Spain he put the
whole thing off. Nevertheless, on 13th July, while he
was visiting Franco, the Palazzo Chigi proposed that Mussolini
and Hitler should meet at the Brenner on 4th August. Indications of Germany's concealed mobilization were multiplying,
and Italian officials and Germans of the Weizsäcker[6] type
hoped that Mussolini might again hold Hitler back, while
Ribbentrop was quite glad of the opportunity to shout
and boast. As the situation sharpened the Duce became
less bellicose and contemplated the pleasures of a bigger and
better Munich; he talked of a plebiscite in Danzig, and
he decided, while Ciano was away, to propose an international
conference on the question; for instructions on the preparation of this he summoned Magistrati from Berlin. Ciano
returned on 19th July and was annoyed to find all this
en train without him. However, when he and Magistrati
went to Mussolini, Ciano was overruled. "Why," said
the Duce, "should not the two chiefs of the authoritarian
countries, accused as they always are of desiring war, make
themselves protagonists of a practical peace plan such as
the project of a conference between Italy, Germany, France,
Britain, Poland, and Spain, a gathering capable of assuring
to the peoples a period of well-being and tranquillity?"[7]

[4] D.D.I. series 8, XII, no. 323.

[5] Diary, 3-7th and 20th July 1939.

[6] Cf. E. Kordt, op. cit.; but the evidence at Weizsäcker's trial
conflicted with this interpretation of his role. See also Weizsäcker:
Erinnerungen—(1950).

[7] Information provided by Count Magistrati. See also D.D.I. series
8, XII, no. 647.

Mussolini did not know that Hitler and Ribbentrop were determined to fight, but he realized that they would dislike the conference idea and say that he was trying to back out of the alliance. Though he insisted that this was not the time to embark on war, he repeated several times that " whenever Germany finds it necessary to mobilize at midnight, we shall mobilize at five to twelve." Finally the Duce fortified Magistrati with a new list of considerations which made open war inadvisable for some time : a war of nerves served the Axis better than its enemies while real war would not now come as a surprise, a conference would provide a popular way of handing Danzig over to Germany, if the others refused to confer they would be in the wrong, and so on : according to Italian information, Poland, France, and Britain were in earnest and intended to fight.[8] Mussolini made it plain that he would not move without Germany's prior agreement, and he naturally asked for secrecy.

On the following Tuesday, 25th July, Magistrati, together with Attolico, visited Ribbentrop in his castle at Fuschl to urge the conference plan upon him. (The conversation, as so often between Axis representatives, was in English.) Ribbentrop was in one of his genius grade II states and uttered long obstructive dissertations such as that suffered by Sumner Welles in March 1940; he prefaced many of his sentences with the words " I will tell you very frankly." Germany could not retreat, neither could he meet the Poles at a conference after their inexplicable refusal of his motorroad proposal. Half-way through he reversed gear for a moment and said that Hitler agreed with Mussolini that a conflagration was undesirable at present and that he would move against Poland only if he were certain that Poland would be completely isolated. Then he objected again to the conference idea because the Axis would thereby be exposed to the attacks of the Jewish-Masonic Press. The great advantage of the Axis should be that it was led by two strong men who could act outside international combinations. Finally, he objected to a draft communiqué in

8 See D.B.F.P. series 3, vol. V, nos. 431, 432, 489, showing that the Foreign Office had made British intentions clear in both Rome and Berlin.

favour of a conference which the Duce had prepared for
the Brenner meeting because, he said, this meeting must finish
with something tremendous, not with something banal.[9]
After a great deal of German prevarication that was the end
of the Brenner project for 4th August, which was replaced
by the Salzburg meeting exactly a week later.

At the beginning of August 1939 Ciano's fluttering attention was diverted by the Collar of the Annunziata which
he was about to reap for his Albanian sowings. It was
on 4th August that the optimism which he based upon
the Steel Pact pledges and which his brother-in-law Magistrati,
encouraged from Berlin, was at last shaken by Attolico.
It might well be. Nostitz told Hassell at about this time
that "at present we are at the third and last phase of
partial mobilization against Poland. On 26th or 27th August
everything is to be ready."[10] The military order for the
German seizure of Danzig had been drawn up on 27th
July, and the necessary crisis was heated up during the
first week in August. Forster, the Nazi boss in Danzig,
was at the Obersalzberg on 7th August, and on 9th August
Germany intervened without any legal right to do so
between the Senate of Danzig and the Warsaw Government. On the afternoon of Friday, 11th August, the League
of Nations High Commissioner for Danzig, the Swiss diplomat and historian, Carl Burckhardt, was with Hitler for
two and a half hours. The Führer was threatening, and one
of his threats was that he could count upon the unstinted
support of Italy and Japan.[11] Burckhardt, however, had
"an impression of slight uncertainty" when Hitler said
"Italy will fight with us whatever happens."

That same morning Galeazzo Ciano arrived by air at
Salzburg. On the eve of his departure from Rome on
10th August Mussolini had ordered him more emphatically than ever before to insist upon the necessity of postponing military action and of calling a European conference. But Ciano found an implacable Ribbentrop determined on war even if the Germans should be given "more

[9] Magistrati. See also D.D.I. series 8, XII, no. 687.
[10] Hassell, op. cit.: entry for 7th Aug. 1939.
[11] D.B.F.P. series III, vol. VI, no. 659.

than they have asked for." Just before lunch at Ribbentrop's mansion at Fuschl, the German Minister quoted the recent Polish statement on the Danzig Senate and added in so many words that Germany was bound to destroy Poland for this. The lunch-party was plunged in the blackest gloom. Ciano, already startled rudely out of his Milan-Berlin illusions, was pale and shaken, and whispered to Magistrati *Siamo alle botte*—we are almost at blows. Mostly there was silence at table; at one point Ribbentrop discoursed upon the difference between woodcock and snipe. Afterwards there was a bleak expedition by car to the Wolfgangsee. The irony was heightened by the fact that the Italians were in uniform and the Germans not.

Ciano had ten hours of Ribbentrop on that Friday. "At times our conversation became pretty dramatic. . . . I realize how little we count in German judgement," he noted in his diary. The tragic bitterness of his disillusionment is almost greater in his Minute of their meeting. Ribbentrop, he wrote, admits that he has changed abruptly from the day when he said the Axis needed two or three years' preparation for war and justifies this by referring to a new situation, and yet he fails to show that the situation has changed in any way. He starts out from two axioms which it is impossible to discuss with him because he simply replies by repeating them. They are (1) that the conflict will be localized, (2) that even if France and Britain wish to react, there is nothing they can do about it. At one point Ribbentrop accepted Ciano's wager that the Western Powers would fight.

When Ribbentrop told Ciano that Russia would not enter into the war and referred to fairly definite conversations between Moscow and Berlin, Ciano pointed out that the secrecy maintained towards Italy with regard to this was difficult to reconcile with the terms of the alliance and with the absolute loyalty observed by Italy towards Germany. Certainly, if we may go by Ciano's Diary, he had, since the Steel Pact, scrupulously informed Mackensen of the development of Italy's relations with Britain and France and with regard to her policy as a whole. It is true that he had discussed Germany's relations with Russia very freely

with a Soviet diplomat in Rome on the strength of the
" deductions " of Rosso, his Ambassador in Moscow.[12]

Ciano repeated Italy's arguments in favour of delay and
tried to urge the conference idea upon Ribbentrop; as a
matter of fact, according to the communiqué drafted by
Mussolini to be published at the end of the Salzburg conversations, he specifically asked only for a tentative intimation
that the Axis Powers had not banged all the doors. The
communiqué had been drafted in French and English by
the Italians, and the following is the English version (as
recorded in the German Minute of the meeting with Hitler
on 12th August):

" The Minister of Foreign Affairs of the Reich, Mr.
von Ribbentrop, and the Italian Minister of Foreign Affairs,
Count Galeazzo Ciano, have examined—in the course of
their conversations at Salzburg—the general situation in Europe
and the problems concerning the common policy of the
two allied countries.

" The two Foreign Ministers were able to[13] realize once
again in [sic] this occasion, the perfect identity of views
existing between their Governments, and reaffirm the common
decision of Germany and Italy to resist the policy of en-
cerclement [sic] promoted by the great democracies, and to
defend their vital rights, opposing by force any attempt of
aggression directed against them.

" At the same time the Foreign Minister of the Reich and
the Italian Foreign Minister wished to reaffirm the peaceful
intentions of their Governments, and, thoughtful of the
destinies of Europe, they agreed to state that, according to
their opinion, it is still possible to reach—through normal
diplomatic negotiations between the various Governments
—a satisfying solution of the problems which trouble, in
such a serious way, the life of Europe."

Ribbentrop objected that the communiqué would be interpreted as weakness, then he admitted that it might be

[12] See Schulenburg's Memorandum of 16th Aug. 1939 in *Nazi-Soviet Relations*.

[13] The German typescript has *zu* in the English text. It has been
corrected by the official translators. See D.G.F.P. series D, vol. VII,
no. 43.

good tactics but went back to the repetition of his axioms. Finally, he refused any precise indication of Germany's plan of action since "all decisions were still locked in the impenetrable breast of the Führer."[14]

When Ciano got to Berchtesgaden after lunch on Saturday, 12th August, he found himself faced, in addition to Hitler and Ribbentrop and the interpreting Paul Schmidt, with an agent of Himmler's now attached to the German Embassy in Rome, a young S.S. Führer called Dollmann.[15] When the official conversations began Magistrati and the other Italians were sent off to drink coffee with a Nazi Party official called Martin Bormann. We shall hear of both of them again.

Ciano's and Schmidt's accounts of these Berchtesgaden meetings do not conflict, but it is interesting to see how Ciano, in summarizing the whole thing for the Duce, sorted out the material which Schmidt probably wrote out in chronological order. It must have been an impossible task to make a coherent record of any 'conversation with' Hitler.

By now Hitler had all but decided to begin the "action" to destroy Poland on 25th August, that is in just under a fortnight. It was all the more important to him that the Rome-Berlin Axis should seem alarmingly strong because he was still uncertain with regard to Russia, and Japan[16] had continued to be elusive; in any case it would be difficult to enjoy the friendship of both, however much one might pretend to be doing so. It was equally important to him to prevent any Italian mediation; he was determined that no *Schweinhund*[17] should prevent this war this time. Thus, knowing Italy's military weakness, Hitler was yet dependent upon her politically, and it is strange to find that Mussolini made no use of this fact. Once he had been made to realize that Italy was in a condition of military

[14] Ciano Minute of Convention, 11th August 1939. See also D.D.I. series 8, XIII, no. 1.

[15] Dollmann went to Rome ostensibly as some kind of cultural attaché, but not in consequence of the Secret Protocol of the Steel Pact which was never really implemented.

[16] Japan was apparently not mentioned by the Germans during the mid-August talks.

[17] This was the term he almost certainly used when addressing his commanders-in-chief on 22nd Aug. See below, p. 212.

exhaustion, the Duce warmed up to the delectable prospect of a new Munich, but his proposals, which might have been imperative, were apologetic, and Ciano dared not risk his displeasure by deviating from his instructions.

The meeting on the afternoon of 12th August lasted for three and a quarter hours. The gist of Hitler's oft-repeated remarks was that an Axis war against Britain and France was desirable while the Axis was led by the two Great Men and before these two should be much older. With this in view Germany and Italy must respectively " liquidate " Poland and Yugoslavia, treacherous friends in their rear; he reverted several times to the desirability of an Italian attack upon Yugoslavia,[18] which as a piece of connivance would be much more useful from a German blackmailing point of view than a mere annexation of Albania. He gave a number of inconsequent reasons for his own imminent attack upon Poland which, he made clear, would occur before the end of August. First there was his *felsenfeste Uberzeugung* that no one else would intervene; if the Western Powers did move it would show that they would have attacked the Axis anyway. The action against Poland could not be delayed because after October Poland might do the most dreadful things to Danzig, and Germany would be unable to react since Poland would then be submerged in fog and mud until the spring of 1940. Another explanation offered by Hitler was that since on geopolitical grounds he was " evacuating " South Tyrol[19] in Italy's favour, which might in the eyes of the world appear like weakness, Italy must understand that he would lose too much prestige if he now allowed Poland to express, unpunished, the indignation which German provocation had aroused in her. Ciano did

[18] Ciano noted in his Diary on 12th Aug. that Hitler only excited himself when he spoke of the destruction of Yugoslavia. In his Minute on the meeting of 12th Aug. Ciano noted that Hitler urged Italy to take Croatia with Dalmatia, but not Slovenia. This also suggests pre-1914 Austria, which included Slovenia, while Croatia was Hungarian; Dalmatia had been Austrian too, but in view of its Italian enclaves Hitler could with difficulty veto its Italian occupation.

[19] Hitler spoke of the South Tyrol more than once, according to later entries in Ciano's Diary.

not bother to take note of Italy's appeal to him to remember
that Danzig was the Trieste of Germany, but this was
recorded in the German Minute by Schmidt.

When Ciano later announced that Mussolini insisted upon
a peaceful Axis gesture and would have liked an international conference to be called, Hitler argued that one
could not leave Russia out now as at the time of Munich,
and since she would vote with Britain, France, and Poland,
Germany, Italy, and Spain, would be in an unsatisfactory
minority. This was the strangest argument of all, since
Russia's presence would only occur thanks to Germany.
The carefully staged arrival of the telegram from Moscow
a little later, according to which, the Germans stated, Russia
was ready to enter into political negotiations with Germany,
also suggested that Russia would be more likely to side with
Germany against Poland. Perhaps this patent discrepancy
contributed to the scepticism of Ciano and his colleagues
with regard to Germany and Russia; in spite of the warnings
of the Italian Ambassador in Moscow,[20] they never really
believed in German-Russian friendship, however temporary,
until Ribbentrop left for Moscow on 22nd August. As
a matter of fact, on Thursday 10th August the Soviet
Chargé in Berlin spoke of the outcome of the negotiations with
the Western Powers as still uncertain, and on Saturday the
12th he announced " that he had received instructions from
Molotov to state here that the Soviets were interested in
a discussion of the individual groups of questions that had
heretofore been taken up. . . . Such a discussion, however,
could be undertaken only *by degrees.* . . ."[21] At this point the
Germans could count on nothing more.

By far the most important paragraph in Ciano's account
of the meeting on 12th August occurs at the point when
Ciano has very briefly recorded his own efforts to re-state the
Italian point of view. " The Führer interrupted me to say
that what I was saying was perfectly true and that he agrees
with Mussolini that two or three years—not more than that
—would be useful to the Axis to improve its position and
preparation. He would have waited as had been agreed.

[20] See M. Toscano, op. cit.
[21] *Nazi-Soviet Relations*, pp. 44-6 and 48-9.

But Polish provocation and the aggravation of the situation make German action urgent—action which will not, however, provoke a general conflict. The Führer is certain, therefore, that where Italy is concerned, he will not have to ask for help according to the existing obligation " (*l'aiuto secondo l'impegno esistente*).

An equivalent paragraph is not to be found in the German Minute, which is much more detailed; it appears by comparison with the German records of the talks on 12th and 13th August that Ciano wrote both his accounts after the meeting on the 13th, since he seems to have attributed several things to the Saturday conversation which Schmidt recorded as having been said on the Sunday.[22] Although Ciano was much more slapdash than Schmidt, there was less likelihood than usual of linguistic misunderstandings, because, while again there was no Italian interpreter present, Dollmann spoke perfect Italian. And finally, though Hitler fought against the defection of Italy even in a localized war until his letter to Mussolini less than a fortnight later, he did then pretty well repeat what Ciano claimed he had admitted on 12th August. It should not be forgotten that in March[23] Hitler had warned the Italians against starting a war before 1941, while in April in Rome Göring had spoken of 1940 as the earliest feasible date.

After his initial talk with Ribbentrop Ciano was *bouleversé*, and with that completeness which is characteristically Italian. The relations between the Axis Powers were now such that the Italian Foreign Minister kept his aeroplane under special guard each of the two nights at Salzburg lest someone should interfere with it. Discussing the position into which Italy had been not even manœuvred but kicked, Ciano, Magistrati, and Attolico—whose anxieties Ciano had earlier regarded as hysterical—took refuge in the bathroom of Ciano's hotel suite; they hoped that the Gestapo microphones did not reach quite so far. There on the evening of the 12th Attolico begged Ciano to regard Italy as freed from

[22] D.G.F.P. series D, vol. VII, nos. 43, 47. D.D.I. series 8, vol. XIII, nos. 4, 21. According to Ciano the Sunday meeting only lasted for half an hour.
[23] See above, chapter IX.

the Steel Pact by the infraction of Article II by Germany and by the release from the obligation in Article III which Hitler had pronounced to him. Ciano was worried. He knew that Mussolini did not want to be released and then left out at the time of a victorious distribution of plunder. He knew that the cause of Fascism would suffer. With Attolico and Magistrati he decided at all events to give up the idea of publishing the communiqué, which was far too emphatic about Axis identity of views; this he conveyed to Ribbentrop before he met Hitler again the next morning. The Führer agreed: " Thus doors were left open on all sides, no one was tied and nothing prevented."[24] Hitler seemed even more decided on the 13th.[25] He ranted marvellously against the Western Powers who, he said, were determined to rule the world and regarded Germany and Italy as *nicht ebenbürtig*. This psychological element was perhaps the worst in the whole situation and could only be ended by a life-and-death conflict, said Hitler.

At the end the Führer indulged in the habitual eulogies. " He was personally fortunate to live at a time in which, apart from himself, there was one other statesman who would stand out great and unique in history; that he could be this man's friend was for him a matter of great personal satisfaction, and if the hour of common battle struck he would always be found on the side of the Duce ' und zwar auf Gedeih und Verderb '."[26] This is Schmidt's version. Ciano only noted " Hitler insisted on often repeating to me how much he wished to meet our Chief, but he did not indicate that political questions were to be discussed, and he added that he would be happy to have him some time as his guest for the musical festival at Bayreuth."

No sooner had Ciano's aeroplane safely left Salzburg for Rome, on the afternoon of 13th August, than the *Deutsches Nachrichten Büro,* in spite of the joint agreement to the contrary, published a communiqué emphasizing the identity of the views of Italy and Germany in the Salzburg conversations; this was quoted by a part of the Italian Press though

[24] Schmidt Minute, 13th Aug. 1939.
[25] Ciano Diary, 13th Aug. 1939.
[26] =" For better and for worse," only it is much more forceful.

ignored by Stefani. Attolico could endure this confusion and bad faith no longer, and on his own initiative he followed Ciano to Rome to try to ensure that Italy should make clear that since Germany had broken Article II, she did not feel bound by Article III of the Steel Pact.[27] Before leaving Berlin he had heard from Dirksen, their Ambassador in London whom Hitler and Ribbentrop simply refused to see, that Britain would certainly fight. As Ciano had indicated on 12th August when Hitler said that the French would be held up by the Italian fortifications ("At this point Count Ciano showed signs of extreme doubt," noted Schmidt), the Italians were greatly afraid of a French occupation of the Po valley, the more since scarcely any of their plans for moving their war industries to the south had been realized. (According to Hitler it was, of course, the Italians who were to break through the Maginot Line.)

Once back in Rome, Ciano's mind was made up, and he did all he dared to back up Attolico. In particular he took steps at last to make Mussolini aware of how strong was anti-war and anti-German feeling in Italy. Many of the people around the Duce were so accustomed to telling him what he wanted to hear that it was difficult to induce them to speak the truth. But even Starace was prepared for anti-German demonstrations now if Germany should attack Poland.

Until the end of the month the battle swayed backwards and forwards in the Palazzo Venezia. Mussolini was at one moment furious with the Germans, but then again he could not face the slur on his honour if he did not march with Hitler, or he remembered that he might miss his booty; or he was suddenly afraid of Hitler's revenge and, if Badoglio is to be believed,[28] spoke of strengthening the defences of the Brenner. On 18th August Attolico was back in Germany. He met Magistrati at Munich and

[27] Canaris had already expressed this view in conversation with the new Italian Military Attaché in Berlin, General Roatta. See D.D.I. series 8, XIII, no. 10.

[28] See Badoglio, op. cit.: but Badoglio's chronology is sublimely vague and misleading. Mussolini was, it seems, afraid of documents which the Germans had found in Vienna.

together they saw Ribbentrop with a message from Mussolini to Hitler insisting that a Polish-German conflict could not be localized; Attolico added that Italy simply lacked the coal and petrol she required if she were faced with war in the Mediterranean. Ribbentrop was more exasperating than ever. " As for coal," he said, " Germany is rich in that and will be richer still when she has occupied the Polish coalfields. She will be able to supply a great deal to Italy, if necessary via Switzerland. Roumania and Russia will look after petrol."[29] That evening Ribbentrop telephoned to Attolico to say that " the decisions indicated to Ciano had now been taken." In other words, Hitler, who had decided at the time of the Danzig crisis over the Polish customs (4-5th August) to go all out for a treaty with Russia, had on 18th August sent a further message to Moscow to this effect.[30]

The next day Ribbentrop met Attolico and Magistrati again at the Oesterreichischer Hof in Salzburg with Hitler's answer; it was more rigid than his attitude to Ciano a week earlier. He could not, he repeated, retreat before Poland's provocations, but the war would without question be localized and victorious. Attolico, noticing that Ribbentrop was increasingly identifying Germany with the Axis,[31] obstinately insisted that Italy could not agree. Thereupon Ribbentrop asked to speak to Attolico alone and Magistrati withdrew. As soon as he had left the room Ribbentrop upbraided Attolico with the indiscretions of the Italian diplomats in Berlin; the Italian Embassy, he said, was the centre of gossip about Axis difficulties, and how was it, he asked, that the Belgian Legation had been informed that Italy was not coming in on Germany's side? Attolico flew into a calculated rage; he immediately called Magistrati back to witness his repudiation of the slur Ribbentrop was casting upon the Italian Embassy and Ribbentrop rather sulkily crumpled up.

On 20th August Mussolini, to the despair of Ciano and

[29] D.D.I. series 8, XIII, nos. 100, 101, 102.

[30] See Ribbentrop to Schulenburg, no. 185 of 18th Aug. 1939 in *Nazi-Soviet Relations*, p. 61.

[31] D.D.I. series 8, XIII, nos. 108, 116.

Attolico (who had returned to Rome), was all loyalty to Hitler, but on the 21st, while the German Press was busy denying rumours that the Duce had reacted negatively in the Polish crisis, Ciano seems to have brought him round. He (Ciano) offered to go to Salzburg again at once and to speak out: " Hitler won't make me put out my cigarette as he made Schuschnigg."[32] They tried to reach Ribbentrop by telephone. When at last he replied at 5.30 p.m. he said he could decide nothing until he had received an important message from Moscow. Five hours later Ribbentrop telephoned again to say that he would prefer to see Ciano at Innsbruck on the next day as he must then leave for Moscow immediately to sign a political pact with the Soviet Government. This piece of news startled Rome that evening as much as it shook the rest of the world in the next few days.[33] The Japanese, too, had been taken completely by surprise. For the moment Ciano dropped his idea of another talk with the Germans.

With Ribbentrop preparing to leave for Moscow, the Führer reassembled his commanders-in-chief at the Obersalzberg on Tuesday, 22nd August, and bade them prepare the attack upon Poland for the Friday night, 25th August, as an essential preliminary to war against the West; the latter was necessary and might follow immediately. Hitler's tirades, two hours before and two hours after a luxurious lunch[34] on 22nd August, appear to have been more than usually Nietzschean.[35] There were masters and supermen on

[32] Ciano Diary, 21st Aug. 1939.

[33] " Wie eine Granate," Hitler boasted.

[34] See Gisevius, *Bis zum bittern Ende* (1946), vol. ii, p. 119.

[35] Texts found in the O.K.W. file at Flensburg, see *Nuremberg Trial Proceedings*, part I, p. 171. Gisevius, op. cit., vol. II, p. 119, says it was forbidden to make a record at the time and there are therefore several versions of these addresses, the O.K.W. ones leaving out several piquant details; it is agreed that they reproduce the general trends quite accurately. The American publication *Nazi Conspiracy and Aggression*, vol. II, includes a version which contains the words " since . . . Mussolini is menaced by the weak-headed King and the treacherous scoundrel of a Crown Prince, I have decided to go with Stalin . . . Stalin and I are the only ones that

the Axis side and none in the West to oppose them. Therefore one must fight at once.

" . . . . Essentially it depends on me, on my existence,
because of my political activity. . . . Furthermore, the fact
that probably no one will ever again have the confidence
of the whole German people as I have. . . . But I can
be eliminated at any time by a criminal or an idiot.

" The second personal factor is the Duce. His existence
is also decisive. *If something happened to him, Italy's loyalty
to the alliance would no longer be certain.*[36] The basic
attitude of the Italian Court is against the Duce. . . . The
Duce is the man with the strongest nerves in Italy.

" . . . . There is no outstanding personality in England
or France. . . . Our opponents are little wormlets.[37] I saw
them at Munich."

In the afternoon came further classic examples of the
brutal German style.

" I shall give a propagandist reason for starting the war
—no matter whether plausible or not. The victor will not
be asked later on whether he told the truth. . . . Shut pity
out of your hearts. Act brutally. . . . The stronger is in the
right.   Greatest ruthlessness."

The next morning Schwerin-Krosigk, who happened to be
in Rome, saw the Italian Foreign Minister an hour or so
before Ribbentrop reached Moscow. The German Minister of
Finance informed Ciano that the whole German people was
of one mind about the urgent necessity for the solution of
the Polish question.

" Count Ciano replied that a great deal would depend upon
the attitude of the Axis peoples. For it would be necessary
to fight with the utmost tenacity, since in case of a defeat
we should have to count on a peace which would practically
mean the end of the Axis Powers. Count Ciano concluded

---

see only the future. . . ." Gisevius was in fairly close touch with
Canaris, who made his own very full notes in the room, and was
horrified. See also D.G.F.P. series D, vol. VII, nos. 192, 193. Also
D.B.F.P. series III, vol. VII, no. 314.

[36] My italics.

[37] Note the double diminutive (= " kleine Würmchen ").

the conversation by stating that despite the great diplomatic success of the Russian Pact he considered the situation as very serious."[38]

On 24th August Hitler flew from the Obersalzberg to Berlin to meet the triumphant Ribbentrop, the greater Bismarck, back from Moscow; on the same day the Nazi, Forster, was declared the supreme chief of Danzig which was equivalent to its annexation. Not since the unexpected Anglo-German naval pact of June 1935, as some said, had Hitler and Ribbentrop felt so exultant, and they waited in a state of feverish exaltation for their great adventure to begin on the very next night, between 25th and 26th August. Before the time was up, however, the master spirit faltered: in the German Admiralty Register on 25th August was written: "*Fall Weiss* already started will be stopped at 20.30 because of the changed political conditions. (Mutual Assistance Pact between Great Britain and Poland of 25th August noon[39] and information from the Duce that he would be true to his word but has to ask for large supplies of raw material.)"

This is not the place to examine the genesis or the making of the Anglo-Polish Treaty. Here it need only be noted that, whereas Hitler had expected the Western Powers to be cowed by his pact with Russia, he was all the more astonished by the British pledge to an almost helpless Poland which Britain was in no position to support. The Anglo-Polish Treaty is, however, relevant to the story of the Axis in that Hitler and Ribbentrop asserted later, and possibly believed at the time,[40] that it was the knowledge of Italy's defection which spurred the British on, while other people believed that Mussolini's letter to Hitler on 25th August was caused by the news that Britain had decided to commit herself to Poland. The truth is that while the British were in a general way fairly well informed about Italy's weakness, the Italians had, it has been seen, all along expected the Western Powers

[38] Schwerin-Krosigk to Ribbentrop, 23rd Aug. 1939, in *Nazi-Soviet Relations*, p. 79.

[39] The Anglo-Polish Treaty was not signed until 5.35 p.m.

[40] Ribbentrop said at Nuremberg that he remembered Hitler saying so immediately: cf. *Nuremberg Trial Proceedings*, part X, p. 183.

to fight; but British and Italian action on 25th August 1939, though each conducive to the delay of the attack upon Poland by exactly a week, were independent of one another. It should be added that people like Weizsäcker[41] seemed to consider that the difficulties made by Italy affected Hitler more than the news from London, though others attributed major importance to the Anglo-Polish Treaty.[42]

Spoiling for battle and believing all to be prepared as he wished, on the morning of 25th August Hitler drew up a letter to Mussolini in which, at last, he clothed with much tardy explanation the naked statement of the conclusion of the German-Russian Agreement.[42a] He had not announced it hitherto, he said, because he had not conceived the magnitude of the scope of the Nazi-Soviet conversations, but at Moscow "the vastest pact of non-aggression to-day existing" had been signed. Twice Hitler insisted that the Moscow Agreement would prevent any attack upon the Axis by Roumania, while it would ensure a modification of the attitude of Turkey.[43] Then he implied that he was about to attack Poland, though he still concealed his time-table from his so greatly revered ally. "And finally," he concluded, "I can assure you, Duce, that in a similar situation I shall offer Italy complete understanding and that you can be certain of my future attitude in every situation of the kind."

Ciano was informed of the arrival of the letter about 2 p.m. and went with Mackensen to deliver it to Mussolini about one hour later. According to Mackensen's subsequent wire to Ribbentrop,[44] the Duce translated the letter correctly to Ciano and then very cautiously indicated his objections, the usual things—it was too soon to start a war, a general conference might have settled everything, and so on. By 5.30 p.m. Ciano had telephoned Mussolini's answer to Attolico

[41] *Erinnerungen*, pp. 253-57 cf. Hassell, op. cit. p. 77.

[42] Ribbentrop certainly did at Nuremberg on 29 Mar. 1946.

[42a] D.G.F.P. series D, vol. VII, no. 266.

[43] Italy constantly showed particular anxiety about both Turkey and Roumania.

[44] Ribbentrop at the Nuremberg Trial said all this had occurred earlier, but Mackensen's telegram is clearly dated and timed.

to be conveyed *quam celerrime* to the Führer. The second
half of the Duce's letter contained the following sentences :

" If Germany attacks Poland and the conflict remains
localized, Italy will give Germany every form of political
and economic help requested of her.

" If Germany attacks Poland and Poland's allies attack
Germany, I propose not myself to take any military initiative, given the actual state of Italian military preparation which
was made clear to you, Führer, and to von Ribbentrop, in good
time and repeatedly.

" Our intervention can, however, immediately take place
if Germany at once provides us with arms and raw materials
to withstand the attack which the French and British will
direct primarily against us. When we met war was always envisaged for a period after 1942 and by then I should be
ready on land and sea and in the air, according to what
we had agreed."[44a]

Mussolini begged for an immediate reply as he had to call
together the chief organs of the régime. Halifax and
Raczynski must have signed the Anglo-Polish Treaty probably
just after Ciano was on the telephone to Berlin :[45] the
German attack upon Poland appears to have been postponed about one hour later, as Roatta immediately telephoned
to Rome.

At 9.30 Mackensen brought a brief reply from Hitler,
asking what exactly Italy needed and by what date. Ciano
noted that Mackensen privately asked him to make a very
long list.[46] The next morning, 26th August, at 10 a.m.,
the Italian military chiefs were summoned to the Palazzo
Venezia to compile the list, and Ciano begged them to drop
all conventional optimism. Italy really had no reserves left,
and the list was staggering. At 12.10 Ciano telephoned
to Attolico that in order to undertake a twelve months'
war Italy's armed forces required at least seven million tons

[44a] D.D.I. Eighth Series, vol. XIII, no. 250.

[45] In a despatch written on 19th January 1940 Attolico refers
to news having reached him in the morning of August 25th that
the Anglo-Polish Treaty was on the verge of signature. See D.D.I
series IX, vol. III, no. 171.

[46] Ciano Diary, 25th August, 1939.

of oil, six millions tons of coal, two million tons of steel, and one million tons of timber, besides small quantities of rubber, copper, and the rarer metals. In order to protect Italy's industrial quadrilateral Turin-Genoa-Milan-Savona, which was half an hour's flight from Corsica, a hundred and fifty A.A. batteries with ammunition were necessary.

In Attolico's car on the way to the Wilhelmstrasse with this message Magistrati said to the Ambassador, " But by when do you suppose all this is to be consigned?" and Attolico looked at him without answering. When he reached his destination an icy Ribbentrop naturally asked him the same thing. " Why, at once," said Attolico, " before hostilities begin." Soon after 3 p.m. Ribbentrop telephoned Hitler's reply this time. For organizational and technical reasons it was impossible to supply the oil and the copper immediately, and only thirty A.A. batteries could be sent at once. In these conditions Hitler understood Mussolini's situation and asked him only to busy the Anglo-French, as he had himself proposed, with propaganda and suitable military demonstrations. In view of his pact with Russia Hitler would not be afraid to solve the Eastern Question[47] even with the danger of complications in the West. For the moment Attolico had helped to save Italy but not Europe; Hitler's hesitation on 25th August had lasted less than twenty-four hours.

At about 7 p.m.[48] the Italian answer to Hitler's recoil was telephoned by Ciano to Attolico. Mussolini repudiated Attolico's ingenious device. But, while saying that his requirements needed to be met only within the next twelve months, he noted that Germany was not in a position to fill the holes made in Italy's military resources by the Abyssinian and Spanish wars. According to his Diary Ciano felt assured by the 26th that Mussolini had really made up his mind, although the Duce writhed with the humiliation of confessing his weakness. But if he was not to fight, all the more he longed to mediate. Already on 23rd August Ciano

[47] In Hitler's language the solution of the Eastern Question meant the conquest of the Slavs, at this moment of the Poles.

[48] Ciano's Diary says about 8 p.m. but 6.42 p.m. is the official timing given by the Italian Foreign Office.

had urged upon the British Ambassador that Germany should have Danzig but the rest be settled by a conference, and Mussolini reverted daily to this theme. His message on the evening of 26th August concluded with the words :

" And it is also for this reason that I allow myself to insist afresh—and certainly not on account of considerations of a pacifist character alien to my spirit, but in the interests of our two peoples and our two Régimes—upon the possibility of a political solution which I still think can be attained, such as to give complete moral and material satisfaction to Germany."[49]

The Duce's insistence upon the possibility of a political solution probably enraged Hitler far more than his military defection. It was the night after receiving this message from Mussolini, about half an hour after midnight on the morning of Sunday, 27th August, that Dahlerus[50] was taken to see Hitler and found him in a wild condition. The Führer asked a great many questions about mysterious England. He then worked himself into a state of hysterics about Germany's strength. Dahlerus describes in his book how he screamed that he would build U-boats and aeroplanes :

" The voice became more indistinct and finally one could not follow him at all, then he pulled himself together, raised his voice as though addressing a large audience and shrieked—shrieked " ich werde Flugzeuge bauen, Flugzeuge, Flugzeuge, und ich werde meine Feinde vernichten."[51] Just then he seemed more like a phantom from a storybook than a real person. I stared at him in amazement and turned to see how Göring reacted, but he didn't turn a hair." Then Hitler asked Dahlerus why he had never been able

[49] = " Ed è anche per questo, che mi permetto nuovamente di insistere e non mai in base a considerazioni di carattere pacifista aliene dal mio spirito, ma in base agli interessi dei nostri due popoli e dei nostri due Regimi, sulla opportunità di una soluzione politica che ritengo ancora possibile e tale da dare piena soddisfazione morale e materiale alla Germania."

[50] Dahlerus was a Swede who knew Göring and tried to intervene to prevent the war. His account of his efforts was called *Sista Försöket* (Stockholm, Norstedt, 1945): an English translation called *The Last Attempt* was published in 1948.

[51] " I shall build aeroplanes . . . and destroy my enemies,"

to come to an understanding with the British, and when he was told, because they had no confidence in him, he exclaimed, " Idiots! Have I ever in my life told an untruth?" Henderson had gone to London the day before with one of Hitler's " last offers," including the usual cavalier alliance offer : it becomes clear that the Führer had decided on war independently of what Henderson was to report to him the day after his return, i.e. on Tuesday, the 29th. This was, in so many words, telephoned by Ribbentrop to Mackensen very late on 26th August, just before Macken-sen was to convey to Mussolini another message from the Führer which was probably sent off immediately before the talk with Dahlerus—it reached Rome at 3.40 a.m. on 27th August. It accepted Italy's non-belligerency, and, as Ciano noted in his Diary, asked only for three things : that Italy's decision should be kept secret as long as possible, that Italy would do all she could to bully the Anglo-French by the means already suggested, and that Italy should send industrial and agricultural labour to Germany. The third request was made as if it involved a very great favour; Ribbentrop telephoned twice within ten minutes later that morning[52] to insist upon the other two.

Meanwhile Loraine informed Ciano of the proposals Hen-derson had brought to London. They had meant little enough to Hitler, but it was first-rate diplomacy to tell the Italians at this moment that Hitler was offering Britain an alliance —on conditions—behind their backs. " The matter of the secret negotiations in London has given the Germans a heavy blow in Mussolini's estimation," wrote Ciano. " He says that Hitler acts in this way out of fear of intervention by the Duce, which would succeed in ending the crisis at the last moment, as occurred at Munich last year, and which would increase Mussolini's prestige of which Hitler would be jealous.[53] There was not quite so much in this as Mussolini would have liked, for Hitler had sent for Henderson to make him the offer[54] just before Attolico's visit to Ribbentrop on 25th August when the Duce's message had hinted once

[52] At 8.40 and 8.50 a.m.   [53] Ciano Diary, 27th Aug. 1939.
[54] D.B.F.P. series 3, VII, nos. 283, 284.

more at a political solution. On the evening of the 27th Ribbentrop telephoned to Mackensen again, belittling the offer to London and saying that war was practically certain,[55] it is clear now that this statement was not made merely, as Ribbentrop liked to say at his trial, to keep the Italians up to the mark : a quarrel was picked with Henderson as soon he as returned.

For the following week the situation now arrived at between Italy and Germany matured. On 1 September, when Hitler had irrevocably crossed the Polish frontiers, the Italians extracted a more definite statement from him[56] that he would not need Italian help, a statement which they immediately published in their press and broadcast; it was similar to what Hitler said to the Reichstag on the same day but was never published in Germany. The Italian newspapers as from 1st September seemed to become less anti-Ally; Bocchini had said to Ciano on 30th August that if there should be demonstrations in favour of neutrality the police and carabinieri would join with the public. All this week, from 27th August to 3rd September, Mussolini and Ciano urged Hitler to accept their mediation and a conference, since, as they repeated each time, Germany was in a very strong position and would get at least Danzig for nothing; they suggested, also, that an exchange of populations might be opportune in the German-Polish case. Ciano sounded the British and French and found the French most eager, for one reason because both Gamelin and Darlan seem to have been as scared of an Italian attack as the Italians were scared of them.[57] At one point it was thought that a conference between Germany, Italy, Britain, France, and Poland might open on 5th September. Several times during this week Hitler thanked Mus-

[55] D.G.F.P. series VII, no. 357.

[56] According to Simoni, op. cit., p. 18, Attolico mysteriously coaxed this from a *trasognato* Führer in the absence of Ribbentrop. See D.D.I. series 8, XIII, nos. 529, 563.

[57] Gamelin in his *Servir—les Armées françaises de 1940* (1946) says that he and Darlan emphasized the importance of the " absolute neutrality of Italy," though some well-placed British observers thought the French rather wanted the Italians in the war as opponents whom they had a good chance of beating.

solini almost obsequiously for his offers of mediation, and on 1st September at 13.10 Mackensen delivered two of the Führer's personal letters to the Duce in which he not only thanked him for all his efforts ' and especially for his offers of intervention,' but added that he had hoped not to expose Mussolini to the danger of acting as mediator in circumstances which would make his efforts vain.[58] For he was determined at all costs to avoid mediation[59] and in this same letter referred with ill-concealed satisfaction to the breakdown of negotiations. Certainly he stopped to ask whether the French and British, in requiring the halting of the German Army if they were not to declare war, were presenting ultimata or not, but it can only have been in order that his forces might advance farther into Poland.

Early on 2nd September the Duce, nevertheless, made one last effort to bring about a conference, and dispatched a telegram to Berlin in which he stated that he still had a possibility of bringing the Powers together : he emphasized that it was the attitude of France which justified his attempt and that a mere halt of the German Army might be accepted all round. Early that evening, however, Rome was informed from London that Britain could only fall in with the Italian mediation offer if the Germans withdrew to the frontier, and Daladier took up the same position in addressing the French Chamber. Mussolini has been condemned for misrepresenting the situation in his telegram to Berlin that day, but if he attempted anything at all it was useless to speak of more than a halt to the Führer. Moreover, he knew through his Ambassador in Paris, Guariglia, that Daladier and Bonnet were not the same thing. Indeed he was justified by a call from Guariglia to Ciano in the following night

[58] D.G.F.P. series D, vol. VII, nos. 500, 504, 507, 508. The shorter of the two letters was the equivalent of the message the Italians had published.

[59] I know that this interpretation has been questioned; Kordt (op. cit.), for instance, rejects it, while producing, as it seems to me, evidence in its favour, e.g. that on 30th August Hitler was planning to demand more than Germany's territory in 1914.

to say that Bonnet had asked whether Mussolini could not obtain " a symbolic withdrawal of German forces from Poland."[60]

On 3rd September came Hitler's final and inevitable refusal in a letter which Mackensen delivered to Mussolini at 9.40 a.m. on 4th September. This reply of Hitler's has been quoted a great many times. It exulted in the German successes in Poland. But it also states :

" I further believe that although our paths are now diverging, Destiny will bind us to one another. If National-Socialist Germany were destroyed by the Western democracies, Fascist Italy would also face a difficult future. Personally I have always been convinced of the indivisible future of our two régimes and I know that you, Duce, feel the same thing."[61]

Hitler's letter lashed Mussolini into bellicosity and enthusiasm for the Axis, and, if Mackensen may be trusted, the Duce would not hear of " the paths diverging." Britain's demand for the complete withdrawal of the German Army was outrageous, he said; by insisting upon this she had forced war upon Hitler.[62] " So France will be the aggressor," Ribbentrop had declared triumphantly to Coulondre when he came to declare war, to which the French Ambassador replied that history would be the judge.[63]

When at last the British, and then the French, declaration of war had reached the Führer on 3rd September 1939, that ' crowning mercy ' day, what was the significance of the Axis and what the relations between Hitler and Mussolini? Had they a common future, as Hitler said?

[60] See L. B. Namier, op. cit., and the sources used by him. Also D.D.I. series 8, XIII, nos. 616, 617.

[61] " Ich glaube aber weiter, dass—auch wenn wir jetzt getrennte Wege marschieren—das Schicksal uns doch aneinander binden wird. Sollte das national-sozialistische Deutschland von den westlichen Demokratien zertsört werden, würde auch das faschistiche Italien einer schweren Zukunft entgegengehen. Ich war mir persönlich dieser Verbundenheit der Zukunft unserer beiden Regime stets bewusst, und ich weiss, dass Sie, Duce, genau so denken." D.G.F.P. series D, vol. VII, no. 565.

[62] Mackensen to Ribbentrop (Most Secret), 4 Sept. 1939.

[63] Coulondre to Bonnet, 3rd Sept. 1939.

It was thought in strongly anti-munichois circles in London and Paris[64] that Führer and Duce were playing each other's game all the time, that Mussolini in fact proposed an international conference in order to gain time for Hitler in Poland. There is no evidence hitherto that this was the case. It was a far stranger situation. According to the extreme version by Gisevius, Hitler had said on 22nd August that this time if any mediator intervened " he personally would throw this swine downstairs even if he had to kick him in the stomach in front of the photographers."[65] This mediator had already in 1938 been ' his friend Mussolini,' the one being whom he was willing to recognize as Superman number two and upon whom he counted as against royal and other influences in Italy. (Certainly the Duce always offered him mediation on extraordinarily favourable terms.) It was part of Hitler's madness that his hero and his devil should have come to be the same person. For there is no doubt that at times Hitler's mental condition in the summer of 1939 was one of what in simple language is termed madness. There is no reason to question Dahlerus's account of him just after his Reichstag speech on 1st September, when he screamed that he would fight for one year, for two years, for ten years, and with this " brandished his fist and bent down so that it nearly touched the floor."[66] But with his madness went a crystal-clear lucidity over military detail and other practical facts, and an unshakeable determination to strive after the realization of his dreams.

It has often been argued that Hitler did not really want Italy to march in 1939—this is another aspect of the connivance theme. No doubt there had been Reichswehr scepticism as to the desirability of Italy as an active ally, but by now the Reichswehr in the person of Keitel and Jodl had become so subservient to the Führer that traditional doubts of this kind did not carry weight. It is clear from the records of the German Navy that they had counted on Italy; the Navy was Germany's weakest spot and Italy's strongest, and Raeder was in particular need of Italian

[64] See *Carnets secrets de Jean Zay.*
[65] Gisevius, op. cit., vol. II, p. 122.
[66] Dahlerus, op. cit. Hitler, incidentally, had peculiarly long arms.

submarines in the fight he planned against Britain; he also wanted the Italian Navy to tie down British ships in the Mediterranean.[67] As for Hitler himself there seem no grounds to question that he had set his heart upon the all-round co-operation of Italy if he were not to be allowed to destroy Poland without 'interference.' The Italian Alliance was the thing that had matured out of his 'boyish thought,' his original scheme of things. The British had remained elusive and impenetrable, and up to now he must have felt something similar about the Japanese; neither of them, in his eyes, had produced supermen worthy of his friendship. He toyed with the idea of promoting Stalin to the super-class, but he always knew that his pact with Russia in 1939 meant, exactly like his pact with Poland in 1934, nothing but the postponement of a conflict which he basically desired. Thus his friend Mussolini was his only friend, and he had wished the friendship to have been demonstrated to the world in September 1939 with more than the mere pageantry of September 1937; after all, on 22nd August, ten days after Ciano's visit, he had still seemed sure of Mussolini's unqualified *Bündnistreue*. He consoled himself now with the conviction that it would not be long before he induced Mussolini to march by his side : and it must have been evident to others that if he were soon to be successful in the West his conviction was completely justified.

[67] See views expressed by Raeder 3rd Sept. 1939 and 1 Nov. 1939 in *Führer Conferences on Naval Affairs*, 1939.

Chapter XI

THE AXIS SHAKEN

At 9 a.m. on 3rd September 1939, since Ribbentrop preferred to make himself scarce, Sir Nevile Henderson was obliged to read the British ultimatum preparatory to a state of war between Great Britain and Germany to interpreter Paul Schmidt; the latter took it to the Reichskanzlei where, according to his evidence at Nuremberg on 28th March 1946, " I found Hitler in his office in conference with the Foreign Minister. . . . When I had completed my translation, there was silence at first. . . . For a while Hitler sat in his chair deep in thought and stared rather worriedly into space. Then he broke the silence with . . . ' What are we going to do now?' " This is how the " phony " war began.

In the relations between Hitler and Mussolini the next few months were characterized above all by Hitler's newly found friendship with Stalin. This fortified Mussolini's desire to mediate, a desire which remained strong so long as the Duce was convinced that he was militarily too weak to take part in the war himself. But it was also better to mediate than to be manœuvred into collaboration with those very Bolsheviks against whom he had made such costly efforts in Spain. In the " Cavallero Memorandum " the Duce had spoken of the importance of the fifth-column work there still was to do (the Germans had already done theirs very thoroughly), and he had believed that, if the West allied with Russia, the alliance would prove a boomerang from the point of view of internal morale. Now the boomerang looked like homing in his own direction, and there were, though he did not seem to know it, a number of Communist cells in Italy intact and ready for 1943.

In the " Cavallero Memorandum," also, Mussolini had spoken of a rapid occupation of the Danubian Basin and the Balkans, and it was clear that Roumanian petrol was

uppermost in his mind. In the middle of September the
Russians marched into the east of Poland which soon
brought them to the East European centre of Lwów and
to the frontiers of Hungary; the Balkans vibrated with
the shock. Ciano professed to be concerned above all for
the Polish Catholics thus callously delivered into Bolshevik
hands; Fascist Italy could never associate herself with
such a thing. But more important was the fact that the
new Rome could not ultimately compete with the new
Moscow in the Balkan peninsula; Italy trembled for her
newly won influence there and doubted the validity of Berlin's
polite assurances which were to have guaranteed it. At
that time the Russians were expected hourly in Bessarabia.
The *Popolo d'Italia* pronounced that it was more absurd
than ever for France and Britain to continue the war, since
if it was necessary to fight Germany it was also necessary
to fight Russia. Needless to say, the Italians were kept completely in the dark as to German-Russian plans—Ciano complained that the Germans always wrapped themselves in
mystery when they were preparing some devastating blow[1]
—and Ribbentrop could not find the time to see Attolico
before he left again for Moscow on 27th September to
sign the Fourth Partition of Poland.

On his return on 30th September he managed to telephone to Ciano a good deal more politely than he had for
a long time and to propose an immediate meeting; he and
Hitler always longed to explain themselves copiously *after*
they had taken a decisive step. With surprising docility Ciano
left for Berlin at 6 p.m. the same evening. There were
some three hours of ' conversation,' nearly all Hitlerian
monologue, at the Neue Kanzlei on 1st October. Ciano
had noted on 1st September that the Duce was calm now
that his decision had been made. On 1st October he
found the Führer positively serene after the frenzies of
August; Hitler, if a little tired in appearance, was not
only tranquil but beguiling, and though the Salzburg-Berchtes-
gaden conversations seven weeks before had put an end
to any pro-German sympathy in Ciano, it is clear that he
softened in the radiance of the Führer's charm. Twice in

[1] Ciano Diary, 26th Sept. 1939.

his Minute of this fresh meeting of his with Hitler and
Ribbentrop he referred to the extreme cordiality of Hitler,
who several times stressed his particular friendship for the
person of the Duce, and at one point referred to Italy's
most helpful action. " Tell him all the same that I am
convinced that Italy's absence from the battlefield and a
German defeat would mean the end of Italy's great imperial
aspirations in the Mediterranean." Further, Hitler " several
times emphasized his appreciation of Italy's collaboration,
not however concealing a slight feeling of grievance that
we had not chosen to fight at Germany's side immediately."
When Hitler spoke of the end of Italy's Mediterranean
ambitions, " he seemed to me," Ciano commented, with
a relapse into *naïveté,* " to be inviting Italy to join him in
the war, but I must add that this was done with extreme
delicacy and without exerting the slightest pressure." Both
Hitler, and more particularly Ribbentrop, while playing
this card of the peril lurking behind a German defeat, were
full of " mathematical certainty " of the invincibility of
Germany. The German Army, Hitler said, was chafing to
fight the French whom it regarded as beaten in advance.
" I shall make my Reichstag speech and that will be my
last attempt [at peace with the West], but I tell you that
if Italy were disposed to march with me at once I would
not even make this speech, but would at once have recourse
to force, in the certainty that Italy and Germany together
can smash France and England in no time and settle their
accounts with those two countries once and for all." Tell
the Duce, Hitler went on, that he need not be afraid to be
without A.A. batteries for the enemy is too greatly scared
of our reprisals to dare to bomb us. Though Ciano wavered
before so much seduction, the Duce, when he read Ciano's
report, was too jealous, as it seems, to respond to these
enchantments.[2]

As for the political situation, Germany had now, Ciano
was told, fixed zones of influence with Russia just as
she had previously fixed them with Italy. Hitler repeated
that he considered that Italy should become the absolute

[2] Ibid., 3rd Oct. 1939.

master of the Mediterranean with "dominant interests in all the countries of the Balkan peninsula which touched the Mediterranean or the Adriatic." With regard to the future of Poland, in which the Italians expressed interest, Hitler indicated that eight to ten million Poles would probably be allowed to live in a state of subjection to Germany about equivalent to the condition of the Czechs. Ciano asked whether the future Poland was to be a sovereign state; he received no clear answer, but it was clear that it was not. He noticed that, whereas in August Hitler had spoken of twenty million Poles in all, these were now reduced to a mere fourteen to fifteen millions. Hitler was, he said, studying various population transfers and would probably find space in former Polish territory for "the Germans of the Dolomites," as it pleased him to call the South Tyrolese.[3]

Ciano and Attolico had already been at work upon the grouping of the neutral Powers in a League over which Italy was to preside; the league was ostensibly to have economic aims. The Italians seemed to wish simply to make use of Italy's non-belligerency in order to increase her influence. At Berlin on 1st October Hitler expressed his satisfaction over the project because Franco-British propaganda was gaining ground among the neutrals and he appealed to Italy to counteract this.[3] Before Ciano left Ribbentrop expressed a desire for a meeting of the two Chiefs at the Brenner at the next practicable opportunity. The sudden violence of Ribbentrop's enthusiasm for Communist Russia Ciano could only describe as sinister and bewildering. This helped him, perhaps, to recover his equilibrium on returning to Rome.

Meanwhile Mussolini was in a chaotic state of mind. Every time a foreign newspaper suggested that Italy was repeating her behaviour in the last World War, he nearly threw all caution to the wind to join Hitler after all. He was deeply envious of the German successes in Poland in September, and for this reason he discounted Hitler's mathe-

[3] Ciano Minute, 1st Oct. 1939 and D.G.F.P. series D, vol. VIII, no. 176.

matical certainty and accepted Italian military intelligence to the effect that France and Britain were strong and tenacious. He was flattered by Hitler's Danzig speech (19th September) when the Führer declared that the war was due to the British refusal of Mussolini's offer of mediation.

In spite of the information his intelligence people supplied, the Duce persuaded himself to share Hitler's professed belief that the West could be induced to make peace once Poland was liquidated. Hitler expressed this view to Raeder on 7th September, though on 23rd September he seemed a good deal less certain.[4] On 6th October he called a special session of the Reichstag and announced before it that Germany's *Lebensraum,* now recognized, must be secured and her former colonies restored, and provided that these conditions were accepted " the great nations must come together and hammer out and guarantee a comprehensive agreement which will give to all a feeling of security and quiet and peace." Mussolini was so foolish as to think his opportunity had come, but Ciano noted that only two voices had been raised in Britain in favour of negotiation with Hitler; they were the voices of two very old men called David Lloyd George and George Bernard Shaw.

Hitler's peace offers were never made very seriously, and in October 1939 the Führer was probably as glad as the Duce was sorry that no *Schweinhund*—this time either— would be able to mediate. His statements to Raeder in September could be interpreted equally well as aimed at dividing France from Great Britain, one of his major objectives which was crowned with only too great success. The Reichstag speech was made primarily as a sop to German opinion. Every witness of the Berliners' reaction to the outbreak of war has confirmed the dismay of the German capital. In spite of gaudy triumphs in Poland, in Germany it was an autumn of remarkable gloom.[5] An Italian diplomat in Berlin wrote in his diary on 23rd November, " I believe that in future years, and above all if Germany should win this war, no one will be able to realize the appalling demoralization which prevailed in

---

[4] *Führer Conferences on Naval Affairs,* 1939.

[5] See Hassell, op. cit., among many other accounts.

THE AXIS SHAKEN

the Reich in these months."[6] In his Minute on the conversations of 1st October Ciano began by saying that his
arrival was interpreted as another Italian effort to procure
peace and, coinciding with the suspension of the black-
out and of the ban on dancing which followed the end
of hostilities in Poland, was greeted with extraordinary enthusiasm. Analyses of German *Stimmung* were always over-
weighted by evidence from Berlin, whose population was
the most sober in Germany; nevertheless, it seems to have
been true that the country as a whole was filled with
forebodings of ill. In 1914, people whispered, we began
with triumphs too, and where did we end in 1918? Hitler's
Reichstag speech on 6th October was intended to prove
to his public that there was no other course possible but
the one he pursued. The alleged attempt on his life at Munich a month later seems to have done nothing to make the
Führer's war more popular, and was in itself treated with
scepticism; according to Gisevius, who claims to have seen
the police reports, it was the work of a genuinely Communist workman, but it was characteristic that the public attributed it either to the Gestapo or to malcontent S.A. people.[7]

An important element in the gloom of Germany was
the feeling of being alone against the world again; this
mingled with a sense of guilt over the appalling behaviour of
the S.S. in Poland, news of which was very soon whispered
around. In varying degrees people felt, "We deserve to
be alone." (Thus the optimistic assumptions of British propagandists were perhaps more justified at this time than in any
later period of the war.) The feeling of loneliness caused
bitter resentment against Italy; it was in Germany more
than in Allied or neutral countries that people spoke of
Italy's treachery "again." Attolico, not very wisely perhaps,
gave an insistent Duce a long account of this state of
things as early as 7th September,[8] and German bitterness
against Italy probably increased when from the middle of
October it became certain that the war would continue. It
is not without significance that at the beginning of the

[6] Simoni, op. cit. Simoni's real name was Lanza—he was Italian
First Secretary in Berlin.
[7] Gisevius, op. cit.   [8] D.D.I. series IX, vol. 1, nos. 80, 81.

war, Göring, who liked to interpret the national mood, had told Magistrati that Italy's neutrality really suited Germany better than Italian participation. At the end of October, however, Göring appears to have twitted Teucci, the Italian Air Attaché in Berlin, with the Ribbentrop thesis that Italy's 'ratting' on 25th August had caused the Polish Treaty to be signed on the same day. On 2nd November Ribbentrop himself made this reproach to Attolico. On 8th November, therefore, Ciano sent a strong refutation to Attolico, pointing out, among other things, that on the night of 31st August the British authorities cut off telephonic and telegraphic communications with Italy as much as with Germany. No one better than Ribbentrop, wrote Ciano, knew Italy's reasons, which were all clearly recorded though the relevant documents had not been published. On 12th November Magistrati called on Göring and soon took up the argument, suggesting that the " Cavallero Memorandum " had surely made Italy's position only too clear. Göring replied with his customary smartness that Germany had not known what to make of it, since a month or so before the Italians were talking of fighting France alone.[9] When he felt tired of the long argument which followed, Göring remarked that it was all ancient history now. At present, he said, 10 per cent. of the Germans are entirely sceptical towards Italy, 10 per cent. are doubtful, and the remaining 80 per cent. are quite content with Italy's behaviour, convinced that it is in accordance with an understanding between the Duce and the Führer; 40, 40, and 20 per cent. would have been nearer to the truth, but Göring liked to be affable. Since the Steel Pact he had been sulking over Italy and the Order which Ribbentrop had figuratively snatched from him, but for the moment he allowed Magistrati to mollify him.[10] A week or so later at a public

[9] Simoni, op. cit.—entry on 13th Nov. 1939, and see also chapter IX, p. 137, above.

[10] Three months later, however, he returned to the charge with the same arguments; this time he referred to Italy's economic weakness as the explanation of a letter to Attolico on 24th Feb. 1940 insisting again that the reasons for Italy's non-belligerency had been purely military.

banquet at Dresden, at which the Italian consul was present, the Gauleiter of Saxony, Mutschmann, proclaimed aloud that Germany should beware rather of treacherous friends than of her enemies. This was important because Mutschmann was an old S.S. stalwart, the type of Party man who had hitherto backed the Führer's Italophile policy against the natural prejudices of the Germans. Mackensen tried to explain the speech away by saying the Gauleiter was probably drunk, to which Ciano might well have rejoined *in vino veritas*.

It was the question of the South Tyrol which particularly and increasingly exacerbated feelings between Germany and Italy during the autumn of 1939. The South Tyrolese seemed to become more and more Nazi, and, when it came to the opting in December, the Germans who were concerned deliberately worked to bring about a demonstrative pro-German plebiscite since Himmler was planning a systematic re-settlement in conquered territory—at this stage there seems to have been no restraining influence from on high. People like Ciano and Attolico said : " *Tant mieux,* let us be rid of them all." But the pro-German South Tyrolese were not obliged to leave before the end of three years, and in any case the Nazi talk now was that if they left they would soon be back, since Germany would certainly annex the South Tyrol at the end of the war.[11] Hitler's declarations to the contrary had, not illogically, ceased to carry any weight. Ciano seems to have been more often exasperated over this matter than any other, and it is difficult not to sympathize with him. After all, Hitler on 12th August had justified war against Poland on the grounds that the evacuation of the South Tyrol had strained his prestige to its utmost limit, and yet a month later the Germans suggested the postponement of the exodus until the end of the war.[12] On 11th October Ciano told Mackensen that the Italians could not excuse the delays, " all the less since—under Russian pressure—the Germans had expelled eighty thousand men from the Baltic States in a few hours."[13] Over the

[11] Simoni, op. cit., 12th Dec. 1939.
[12] Ciano Diary, 12th Sept. 1939.   [13] Ibid., 11th Oct. 1939.

South Tyrol at least Mussolini and Italian public opinion were at one, and Ciano lamented the lack of Franco-British propaganda on this subject about which its effects might, he thought, have been really inflammatory.

The climax was reached with the Pfitzner revelation just before Christmas. Professor Pfitzner had been a professor of history at the German University in Prague, although he was young, for a number of years, and as such he had been recognized as one of the leading Sudeten German "intellectuals"; he was in fact everything that this designation could imply. When the Germans seized Prague they made him its vice-mayor. In the middle of December he delivered one of his customary addresses before what he presumed to be a loyal German audience, and he proclaimed that Greater Germany would require, not a mere South Tyrol and Trieste,[14] but the whole valley of the Po. Ciano's evidence for the incident, coming via Muti,[15] might have caused one to doubt, but everything combined to justify that young hero in this case. Pfitzner, like other Sudeten German professors, had always talked in this manner, and the seizure of Bohemia and the destruction of Poland had naturally fired his imagination. Attolico seems to have got hold of independent confirmation of the statement in question, and the anxiety of Mackensen suggested that, however much he denied it, it was true.

Just as in other days Ciano had been concerned to discover enthusiasm for the Axis in Germany or Italy, since Salzburg he wanted to find depression in the Reich and anti-German feeling in Italy. But all other witnesses in this case bear him out. Except for a small minority of the Fascist *gerarchi* such as Farinacci and Alfieri, the Italians were anti-German from top to bottom, and it is significant that Interlandi's anti-Semitic paper *Il Tevere*[16] was called the "Rhinegold" in Rome. In some cases Italians were anti-German only because they feared that Germany would drag them into

[14] Songs about getting back Trieste were current in Vienna, as the Italians knew.

[15] A young and foolish Fascist who succeeded Starace as Secretary of the Fascist Party.

[16] Ciano Diary, 13th Sept. 1939. See above, p. 111.

war, in others out of profound objection to National-Social-
ism, but in most cases out of simple humanity : the ordinary
people in Italy were quick to know that Hitler's Germany
was an engine of cruelty, though they could not at first
have conceived to how great an extent. They hated going
to Germany to work, but it was from many of those who
had to go that stories of horrible brutality, in some cases
experienced at first hand, trickled back to Italy.

It was a remarkable thing that though Gayda announced
the death of Poland as early as Hitler could have wished,
recognition was not withdrawn by the Palazzo Chigi from
the Polish Embassy in Rome. On 15th November Simoni
noted that the Italian Embassy in Berlin was becoming a
sort of Ministry for the territories occupied by the Germans.
. . . " Above all the poor Poles give us a great deal of work,
but I believe that no bureaucratic efforts were ever made with
so much goodwill and sincere warmth of feeling. From
Rome we are ordered to grant as many entry permits as
possible with the greatest liberality to Poles and Jews."
At one moment the Italian officials in Berlin thought they
might be going too far, but, on inquiring from Rome, they
were told to go straight ahead. On 18th November Ciano
noted that the troops on the French frontier were fraterniz-
ing, while everything was inflaming Italian hatred of the
Germans whose Military Attaché, Rintelen[17]—to take a single
example—had been addressing Italian officers as if he were
inspecting them. On 12th December Simoni noted an instance
that had come to the notice of his Embassy : at the
moment of the outbreak of war five officers of the Fascist
militia were on a visit to a German police unit. On 1st
September they were put into S.S. uniform and forced to
serve on the Siegfried Line. The affair had, however,
as Simoni wrote,
" a useful aspect in so far as these five will return to
their country completely *orientati* about the Germans and they
will certainly not be good propagandists for the Axis. . . .
They are, among other things, terrified by the mentality
and behaviour of the S.S. whom, however, they only saw at
work in a purely German area."

[17] Not to be confused with the Styrian Rintelen, see chapter II.

In the Fascist Party, as in keenly Catholic circles in Italy, Hitler's pacts with Russia had done most to make him unpopular, and when, on 30th November, Russia attacked Finland, Italian indignation became extreme. Since anti-Russian demonstrations were allowed there were a great many of them, but Ciano believed that the participators would have been better pleased to demonstrate against Germany.

Ciano was compelled to observe that Mussolini himself was as often exasperated by the Allied blockade. Nevertheless, after a promising intrigue against Ciano, a number of his friends were promoted when the Duce reshaped his Cabinet at the end of October. The rumours of an immediate German attack in the West riled Mussolini, for he was terrified of its success. In November, if Ciano is to be believed, the Duce instructed the Italian consul in Prague to advise the Czechs to call themselves Communists in order to make things difficult between Moscow and Berlin. On 4th December Ciano wrote in his Diary:

" I have shown the Duce a report from an Italian—Grand Uff. Volpato—the only foreigner to have been in Posen so far. He describes, with a simplicity which increases the horror of the facts, exactly what the Germans are doing : atrocities without name and without reason. The Duce him-self was indignant : he advised me to convey the information in this report round the necessary corners to the French and American press. The world must know."

At this moment Ley, after an interview in Venice with his opposite number, Cianetti, rushed to Rome to express the Führer's thoughts to the Duce. From the amount of comprehension he was charged to convey to Italy from Hitler and " all authoritative German circles,"[18] though not Ribbentrop, there must have been real anxiety in Berlin about Italy's insubordination. At naval conferences on 10th November, and especially on 22nd November, Hitler was thinking in terms of Italy's soon joining him, but on 23rd and 25th November he emphasized that only " the Duce and his Fascists " were in favour of this : on 23rd

[18] Ciano Minute of his conversation with Ley, 5th Dec. 1939.

November Hitler specifically stated "Italy will not attack until Germany has taken the offensive against France."[19] Of all the Nazi leaders Ley was the most disastrous envoy it was possible to send; his notorious drunkenness, which might be regarded as good fun in northern and Slavonic countries, was considered as merely disgusting among Latin peoples.

It was on 5th December that Ley was in Rome. He had obviously been instructed to put the Italians right about the Russo-Finnish war. So he explained laboriously how the Nordic countries, including Finland (alas for Rosenberg), had always shown an ideological aversion towards Italy and Germany—it was the Swede, Sandler, who had proposed sanctions against Italy. Russia, on the other hand, was a harmless giant who could easily be pushed back into Asia when the time came; until England was beaten the harmless giant must be humoured. Russian influence in countries like Bulgaria need not be feared because "the Germans can easily tame Slavs everywhere."[20] This being the case Ciano was unable to get any satisfaction from Ley with regard to the restoration of some kind of Polish national state, a theme to which the Fascist Government recurred until its fall; there was, in fact, no more frequent divergence between Fascists and Nazis than over this kind of theme. But it did become plain to the Italian Foreign Minister that Germany was preparing to attack Britain through an invasion of Holland. In fact Ley gave enough away for his visit to have been worth while from the Italian point of view; in so far as he answered the questions put to him it was obvious that he echoed Hitler mechanically, and this compensated for the growing taciturnity encountered in Berlin by Attolico, who, like Ciano himself, was by now darkly suspect to Ribbentrop. As the Fascist Grand Council had been convened for 7th December Ciano

[19] D.G.F.P. series D, VIII, no. 384; on 23rd Nov. Hitler addressed his commanders-in-chief rather as he had on 23rd May. On 25th Nov. there was a further naval conference.

[20] Ciano Minute, 5th Dec. 1939. cf. D.G.F.P. series D, vol. VIII, no. 436 which shows that Ley, while disregarding Ribbentrop, had been briefed by Hitler.

had written to Attolico on 24th November[21] to ask the old question " What does Germany intend now?", but Ley's visit on 5th December was in the nick of time. Ciano read to the Council all his documents relevant to the Axis and felt satisfied that Italian indiscretion would prevail and the knowledge be diffused over the country.

All through the autumn Mussolini, tormented by the humiliation imposed upon him as the un-dynamic dictator, and afflicted by ills[22] which accentuated his instability, had been seeking before everything self-justification. Already towards the end of October he had decided not only that that rarely assembled body, the Grand Council, should be convened but also that Ciano should vindicate his Duce's foreign policy before the Chamber of Corporations and the world. The speech for this purpose seems to have been written entirely by Ciano but approved by his father-in-law without alteration; its underlying theme was "not we the traitors. . . ." At 9 a.m. on Saturday, 16th December, with Grandi presiding at Montecitorio and in the presence of the Duce, Ciano delivered his oration for the space of nearly two hours. The trappings were conventionally Fascist—Italy had but one heart, one faith, one will, that of her Duce—and the tone of the speech was before everything anti-Communist. He described the Axis as an integral part of anti-Comintern policy, originally operative in Spain, and then disclosed how Germany had made her pact with Russia on 23rd August after informing Italy only on the night of the 21st. He recorded his meeting with Ribbentrop in Milan in the previous May and stated clearly that while Italy had estimated that the Axis could not face the risk of war until 1942, Germany had preferred to allow four to five years to complete the necessary military preparations. He read aloud the communiqué which he had proposed in vain at Salzburg, where he first learnt of Germany's decision to take military steps against Poland instead of attempting a political solution. He referred to the Duce's peace efforts on 31st August and insisted

[21] D.D.I., Ninth series, vol. II, no. 315.
[22] See Ciano Diary, especially 27 Dec. 1939.

that until 1st September only Germany knew that Italy
was not to fight.

Though the Allies were reproached with a number of
things and Britain blamed for killing last-minute hopes of
mediation, the speech was a piece of audacity towards
Hitler. It was hailed in Italy as a denunciation of the
Steel Pact and the 'funeral march of the Axis,' and for
a time Ciano persuaded himself that he had cut the bonds
that bound Mussolini to Hitler. On 19th December the
Italian Press received instructions in future to report all
warlike operations impartially.[23] The Italians breathed again;
they also felt great satisfaction over the exchange of visits
between the Pope and the King before and after Christmas;
the Pope, particularly, was regarded as an anti-Nazi stalwart,
and that the Vatican and Quirinal should ostentatiously draw
together at this moment was felt to be damaging to Hitler.

The climax was reached not on 16th December but early
in the New Year, 1940, when Mussolini brought himself to
the point of writing a long personal letter to Hitler. This
began by stating that Ciano's speech " from the first to the
last word " expressed nothing but the Duce's own views :
he then referred to Ciano as one of the most convinced
champions of Italo-German friendship. Mussolini went on
to say that the German-Russian *entente* had damaged Germany
and Italy in Spain to the Western Allies' advantage. Though,
as he pointed out, Ciano's speech had not mentioned Finland,
the Duce described the strong sympathy felt in Italy for
this small but brave nation.

While trying to deny the existence of sympathies for
Britain in Italy Mussolini complained to Hitler that British
propaganda (he admitted that the B.B.C. was listened to
by the Italians) was making successful play of Germany's pact
with Communism and of the treatment of the Poles; therefore he urged the creation of a Polish national state under
the aegis of Germany. He was, he said, profoundly convinced that Britain and France could never bring Hitler's
Germany helped by Italy to capitulate, but might it not
cost too much to beat the Allies to their knees?

[23] Simoni, op. cit.

" Is it worth while, now that you have secured your eastern frontiers and created the greater Reich with ninety million inhabitants, to risk everything—including the régime—and to sacrifice the flower of Germany's youth in order to hasten the falling of an over-ripe fruit which should in any case fall to us, the representatives of the new forces of Europe? (The great democracies bear within themselves the seeds of their inevitable decay.)"

Politically, Mussolini continued, he understood that " since Ribbentrop's forecast that Britain and France would not intervene was mistaken, you avoided a second front" by making terms with Russia. "But I who was born a revolutionary *and have never changed my revolutionary mentality must tell you* that you cannot permanently sacrifice the principles of *your* Revolution to the tactical exigencies of a certain political moment. . . . The solution of your *Lebensraum* problem is in Russia alone. . . ."

This astonishing manifestation had been brought to maturity by the multiplication of the signs of a German offensive to be launched against the West around the date of 20th January. The letter had certain weaknesses such as its equivocal reference to the Balkan block idea which Mussolini now disowned. The manuscript of this letter shows the alterations made by the Duce in his original text; they illuminate the workings of his mind but do not reveal radical changes.[24] The letter went off to Berlin on 5th January 1940, and was delivered into Hitler's hands by Attolico on the afternoon of 8th January. This was the zenith of the liberation of Mussolini's spirit from that of Hitler; in this fashion he could say his say uninterrupted by the endless monologues of the Führer. But the effort to assert himself proved to be too great for Mussolini; he succumbed very shortly afterwards to what was perhaps an inevitable reaction, rather as if he had tried to force himself to take a cold bath, then, shivering, had turned on the hot tap further and further.

---

[24] The original draft of the last sentence above ran as follows: " But I, who was born and shall die a revolutionary, must tell you that you cannot permanently sacrifice the principles of *our* Revolution to the tactical exigencies of a certain moment."

Chapter XII

THE MISSION OF SUMNER WELLES

In spite of the Duce's unsteady performance as Pollux to his own Castor the Führer had confidence in his power over Mussolini. Apart from his thin-skinned vanity and not unjustified sense of common interest with Hitler, Mussolini was kept in a state of irritation by the British blockade which reminded him incessantly that the Mediterranean was not yet an Italian lake. The German coal upon which Italy so much depended originally came by sea, via Rotterdam. On 27th November 1939 Britain declared German exports as well as imports to be contraband, though it was not until 1st March 1940 that British ships actually stopped German coal bound for Italy. Hitler knew very well that the Allies' blockade would do a good deal to bring Mussolini into the war on his side. On 22nd November at a Führer Conference on Naval Affairs it was stated that " Italy will be asked for submarines once more as soon as her attitude is clarified. It seems to be crystallizing by degrees, as witnessed by the note to Britain concerning the molesting of Italian ships." Ciano noted as early as 27th September that Mussolini was in favour of acceding to all German requests for naval assistance, but he claimed that he and Admiral Cavagnari had been able to sabotage the whole idea. This was not quite true, and there was a certain exchange of intelligence all the time. The Germans had marvellously arbitrary ways of impressing Italians into their ranks, as witness the affair of the five militia officers. At a Naval Conference on 8th December, Hitler advised " somewhat delaying the embarkation of Italian officers aboard submarines, but he [Hitler] has no fundamental objection."[1]

Three days after this Ley arrived back in Berlin from Italy. According to the information received by the Italian Embassy[2] he went straight from the Anhalterbahnhof to

[1] *Führer Conferences on Naval Affairs*, 1939.
[2] Simoni, 11th Dec. 1939.

a two hours' interview with Hitler in the morning and was with him again in the afternoon; Ribbentrop was not present. Ley complained of an icy impression in Italy to start with, though things had improved after he had seen Mussolini. The Leader of the *Arbeitsfront* was not among Hitler's more influential colleagues, but he was the first German Minister to have visited Italy since the outbreak of war. A few days later came Ciano's speech. It was almost entirely suppressed in the German papers, but the official world soon came to know what it had contained. German reactions to it were slow but strong,[3] and Himmler arranged to go to Italy at once to see his agents on the spot, the opting then in progress in the South Tyrol giving him an excellent excuse.

The Germans began to be afraid that it might really be 1915 again, that is, that the Italians would join in on the other side. It has been seen that Raeder wanted Italy as his ally. General Marras, the new Italian Military Attaché in Berlin, now picked up the impression from Reichswehr staff officers that they " would rather see us in the war on their side, even with all our weaknesses—by now well known to them—than have us, as they fear, as enemies."[4] Attolico heard from Hewel, liaison official between the German Foreign Office and the Nazi Party, that Ribbentrop was absolutely enraged : the Foreign Minister considered that Ciano's speech had been positively damaging to the interest of the Reich. The statement, he affirmed, that Italy had required three years' time from May reduced *ad absurdum* her ' potential ' help to Germany, while the fact that Germany had named an even longer period might suggest to the enemy that the Reich also was unprepared and in fact only bluffing.[5] It would not be fantastic to suppose that Ribbentrop was already contemplating a terrible revenge against Ciano.

[3] The Mutschmann and Pfitzner incidents, though they attracted attention at much the same time, had occurred independently of Ciano's speech.

[4] Simoni, 24th Dec. 1939. Marras had been Military Attaché in Berlin before Roatta too.

[5] Idem, 28th Dec. 1939.

Hitler at this time was in fine fettle, quite undaunted. Though the attack on the Low Countries had to be put off several times,[6] he was licking his lips over the prospect. On 20th December he paid his traditional Christmas call on his old friends, the Bruckmanns, and found time to stay an hour and three-quarters; he seemed well, confident, and totally unrepentant when the destruction of Warsaw was mentioned. He signed the Bruckmanns' visitors' book and appended to his signature " In the year of the battle for the setting-up of the great German-Nordic Empire."[7] He was full of plans for titanic reconstruction at this time.

At 3 p.m. on 8th January 1940 Attolico was led into the presence to deliver the Duce's letter; the inevitable Ribbentrop was in attendance. Hitler read the letter " almost with avidity," stopping to agree over a sentence which stressed the necessity for Germany to maintain peace in the Balkans —in August, it may be remembered, Hitler did his best to incite Italy to attack Yugoslavia but his friendship with Russia had reversed this programme too. After reading and re-reading the Duce's words, the Führer said to Ribbentrop, " I must write a letter in reply." Then after some rumination he asked Attolico whether there was really so much sympathy in Italy for Finland, to which Attolico naturally replied that there was. This offended against the geo-political thesis that only the Great Powers should count since only they were strong, and Attolico was treated to the assertion that Russia had not been exorbitant. With the expression of the Führer's faith in victory in 1940 the Ambassador was dismissed; Hitler said he would answer Mussolini in due course.[8]

It was the old story. Just when the choicest dishes were about to be served Hitler found Mussolini asking him to rise and leave the dining-table. The Duce had ended his letter by expressing his wish to be an economic and military, but also a diplomatic, reserve for Germany " in the case of your wishing to arrive at a negotiated solution ". It seems that soon after Attolico had left him the Führer sent for

---

[6] The order for this attack was originally issued on 9th Oct. 1939.

[7] Hassell, op. cit., p. 111. Deutsch-germanisch was the adjective he actually compounded.

[8] D.D.I. series IX, vol. III, no. 550.

Göring, and with Ribbentrop the three of them angrily discussed the Duce's letter for more than five hours. Hitler then withdrew into an Olympian reserve, sending out his captains to face the latest peace offensive. Meanwhile the senior staff of the Wilhelmstrasse read Mussolini's letter with secret satisfaction and whispered their approval to one another.

Ribbentrop saw Attolico on 10th January, and Göring saw Attolico on the 12th and Magistrati on the 15th. The Nazi chiefs were intransigent. Their argument was: "Of course *we* don't want war but England forces us to fight because she is determined upon our annihilation." Ribbentrop tried to be diplomatic over Russia, curbing the enthusiasm he had expressed to Ciano in October; now he assured Attolico that Germany had only one ally, Italy, and would never come to an alliance with Russia. Thus January dragged on and Attolico waited in vain for Hitler's answer to Mussolini. There is relatively little direct evidence of the Führer's state of mind at this time except the following: at his conference with Raeder and the others on 26th January it was noted that "the Führer believes that Italy will enter the war only in the event of great German successes and preferably only against France; he sees no great advantage for Germany in Italy's participation in view of the fact that Germany would probably then be burdened with the obligation to make more deliveries to Italy."[9] Many other Germans had said this before now, but never Hitler. For the moment the Führer was content to wait. He instinctively knew that, left in suspense, Mussolini would relapse into flamboyant bellicosity and dependence therefore upon Germany. It was this indeed which Ciano witnessed and Attolico sensed during February. "The delay of the Führer's answer to the Duce's letter exasperates him," Simoni noted of Attolico on 8th February; "he does not know how to explain it, and fears more and more that this silence may precede some evil surprise." On the 19th he wrote, "Attolico feels that he is in process of losing his battle in which the position, and perhaps the fate, of our country is at stake." His failing health seemed to sharpen Attolico's perception.

[9] *Führer's Conferences on Naval Affairs,* 1940.

Hitler knew that the British Navy was to stop the transport of German coal from Germany to Italy as from 1st March, and soon after that he intended to have seductive deeds of his own, not merely words, to offer the Duce—it was on 1st March that he decided upon the plan for the action against Norway. Meanwhile he sent the inevitable Philip of Hesse to Rome to propose, rather vaguely, a personal meeting of the Chiefs at the frontier. Mussolini seemed delighted and told the hideous Prince that he hoped to fight at Hitler's side as soon as Italy could thereby help Germany and not burden her—this interview was on 8th February. At about the same time Mussolini refused to sell arms and munitions to the British, and, with this, put a stop to expanding Italo-British commerce, since the British had made the sale of arms a condition for the resumption of commercial negotiations. Until now non-belligerency had made possible something of a trade-boom in Italy, since orders had been given to drop autarkic principles for the moment and to buy up raw materials and accumulate foreign exchange. The refusal to Britain was the beginning of the economic end. The Duce followed it up by forcing his own representatives to make most unwilling concessions to Clodius in the Italo-German commercial agreement which was concluded on 24th February; even copper, of which Italy was in great need and which was now to be confiscated from private houses and from the churches, was promised to Germany.

Suddenly all eyes were focused on Sumner Welles, and even Attolico's hopes flickered brightly before they died. President Roosevelt's representative was to make an exploratory visit to Europe to see whether there was still a possibility of the re-establishment of peace. More precisely his journey was intended to counteract Germany's pressure upon Italy to join in the war. " Only in Italy," Sumner Welles wrote later, " was it remotely conceivable that the policy of this [the American] Government might have some concrete effect. If by some means the United States could prevent Italy from actually taking part in the war against France and Great Britain, if Hitler could not obtain the active participation of his southern partner in an attack upon France, the outcome of the war might be less certain than it then seemed."[10] So Sumner Welles came to Europe, as it were to fortify Ciano against Hitler and Ribbentrop, and it is not surprising that Berlin reacted frigidly. But for the American envoy to have had any chance of success he should have arrived in Europe two months earlier.

Sumner Welles's admirable account of his visits to the four chief European capitals is available to the English-speaking world. Here it is relevant to pick out one or two of his impressions. He arrived in Rome on 25th February and left for Berlin on 29th February. He found Ciano just as we still find him in his diary—indeed Sumner Welles's testimony is the best confirmation of its authenticity.[11] The difference between the attitudes of Ciano and of Mussolini was patent; the two only coincided in condemning the Western Allies' idea of restoring the independence of Austria and Czechoslovakia. Ciano[12] was alarmed by Mussolini's coldness towards his American visitor (whom he received on 26th February), but Welles himself was more taken aback by the Duce's appearance. " The man I saw before me seemed fifteen years older than his actual age of fifty-six. He was ponderous and static rather than vital. He moved with an elephantine motion; every step appeared an effort. He was heavy for his height, and his face in repose fell in rolls of flesh." Since Sumner Welles shows no tendency whatever towards over-statement his description confirms all that Ciano's Diary indicates about the state of Mussolini's health in the winter 1939-40.

Towards the end of his interview with the Duce, Sumner Welles plunged straight into the theme—so oddly related to the motive of his own journey—of Mussolini's letter to Hitler. " Do you consider it possible at this moment," he asked, " for any successful negotiations to be undertaken between Germany and the Allies for a lasting peace?" " Yes," came the answer, " but I am equally sure that if a

[10] Sumner Welles, *The Time for Decision* (Harpers, 1944), chapter 3, " My Mission to Europe 1940."

[11] Quite apart from Welles's preface to the Diary.

[12] Ciano acted as interpreter His Minute has a differently arranged account of this conversation.

' real ' war breaks out, with its attendant slaughter and devastation, there will be no possibility for a long time to come of any peace negotiations." It should be added that Mussolini spoke to Sumner Welles with great bitterness of Britain, and with great insistence upon the satisfaction of Italy's claims.

Early on 1st March Sumner Welles arrived in Berlin and was received by Ribbentrop at noon. Never can even this man have behaved more intolerably. He who carried on so many of his political conversations in English suddenly found himself unable to understand a single English word. While Mussolini had kept his eyes shut for " a considerable part of the time," Ribbentrop " sat with his arms extended on the sides of his chair and his eyes continuously closed " and held forth for well over two hours. It was all the usual rigmarole about Germany's innocence, covered this time with American icing, for he declared that the Reich only asked for her own Monroe doctrine in Central Europe : the analogy was as false as the whole of Ribbentrop's peroration.

On 3rd March Welles saw Hitler, who seemed in " excellent physical condition," and, as was always the case, expressed much the same as Ribbentrop, but with some flexibility and grace. The *leitmotiv* continued to be " England wishes to destroy us utterly, therefore we have no choice but to strike at her as hard as we can." " I believe," said the Führer, " that German might is such as to make the triumph of Germany inevitable but, if not, we will all go down together, whether that be for better or for worse." And then, the only moment of raucous stridency for the inevitable play-acting of the paranoid, " I did not want this war. It has been forced upon me against my will. It is a waste of my time. My life should have been spent in constructing not in destroying." It should here be noted that, while Mussolini only once referred to the Axis by inference when he said that Italy could not be ranked among the neutrals on account of her special relationship with Germany, neither Hitler nor Ribbentrop mentioned Italy to Sumner Welles. In his speech at Munich on

24th February, Hitler had made much with "To-day Italy is our friend" when he made his routine list of Germany's advantages as compared with the last World War.

Ciano misinterpreted the American's reaction to his talk with Mussolini: Sumner Welles left Rome with the old François-Poncet illusion,[13] dearer still to Mussolini himself, that the Duce and the Duce alone might be able to restrain the Führer. But in Berlin Welles easily grasped the asymmetry of the Axis and the hopelessness of the situation. He made the usual foreign statesman's visit to Karinhall and saw Hess and Schacht and Weizsäcker; the State Secretary finally ventured upon the assertion that "here [i.e. in the German Foreign Office] the relations between Germany and Italy have *narrowed* greatly."

In the long run Sumner Welles's visit probably changed nothing, but it profoundly agitated Hitler and Ribbentrop; powerful competitive influence was being exerted in Rome to reinforce those deplorable Mussolinian tendencies towards peace-making against which Hitler had to contend. He knew that the Allies were exceedingly vulnerable in the immediate future and believed Sumner Welles was simply trying to gain time for them, thus defrauding him of the full glory of the offensive he had planned. When he sent for Schacht to school him for his interview with Sumner Welles, it is interesting that Hitler admitted that from now on time might work against Germany—"Who knows," he added, "where Stalin or Mussolini will stand in a year's time?"[14] So early as 28th February Madame Tabouis— was this through her Russian sources or merely a good guess?—had prophesied an imminent Ribbentrop journey to Rome, and on the 29th the Italian Embassy in Berlin received an irritable letter from Ciano asking why Hitler still did not answer Mussolini. Quite suddenly on Friday, 8th March, Mackensen informed Ciano that Ribbentrop would arrive in Rome on the Sunday, bearer of the long-delayed

[13] This illusion was the cause of François-Poncet's request to be transferred from Berlin to Rome after the Munich Agreement.

[14] Hassell, op. cit., p. 136. Hassell saw Schacht on 8 Mar. Sumner Welles could not mention Schacht in his book, as it came out in 1944 when Schacht was in prison and in danger of his life.

reply; after two months it was now possible to concoct a long letter dated 8th March with, as Hitler might have said, lightning speed. If American diplomacy unwillingly precipitated this letter it helped to re-harness Mussolini to Hitler's chariot.

Hitler's letter, like Mark Antony's funeral oration, was primitive enough, but it was such as most surely to whet Mussolini's appetite, to whip him into an ecstasy of combative zeal. The Führer began with the usual vindication of the German attack upon Poland: Italy, he said, would not have endured five per cent. of the martyrdom supported by Germany at Poland's hands, and he had been compelled to act above all for motives of prestige at home. There followed a gush of enthusiasm for *Italy,* his first but his eternal friend, for the sake of its people, its system, but above all its Chief.

" I fully understood your decision," wrote Hitler, " and have appreciated your support. . . . We can nevertheless have no doubt about one point: the outcome of this war will also decide the future of Italy. If this future is considered in your country in terms of merely perpetuating the existence of a European state of modest pretensions, then I am wrong. But if this future is considered in terms of a guarantee of the existence of the Italian people from a historical, geopolitical, and moral point of view, or according to the rights of your people, those who are fighting Germany to-day will be your enemies too. I know you think the same. I, too, believe that the destinies of our two States, of our two Peoples, of our two revolutions, and of our two régimes are indissolubly linked."

Ribbentrop left Berlin on 9th March with Gaus, Clodius, all their secretaries, and thirty-five other people, including barbers, a doctor, a masseur, a gymnastic teacher, and a ' student ',[15] the size of the ' delegation ' was not unusual but it is worth noting the absurdity of it in time of war. On Sunday, 10th March, Ciano and a crowd, which the *Federale* found difficult enough to assemble,[16] greeted the Nazi Minister very coolly at the station at Rome. There followed a long, long interview with Mussolini during which,

[15] Simoni, 8 Mar. 1940.   [16] Ciano Diary, 10th Mar. 1940.

as Ciano said, "Ribbentrop expands in many words" the points of Hitler's letter after a very poor explanation of its delay. In addition to the common destiny of Italy and Germany, another main theme was that Germany (who of course desired peace) was on the eve of a necessary and breath-taking triumph of which the United States evidently wished to cheat her by loose talk about restoring peace. Ribbentrop dilated considerably over the "enormous responsibility" of America in bringing the war about, producing in evidence documents found by the Germans in the Polish Foreign Office. The Jewish world-plutocracy was at the root of it, of course, to which Mussolini made the interesting rejoinder that it was a matter of the three hundred who rule the world and to whom Rathenau referred long ago.[17]

In his letter Hitler had also vindicated his friendship with Russia along similar lines. Formerly, he claimed, Russia had aimed at the destruction of the non-Jewish peoples, but now, since Litvinoff had been *écarté,* one could work unexceptionably with the nationalistic Russia of Stalin. Ribbentrop, needless to say, let himself go in expanding this point—on his second visit to Russia the members of the Politburo had seemed like old comrades. He also used the occasion to state that the Nazi Party had approved without reserve of the pact with Russia to which Mussolini in his New Year letter had objected because, *inter alia,* it must certainly have distressed many good Nazis. The Reich Foreign Minister also found all kinds of ingenious arguments to justify his own behaviour in the past: now he claimed that he had always known that there would be war between Britain and Germany—indeed, he had reposed his one hope to the contrary in the person of Edward VIII.[18]

When Hitler was drafting his letter the coal-ships had been stopped and the Italian position was consequently critical. He therefore assured Mussolini that he was instructing his people to make Italy independent of coal from the

[17] "Three hundred men, all acquainted with each other, control the economic destiny of the Continent," wrote Rathenau in the *Neue Freie Presse* (Vienna) in 1909 when Mussolini was in Trent.

[18] All this is recorded in the German Minute of 10th Mar. 1940, D.G.F.P. series D, vol. VIII, no. 665. See above, chapter VI, p. 111.

West.[19]   Anyway he believed in principle that men like the Führer and the Duce always find a way of putting an end by economic as well as by military means to anything of the nature of "these democracies' terroristic blockade." This was like an echo of the foolish remarks to which Mussolini had treated Ciano ever since the coal situation had become threatening, though to Ribbentrop he said "No cannons without coal." On 9th March, however, Italy came to terms for the moment with "these democracies" over the blockade and on the 10th Ribbentrop consequently redoubled Germany's offers, explaining that Hitler was convinced that Britain wished to strangle Italy commercially. It was astonishing with what rapidity Clodius now became able to supply not only twelve million tons of German coal per annum, but also all the necessary coal-trucks for their transport by land. This completed the process begun in 1935; from now until Germany's collapse, all Italy's imported coal came from the greater German Reich. It was one aspect of the break with the West already. From this time onwards the Swiss watched coal-trucks streaming, as it seemed, interminably from Basle to Chiasso. As the war years passed strange things came to be hidden under the coal, men of all nationalities pursued by the Gestapo, wondering whether they would be suffocated with coal-dust before they enjoyed the exquisite luxury of reaching neutral Swiss territory.

On 11th March the Duce received Ribbentrop for the second time—it was now his turn to talk. He began by a reference to the visit which Ribbentrop had made earlier that same day to the Pope whose pacific machinations were as distasteful to Hitler as any others. Mussolini went on to refer to some documents claiming to reveal the intrigues of Otto of Habsburg, documents which the Duce had actually handed to his visitor the day before. This trivial attempt to curry favour with the Nazis only deserves mention in view of the past history of the Axis. More immediately relevant was the Duce's fresh request that the telegram Hitler addressed to him on 1st September should be published in Germany—it

[19] At the end of his letter Hitler reverted to the coal question which, he suggested, was particularly infuriating for Mussolini.

never had nor would be.[20] Mussolini then underlined his
recent "No" to the "arbitrary" British demand to buy
arms and munitions from him, and accepted notice given by
the Germans that they were preparing to send submarines to
the Mediterranean. With regard to the major question of
Italy's military participation in the war, the Duce stated that
it would undoubtedly occur—though he did not yet know
exactly when—as a war "parallel" with that waged by Germany; it was essential for Italy to free herself from her imprisonment in the Mediterranean. Mussolini insisted that all
along Italy had been a perfect ally to Germany, supplying her,
for example with large quantities of essential vitamin-C foods.
The second Ribbentrop interview ended with the understanding that Hitler and Mussolini should meet at the Brenner after
19th March.[21]

There was an odd little pendant to this visit of Ribbentrop to Italy. On 13th March the Italian Embassy in
Berlin received a telegram to say that a German school
was to be opened in Trieste[22] This, as far as the available
evidence goes, was an unsolicited gift such as Mussolini
loved to bestow upon Hitler; the persecution of the Jews
had probably been the same thing upon a vaster scale. The
Italians who knew of these superfluous gestures of generosity
found them particularly exasperating.

To Ciano Mussolini seemed less pleased and he kept
saying either that he did not believe in the pre-announced
German offensive in the West or that he wished to see
Hitler in order to continue to dissuade him from it. Ribbentrop's report in Berlin cannot have allayed his master's fears,
for on 13th March the Reich Foreign Minister telephoned
to ask for the Hitler-Mussolini meeting to take place, not
after the 19th, but on the Monday morning, 18th March.

Sumner Welles arrived back in Rome, after visiting
Paris and London, on 16th March, and immediately saw

[20] See above, Chapter X, p. 209. Ciano had complained about this
in his letter to Attolico on 8th Nov., see above, chapter XI.
[21] D.G.F.P. series D, vol. VIII, nos. 669, 670.
[22] Simoni, op. cit.

Ciano and then the Duce. His second and friendlier interview with Mussolini on 16th March is a little difficult to reconstruct, since his account and Ciano's Minute do not coincide. At all events it can be affirmed that Sumner Welles stated that the Western Allies would be ready to negotiate if there were a serious possibility that Hitler would keep his word, but without this there was no basis for any attempt at making peace. Mussolini played up as best he could to the implication that all eyes were fixed on him. He said that he believed the German offensive to be very near and that Europe could not stand a real war. But Germany must be guaranteed her *Lebensraum*; in addition, all Italy's claims and the just claims of Hungary must be considered. According to Sumner Welles he said that a " just political peace " was the indispensable *first point*: according to Ciano he announced that the Four Powers who were assembled at Munich were the only possible guarantors of such a peace and that *his* Four-Power Pact idea should be revived. The Duce asked to be able to communicate Sumner Welles's impressions of London and Paris to Hitler, but when Welles telephoned to Washington for permission Roosevelt refused. As the American rose to leave, Mussolini said to him, " You may wish to remember that, while the German-Italian Pact exists, *I* nevertheless retain complete liberty of action."[23] According to Ciano " At the conclusion of the interview the Duce confirms his political solidarity with Germany."[24]

On the next day, Sunday, 17th March, at 1.30 p.m. Mussolini and Ciano set out for the Brenner. It was snowing there, as it so often is. The Italians arrived first on the Monday morning and Mussolini waited for Hitler with a feeling of " anxious pleasure ": " of late he has reacted more and more to the fascination of the Führer : the causes of this are the military successes, the only successes which Mussolini really appreciates and desires."[25]

Hitler arrived still in good health and temper, as Sumner Welles had found him a fortnight earlier; the signs of fatigue which Ciano noticed in October had left him. It

[23] Sumner Welles, op. cit.   [24] Ciano Minute, 16th Mar. 1940.
[25] Ciano Diary, 18th Mar. 1940.

was the first time he had seen the Duce since Munich. Hitler joined Mussolini in his train on the Italian side of the frontier. Needless to say he talked and talked; Mussolini listened " con simpatia e deferenza," and was able to say little.[26] Apart from the endless repetitions, grotesque abuse of Poland and a great deal of military reminiscence and prognostication, the Führer made full use of his Mark Antony technique. *If* Italy had taken up a strong position in August and had thus induced Britain and France to keep out of the war, that would of course have been opportune, he said. But if they could not have been prevented then it was no doubt better for Italy to have kept clear of the conflict.

" He had not," Hitler said, " come to ask for anything with regard to Italy's attitude, but *simply* to explain the situation and to convey his own expectations with regard to the future development of the war. Then the Duce could . . . make his own decisions. Undoubtedly . . . the defeat of Germany would mean the end of the Italian Empire. . . . He [the Führer] is a realist and would *never* in any way desire the Duce to do anything which conflicted with the interests of the Italian people, for he was not like the English who expected other nations to snatch the chestnuts out of the fire for them."

It was true, Hitler confessed, that in *Mein Kampf* he had said that Germany should ally with England. Yet since England had been determined to fight Germany he had decided for Russia. " This decision matured in him after much thought and will never be changed . . . the Führer is determined always to preserve friendly relations with that country." This was an odd and inconsequent and perhaps daredevil change from the instruction he had obviously given to Ley in December, and a flouting of the Duce's reproofs in his letter of January. It was rather as if Hitler were saying, " So little can you resist me that I shall make you happily eat your own words."

When the Duce had a chance to speak he first of all agreed with everything Hitler had said—his habit of agreeing with his companion of the moment, whatever this involved, was

[26] D.G.F.P. series D, vol. IX, no. I.

growing upon him.[27] He then stated that Italy's entry into
the war at Germany's side was inevitable, it was simply a
matter of choosing the right time. He made one perfectly
sensible reserve, all the stranger since he often shared
Hitler's pose of " We heroes are above mere economics " :
he specifically stated that Italy's finances could not stand a
long war.

Finally, Mussolini referred to his talks with Sumner
Welles.[28] It is not quite clear from the Minute whether, as
Ciano had feared in anticipation, he quoted Sumner Welles's
remarks about the willingness of Britain and France to make
peace as the evidence, but in connexion with the American
visitor he spoke of poor morale in the Allied countries.
As Sumner Welles had been to Berlin before London and
Paris, and in any case would have been far more cautious
in Berlin than in Rome, the implication was of the greatest
interest to Hitler and may even have clinched his decision
to strike soon; he made it clear, however, that owing
to meteorological considerations the German offensive would
not follow immediately.

Sumner Welles had waited in Rome to see Ciano who, on
his return on 19th March, was able to pass on this piece
of information, and to state that no change in Italy's position
had been decided upon. The two agreed that Italy should
remain in contact with the United States, each bearing
in mind the possibility of some joint step in the direction
of peace; Ciano says that they even spoke of the possibility
of a Mussolini-Roosevelt meeting in the Azores. Ciano made
the rash prophecy that Italy would never enter the war while
he was Foreign Minister. Altogether, the extraordinary way
in which he advertised his difference of view from that of
his chief can only be explained by his belief at that time
that Germany would be beaten and that he could then
persuade the Allies to accept him as the Duce's successor.

While Sumner Welles was waiting for Ciano's return
from the Brenner, he saw as many other Italians as possible,

[27] Cf. C. Senise, *Quando ero Capo della Polizia* (Ruffolo, Rome,
1946).
[28] On this occasion it had suited Hitler " loyally " to send Mussolini the records of the German conversations with Sumner Welles.

" both those in official positions and those who played some part in the business and intellectual life of the country. Without a single exception they not only expressed their bitter opposition to Italy's involvement in the war but pled almost hysterically that the President of the United States exercise his influence to prevent that from happening."[29] (To his cousin Blasco d'Ajeta, an important official at the Palazzo Chigi, he himself seems to have spoken with the greatest pessimism of the outlook for Germany.)

The veritable panic in Italy over the prospect of being drawn into the war expressed itself in another way. Not only had Sumner Welles been hailed for the olive-branches he was thought to be bearing with him, but the Italian public so much longed to do so that it succeeded in interpreting the Brenner meeting as part of the peace action which it hoped Sumner Welles had initiated : Rome itself was described as " festive " on 18th March. Simoni found exactly the same thing in Berlin : Mussolini, people said, had certainly persuaded Ribbentrop of the necessity of a compromise peace. Even people in high official positions made this guess, for they still regarded Mussolini as faintly like Hitler's good angel, able to restrain him at least occasionally.[30] The news that Hitler had left for the Brenner inflated these hopes. As for the idea of Italy's joining in the war, the normal Berlin reaction was to say " Mussolini is not such a fool."[31]

Ironically enough all the journeys of Sumner Welles and Ribbentrop and the two dictators were to bring not peace but a sword; it has been seen that if Roosevelt's envoy achieved anything it may have been to make even more certain the German offensive which was to sweep France off her feet and to justify Ribbentrop's boast, when he got to Rome on 10th March, that in a few months' time there would be no British left on the Continent but prisoners of war. Ciano himself was too close to the Duce, saw him too constantly, and heard him change his mind too often, to

[29] Sumner Welles, op. cit.

[30] See Hassell's indication about Weizsäcker and Nostitz; also Hassell on the " man in the street " in Germany, p. 138.

[31] Simoni, 18th Mar. 1940.

be clear as to the way in which the situation was developing. He was now so anxious to keep out of the war that
he exaggerated the value of a little respite and interpreted
the passing ill humour of Mussolini as of permanent significance. How eagerly he recorded on 19th March that
Mussolini was angry because, having meant to say so
much at the Brenner, he had scarcely been allowed to speak!
" To which he is not accustomed as a dictator, or rather
as doyen of the dictators."[32] This was perfectly exact but
it did not count.

In his almost frantic desire to keep out of this war Ciano,
one feels, was beginning to lose his young Fascist ardour for
waging war at all. Not so the Duce. It was splendid if one
could be fêted as the saviour of peace, as in 1938, in order,
however, to prepare for a safer and more magnificent
war later on. While the Italians as a whole—apart from
convinced anti-Fascists like those who had fought for the
Republic in Spain and wished Italy to fight against Hitler
from the beginning—desired above all to keep out of the
war, over one thing Mussolini did not vacillate : all along
he intended to come in on Germany's side at what seemed
to him to be the right moment. This is clear from Ciano's
Diary and from every other indication. The idea of neutrality
repelled him. When his diplomats urged upon him that
Germany's behaviour had freed him from the Steel Pact
obligations he ignored them, for he did not wish to be
freed.[33] And while he kept the Brenner well fortified, he
would never have led Italy into the war against Germany for
many reasons, among them that since his visit to Germany in
1937 he would have been afraid to do so.

In the maturing of Mussolini's state of mind towards
rapid intervention, the visit of Ribbentrop on 10th and 11th
March, bearing Hitler's letter, seems to have had more
influence upon him than any other single event before
Germany's military triumphs in May, and a more decisive
influence than these. That this was the case was felt

[32] Ciano Diary, 19th Mar. 1940.
[33] His remark to Sumner Welles quoted above was most unusual
even for the vacillating Mussolini; it was perhaps a convenient
thing to say to Roosevelt's representative.

by the—in this case hypersensitive—Italian Embassy in Berlin; it is recorded in Simoni's Diary, which is sometimes unreliable with regard to extraneous detail, but which faithfully conveys the Embassy atmosphere and reflects the state of mind of Attolico. The same thing was conveyed to Weizsäcker[34] by Ribbentrop and his retinue upon their triumphant return from Rome. The most impressive witness, however, is Sumner Welles who wrote that on 16th March:

" I found Mussolini looking far better physically than he had when I had seen him two weeks before. He did not seem to be labouring under the physical or mental oppression which had been so obvious during my first conversation with him. . . . He seemed to have thrown off some great weight. Since that time I have often wondered whether during the two weeks which had elapsed since my first visit to Rome, he had not determined to cross the Rubicon, and during Ribbentrop's visit had not decided to force Italy into the war after Germany's all-out offensive commenced."

In this case Hitler, two days later at the Brenner had nothing to do but inspect and approve the work of his Foreign Minister. One might have supposed that Ribbentrop would ruin any delicate situation and that in March 1940 he had thrust himself upon Mussolini so brusquely as to injure the Axis irreparably. The German rulers themselves seemed surprised by the change in Mussolini after 10th March 1940. Yet Hitler must have known that the effect of his letter would be potent after all the uncertainties of the winter; he had felt sure all along that Mussolini would intervene on his side in the end.

[34] See Hassell, p. 139. Donosti, op. cit., also confirms the importance of Ribbentrop's visit to Rome in March 1940.

Chapter XIII

MUSSOLINI DECLARES WAR

The period of Italy's intervention in the war in the summer of Germany's triumph might, one would have thought, have been the one period of the smooth working of the Axis. But there was little but irritation and sabotage on both sides except between the Leaders themselves, and even Mussolini was seldom content. From now on Führer and Duce were to meet more frequently.

A change intended to oil the machinery was brought about in the spring of 1940. For months Philip of Hesse had been urging in Rome that Attolico should be recalled, and in April Mackensen was instructed to complain that he did not contradict hostile rumours.[1] He went so far in conversation with Ciano on 24th April as to ask for Farinacci or Alfieri[2] in Attolico's place. Ciano ruled out Farinacci, but suggested his own *chef de cabinet,* Anfuso.[3] Attolico, who had started life as an ardent anti-Fascist and had then changed rather suddenly,[4] was not the enemy to the Axis depicted by some of his friends. But he was intelligent and competent. His parting words (in English) to a Wilhelmstrasse friend, presumably Kordt himself, are reported as follows : " Everybody wants me to say Italy is strong. I think it more honest and personally stronger to say she is weak. Don't you let Italy enter the war too soon—otherwise you will be sorry about it."[5] It was not until the end of April that the change was officially announced, and it was the middle of May before Alfieri, the Duce's choice, was established as the new Italian Ambassador in Berlin. The

[1] D.G.F.P. series D, vol. IX, no. 164.

[2] Hitherto Minister of ' Popular Culture,' he was succeeded by Pavolini. Like Attolico, Alfieri could speak no German.

[3] D.G.F.P. series D, vol. IX, no. 165. In 1936 and in 1937 Mussolini had asked for Hassell's recall. Anfuso succeeded Alfieri in Berlin in 1943. See below.

[4] F. S. Nitti *Mediterazioni dell'Esilio* (1947).

[5] Kordt, op. cit.

importance of the change was considerable, for it is not too much to say that Alfieri was fatuous and futile and positively servile in his behaviour to the Nazi chiefs. He tried to stage a ludicrously pompous entry into Berlin and was annoyed to find that the wives of his Embassy staff had no uniforms to put on for the occasion. The Germans were willing to put up with nonsense of this kind from Göring but not from a foreigner; as for Alfieri's Embassy colleagues, they despised and deplored him from the start. Alfieri, however, was *persona grata* with Hitler as a Fascist who had taken Germany's side in July 1934 when Mussolini made "the one political mistake of his life."[6]

It should also be noted that Magistrati, whose wife, Ciano's sister Maria, had once upon a time had a lot to do with the decisive Italo-German *rapprochement*,[7] had been transferred from Berlin in February 1940 to become Minister in Sofia; the Germans made it clear that they were glad to see the last of Ciano's brother-in-law and they specifically vetoed his succession to Attolico. The most notoriously and energetically anti-Nazi figure at the Italian Embassy in Berlin was the Press Attaché, Antinori; he was a cousin of Baroness Braun von Stumm[8] who had forbidden him to come to her house. It was miraculous that he should have survived so long, and the arrival of Alfieri sealed his doom, though it was not until the Italian declaration of war that the Nazis insisted upon his immediate recall. And although Ciano's behaviour was sometimes vulgar and servile, it is fair to remember that all these people were transferred to good positions (Attolico became Ambassador to the Holy See,[9] "from the devil to holy water" as he said), just as Ciano made efforts on behalf of Schuschnigg in 1938 and the British Ambassador in Belgium in 1940,[10] efforts which were not likely to improve his stock in Germany.

The whole situation was swiftly reconditioned by the Nazi triumphs in Scandinavia in April and then in May in the Low Countries and France; it was against this

[6] *Hitler's Table Talk* (1953), pp. 416-417.
[7] See chapter III, above; she died in Oct. 1939.
[8] See chapter III, above.   [9] Attolico died in 1942.
[10] Simoni, 10th June 1940.

tempestuous and terrific background that the drama developed. Towards the end of May Simoni made an analysis of German opinion with regard to Italy's intervention; other witnesses bear him out. The typical Party view shared by a large number of officers was now angrily opposed to Italy's participation in the war. Germany had won without Italy's help, but in this way Italy would lay claims to gains which she had done nothing to deserve. More politically experienced people, among them diplomats and businessmen, were, according to Simoni, aware that the war was by no means over and felt that Italy's intervention was a trump to be played later at a time when the German population might have been discouraged. Others, and he thought the most intelligent, were strongly in favour of immediate Italian intervention, since later developments might cool Fascist ardour. It was not generally realized in Germany how ill prepared Italy still was, Italian bluff being clever and fairly successful.

In spite of Hitler's reckless promises and commands for deliveries to Italy, it was habitual during the winter of 1939-40 for all the essential military supplies earmarked for Italy to be requisitioned at the last moment for the Reichswehr. It is possible that Göring was partly responsible for this. It has been recorded that his attitude towards Italy had been unfriendly and reproachful since the signature of the Steel Pact; his mentality was so grotesquely childish that it is not as fantastic as it sounds to attribute his spleen to that Collar of the Annunziata which had gone to Ribbentrop. After the meeting of Hitler and Mussolini on 18th March Göring appeared to facilitate certain deliveries to Italy, and in the end, much against the King of Italy's will, the first birthday of the Italo-German Military Alliance brought Göring his reward. The Italians complained that they observed the Clodius agreements while the Germans still kept much that was promised to Italy for themselves.[11] Certainly the improvement in Italy's equipment during the period of her non-belligerency seems to have been slight.

There is no doubt that in the Fascist Party and in all jingo and *exalté* Italian circles Hitler's dazzling military

[11] Simoni, 21st Apr. 1940.

successes, and the helplessness of the French and British in the face of them, created a keen desire to plunge blindly into war; it cannot be said that the Germans became more popular in Italy, but the German alliance certainly did. Until the spring of 1940 scarcely any Fascist leader, except Farinacci and Alfieri, was pro-German; now the Mutis and Riccis[12] and the Buffarini-Guidis[13] were all enthusiasm at least for intervention. There was much talk of the dismissal of Ciano. On 10th May his wife, the fiery Edda, the daughter to whom Mussolini was said to listen, went to the Palazzo Venezia to insist to her father that the country longed for war and would be dishonoured if it remained neutral. Grandi, who had returned from London, as the Duce complained, in far too anglicized a condition, held out against the seductions of the time until about 20th May; then he, too, decided that one must adapt oneself to the new period.[14]

There was another element in the situation. For many years many Germans had felt an unshakable affection for England, like that of an admiring youth for an elder and more successful brother who seems indifferent to him. In spite of all Goebbels' efforts, the last war, so long as it lasted, did little to weaken this love. A similar type of Italian felt an almost possessive attachment to France, perhaps more like that of a despised elder brother. He felt that however much Mussolini pretended about Rome, Paris was the true capital of the civilized, which meant more particularly the Latin, world. The collapse of France before what these Italians had always regarded as the savage German hordes was like the collapse, all over again, of the Roman Empire. As each day in May 1940 passed, intervention became a more dastardly thing. Even chauvinist Italians often had some of these feelings towards France, while Britain was something farther away from them. As for the politically conscious anti-Fascists, they had the one consolation that Italy

[12] Renato Ricci had been at the head of the Fascist Youth Organisations since 1925 and became Minister of Corporations in Nov. 1939.

[13] Buffarini-Guidi became Under-Secretary for the Interior in Feb. 1943: he was a friend of the Petacci family.

[14] Ciano Diary, 20th May 1940.

was so ill prepared for war that even in alliance with Germany the Fascist régime was risking its survival. The 'stab in the back of France' was certainly no worse morally than Germany's far more ruthless destruction of all her small-nation victims, Czechs, Norwegians, Dutch, Belgians— there were more Poles but they were equally helpless— and yet how much more guilty the Italians felt and how strongly they made the world feel their sense of guilt!

An interesting side-light was thrown on Italian opinion in the spring of 1940 by the popularity of the *Osservatore Romano,* which pursued a strongly anti-interventionist policy and in which on 10th April Professor Gonella clearly censured the German invasion of Denmark and Norway. The circulation of the one Italian newspaper which was able to condemn German policy and action increased sensationally. Mussolini objected, but the Pope at first refused to give way, and when the *Osservatore* published the Papal condemnation of the German invasion of Holland and Belgium its circulation beat all records. Thereupon the Fascist Party was mobilized and those who distributed or bought the *Osservatore* were often beaten up very nastily in the next few days, so that Pius XII decided to give way, and after 16th May no political news was published in the organ of the Vatican; as a result its circulation melted away.[15]

For Ciano the Germans continued to be the most exasperating allies. Hitler and Ribbentrop had a not unjustified fear of Italian indiscretions; certainly if in defiance of the consultation clause in the Steel Pact they had treated Italy to *faits accomplis* before the outbreak of war, they were not likely to change now. At the beginning of April 1940 the Germans focused attention upon Roumania and suggested to the Hungarians that the Russians were eyeing Bessarabia more actively and that they, the Germans, might need to march across Hungary to occupy the rest of Roumania. Teleki sent a messenger to consult with Rome about this. The news, not unexpected, was nevertheless particularly agitating for Italy from every point of view. Since the Russian pact the Germans had vetoed the slightest modifica-

[15] See C. Cianferra, *The Vatican and the War* (Dutton, 1945). Mr. Cianferra was well informed about Vatican policy.

tion of the Balkan *status quo,* though it had always been
agreed before that Italy should take what she wanted from
Yugoslavia[16] and it had long been evident that she hoped
to win the race to Ploesti. Indeed the Italian Embassy in
Berlin was tired of enquiries from Rome as to Germany's
intentions towards Roumania.

At 2 a.m. on 9th April a message arrived at Ciano's house
from Mackensen asking to see Mussolini at 7 a.m. This
was to inform him of a German occupation, not of Roumania,
but of Denmark and Norway—" the usual letter in the usual
style to announce a coup which has already taken place."[17]
Göring told Renzetti[18] at the end of April that the Duce
would be given at least a fortnight's warning before the
German offensive in the West. But on 10th May Mackensen
was even more exasperating than the time before, for Ciano
was actually his guest to dinner on the 9th. When the
Italian left the Mackensens half an hour after midnight his
host murmured to him that he might have to disturb him
during the night with a message he was expecting from
Berlin. Surely enough at 4 a.m. he telephoned to the
unfortunate Ciano to say he had just received orders to
see the Duce at 5 a.m. precisely, and then turned up with
a bundle of documents which, as Ciano remarked, certainly
did not arrive by telephone; they were said to have been
in the custody of a courier who had been forbidden to leave
his hotel before the appointed time.

During the winter Mussolini had really wished to stop
the war, for one thing because his military advisers regarded
the 1942 date as almost too soon for Italy to be prepared.
As the winter turned into spring Mussolini several times
anticipated the intervention date and from the middle of
April it had become 1940 itself, but after the harvest was
in—three months' breathing-space, Ciano noted on 20th April.

[16] Cf., for instance, the Hitler-Ciano talks in the middle of Aug.
1939; Hitler's incitement of Italy against Yugoslavia at that time
confirms the suspicion that the Germans were by no means so
sure of Russia then as they tried to make the Italians believe.

[17] Ciano Diary, 9th Apr. 1940.

[18] Simoni, 30th Apr. 1940. On this occasion Göring seems to have
gone back to Hitler's idea of 23rd May 1939, that the Italians
should attack the Maginot Line.

From the moment of his invasion of Scandinavia, Hitler suddenly found an astonishing amount of time to write to Mussolini long, theatrical accounts of the heroic exploits of the Germans in Norway with references to the absurd writhings of those ludicrous pygmies, the British and the French. There was a lengthy outburst on 9th April, another on the 10th, and yet two more on 18th April and on 3rd May respectively. Each letter suggests some overgrown, rather macabre schoolboy playing with new toys and indeed reminds one forcibly of Marshal Göring playing with his electric trains. There were rumours at the time, and they were current in the Italian Embassy in Berlin, that these letters of Hitler were intended to cool Mussolini's ardour : this was specifically stated about Hitler's letter of 18th April which was brought to Rome by the Prince of Hesse in a special aeroplane in the very best Axis tradition. But it was quite untrue that there was anything restraining about Hitler's letters. On the contrary they were cleverly composed so as to whet Mussolini's appetites and whip him into a frenzy of desire to join in the game. Hitler's letter from hero to hero on 10th April ended with " He who, like you and me, dares greatly, will always be alone. All the stronger, especially in these hours, is the thought and the mark of friendship." It is significant that already on 4th April Hitler had ordered the resumption of Staff talks with the Italians.[19]

It was after 10th May and the Pope's condemnation of Germany's action that Mussolini felt more aggressive in his isolation and spoke to Ciano of liquidating Papacy and Monarchy together, for the dynasty was making plain its dislike of coming into the war on Germany's side. Hitler's letter which Mackensen was constrained to deliver at 5 a.m. on 10th May had announced that Hitler had crossed his Rubicon (the Führer, too, used the phrase),[20] and after this Hitler poured out exultation in three more long letters, dated 13th, 18th, and 25th May, to the Duce ;[21] nearly every

[19] D.G.F.P. series D, IX, no. 46.
[20] Cf. Sumner Welles on Mussolini, quoted in chapter XII above.
[21] Mackensen took the letter of 13th May to Ciano at 1 a.m. on 14th May; as Mussolini had requested to be left in peace

time he thanked Mussolini, as he had after the Anschluss, for his comprehension, and nearly every time the gratified Duce thanked him for finding time to write. On 18th May Hitler announced a breach more than 100 km. long in the Maginot Line; to this Mussolini replied on the following day that " the Italians," a phrase he used when speaking of himself,[22] were convinced that their days of non-belligerency would very soon be ended. The times were changed indeed : on 20th May Simoni noted that " all visas to Polish citizens for entry into Italy—granted generously hitherto—are suspended." Roosevelt's messages, in which he tried to deter Mussolini, served no purpose but to be passed for inspection to Berlin.

Badoglio[23] declares that on 26th May Mussolini very solemnly informed him and Balbo together that he had dispatched a letter to Hitler the day before announcing that Italy would be ready to join in the war any day from 5th June onwards. According to his own account Badoglio protested vehemently, declaring this was national suicide. There is, unfortunately, no confirmation of Badoglio's assertions. What is certain is that Mussolini convened his chiefs of staff to the Palazzo Venezia at 11 a.m. on 29th May and referred incidentally to having read Hitler's letter of the 25th to Badoglio on 28th May. Badoglio, Cavagnari, Pricolo, and Graziani were present. On 31st March, that is between the various conversations in March and the German offensive, Mussolini had drawn up a memorandum to the effect that Italy must sooner or later intervene on Germany's side, but the time indicated for doing so had been the spring of 1941. After the easy conquest of Norway and the subjection of Denmark, he said, he had decided upon the beginning of September 1940, but following more recent events still, " I consider any day good for our entry into the war from 5th June onwards. . . . If we delay a fortnight or a month we shall not improve our position while we shall give Germany the impression of arriving after all the work is done and when the risks are at a minimum,

---

unless an immediate decision were required it was not delivered to him until 9 a.m. See D.G.F.P. series D, vol. IX, no. 242.

[22] Ciano often did the same.   [23] Op. cit.

apart from the consideration that it is not our habit to strike at a man who is falling. . . ."[24] The Duce confirmed his military directives as defined on 31st March : to remain on the defensive on land except possibly in the direction of Yugoslavia,[25] but a vigorous, aero-naval war was to be initiated on all the frontiers. The immediate outcome of the meeting on 29th May was the creation of the Italian High Command under Mussolini as Commander-in-Chief, in spite of Victor Emmanuel's unwillingness to make way for the Duce. No protest of any kind is recorded from Badoglio or the others with regard to the decisions taken,[26] and the King, who might have made a daring bid for popularity —one which might well have saved the dynasty—merely sulked[27] : at this fateful moment Mussolini did not convene the Fascist Grand Council. It was not mere rhetoric to say that one Italian alone forced Italy into the war in June 1940.

Thus on 30th May the Duce was able to answer Hitler's letter of 25th May with the offer to come in on his side within a week's time; he offered to the Führer to choose the actual day so that they could correlate their military plans. At midday the Italian Embassy in Berlin was warned to prepare for a code message of " extraordinary importance," and the Embassy staff was filled with gloomy foreboding.[28] At 5.30 p.m. the message began to come through, at 6.30 the deciphering was complete, but not till midnight was it possible even to arrange for its delivery by Alfieri to the Führer. For this purpose the new Italian Ambassador was flown early the next morning to Hitler's headquarters at Godesberg. Simoni, who accompanied Alfieri, was struck by the contrast between the Berlin atmosphere and that which exuded from

[24] *Hitler e Mussolini: Lettere e Documenti* (Rizzoli, 1946), Document 24.

[25] There was talk, also, of an immediate Italian offensive in the direction of Djibuti.

[26] In the official *verbale* of the meeting, see *Hitler e Mussolini*, pp. 43-7; but of course the record of any protest made may have been deliberately omitted.

[27] Ciano told Mackensen that the King showed understanding. See D.G.F.P. series D, vol. IX, no. 366.

[28] Simoni, 30th May, 1940.

Hitler's headquarters. "All the enthusiasm of Germany," he wrote, "seems to be concentrated in these thirty or forty people who live in the intimate proximity of the Führer and see nothing beyond their hopes and projects."[29]

Hitler's response, dated 31st May, was delivered by Mackensen to Mussolini on 1st June. It was a reply of perfect gratification. For obvious reasons the Führer welcomed the appointment of the Duce as Commander-in-Chief and approved the suggestion he had made of a declaration from him to reassure the Balkan countries that Italy's intervention would not disturb their neutrality. Hitler adds that the complete defeat of France will assure the geographical and political domination of the Mediterranean to Italy. As for the day, Hitler asks for a delay of at most three days on account of a plan he had made for destroying the French Air Force which may make fresh dispositions in view of the new threat from Italy. As between 6th, 7th, and 8th June, Hitler asks for either the 6th or the 8th as the 7th is a Friday, "a day which is perhaps regarded by many as not suitable for a fortunate beginning (this belief exists among the Germans)"; he is, however, most willing for Mussolini to stick to 5th June if he prefers, and in any event Hitler will guard the secret jealously. His letter includes a modestly expressed query as to whether Mussolini would like to see him.

Thereupon the Duce decided upon 11th June.[30] Mackensen brought him a message on 2nd June that Hitler would after all have preferred an immediate Italian declaration of war. It is quite untrue, although it was believed at the time and has been repeated ever since, that Hitler offered any opposition to Mussolini's concrete proposals for his entry into war. The Führer was only a little evasive about the Italian troops Mussolini offered to the German Army in evidence of Italo-German comradeship, but he made a return offer of German mountain-troops.[31]

[29] Ibid., 31st May, 1940.
[30] Because Balbo persuaded him that an armoured unit must be moved from Albania to Libya. See D.G.F.P. series D, vol. IX, no. 371.
[31] See Hitler to Mussolini, 9th June 1940.

The Italian declaration of war was made on Monday, 10th June, and hostilities began on 11th June. As Ciano said, the news surprised no one and " did not arouse excessive enthusiasm."[32] The position of France was so much more tragic by now that Italy's action had become much uglier. The Duce spoke from the balcony but without his usual conviction.[33] In Berlin there was a special edition of the papers. to announce that Germany had an ally, but no one bought it.[34] Within a week France had capitulated. Poor Mussolini! He had really had scarcely a moment's satisfaction over his war, except perhaps the anticipation of it which followed Ribbentrop's visit in March and flowered in the memorandum of 31st March. After that he was in a perpetual state of anxiety lest he should arrive too late, but when at last he had brought Italy to the point of war he was caught in the " outbreak of peace," as Ciano called it. It was decided that Führer and Duce should meet at Munich on 19th June to discuss the armistice terms to be imposed upon France; on the journey on 18th June Mussolini was uneasy and could not conceal his disappointment from Ciano. It was Hitler who had won the war and would not only have everything to say but would have an incontestable right to say everything this time; in their few days of fighting the performance of the Italian troops had been anything but brilliant; evidently both conviction and equipment were lacking.

At Munich Mussolini and Ciano found Hitler and Ribbentrop miraculously peace-loving and magnanimous[35]—as usual Ribbentrop's remarks to Ciano were little more than an echo of the Führer's to the Duce; to both Italians Hitler seemed like a successful gambler who is anxious to withdraw from the game with all his gains intact. Thus Mussolini, ironically enough, showed himself more acquisitive. The Italians claimed Nice, Corsica, French Somaliland,

[32] Ciano Diary, 10th June 1940.

[33] Cianferra (op. cit.) was one of the witnesses.

[34] Simoni, 10th June 1940.

[35] See D.G.F.P. series D, vol. IX, no. 479 and Ciano Diary and Minute of 19th June. Mussolini had refused to meet Hitler again before Italy had gone to war.

and Tunisia with its frontiers "rectified" at Algeria's expense. They also claimed Malta for Italy, Gibraltar for Spain, and the demilitarization of all British bases in the Mediterranean, while they expressed the desire to acquire an Atlantic outlet in Morocco and to replace Britain in relation to Egypt and the Sudan. The Germans spoke of adding the Belgian Congo and at least a part of Morocco to their pre-1914 Empire. France was to be punished for her "aggression" and her frontiers determined once for all; the South Tyrolese would now be sent to Alsace. But primarily Hitler and Ribbentrop were concerned to force Britain to make peace—Ribbentrop told Ciano feelers were operating through Swedish channels. In order to induce the British to negotiate it was necessary to intensify the isolation of Britain and precisely this required at least a show of magnanimity towards France to prevent the French Government from leaving France for North Africa and above all to prevent the French fleet from going over to Britain. It was for this reason that armistice terms were agreed to according to which both Germany and Italy promised France to make no use of her fleet in the war, though Italy had originally wished to claim it. At Munich Mussolini intended to occupy the left bank of the Rhône, Corsica, Tunisia, and Djibuti, but on 22nd June, after seeing the terms of the Franco-German armistice signed on 21st June, he decided to impose nothing but the demilitarization of a fifty-kilometre strip along the French side of the frontier and full use of the port and railway of Djibuti. The Franco-Italian armistice was signed near Rome on 24th June.

Hitler was immensely affable about all this, expressing his appreciation of all that Mussolini had done. Against the Duce's will he insisted upon two separate armistices, for he would not be cheated of the signature of Compiègne where the humiliation of the French must be an unadulteratedly German action.[36] But he sent a message to Mussolini on 22nd

[36] See Shirer, *A Berlin Diary* (1941). DeWitt C. Poole, op. cit., wrote: "At Compiègne . . . Hitler emerged triumphant not only over Germany's hereditary foe but hardly less so over his own generals."

June saying: "Whatever you may decide [about the areas Italian troops are to occupy] France has been informed that the armistice will come into force only if you arrive at the same result."[37] It suited him admirably that his troops in France should reach the Spanish frontier on 27th June to menace Africa across Franco's Spain,[38] and it suited him admirably to have Italy at war with Great Britain in order at this moment to threaten the vital communications of the British Empire in a way which, without the Italian Navy, he could never have done.

The armistice negotiations intensified the difficulties between the Axis partners over France. Before everything Mussolini hoped to inherit the French Empire and he had stampeded Italy into the war in order not to miss the chance of doing so. Hitler, as far as one can judge, for all his big phrases about Italy and the Mediterranean, cared very little about the fulfilment of the Duce's aspirations. He intended to beat Britain and destroy Russia; he was only not quite sure which task to undertake first. It has been seen that he spoke peaceful language to Mussolini at Munich on 19th June; this meant that he was contemplating peace with Britain in order to march against the U.S.S.R.,[39] a war in which Italy had no conceivable interest to become involved. In order to induce the British to negotiate it was desirable to have shown oneself not ungenerous to France and to have enrolled France on the side of the Axis to face Britain with a solidly pro-Axis Continent; this could be attempted by cheating Italy, who had made herself ridiculous by declaring war so late, of the naval and imperial gains upon which she had been led to count. The day before the dictators met at Munich in June, a certain General de Gaulle had raised the banner of a free France on the British soil he had successfully reached. In the end he became the central figure in all Europe's resistance to tyranny. Hitler had quite enough intuition to scent danger. If France and Europe should respond to de Gaulle, Britain was much

[37] Hitler to Mussolini, 22nd June 1940.
[38] See Lord Templewood's *Ambassador on Special Mission* (1946).
[39] Jodl bore witness to this.

more likely to fight; worse still, the war might be a long war, and the longer it lasted the less likely was Germany to remain victorious.

Thus over France the interests of Hitler and of Mussolini appeared to be diametrically opposed. On 5th July the Duce grumbled to Ciano that France was edging her way into the Axis camp—" he is afraid that this may lead to our being defrauded of our booty." Two days later, on Sunday, 7th July, Ciano arrived in Berlin again and tried to urge the Italian view over this upon Hitler, who was very accommodating and said that of course France must be made to pay dearly for her faults. The Italian Foreign Minister produced larger and more specific demands than those made by Mussolini three weeks earlier at Munich. They included Italian domination of the Middle East and the Italian occupation of Aden, Perim, and Socotra. Tunisia (plus important Algerian mines) was requested only as an Italian Protectorate. The Führer agreed in principle with regard to the Mediterranean and the Red Sea,[40] but as he did not intend to make a formal peace with France the discussion remained conveniently academic. Ciano spent about two hours with Hitler that Sunday morning. Afterwards came a marvellous lunch. " A profusion of flowers and wines. The most famous French cellars must have con- tributed a great deal, to the great joy of the S.S. officers, coarse creatures. . . ."[41]

Both Hitler and Ribbentrop were far less sanguine than they had been on 19th June about ending the war, but they seemed mysterious and uncertain, waiting, they said, for the plans for the invasion of Britain to be worked out. Propaganda demanded, however, that another public peace gesture be made towards London; in spite of all the victories it was still particularly important from the point of view of German morale. On 19th July Ciano was in Berlin once more for this performance, a savage speech—for all the grief for future sacrifices he expressed—from the Führer before the Reichstag, upon which occasion Hitler promoted all his victorious generals to be Field-Marshals and Göring a

40 Ciano Minute, 7th July 1940.
41 Simoni, op. cit., 7th July 1940.

Reichsmarschall. Shirer thought Hitler in brilliant form that day. " Count Ciano," he added, " who was rushed up from Rome to put the seal of Axis authority on Hitler's ' offer ' of peace to Britain, was the clown of the evening. . . . Without the slightest pretext he would hop to his heels and expand in a salute. Could not help noticing how high-strung Ciano is. He kept working his *jaws.* And he was not chewing gum."[42] Ciano's countryman, Simoni, who had met him for the first time this July, wrote of him (on 10th July): " He seems intelligent but frivolous, capricious, without character and spoilt by a circle of weak courtiers who surround him and flatter him and satisfy his every whim with repulsive subservience. . . ." On 20th July, when it was clear from their press that the British had no intention of giving way, Hitler received Ciano once again. It would be war to the death with Britain; Hitler would suggest another meeting with Mussolini at the Brenner as soon as military plans had matured. There was no talk now of when the war would be over. It might, indeed, last for some time. Mussolini had tormented himself because he thought he had joined in the *Blitzkrieg* too late : in reality he had entered the Six Years' War a great deal too soon.

[42] Shirer, op. cit.

Chapter XIV

THE ATTACK UPON GREECE

Stalin, like Mussolini or indeed like any of the rest of us, had not expected France to have such feet of clay, but he drew the consequences with promptitude. The day the Germans entered Paris, the Russians seized the only important towns in Lithuania, the capital Kaunus, and Vilna, which had been recently re-acquired when Poland collapsed, after nineteen years' argument about it. By 21st July Estonia and Latvia had been swallowed up by Russia too. On 27th June, the day the Germans reached the frontiers of Spain, the U.S.S.R. presented an ultimatum to Roumania demanding in decently polite terms the cession of Bessarabia and a northern portion of the Bukovina. Thus the frontiers of Tsarist Russia were to be very nearly restored.

Although it had been agreed between Berlin and Moscow that the Russian zone included the Baltic States[1] and Roumania east of the Pruth, the Soviet ultimatum to Bucharest was like an incendiary bomb dropped into Balkan politics. Mussolini, it has been seen, was watching the Roumanian oil-fields nervously, hoping to reach them before Hitler and determined to invade Yugoslavia if a Balkan landslide were imminent. There are indications, so early as this June of 1940, of Hitler's first project for turning on the U.S.S.R. Though Roumania was not mentioned between them on 7th July, Ciano noted that the Führer's attitude towards the U.S.S.R. had changed. In fact, at this stage, just when the Italians were celebrating their entry into the war by trying to arrange a superficial *rapprochement* with Russia, Hitler reversed his policy once again. From this time on the

[1] That is to say Estonia and Latvia, but not Lithuania, until the signature of the Secret Supplementary Protocol of 28th September 1939, when Germany accepted the province of Lublin and most of that of Warsaw, in exchange for Lithuania. In June and July 1940 the Russian occupation of the Baltic states comprised full annexation after mere garrisoning since the autumn of 1939.

German forces on the eastern frontiers were steadily augmented.

At all events the Roumanian question had become critical. Roumania was a Versailles Successor State and her frontiers had been drawn a little generously in 1919. With Poland she had accepted a British guarantee in 1939 and was for this reason, too, in bad odour with the Axis; she was advised both in Berlin and Rome to yield obediently to the Russian demands which were inevitably followed by those of Bulgaria and Hungary. The Dobruja frontier with Bulgaria was relatively simple to redraw, but the infinitely complicated question of Transylvania had poisoned the relations between Roumania and Hungary since the days when Maniu led the Roumanian opposition in the Hungarian Parliament before 1914.

For years now Mussolini had been the foremost champion of Magyar revisionism which claimed for Hungary the whole of Transylvania, in spite of a considerably larger and more rapidly increasing Roumanian than Magyar population there. Hitler, on the other hand, had until November 1938 preferred Roumania, partly because the German minorities there were better treated than the Magyar minorities or the Germans in Hungary, and because the Transylvanian Saxons were definitely opposed to revision in Hungary's favour; but Hitler also felt sympathy for Roumania on account of Codreanu. Zelea Codreanu was the leader of the Roumanian Fascists or Iron Guard, and, although he had founded his movement independently of National Socialism in Germany, he had early established contact with it. Further, he was said to be blessed with German blood on his mother's side, and if the Iron Guard had a merciless programme with regard to the minorities in Roumania, Germans included, Hitler seems, nevertheless, to have felt a vague parentalism towards Codreanu. King Carol of Roumania, who displayed the same kind of courage in the face of Nazi Germany as Prince Starhemberg, was the one lesser European ruler who followed up a visit to Berchtesgaden—in November 1938—with an act of defiance to Hitler. Codreanu was already under arrest, but the King was scarcely back from his journey (which had taken him to London and Brussels beforehand) when

the Iron Guard leader was shot by his guards "while trying
to escape." Hitler knew that formula too well to hesitate
as to its meaning; he for one was certain that the King
had ordered the 'liquidation' of Codreanu. It is interesting
to find in Ciano's Diary[2] that in August 1939 the Führer
spoke to Ciano with great bitterness of this incident—it
was one of the things Hitler would never forget. Thus
from November 1938 until the abdication of Carol, although Hitler obviously disliked Hungary and its aristo-
cratic flavour with all his Austrian *petit-bourgeois* heart,
Führer and Duce concurred in frowning upon Roumania;
though it had veered right away from Titulescu and even lip-
service to democracy it was a relic of the Little Entente,
and, whereas Stoyadinović had been a false friend to Czechoslovakia in its hour of need, King Carol had done what
he could to be loyal to Prague.

Few words need be wasted upon Roumanian policy at
the moment of the Russian ultimatum, for it consisted of
nothing but a few unheard cries for help. Since the outbreak of war the Hungarians had tried to play everything
on the Italian card and there is no doubt that Teleki,[3] as
Prime Minister, was profoundly aware of the dangers of
National Socialism, especially for Hungary. The Magyars
were thankful that Italy kept out of the war during the
winter of 1939-40, and they appeared to be seriously considering the elevation of a prince of the House of Savoy
to the throne of St. Stephen, left vacant since the débâcle
of the last of the Habsburgs in 1918. At one point when
Germany was demanding to march across Hungary,[4] the
Magyar leaders had nursed the illusion that Italy might back
them—should they resist—with something of the vigour of
July 1934.

With the Russians marching into Bessarabia at the end
of June 1940, the Hungarians could scarcely contain their
Transylvanian appetites a moment longer. Hitler complained
of their impatience to Ciano at the interview in Berlin on
7th July and summoned them to a tripartite confabulation
at Munich three days later; there the Magyar leaders were

[2] 17th Sept. 1939.   [3] Himself a Transylvanian.
[4] Ciano Diary, 9th Sept. 1939.

given permission to attack Roumania at their own risk, but both Germany and Italy made it clear that their hands were too full for them to become in any way involved. From Munich the Italian and Hungarian parties were motored to Salzburg where their trains were waiting : witnesses agree that the demonstrations at Salzburg were fervid—" the Austrians," observed Simoni, " always take the lead in manifestations of Nazi enthusiasm."[5]

On 15th July Hitler wrote an exceedingly unpleasant letter to King Carol around whom disaster was piling up as it had around President Beneš two years before. Like some scolding school prefect Hitler told him that he had better give up trying to be clever; instead he should act according to principle, even if he found that difficult, and abandon the attempt to play off Bulgaria against Hungary. The Führer expressed solidarity with the Duce and declared that Roumania must make up her mind to lose territory. He added the extraordinary statement that Germany was indifferent to Roumania's fate (owing to her recognition of Russia's claims) and was prepared, if necessary, to do without Roumanian oil. Mussolini immediately expressed his acquiescence to Mackensen and repeated it in a letter to Hitler dated 17th July in which he also gratefully acknowledged a recent gift from the Führer of two armoured railway carriages.[6] It is clear that the Führer's assertion of indifference was made for Russian consumption. The situation had become so acute that Hitler had begun to fear that Russia might move still farther west the moment he himself was fully engaged in the invasion of Britain. He abandoned the idea of attacking Russia for the moment, but he was all the more determined to settle his accounts with her as soon as the British were beaten.[7] Until then he was more intent than ever upon preventing any kind of explosion in the " Danubian-

[5] Simoni, 10th July 1940.

[6] During Mussolini's journey back from Munich on 19th June his train had been attacked by enemy aircraft. Hitler decided this precious life must be better protected in future.

[7] On 31st July at the Berghof, Hitler told his generals that " Russia must be disposed of. Spring 1941." See D.G.F.P. series D, vol. X, p. 373.

Balkan sector." Once again he insisted on this in his conversation with Ciano on 20th July—it was the task of the Axis Powers to induce moderation and caution in both Roumania and Hungary; he approved of Bulgaria's claims, but wished to avoid any part in the negotiations, which should be directly engaged between the parties concerned.

The representatives of Roumania were sent for now, to the chagrin of Budapest; it was clear that they would try to buy Axis patronage and protection. They went first to Salzburg on 23rd July to be scolded, then to Rome on 27th July; according to Ciano, Mussolini had received the German minutes of their meeting in time to repeat what Hitler had said. But all these admonitions from the Supermen did not bear fruit; when the Hungarians and Roumanians met on their own at Turnu Severin in the middle of August they could still not agree. At last on 26th August Ribbentrop lost patience and summoned everyone to Vienna for another Vienna award. On his way, as it were, Ciano was invited to lunch with the Führer at Berchtesgaden on 28th August. With regard to the question under consideration Hitler expressed irritation against the incontinent behaviour of the Magyars, and on the following day Prince Eugene's palace of the Belvedere was once again desecrated by the political puerility of Ribbentrop and Ciano. Without any serious study of the problem they drew their pens across Transylvania in utter disregard for its historical frontiers, with no more constructive conception than the German formula that Hungary should be given two-thirds of her claim. When Manoilescu, the Roumanian Foreign Minister, saw the new frontier on the map, he performed what may have been the only honest action of his life—he fainted. Roumania seemed to be disintegrating completely and a few days later King Carol abdicated in favour of his son. With the elimination of Carol the Germans breathed again, Simoni noted.[8] The good Fascist General Antonescu now became Roumanian Prime Minister and dictator; he got on well with Hitler who frequently praised his " fanatical nationalism," and while his power lasted—until August 1944— he lined Roumania up as an obedient Axis satellite. The

[8] 6th Sept. 1940.

Hungarians, on the other hand, maintained a show of independence until March 1944.

Over few questions did the Nazis treat the Fascists worse than over that of Yugoslavia. When Germany was devouring Czechoslovakia one year or Poland the next, she had always made rough gestures towards Yugoslavia, another of the heterogeneous "creations of Versailles." In August 1939 morsels of Yugoslavia had almost been pressed into Mussolini's watering mouth. From the time of the German-Soviet Pact, however, every German-Italian talk was loaded with elaborate explanations to the effect that, of course, the Yugoslav problem should be solved in an Italian sense, only not yet. On 7th July 1940 it was agreed that Yugoslavia had no claim to exist as a member of the Axis New Order, but Hitler insisted that Italy was on no account to move against her, not only because Russia might come to her help, but also because a common Anglo-Russian interest might be created. Ribbentrop missed no opportunity of telling the Italians how much the Yugoslavs hated them.[9]

On 16th August 1940 Ribbentrop sent for Alfieri to rap him over the knuckles. Once again he repeated the monotonous refrain of "Hands off Yugoslavia," complaining that he had had information from his Military Attaché in Rome that the Italian General Staff was working out an anti-Yugoslav plan without German "permission." Ribbentrop also specifically objected to the improvement in Italo-Russian relations which Mussolini had initiated in the spirit of Axis solidarity or in other words in subservience to Hitler. An understanding with Italy, the German Foreign Minister now declared, might impel Russia in the direction of the Straits, and this in its turn might serve Britain. Thirdly, Ribbentrop stated that an Italian move against Greece would be most unwelcome. "This is a halt called all along the line," is the entry in Ciano's Diary.[10]

When Mussolini declared war against Britain and France from the notorious balcony of the Palazzo Venezia, by prearrangement with Hitler he added: "I solemnly declare that Italy does not intend to draw the peoples who live along her land or sea frontiers into war. Let Switzerland,

[9] Simoni, 25th July 1940. [10] D.G.F.P. series D, vol. X, no. 353.

Yugoslavia, Greece, Turkey, Egypt take note of these words of mine. It depends upon these countries and upon them alone whether they remain at peace or not." In October, when he ordered the generals to attack Greece, Mussolini asserted that he had been thinking out this plan since before June. The truth is that Ciano and his friend Jacomoni, the Governor of Albania, were inordinately pleased with themselves over their easy descent upon that country which had brought Italian troops to the frontiers of Greece, and they often thought that it would be exhilarating to play another round of this game which might lead to the subjugation or partition of Greece itself—indeed their attitude was not entirely unlike that of Ribbentrop towards Poland in 1939. But there is no trace of any planning of such action before August 1940, and no trace at all of serious planning.[11]

While Greek popular sentiment was pro-British and anti-Italian, it should not be forgotten that the Metaxas régime aspired to totalitarianism and Metaxas himself was an enthusiastic Germanophile. The naval war was bound to create friction between Italy and Greece, more particularly on account of the Dodecanese, islands of strategic importance in the eastern Mediterranean owned by Italy but inhabited by Greeks. Into the bargain the Military Governor of Rhodes was the old Fascist Quadrumvir, De Vecchi, whose *bête noire* was Greece,[12] so that he blamed " Greek treachery " for all his own failures. It is true that this is the account given of De Vecchi by the last pre-war Italian Minister in Athens whom De Vecchi accused of being no more than the servant of Greece. The Minister in question was Emanuele Grazzi, a brother of Umberto Grazzi who was Italian Chargé d'Affaires in Vienna when Dollfuss was murdered.[13] Though he belongs to the large company of Italian diplomats who have protested almost too much against the policy of the régime they served while it lasted, it is certain that he did what he could to send accurate dispatches

[11] It is interesting that Stalin asked Ribbentrop about Italy's intentions towards Greece in August 1939; see *Nazi-Soviet Relations,* p. 73.

[12] See E. Grazzi, *Il Principio della Fine* (1946).

[13] See chapter II above.

from Athens to Rome. He reported that the Greek Government was extremely correct because it was particularly anxious to avoid a conflict with Italy, but he also made clear that the Greeks would resist Italian aggression with all their might. Ciano, however, did not want to receive information of such exactitude, and if he read it at all he ignored it, and, further, kept Grazzi completely in the dark as to Fascist intentions.

The fact was that at the beginning of August 1940 Mussolini was plunged once again into a fever of anxiety lest, as Ciano said, peace might break out, finding him with nothing but Menton in hand. Not only was Hitler not proceeding against Britain in spite of the extraordinary confidence of his Nazi entourage, not only was the German excuse that the weather was too bad wearing thin, but the Italians had again heard disconcerting rumours that Anglo-German negotiations were in process via Sweden. If the Germans did make peace with the British, it seemed likely that Italy's African claims against France would simply be forgotten, so that the Duce began to speak of action against Yugoslavia or Greece in September.[14] Ciano preferred aggression against Greece, and by the middle of August everything—except the Italian armed forces—was ready; a nice Greek-Albanian frontier incident had been concocted and Greece was to pay for it with Cephalonia and Corfu. Metaxas, however, appealed to Berlin, and this led to the scolding which Ribbentrop administered to Alfieri on 16th August. The Italians gave way obediently in a prompt telegram from Ciano, though Mussolini could not refrain from complaining a great deal against Greece and Yugoslavia in a letter delivered to Hitler on 27th August; in it he declared that both these countries had already mobilized almost completely.[15]

Every sign indicates that Hitler's apprehension about Russia was growing. This was one reason for the summons to

[14] See Ciano Diary, 6th Aug. 1940, where Ciano adds that he does not think Hitler " will allow any disturbance of the Balkan *status quo.*"

[15] Mussolini began to write this letter on 23rd Aug. There are several drafts of it extant but the variations are inessential.

Vienna for a settlement to be dictated to Hungary and
Roumania. After seeing Hitler on 28th August, Ciano sent
a telegram to Mussolini from Vienna the next day, one
paragraph of which ran as follows :

" I should particularly emphasize that both from Hitler's as
from Ribbentrop's statements a marked distrust is revealed of
Russia, which they say is ready to exploit possible complications
to the uttermost, and to advance with the complicity of
Bulgaria and Yugoslavia ' as far as the Straits, the Aegean,
and even the Adriatic.' "

The reference to the Adriatic was inserted expressly to
alarm the Italians, for it does not appear in papers for
German consumption only.[16]

The second Belvedere Award was, however, a provocation
rather than a sop to Russia, since the new frontiers were
guaranteed by the two Axis Powers, and the Russians en-
quired curtly against whom this guarantee might be considered necessary.[17] It rapidly became clear that Antonescu's
Roumania was to be an Axis preserve. Genuine resistance
(which sometimes took pro-British forms) to the establishment of the new Roumanian frontiers was harshly suppressed
and Codreanu's successor, Horia Sima, became Deputy Premier,
though it was not until October that Antonescu himself
publicly appeared in a green Iron Guard shirt. More interesting
still, on 11th September " several hundred S.S. men in
uniform were reported to have arrived at Galatz, to help
in the repatriation of the Germans from Bessarabia,"[18] and
German experts of all kinds now poured into Roumania;
it was explained that the Reichswehr officers had kindly
responded to an appeal from General Antonescu to reorganize
the Army.

On 13th September Ribbentrop telephoned to Ciano, and,
as usual, invited himself to Rome; this time he gave

[16] Ciano *Europa* pp. 581-83. D.G.F.P. series D, vol. X, no. 407.
[17] Simoni on 25th July 1940 reports Ribbentrop as saying a guarantee could not be given because it would lead to trouble with
Russia.
[18] *Bulletin of International Affairs*, vol. XVII, no. 19, 21st Sept.
1940. p. 1257.

the Palazzo Chigi nearly a week's notice, but he seems to have divulged nothing more by telephone than that he wished to discuss Russia and America. He arrived on 19th September, and must have brought a letter from the Führer to the Duce dated 17th September which was the day the invasion of Britain was " postponed indefinitely."[19] The letter, as usual, contained a mass of military detail, this time about the security of Germany's frontiers, especially those to the east. This was particularly necessary, Hitler wrote, because of the uncertainty of the Roumanian situation and the need to be prepared for every kind of eventuality and intrigue. For the first time he admitted to Mussolini the impossibility of winning the war that autumn and referred to the unfortunate fact that " we are not the rulers of the seas." Finally, Hitler concluded, Japan remained the best ally of the Axis in the East as a bastion against the United States.

Ribbentrop proceeded to explain to Mussolini and Ciano that the continued resistance of Britain could only be explained by her hope of American and Russian intervention, and in order to shatter this hope he drew out of his hat a familiar rabbit of his, a military alliance with Japan. This was to " paralyse " America by strengthening the isolationists against Roosevelt before the Presidential election, and he expressed confidence that it would paralyse Russia at the same time.[20] So off Ciano had to go to Berlin once more to take his part in the realization of Ribbentrop's belated dream, the German-Italian-Japanese Tripartite Pact signed at the Neue Reichskanzlei on 27th September 1940.

The text of the most important article (III) of the new pact ran as follows : " Germany, Italy, and Japan undertake to assist one another with all political, economic, and military means if one of the high contracting parties should be attacked by a Power not at present involved in the European war or in the Sino-Japanese conflict." Article V added that " the aforesaid terms do not in any way affect the

[19] *Führer Conferences on Naval Affairs,* 1940.

[20] Ciano Minute, 19th Sept. 1940. Also D.G.F.P. series D, vol. XI, nos. 73, 79, 87.

political status which exists at present between each of the three contracting parties and Soviet Russia," in other words they were aimed against the United States.

On 27th September Shirer noted in Berlin:

" The bally-hoo to-day has already been terrific, pushing all other news completely off the front page. The German people are told that the Pact is of world-shaking importance and will shortly bring final ' world peace.' The ceremony of signing . . . was carried through with typical Axis talent for the theatrical. In the first place the surprise of the event itself. Then the showy setting. When Ribbentrop, Ciano, and Japanese Ambassador M. Kurusu, a bewildered little man, entered the gala hall of the Chancellery, Klieg lights blazed away as the scene was recorded for history. Brightly coloured uniforms all over the place. The entire staffs of the Italian and Japanese embassies present. (The Russian Ambassador was invited, but replied he would be out of town this noon.) The three men sit themselves at a gilded table. Ribbentrop rises and motions one of his slaves, Dr. Schmidt, to read the text of the Pact. Then they sign while the cameras grind away. Then comes the climactic moment, or so the Nazis think. Three loud knocks on the giant door are heard. There is a tense hush in the great hall. The Japanese hold their breath. The door swings slowly open and in strides Hitler. Ribbentrop bobs up and formally notifies him that the pact has been signed. The Great Khan nods approvingly but does not deign to speak. Hitler majestically takes a seat in the middle of the table, while the two Foreign Ministers and the Japanese Ambassador scramble for chairs. When they have got adjusted, they pop up, one after another and deliver prepared addresses which the radio broadcasts round the world."[21]

Simoni gives a similar account; he notices that during these addresses Hitler's eyes strayed two or three times to Ciano's crooked little legs.[22]

When Hitler received Ciano this time he told him that the invasion of Britain had been given up[23] and they spoke in

[21] Shirer, op. cit.   [22] Simoni, 27th Sept. 1940.

[3] *Niente sbarco* was what Ciano noted. See Diary, 27-8th Sept. 1940.

terms of the inevitable continuation of the war; he asked
to meet Mussolini at the Brenner on 4th October to discuss
Spain. Ciano noted of Hitler and Ribbentrop this time that
" they are impeccably friendly towards us,"[24] for they felt
in greater need of their allies. The atmosphere in Berlin
was gloomy, not only because the end was no longer even
said to be in sight, but also because the public was feeling
the first strain—before becoming more hardened—of the
R.A.F. raids which were robbing the capital of a good deal
of sleep. Shirer gives an excellent account of the blood-
thirsty enthusiasm of the nurses to whom Hitler made
his *Winterhilfe* speech on 4th September, but the enthusiasm
was patently hysterical. Just about this time a squadron of
Italian planes, after much insistence from the Germans
after all, had at last arrived on the coast of Belgium to
help raid Britain, but Simoni noted that the Berliners only
thought it depressing to have to call in Italian help.[25] The
Tripartite Pact had not dissipated their pessimism : when
he paid a brief visit to Milan and Rome at about this time
Simoni felt the Italian mood to be rather callous than gloomy,
for the people did not care about Mussolini's war.

If Ciano is to be believed Hitler actually agreed with him
on 7th July that " England may occupy the Ionian Islands
to transform them into anti-Italian bases, and he declared
himself definitely in favour of action on our part to forestall an English move of the kind."[26] Over two months
later, when Ribbentrop reached Rome on 19th September[27]
radiant with the certain solution he brought with him
of the problem of quick victory, he seems, according to
Ciano's Minute of the conversation, to have been scarcely
less indiscreet. As exclusively Italian interests were concerned
in Greece and Yugoslavia, he said, it was for Italy alone

[24] Ibid.   [25] Simoni, 28th Aug. 1940 and 1st Oct. 1940.
[26] Ciano Minute, 7th July 1940. According to the German Minute
Hitler did not commit himself. See D.G.F.P. series D, vol. x, no.
129. In the Minute of a German naval conference held on 4th Nov.
1940, it is stated : " On no occasion was authorisation for such
an independent action given to the Duce by the Führer." *Führer
Conferences,* 1940, p. 112.
[27] The Italians had started a clandestine Greek wireless station
the day before.

to choose how these questions should be settled. The chief effort was to be made against Britain, "but he confirms that Yugoslavia and Greece are two zones of Italian interest in which Italy can adopt whatever policy she chooses with Germany's full support."[28] Germany only reserved the district around Maribor for herself, an area which had been part of Styria in old Austria; the reference to Maribor made Germany's acquiescence seem concrete. To all this the Duce had replied that Greece was for Italy what Norway had been for Germany before April, and it was therefore essential for Italy to proceed with the liquidation of the Hellene State. In spite of his scene with Alfieri on 16th August, it does not appear that Ribbentrop objected nor yet that the subject was mentioned when Hitler and Mussolini met at the Brenner on 4th October. In the next few days, especially on 7th and 8th October, so many German troops arrived in Roumania, which had not been mentioned either, that it had to be admitted that the Germans had occupied that country and its oil-fields—solely by invitation. This time it is particularly easy to understand Mussolini's indignation.[29] He tried to be invited, too, and a few Italian Air Force officers arrived in Bucharest on 14th October. It was apparently the occupation of Roumania which determined the Duce to try to "spring" the invasion of Greece upon Hitler; he had already given unmistakable evidence of his intention to make the attempt before the autumn should be gone.

Thus Hitler had no grounds for complaint that he had not been informed of Mussolini's attack upon Greece, but it was stage-managed with a servile imitation of Nazi brutality-cum-falsity at the expense of the Greeks. The Duce had a meeting with Ciano, Jacomoni, and his military chiefs at the Palazzo Venezia on 15th October when the action was decided and Ciano promised to provide a provocative incident which would require the punishment of the Greeks. Ciano also guaranteed that only a thin top layer of Greek plutocrats was Anglophile, the people as a whole being completely indifferent, and it was hastily presumed that most of

[28] Ciano Minute, 19th Sept. 1940.
[29] Cf. D.G.F.P. series D, vol. XI, no. 192.

the Greek generals had been bought. The Greeks had in fact
prepared to be attacked in August, but later they believed,
as Ribbentrop had assured Athens,[30] that Berlin would hold
back the Italians. A gala performance of *Madama Butterfly*
to inaugurate the new opera-house at Athens was fixed for
25th October to mark at least a cultural Italo-Greek *rapprochement,* and the Greek Government invited Puccini's only
son and his wife as official guests. The Puccinis arrived
in Athens by train on 24th October, having been urged
by the Italian Minister, Pavolini, not to cancel their journey.
About a week before this the journalist, Curzio Malaparte,[31]
arrived on behalf of the *Corriere della Sera*; he informed
the Italian Minister that he had brought him the following
message from Ciano : " Tell Grazzi that he can write what
he likes but I shall make war on Greece just the same."
While Grazzi was giving a big reception on 26th October
by way of returning the hospitality offered to the Puccinis,
the Italian ultimatum to Greece was being deciphered by his
staff : when his guests went home at five in the morning of
27th October it was ready for the Minister to read. He
was to wake up Metaxas, who was over seventy and had
had a stroke, in the middle of the following night to give
him three hours' notice of the Italian invasion timed for
6 a.m. on 28th October. The unhappy Grazzi, sitting in
Metaxas's parlour at the fateful moment, could not help
noticing that it was furnished with just about the same
suburban taste as that of Mussolini's wife at the Villa
Torlonia.

Late on 19th October Mussolini, having made his dispositions on 15th October, wrote a long letter to Hitler
from Rocca delle Caminate. It was largely concerned with
the equally burning question of France, but it then passed
on to the subject of Greece. " With regard to Greece
I have decided to put an end to the delays and to strike
very soon," since Greece remains one of Britain's continental
bases, just like Turkey, Portugal, and Switzerland. With

[30] Simoni, 24th Aug. 1940. " Ribbentrop . . . ha dato, senza
consultarci ampie assicurazioni a questo Ministro Ellenico. . . ."

[31] Author of *Technique of a Coup d'Etat* quoted in chapter 1
above.

the Germans in Roumania, writes Mussolini, the Turks will probably not move, and Italy will synchronize a move against Greece with a further push towards Egypt. On the following day, Sunday, 20th October, Bismarck, who was Counsellor at the German Embassy, told Ciano in Rome that Hitler would be in occupied France towards the end of the week in order to meet Franco and the leaders of Vichy France. On Tuesday the 22nd, the day on which Hitler met Laval, the Duce returned to Rome and showed his draft letter to Ciano; there is no evidence that he altered it as the result of Bismarck's message. It arrived in Berlin marked *urgentissima* by special messenger on Thursday, 24th October.[32] The gist of this letter was conveyed to Hitler, by the German Foreign Office, at Yvoire on his return from Montoire late the same evening. Ribbentrop immediately telephoned from France to Rome to suggest that Hitler should return to Berlin via northern Italy in order to report to the Duce on Pétain and Franco. In Munich the Führer found an invitation from Mussolini to his favourite city, Florence. It has always been presumed that the Duce timed his letter to miss Hitler in Berlin,[33] but there is no proof of this, for Hitler had left Berlin sooner than Bismarck had indicated—indeed he had already left when Bismarck saw Ciano.[34] When the Führer arrived in Florence on Monday, 28th October, the Duce had only managed to surprise him in that the attack upon Greece had begun without Hitler's knowledge of the chosen date. But the Führer had had a good three days' official notice that the invasion was about to take place, and when he reached Florence he knew that it had. "Attack in Albania and conference in Florence," was the entry in Ciano's Diary.

[32] Simoni, 24th Oct. 1940.

[33] I cannot agree with the note by Professor Klibansky on the Italian invasion of Greece in *Mussolini's Memoirs* (Contact, 1949).

[34] See E. Kordt, op. cit. As a senior Wilhelmstrasse official he was in a position to be accurately informed about facts like these; Donosti, op. cit., provides some confirmation. Kordt says that Hitler left Berlin by special train at 5 a.m. on 20th October and that Anfuso had already told Bismarck that Greece would be attacked.

Chapter XV

THE AXIS AND FRANCO

When Hitler came to Florence on 28th October 1940 he
had come to give Mussolini his directives for the prosecution
of the Mediterranean war. The conquest of France and
the intervention of Italy had transformed the war into something extra-European; the Führer thought in terms of con-
tinents now, and Africa had become his key to everything,
whether in strategy or economics.[1] He thought that he
had frightened the United States and diverted the U.S.S.R., and
he had decided to seize Gibraltar and Suez without further
delay by sending German detachments, in the " corset " role
they had played to the Austro-Hungarian armies in the
previous war, to brace up the Spaniards and Italians.

It has been seen that the question of France brought German
and Italian interests, both with regard to an ultimate settlement and particularly with regard to the prosecution of the
war, into sharp conflict. There was not only the matter
of the French fleet, but also that of metropolitan France
and the French Empire in Africa. Hitler wished to have
France on his side, a matter of no importance to Mussolini
who persistently asserted that Vichy was in league with de
Gaulle.[2] In order to have France on his side apparently
by her own choice, Hitler tolerated the Vichy Government
in the unoccupied zone; he hoped that the French colonies,
if they were not attacked by the Axis forces, would continue
to pay allegiance to Vichy and thus indirectly to himself;
for this reason he opposed Mussolini's plans to take over
the French North African ports. Should the French colonies
rebel, he regarded it as essential, as he had written to Mus-

[1] Cf. Hitler's and Ribbentrop's remarks to Molotov about Africa on
12-13th Nov. 1940 in *Nazi-Soviet Relations,* pp. 221, 231.

[2] See Mussolini to Hitler, 19th Oct. 1940, quoted below, and
elsewhere. Also Hitler's interview with Molotov, 13th Nov. 1940,
where he enumerates France as an Axis Power (*Nazi-Soviet Relations*).

solini on 17th September, to control Spain as the bridge to Africa.

Guderian[3] thought that Hitler should have crashed straight on in best steam-roller fashion right across France and her possessions. Certainly his attempt to be more subtle cost him much anxiety. At a conference with Raeder and Keitel[4] on 6th September it was admitted that

" In the French possessions in Equatorial Africa there is an open break with Pétain's Government and a swing over to General de Gaulle. There is danger that unrest and revolt might spread to the French West African colonies. The economic situation in the colonies, particularly as regards foodstuffs, is used by Britain as a means of exerting pressure. An agreement between the colonies and Britain, and revolt against France, would jeopardize our own chances of controlling the African area; the danger exists that strategically important West African ports might be used for British convoy activities and that we might lose a most valuable source of supplies for Europe. . . ."

The appeasement of France was to be combined with the exclusion of Britain from the Mediterranean, and it had been hoped that Italian East-Mediterranean ambitions might be satisfied by attacking Egypt and Suez. But Graziani's advance into Egypt, which began in the middle of September, had come to a standstill by the middle of October, and the Italian menace to Suez was not serious. As for Gibraltar, it had been taken for granted by Hitler and Mussolini, from the day the Germans arrived on the Spanish frontier, that Spain would follow Italy's example and declare war on Britain. She had made enough lofty declarations of solidarity with the Axis to warrant at least this. But Franco drove harder bargains than Mussolini, or possibly, as Lord Temple-wood suggests,[5] he learnt from the Duce's mistakes. On 8th August[6] the German Ambassador noted that the Caudillo

[3] See DeWitt C. Poole, op. cit.

[4] *Führer Naval Conferences*, 1940, p. 95.

[5] Lord Templewood, *Ambassador on Special Mission* (1946).

[6] See Secret Memorandum by Stohrer on " Conditions for Spain's entry into the war " (published in *The Spanish Government and*

asked for Gibraltar, French Morocco, a part of Algeria, and the extension of some of Spain's existing colonies; he also required substantial economic assistance and he refused to move without having received it. When Suñer came to Berlin in September it all seemed—as Ribbentrop told the Duce on 19th September—to be arranged, but Germany could not arm herself, Italy, and Spain; as it was the Italians were left without long-promised supplies, some of which were, however, sent east to satisfy the Russians.[7] No British decision was wiser than the one made to put up with numberless affronts in Madrid in order to keep Spain economically dependent upon Britain rather than Germany.

The day before the signature of the Tripartite Pact, Hitler had a long discussion with Raeder alone. It was laid down by the Admiral that Gibraltar must be taken and that this required that the Canary Islands be secured in advance. It was also laid down that

" The Suez Canal must be taken. It is doubtful whether the Italians can accomplish this alone; support by German troops will be needed. An advance from Suez through Palestine and Syria as far as Turkey is necessary. If we reach that point Turkey will be in our power. . . .

" The question of North-West Africa is also of decisive importance. All indications are that Britain, with the help of de Gaulle France, and possibly also of the U.S.A., wants to make this region a centre of resistance and to set up air bases for attack against Italy. Britain will try to prevent us from gaining a foothold in the African colonies.

" In this way Italy would be defeated.

" Therefore action must be taken against Dakar. . . .[8]

" . . . In general, it appears important to co-operate with France in order to protect North-West Africa—after certain concessions have been made to Germany and Italy. The occupation of France makes it possible to compel her to maintain and defend the frontiers advantageous to us."

---

the Axis (U.S. Department of State, 1946) as No. 1. Spain had occupied the Tangier International Zone on 14th June.

[7] Simoni, 2nd Sept, 1940.

[8] Raeder constantly insists upon the importance of Dakar.

Hitler was in general agreement.

"Upon completion of the alliance with Japan he will immediately confer with the Duce, and possibly also with Franco. He will have to decide whether co-operation with France or Spain is more profitable; probably with France since Spain demands a great deal more (French Morocco) but offers little."[9]

This conclusion of the Führer's was the result of the German interviews with the Spanish Minister of the Interior, Suñer, and of a letter from Franco dated 22nd September. Hitler's talk with Ciano in Berlin on 28th September was very largely concerned with the question of Spain, and one cannot help admiring Spanish technique if it had reduced the Führer to the ruefulness indicated in Schmidt's official Minute —it makes one feel that Franco was worth ten Mussolinis. The Spaniards, Hitler said to Ciano, ask for 400,000 to 700,000 tons of grain, the furnishing of all the fuel they will require, the military equipment they lack, and the troops and weapons necessary for the capture of Gibraltar; they also ask (see above) for Morocco and smaller gains. In return they promise their friendship. There is no trace of amusement on Hitler's face for he was a man without laughter. It is not that he himself has forgotten how to be false for he talks to Ciano as if Germany had made greater sacrifices than Italy for Franco. The impression one receives is that he was really nonplussed, for he even remarked to Ciano that the Spaniards with their talk of high ideals made him feel like a Jew who was willing to exploit the most sacred human heritage.[10] Ciano must have had very mixed feelings, the more since he knew that Italy needed a lot of the supplies for which Spain was asking.

A week later Hitler and Mussolini met at the Brenner. Hitler was still obsessed by his Franco-Spanish problem and in a state of consternation over the voracity of Spain.[11] As for Morocco, if France were to forfeit that, then Hitler intended to make good the failure of William II rather than

[9] *Führer Conferences on Naval Affairs,* 1940, p. 106.

[10] D.G.F.P. series D, vol. XI, no. 124.

[11] D.G.F.P. series D, vol. XI, no. 149. See also Ciano Minute 4th Oct. 1940.

hand over the whole of it to Spain; after all he was planning for the return of the pre-1914 colonies to Germany which, as we have seen, was to become, among other things, a great African power. Above all, he said to Mussolini, he feared that it might become known if Morocco were promised to Spain that this would have two dangerous results, one that the British would occupy the Canaries and the second that all French North Africa would join de Gaulle. Mussolini suggested that it would be necessary to offer Spain something in order to combat enemy pressure, but she might be left to hope for Morocco when it came to the final peace. In his letter from Rocca delle Caminate on 19th October he changed his position, saying that he would now prefer Spain not to declare war for the present, so as to give her more time to prepare; perhaps he had other reasons of his own. At the same time he wrote rebelliously about France " who thought, because she had not fought, that she had not been beaten." Vichy, he went so far as to declare (not without some reason), is in touch with London via Lisbon. One could not and should not think of collaboration with the French who must soon be reduced to be a nation of 34 to 35 millions.

Hitler was as impervious as ever to any dissent from his own view; his policy towards France undoubtedly impeded the smooth internal working of the Axis itself and contributed to the failure of Axis policy towards Spain. It has been suggested that Hitler was affected by some particular tenderness towards France, quite apart from the strategic importance of her Empire. His old desire for British friendship was illustrated by at least two references so late as this to the possibility of a German-British compromise.[12] It may be that the French had really won him by their extraordinary submission at this time. " Their hope is that France may become Germany's favourite province," Bullitt wrote to Washington on 1st July.[13] Perhaps Hitler felt that this was the beginning of the comprehension he sought not only from Mussolini and the Germans, if his

[12] The first was to Franco on 23rd Oct. and the second at Florence on 28th Oct. 1940. See Ciano Minute of this date.
[13] See W. L. Langer, *Our Vichy Gamble* (1947).

dream of Nietzschean caste-imperialism was to be fulfilled.
By October 1940 the whole French-Spanish complex had
become so important to the Führer that he made the unprecedented gesture of going to visit both Pétain and Franco
instead of ordering them to mount to the Berghof—hitherto
he had never left his headquarters of the moment for anyone
less than the Duce.

Hitler met Laval at Montoire on his way through to
Hendaye on 22nd October, and Pétain at the same place on
his way back on 24th October. He told Mussolini on 28th
October that while Laval was a corrupt democratic politician
who was only pro-Axis in order to save himself, Pétain
had made an excellent impression on him.[14] Among mere
mortals and apart from supermen, Antonescu and Pétain both
succeeded in gaining the approbation of the Führer—in
Berlin Hitler was afterwards said to have spoken of Pétain
as " a more spiritual Hindenburg."[15] But the current version
of what occurred at Montoire on 24th October, that " Hitler
had assured Pétain and Laval that the French colonial
Empire would be kept intact,"[16] is misleading. It is difficult
to recall any other week in Hitler's life in which he behaved with so much sense and honesty. He said to the
French approximately : " If you contribute to the defeat
of Britain, then Germany, Italy, and Spain will satisfy themselves at British rather than at French expense." Pétain, who
expressed himself ' in favour of the principle ' of coopera-
tion with Hitler, also said that " he could enter no binding
undertaking without consulting the French Government."[17]
He is said to have commented to a friend afterwards, ' It
will take six months to discuss this programme and six
more to forget it.'[18] To Mussolini on 28th October Hitler
" twice solemnly declared that he would sign no peace treaty
with France if all Italy's requirements were not previously

[14] Ciano Minute, 28th Oct. 1940.

[15] Simoni, 3rd Nov. 1940.

[16] This was Göring's statement later, quoted by DeWitt C. Poole,
op. cit.

[17] D.G.F.P. series D, XI, no. 227.

[18] *Le Procès du Maréchal Pétain* (Editions Albin Michel, Paris,
1945), vol. II, p. 876.

satisfied, requirements to be regarded as extremely modest and
certainly less than the French had expected,"[19] and he clearly
emphasized his solidarity with Italy to the French. To both
Franco and Mussolini, if not positively to Pétain, Hitler said
said that of course if the war with Britain ended in compromise, France would have to pay everyone's bill.

The historic meeting of the Führer and Caudillo on
23rd October was, from the German point of view,
nothing short of a fiasco. Hitler made his usual survey
of the general situation, with the main emphasis placed
upon the question of the French. " The great problem that
was to be solved at the moment consisted in hindering the
de Gaulle movement in French Africa from farther expanding itself, and [hindering] the establishment, in this way,
of bases for England and America on the African coast."[20]
The Führer proposed an immediate German-Spanish alliance,
Spain to come into the war in January 1941 when German
forces with Spanish support would attack and take Gibraltar
for Spain. But Franco, who was never so keen as Suñer[21]
to ally with Germany, boggled at German co-operation in
the conquest of Gibraltar (which should be a Spanish feat)
and returned to the whole of French Morocco and a part
of Algeria for Spain as the absolute condition of her
entry into the war.[22] Hitler told Mussolini at Florence that
this had, of course, been unacceptable, and that a secret
protocol with only a vague reference to the Spanish claims
had at last been worked out with infinite trouble after
a discussion which lasted nine hours; " rather than go
through that again the Führer would prefer to have three
or four teeth out."[23] Hitler thought Franco perhaps a brave
man, but one who must have become leader by sheer
chance;[24] he was certainly no organizer, for Hitler said his
chief impression of Spain was one of great confusion.[25]

With what accumulated frustration was Adolf Hitler faced

[19] Ciano Minute of 28th Oct. 1940.
[20] D.G.F.P. series D, vol. XI, no. 220.
[21] He had become Foreign Minister on 17th Oct.
[22] W. L. Langer, op. cit.   [23] Ciano Minute, 28th Oct. 1940.
[24] Perhaps Hitler knew that this was the case.
[25] Ciano Minute, 28th Oct. 1940.

at the end of October 1940! He had conquered Europe
in a manner militarily worthy of Alexander or Napoleon,
yet Britain defied him, France and Russia perplexed him,
Spain lacked " the same intensity of will for giving as for
taking,"[26] and his comrade Mussolini upset all his plans
by using, only three and a half months later, the *carte blanche*
regarding Greece which he, Hitler, had handed him in July.
It appears that Greece was not in fact mentioned at Florence
beyond an offer, at the opening of the leaders' talk, of " complete German solidarity," and also of German parachutists
when Italy should wish to operate against Crete. Later
Hitler wrote to Mussolini that he had felt it to be useless
to say more about Greece that day.

" The meeting at Florence was primarily for the purpose
of removing certain objections raised by the Duce, who believed that Germany is allowing the French too much freedom and that the Italian requirements are thus receiving no
consideration.

" The Führer is, in principle, pursuing the definite policy of
keeping France weak in order to eliminate any threat to
the Axis Powers. There is no doubt that France will be
forced to meet the territorial demands of Germany and
Italy."[27]

In spite of this the Florence meeting was clouded by Hitler's
flat contradiction of Mussolini's letter of 19th October, for
he declared that he had convinced himself at Montoire
that the fight between Vichy and de Gaulle was genuine
and that Spain must be brought into the war at once. The
secret protocol of Hendaye, which had cost so much struggle
on 23rd October, and which Mussolini approved at Florence
on the 28th, involved nothing but a Spanish adherence to
the Tripartite Pact. Even this was softened down, thanks
to the Italians, when it came to be signed at Schönhof in
November; it was, in fact, nothing but a sterile face-saving
device.[28]

The month of November only darkened the Axis outlook.

[26] See German minute of Hitler-Ciano conversation, 28th Sept. 1940
(one translation reads *talking* instead of taking).

[27] *Führer Conferences on Naval Affairs,* 4th Nov. 1940.

[28] D.G.F.P. series D, vol. XI, nos. 221, 294 and note p. 466.

The Italian war against Greece made it possible for the
British to improve their Mediterranean position by the occupation of Crete, Lemnos, and other islands. And it proved
so great a fiasco that the psychological atmosphere of Europe
changed noticeably; even in Madrid there was open satisfaction over the misfortune of the ' macheronis.'[29] When
Molotov came to Berlin in the middle of the month he
seems to have made an early display of the obstructive ability
which became notorious in later years, and all Ribbentrop's
attempts to induce Russia to commit herself to an agreement with the Tripartite Powers—he offered her the Black
Sea and the freedom of the Straits[30]—fell flat. With the
Balkans in a ferment, the Russians were not going to be
bought off; on the contrary, they were developing their
political foothold in Bulgaria and inducing King Boris
to resist Hitler's offers. The adhesion of Hungarians,
Roumanians, Slovaks, and in secret of the Spaniards, to the
Tripartite Pact between 20th and 24th November was a
flimsy consolation for the attitude of the U.S.S.R.

Ciano was back in Austria for the ceremony of the
Magyar signature of the Tripartite Pact on 20th November
in Vienna. He stayed at Salzburg and on 18th November had
had a talk with Ribbentrop and also Suñer, who criticized
German policy towards France in a Mussolini vein. Both
on 18th and 20th November Ciano saw Hitler, who was in
the process of composing a letter of reproof to Mussolini
for all that had gone wrong; on the 18th Ciano himself
sent a letter to the Duce to prepare him, as it were, for
what was to come from the Führer. Hitler's letter expounded
the psychological and military effects of the Greek campaign;
he was particularly concerned that it should have given the
R.A.F. bases within easy reach of the Roumanian oil-fields
on the one hand and of southern Italy and Albania on the
other—" it is the [air] attack upon the Italian cities which
will be decisive," he wrote, and no effective counter-action

[29] Templewood, op. cit.
[30] He announced that he intended to do so when Ciano visited
him at Schönhof a week earlier—see Ciano Minute, 4th Nov. 1940,
but spoke in hostile fashion of Russia on 18th Nov.—see Ciano
to Mussolini, 18th Nov. 1940; see also chapter XVI, pp. 291-292.

could be attempted before March 1941. As political remedies Hitler proposed that Spain should intervene immediately,[31] that the German troops in Roumania should be reinforced and that Yugoslavia should be coaxed into collaboration with the Axis. As regards military action the Führer urged Mussolini to reach at least Mersa Matruh so that the British could be driven from Alexandria and Suez through Axis action, after which an all-round offensive could be launched in the spring. As part of his plan he requested the Duce to withdraw his Air Force (*not* his submarines) from the Channel.[32] Using his perennial climatic argument, he intended, he said, to send a Luftwaffe force to the Mediterranean instead—he would require it to be sent home by the beginning of May.[33]

In conversation with Ciano it appears that Hitler excited himself most over the matter of the seduction of Yugoslavia to be effected through the offer of Salonica; when Ciano expressed his belief that Mussolini would agree, the atmosphere cleared and Hitler became friendly. Why, in that case the Greek affair would become one of the great Axis successes, he declared.[34] When they parted in Vienna on 20th November, Hitler gave Ciano the letter for the Duce, and added : " From this city of Vienna I sent Mussolini a telegram to tell him that I would never forget his help on the day of the Anschluss. I repeat it to-day and I stand by his side with all my might." " There were big tears in his eyes," Ciano added in his Diary. " What a strange man ! "

Mussolini did not seem crestfallen and answered Hitler immediately. It was all the fault of the weather, of the Albanians who had deserted, and of the Bulgarians who had helped the Greeks. He agreed that a Yugoslav alliance should be sought, but made the childish condition that Yugoslav troops should not come into action until the

[31] This meant January, with a simultaneous Axis attack upon Gibraltar.

[32] Thirteen Italian planes were shot down over Harwich on 11th Nov., but very little else was ever heard of the Fascist Air Force in the north.

[33] Hitler to Mussolini, 20th Nov. 1940.

[34] Ciano to Mussolini, 20th Nov. 1940.

Italians had dealt Greece ' a first blow.'[35] On 6th December, Field-Marshal Milch arrived to arrange about the loan of a detachment of the Luftwaffe to Italy and with another letter from Hitler dated 5th December announcing that he had begun his approaches to Belgrade. It is interesting, however, to find that the longest paragraph in the Führer's letter was still devoted to Spain and France; Hitler was exasperated with the Spanish delay and uneasy that Pétain should have sent Weygand to French North Africa; he even admitted to feeling less sure about the enmity between Vichy and de Gaulle.

By now Mussolini had replaced Badoglio as Chief of Staff by Cavallero, but his Balkan fortunes had not mended, and on 9th December the British counter-attacked with success in North Africa. It seems from the entry in Ciano's Diary and from subsequent developments that Mussolini really panicked on 4th December, but it is a little difficult to be certain of the upshot as one or two of Mussolini's letters to Hitler at this time seem to have disappeared. At all events on 5th December the Italian Embassy in Berlin suddenly learnt that the Ambassador, who had been away ill for a long time, would return that day. He had been dispatched from Italy by special aeroplane, but owing to bad weather over the Alps he did not arrive in Berlin until 7th December—in this way his journey crossed with that of Milch. At 5 p.m. on 7th December the incredibly incompetent Alfieri saw Ribbentrop and begged for some kind of German threat against Greece via Roumania or Bulgaria on the one hand, and an unspecified amount of help in the shape of arms and raw materials on the other. Hitler saw Alfieri on 8th December : he recommended " barbaric means," such as " the shooting of generals and colonels "[36] to restore Italian morale in Albania, and he asked for an early meeting with Mussolini. The Duce refused to face him. On 18th December a letter from Ciano to Alfieri, dated 17th December, rather in the vein of the famous letter of 25th August 1939, arrived in Berlin; Ciano pointed out, however, that Italy was asking for a good deal less than

[35] Mussolini to Hitler, 22nd Nov. 1940.
[36] D.G.F.P. series D, vol. XI, no. 477.

in 1939, while Germany to-day controlled not only the
Great German Reich but the resources of virtually all Europe.
A list of raw materials was appended to this dispatch, some
items being urgently required within a month. At the same
time Italy asked for an extra 100,000 tons of coal monthly.[37]
Hitler saw Alfieri again on 19th December and said, approximately, " Yes, I will come to your help but I will not
send you raw materials without knowing how they will be
used; you will send thousands more of your workmen to
Germany and I will deliver finished products to you according
to the advice of my economic experts who will visit Italy
to see what to give you and on what conditions." This interview was a landmark in the history of the Axis, for it was
an important stepping-stone on the way to a German occupation of Italy. Hitherto the Italians had had endless vexa-
tions because the Germans did not send what they had promised, often diverting from the Axis ally supplies with which
they preferred to buy off the potential enemy, Russia. From
now on German economic experts and all the Gestapo and
military agents who chose to dress up in " economic expert "
clothes took up key positions in Italy, and the Italians were
no longer masters in their own house. Simoni indulged in
a Latin extravagance when he groaned that Italy was fast
becoming another Roumania,[38] but he was not altogether
wrong. He noticed that Germans often asked one now
whether Mussolini's position was still secure.[39] The arrival of
a Luftwaffe detachment in Sicily, the Italian " centre of
gravity,"[40] soon laid the foundations of a military occupation.

On 31st December 1940 Hitler wrote Mussolini a long
letter from the Obersalzberg to wish him a happier New Year.
It was remarkable rather for its moderation than for anything else : the fortunes of war, said the Führer, are bound to
ebb and flow. He dealt with Russia, the Balkans, and
North Africa, but he was still as if obsessed with the questions of Spain and France. Franco, he writes grimly, impressed by recent events, has refused to intervene, and we

[37] See Ciano to Alfieri, 17th Dec. 1940.
[38] Simoni, 12th Dec. 1940.   [39] Idem, 17th Dec. 1940.
[40] As Mussolini had said to Ribbentrop on 6th Nov. 1937 : see
chapter VI.

must give up the idea of crossing the Spanish frontier on 10th January. It is interesting that though Hitler was to write the Caudillo a very strong letter on 6th February 1941, in which he told him fairly roughly to stop his idle excuses, and in which he offered him the delivery of a million tons of grain at the moment he declared war on Britain, on New Year's Eve he already seems to have felt that the Spanish refusal was final: "I fear," he wrote in his pontifical way, "that Franco is making the greatest mistake of his life." The chief practical result of Mussolini's visit to the Berghof on 19th to 20th January 1941 was that he agreed to meet Franco himself in order to overcome his reluctance.[41] The upshot of the Duce-Caudillo meeting at Bordighera on 12th February was, however, little more than that both parties agreed in deploring the illusions the Führer had nursed about their traditional and incurable enemy, France. Though the Italians were unpopular in Spain, Franco undoubtedly preferred Italian patronage to that of Hitler, while Mussolini had really regarded Spain as his, not an Axis, affair ever since the secret agreement he had signed with Franco in November 1936;[42] at Bordighera the Duce showed more sympathy for the Spanish view than ardour for an Axis capture of Gibraltar.[43] A fortnight later the Caudillo addressed a letter to Hitler which the latter described to Ciano in March as a practical denunciation of the secret protocol of Hendaye which had been ratified at Vienna.[44]

On 13th December Pétain had replaced Laval by Flandin. Hitler still believed in Pétain, he wrote, but one could not be sure and Weygand's intentions were undoubtedly hostile. Here he was not sufficiently generous to admit that he was adopting Mussolini's view. As a matter of fact three days before the eviction of Laval—presumably the Germans were pre-informed

[41] D.G.F.P. series D, XI, no. 672.   [42] See above p. 94.

[43] See Italian Minute of Bordighera meeting, 12th Feb. 1941, and see also Hitler to Mussolini, 5th Feb. 1941, and Mussolini to Hitler, 22nd Feb. 1941.

[44] Franco's letter was dated 26th Feb. 1941. Hitler's remark is quoted in the Minute of Ciano's meeting with the Führer at Vienna on 25th Mar. 1941.

R.B.A.

—Hitler had signed Directive No. 19, Operation Attila, for the swift occupation, at a given moment, of Vichy France. This Directive ended with the words: "The Italians must not have any knowledge of the preparations made or action contemplated. (Signed) Adolf Hitler." One day later, on 11th December 1940, Operation Felix, aimed at the capture of Gibraltar, was postponed indefinitely.

At the end of 1940 Italian disasters had wrecked Hitler's plans while he himself was propounding the very things that he had scornfully denied when they were put to him by Mussolini two months earlier, that it was useless to wait for Spain and that the Axis should not trust Vichy. Beneath the surface of Hitler's faith in the fraternity of supermen and the fascination of his success for Mussolini, Italo-German discord was chronic. It was due to the fundamental divergence between the national character and interests of Italy and Germany; over it was spread the brittle crust of Nazi-Fascist theories and of individual whims and vices.

Chapter XVI

OPERATIONS MARITA AND
BARBAROSSA

The climax in Hitler's career was always to have been a
Germanic crusade against the peoples of Russia whose soil
should then nourish the German master-race. But the Führer's
vision of his Russian war had been one with a subjugated
Europe and a humbled Britain in his rear. Thanks not
only to the British but also to the vanity of Mussolini, the
obstinacy of Franco, and the intrepidity of de Gaulle, he
decided to fling his armies against Russia as an *entr'acte*
between the scenes portraying the destruction of the British
Isles. He was also impelled to take this suicidal plunge by the
chronic inadequacy of the raw-material situation, which had
clouded his relations with Rome and Madrid. And in considering the drama of 1941 it should be emphasized that both
Sofia and Belgrade were, psychologically at any rate, outposts
of Russia. Hitler had good reason to fear that if he involved
himself in perilous operations in the English Channel or
the Mediterranean, Russia might well be able, since Mussolini
had set the Balkans in motion, to induce a political transformation in both Bulgaria and Yugoslavia; should Russia
succeed in unseating the more or less pro-Axis rulers of these
countries, the profoundly pro-Russian sentiment of their
peoples would certainly make itself felt, and all kinds of Pan-
Slav and contagious social-revolutionary emotions be unchained. Balkan economic resources, to which Hitler, the
Austrian, attached a half-morbid importance, would then be
jeopardized too.

When on 4th November 1940 Ciano went shooting with
Ribbentrop on one of the latter's many estates—on this
occasion it was at Schönhof near Carlsbad—it has been
seen that the German Foreign Minister spoke of offering
Russia a declaration in the sense of the recognition of the
Black Sea as a Russian lake together with the freedom of the
Straits which were not, however, to be held by Russia.

At about this time Ribbentrop also spoke more than once, in the best traditional manner of the enemies of Britain, of turning Russia's gaze towards India. It was obvious to Ciano when he saw Hitler and Ribbentrop on 18th November that their attitude towards Russia had changed, and this was confirmed by Hitler's letters of 20th November and of 31st December to Mussolini. The change has usually been interpreted as the result of Molotov's visit to Berlin and of that of King Boris to the Berghof on 18th November, but it is interesting to find in Hitler's Secret Directive No. 18, dated 12th November, orders " in the event of its becoming necessary, to occupy that part of the Greek main-land in the North of the Aegean operating from Bulgaria . . ." and for the attack upon Russia. This directive is dated the day of Molotov's arrival in Berlin and was drawn up before the talks with him; under the heading *Russia* it states : " A political conference will be held in the near future to clarify the Russian attitude. At the same time, whatever result the conference has, preparations are to be made for the Eastern campaign."[1] It was in this spirit that Hitler received Molotov on the evening of 12th November and again on 13th November when he told the Russian Minister that German troops would remain in Finland so long as he needed Finnish nickel. Later Hitler was " visibly irritated by Molotov's insistence" upon a clearer definition of the twin questions of Bulgaria and the Straits. On the evening of the 13th, in the German Foreign Minister's air-raid shelter, Molotov, far from accession to the Tripartite Pact, conveyed to Ribbentrop the startling suggestion that Russia desired egress from the Baltic, that sacred, German sea.[2]

We know that the Italians, thanks to the disaster of their war in Greece, were at their wits' end in December, and it was not unnatural that they should make a fresh effort to improve their relations with Russia, partly in order to ease Balkan tension and largely in order to try to reduce their

[1] *Führer Conferences on Naval Affairs,* 1941, p. 3. The so-called " definitive" order for the preparation of the Russian campaign was passed to the German General Staff on 18th Dec. 1940 (Directive No. 21).

[2] D.G.F.P. series D, XI, no. 329. See also nos: 325, 326, 328.

political and economic dependence upon Germany. There was a time when Mussolini had expressed his disapprobation of German-Soviet friendship in no uncertain tone, but in June 1940[3] he had agreed that a tentative Italian advance to Russia should be made. It had led to no result. Now, as Ciano confidentially informed Alfieri on 16th December, Molotov dined at the Italian Embassy in Moscow on 13th December; on 28th December Ciano wired to Rosso to go ahead with the conversations, and this was done on 30th December. It was natural enough that Ciano wished to take action independently of Berlin, but it was clumsy to do this if he dared not risk carrying it to a conclusion without asking German permission. With the New Year he decided that Ribbentrop must be informed, and this was done by Alfieri on 6th January 1941.[3a] Ribbentrop was an excessively vindictive character, and, as Simoni noted, he was just back from his father's funeral which had not improved his temper. After all his boasts in 1939 about Russo-German friendship he could not bear Ciano to compete in any way, still less since Molotov had been so provoking in Berlin. Although a German-Russian commercial treaty was rather ostentatiously signed on 10th January[4] and was regarded as satisfactory cover for the Barbarossa plan against Russia, Ribbentrop went off to the Berghof with Keitel and Mackensen[5] and brought back a veto on the Italian-Russian negotiations just before the Duce himself was expected at Berchtesgaden. After being suspended in mid-air without instructions for a fortnight, Rosso had to explain all his soundings away. Apart from the disagreeable character of Ribbentrop's behaviour to his ally, the effect upon Molotov must have more than cancelled out the German-Russian trade treaty. When Ribbentrop and Ciano met on 19th January at the Berghof, the former made a very lame statement pre-

[3] In Mar. 1940 Hitler had urged the Italians to arrive at a *détente* with Russia; it took them three months to follow this up.

[3a] D.G.F.P. series D, vol. XI, nos. 610, 646.

[4] With a Secret Protocol by which Russia agreed to pay 7½ million gold dollars for the last strip of Lithuania: see *Nazi-Soviet Relations,* pp. 267-8. A major economic agreement had been made between Germany and the U.S.S.R. on 11th February 1940.

[5] See Simoni, 8th Jan. 1941.

faced by strong emphasis on Russia as the most important problem of the day.[6] The reason given for his veto was that it could not be tolerated that the Soviet Government should question the actual Balkan *status quo* and seek a foothold on the Straits.[7] In fact on 17th January the Russian Ambassador in Berlin had declared that according to all reports the Germans were preparing to march from Roumania into Bulgaria, Greece, and on to the Straits, "that the Soviet Government has stated repeatedly to the German Government that it considers the territory of Bulgaria and of the Straits as the security zone of the U.S.S.R. and that it cannot be indifferent to events which threaten the security interests of the U.S.S.R."[8]

The tension which surrounded Mussolini's visit to the Obersalzberg in January 1941 was great. It was three months since Führer and Duce had met at Florence, three catastrophic months for Italy. Mussolini had been shirking the encounter, and on 18th January he left Rome in considerable trepidation.[9] In addition to all the obvious reasons for anxiety on the Italian side and the irritation felt over the veto on Rosso's conversations with Molotov, the prospect of more Italian workmen being sent to Germany inflamed the running sore. Most Italians hated the war, and of those who were sent to Germany some were Communist or Socialist—since the Fascist Party preferred to get its opponents out of the way—and many were down-and-out labourers from the south. The Italian workers in Germany were in fact frequently obstructive and were then punished

[6] See Ciano's Minute. This is, of course, the Italian account but there is no trace of resentment on Ciano's part.

[7] In reply to Molotov's question to Rosso on 30th December whether Italy understood Russia's interest in the Straits, Ciano had replied that "while Italy was particularly interested in the Balkans she did not claim to exercise a decisive influence there." See Simoni, 5th Jan. 1941.

[8] See *Nazi-Soviet Relations*, p. 268.

[9] Ciano Diary, 18th Jan. 1941. See also Simoni, 5th Jan. 1941, who says that at that point Mussolini only agreed to meet Hitler in secret and at some unknown destination, their respective trains to stop somewhere in open country.

brutally by the Nazi authorities; the Embassy and, of course, the Consulates had many dossiers full of incidents. Italian confidence in the Germans was scarcely increased by the evidence which became convincing before the end of 1940 that mentally deficient Germans were being systematically killed by gassing;[10] this was largely ' experimental ' with a view to ' liquidations ' of the members of other races on a much larger scale.

On the German side there was not only extreme contempt and irritation over the Italian performance against Greece, but serious anxiety over the stability of the Fascist régime. On 9th January Alfieri saw Himmler, who was naïve and probably said exactly what the information he received from Gestapo agents in Italy led him to believe. Two dangers faced Italy, he declared, " the action of the Catholic Church and the threat of a move against the Duce." The Church, he said, affected Axis policy in a deplorable way and was, of course, responsible for Franco's recalcitrance; while Mussolini was in constant danger from the enmity of the King.[11] After the Conferences (8th and 9th January) at the Berghof to which Ribbentrop had gone, on 8th January Raeder reported that :

" The Führer is of the opinion that it is vital for the outcome of the war that Italy does not collapse, but remains a loyal member of the Axis. The Duce is emphatically pro-Axis. On the other hand, the military and political leaders are *not* pro-Axis and reliable to the same extent. Count Ciano has been sharply attacked by Fascist and military circles. However, the Führer does not believe that in the present situation Ciano would oppose Germany.

" The well-known Italian mentality makes it difficult for the Germans to influence the Italian leaders. The Führer is of the opinion that if the Italians are to be kept in line he must not go too far in matters of leadership. We should not make *demands*; too great demands may cause even Mussolini to change his attitude. Besides there is the danger that then the Italians in turn might make undesirable demands. (For example, the Italians may desire information

[10] See Simoni, 16th Jan. 1941.   [11] Simoni, 9th Jan. 1941.

about German operational plans. The Führer considers that caution is necessary, especially in this connexion. . . . There is great danger that the Royal Family is transmitting intelligence to Britain.)"

Only a fortnight earlier Hitler had said to his naval and military chiefs : " There is a complete lack of leadership in Italy. The royal house is pro-British; it will have to be eliminated if it works against Mussolini."[12]

When the Duce arrived at Berchtesgaden on Sunday the 19th, Ciano was astonished by the spontaneous warmth manifested between Mussolini and Hitler. On this difficult occasion Hitler seems again to have managed the Duce with skill and to have sent him back to Italy more fascinated than ever. It has already been recorded that to Mussolini was entrusted the task, as Ciano said, of bringing home the Spanish prodigal son. On Monday, 20th January, a military conference was held with the Führer, Ribbentrop, Keitel, Jodl, von Rintelen, von Puttkamer, Schmundt, and Paul Schmidt present for the Germans, and Mussolini, Ciano, Guzzoni, Marras (Military Attaché in Berlin), and Gandin for the Italians. Indications were made to the Italians of the programme drawn up by the Germans on 11th January for the purpose of coming to their aid in Libya and the Balkans; Sicily was already a Luftwaffe base since Hitler had ordered a German squadron to go to the rescue on 10th December in response to Alfieri's *cri de cœur* of 7th December.[13] The Führer insisted at least twice that German help to Italy would not be like that of the British to the French, but would be effectual.

Hitler's declamation on this occasion,[14] apart from recriminations against France and the blackmail of Weygand and a reiteration of " Attack upon the British Isles is our ultimate aim," consisted of an anti-Russian outburst. The Russians, Hitler said, had protested against Germany's troops in

[12] *Führer Conferences on Naval Affairs,* 27th Dec. 1940. See also D.G.F.P. series D, vol. XI, p. 987 footnote.

[13] Cf. D.G.F.P. series D, XI, no. 583.

[14] See German Minute U.S. Document C. 134. Cf. D.G.F.P. series D, XI, no. 679.

Roumania, for which they would be snubbed :[15] the German soldiers were there in preparation for the operation against Greece, to protect Bulgaria against Russia, and to implement the Axis guarantee of Roumania. The Führer complained also that he was suffering from Russian obstruction in the matter of Finland's nickel which was essential to Germany. He declared that Russia was a far greater menace than the United States, and was pinning down such large German forces on the eastern frontiers as to impose a serious drain of man-power away from the manufacture of armaments.

On 31st December Hitler had written to Mussolini that so long as Stalin was alive he did not fear hostile Russian action, but one must not forget that Pilsudski's successors had betrayed their Germanophile heritage. At the Berghof in conference with his own chiefs ten days later he announced that " Stalin must be regarded as a cold-blooded blackmailer ; he would, if expedient, repudiate any written treaty at any time." Now on 20th January to the Italians, with the help of the half-crazy anti-Semitic formulae in which he devoutly believed, Hitler compromised between his various assertions. " As long as Stalin lives," he repeated, " there is probably no danger ; he is intelligent and careful " (seventeen months before he had been accepted as a third superman). " But," Hitler added, " should he cease to be there, the Jews, who at present only occupy second or third rank positions, might move up again into the first rank." Finally he asserted that Russia was no danger on land, but was to be feared because she could menace the Roumanian oil-fields. The clash which was at that moment occurring between Antonescu and certain Iron Guard leaders (a disturbance for which Hitler, of course, blamed Russia) made the Roumanian situation particularly delicate, but Hitler indicated on 20th January that Germany would maintain his cherished Antonescu. It was only known later that Horia Sima, who had opposed Antonescu, was spirited away to Germany to be saved for future use. The subject of Roumania gave the

[15] On 21st January Ribbentrop (from Fuschl) ordered Weizsäcker to tell the Russians that " the German Army will march through Bulgarian territory should any military operations be carried out against Greece." See *Nazi-Soviet Relations*, p. 271.

Führer an opportunity to dilate on the matter of revolutions among which, he explained, only the two perpetrated by Mussolini and himself had had " an immediately constructive effect."

So much for Russia for the moment. Apropos Stalin Hitler on 8th January had also said to his own chiefs :

" Britain's aim for some time to come will be to set Russian strength in motion against us. If the United States of America and Russia should enter the war against Germany, the situation would become very complicated. Hence any possibility for such a threat to develop must be eliminated at the very beginning. If the Russian threat were non-existent, we could wage war on Britain indefinitely. If Russia collapsed, Japan would be greatly relieved; this in turn would mean increased danger to the U.S.A."[16]

It is extraordinary to see how the remote scent of danger or conflict so intoxicated Hitler that he ran to meet it and to provoke his potential enemy. But to the Italian ally he neither indulged in these vast cogitations nor hinted at the military directives which were already prepared. The Germans, wherever they went, still claimed with assurance that the war was already won, but Ciano was taken aback to hear Ribbentrop admit at this January meeting that it could scarcely be over before 1942.

The immediate objective at the beginning of 1941 must be to put the Axis ally on her feet. The news from both Italian fronts continued to be bad, and, though Mussolini had assured Hitler at Berchtesgaden that the régime was unshaken, on 5th February Hitler wrote to him to express anew his desire to " overcome a situation which is bound in the long run to have unfortunate psychological effects not only upon the rest of the world but also for your own people." In this letter Hitler proposed that Rommel with a small staff should join Graziani at once in Africa. Mussolini only answered on 22nd February, after he had seen Franco at Bordighera. He confirmed the Caudillo's view that Spain was incapable of war at present. Angrily he wrote that the Italian people had not been shaken by the bad news from the fronts, and added that only the British

[16] *Führer Conferences on Naval Affairs*, 1941, p. 13.

could have been so stupid as to think that the Fascist régime was endangered.

The Germans had grave doubts as to the men and material they were sending to Libya[17]—whether it was worth while, or simply pouring one's resources down the drain. They felt that they should at least insist upon the placing of the Italian forces under German command. At the Berghof meeting at the beginning of the year Raeder " expressed the view that the Italian armed forces need to be strictly organized under German leadership."[18] This was the beginning of a long Axis tussle in which the Italians lost the first round when the Duce, in the same letter of 22nd February, accepted the Führer's proposal to put the Italian armoured and motorized divisions under Rommel in order to assure unity of action. " We shall win," Mussolini concluded, " for many reasons, the first being that we are putting our men and means together to fight for our revolution."

To rescue the Italian position in the Balkans Hitler had planned Operation Marita since November 1940 : this meant to force Yugoslavia to adhere to the Tripartite Pact and to bring up German troops from Roumania across a helpless Bulgaria into Greece by about the end of March. From the time of Ciano's visit to Austria in November Ribbentrop had been working upon Belgrade, but just as King Boris could not completely flout the Russophile sentiments of the Bulgars, so Prince Paul and his Ministers insisted that the furthest length to which they could go with Germany was a non-aggression pact. There was much in Ribbentrop's spiteful insistence upon the obstacle created by anti-Italian feeling in Yugoslavia, which was strongest in Croatia on account of the Dalmatian claims of Italy. On the other hand, the Croat quarrel with the Serbs was based on a claim to be more civilized which was associated with an orientation towards Vienna[19] like that of ex-King Zog. This was a trump in the hand of Hitler, more particularly when it was

[17] See Simoni, 30th Jan. 1941, 3rd Feb. 1941.

[18] *Führer Conferences on Naval Affairs* of 8-9th Jan. 1941, p. 8.

[19] Cf. Hitler's statement to his generals on 27th March 1941 : " Serbs and Slovenes were never pro-German," the Croats being ostentatiously excepted. Nuremberg Trial Proceedings, part II, p. 221.

a matter of his war with Russia, incipient here in the
Balkans somewhere between Zagreb and Belgrade. But,
though some Croat leaders were in German or Italian pay,
Maček, the idol of the Croat peasantry, could never have been
bought by the Axis.[20] He was true to his Slav inheritance,
and all these Slav peoples were dimly conscious of what
they had to fear from Germany. Meanwhile, the Russians
looked on in anger and apprehension, and perhaps with some
contempt.

For during February Rome and Berlin, far from co-operat-
ing at Belgrade, behaved like a couple of jealous women
in rivalry for a beau's favours. Mussolini oscillated between
dangling the bait of Salonica before Yugoslavia in order to
win her quickly enough to demoralize the Greeks, and
protesting to Hitler that Salonica could only be allowed to a
true friend of the Axis which Yugoslavia could never be.[21]
The German game was played more quietly and more falsely.
On 14th February the Yugoslav Premier and Foreign Minister
were induced to make the inevitable pilgrimage to Berchtesgaden, and Prince Paul himself slipped off secretly to see
Hitler on 4th March. While telling the Italians to lay off
Yugoslavia because it was desirable to be extremely cautious
and to gain time, Hitler and Ribbentrop themselves offered
the Yugoslavs Salonica as well as a territorial guarantee
obviously directed against Italy; at the same time they
offered a guarantee that the German Army would not cross
Yugoslavia's frontiers and that they (the Yugoslavs) would
not be expected to co-operate against Greece. Hassell, who
was in Belgrade for about a week in March, is probably
reliable about these negotiations, since he was informed by
Prince Paul and the German Minister both of whom he knew
intimately; he observed that the Croats and Slovenes in the
Cabinet favoured accepting the German offer for the sake
of security against Italy.[22]

[20] The S.S. officer, Veesenmayer, who was sent to negotiate with
him at the beginning of April, failed to enrol him in the German
cause.

[21] Mussolini to Hitler, 22nd Feb. 1941.

[22] Hassell, op. cit., p. 188 et seq. On the other hand, he speaks
on 4th April of Maček as asking for Italian mediation.

On 8th February Hitler induced both Roumania and Bulgaria to sign a pact with Germany against Greece,[23] and on 19th February, immediately after the Yugoslavs had been to Berchtesgaden, Hitler fixed the dates for the move across Bulgaria; on 28th February the first part of Operation Marita began to be executed so that on 1st March Bulgaria adhered to the Tripartite Pact as the German troops were crossing the Danube. The Germans moved very slowly towards Salonica, in order, as they confidentially informed the Italians,[24] to induce the Greeks to give in to them without fighting. Mussolini nearly lost his head again and he rushed off to Albania to order a fresh offensive so that Greece should at all costs surrender to Italy, not to Germany; the offensive proved to be a failure again. Meanwhile, fat little General Guzzoni[25] had been telephoning to Marras to protest against the idea of the Germans peacefully entering Greece " while our people are fighting and dying."[26]

On 20th March Ribbentrop informed Alfieri that Yugoslavia had agreed to adhere to the Tripartite Pact. This statement was as false as the rest of his behaviour all through this affair. On 21st March, indeed, a Cabinet crisis in Belgrade made Yugoslav acquiescence less probable. Thereupon Berlin addressed an ultimatum to Yugoslavia, and a fresh Tripartite Pact ceremony was arranged to take place at the Belvedere Palace in Vienna on Tuesday, 25th March. Ciano who, like all the Fascist Ministers, had been on active service, now went back to his work as Foreign Minister and appeared in Vienna to sign once again on behalf of Italy.[27] When the Yugoslav Prime Minister, Cvetković, had returned, on the night of 26th March, there was a revolution in Belgrade, an event as exciting and important as de Gaulle's

[23] See captured documents 1746-PS (p. 303 below) and D.G.F.P. series D, vol. XII, no. 30.

[24] Simoni, 3rd Mar. 1941.   [25] See Ciano Diary, 17th Jan. 1941.

[26] Simoni, 9th Mar. 1941.

[27] He saw Hitler who spoke openly of his four quarrels with Russia—Finland, Bulgaria, Roumania, the Straits—and added that he had more faith in the German troops on the Russian frontier than in the existing pacts—see Ciano Minute, 25th Mar. 1941. Kordt (op. cit.) says that Hitler complained that the official banquet on this occasion had seemed like a funeral party.

defiance of brute force in the previous June. The Prince Regent disappeared in favour of young King Peter, and General Simović headed a new Government. The enraged Hitler immediately held a Council of War (27th March) and Operation Marita was speeded up with lightning speed while Yugoslav atrocities against helpless Germans suddenly poured from the German wireless. " The Führer is determined," we read in the Minute of this meeting, " without waiting for possible declarations of loyalty from the new government, to make all preparations in order to destroy Yugoslavia militarily and as a national unit. No diplomatic enquiries will be made nor ultimata presented. . . . The attack will start as soon as the means and troops suitable for it are ready." At midnight an excited message, emphasizing before everything the need for discretion, was sent from Hitler to Mussolini. Mackensen delivered it personally to the Duce (alone) at 2 a.m. on 28th March and reported back that Mussolini, " who made the impression of the greatest fitness and calm," seemed well content and came out with the right phrases about Versailles and Sarajevo.[28] Without loss of time the Duce drafted a reply adding to Hitler's enumeration of Hungary and Bulgaria as essential vassals in the new crisis the name of Pavelić " who happens to be not far from Rome."[29]

On Saturday, 5th April, the day before the Germans bombed Belgrade, Hitler informed Mussolini that the attack was about to begin. His message this time was chiefly concerned with proposing to the Duce that in this whole operation he should accept Hitler's strategic orders for all the Italian forces concerned. The Führer tactfully suggested that these orders would be communicated to Mussolini personally in the form of ' recommendations ' and ' wishes.' " This only involves a personal understanding between the two of us and will not be known to the world." After sententiously reiterating that " Yugoslavia is the most authentic creation of Versailles and deserves her fate," the Duce on 6th April accepted the yoke against which his generals, had they known, would have protested bitterly. Mussolini's

[28] D.G.F.P. series D, XII, no. 226.
[29] Mussolini to Hitler, 28th Mar. 1941; see also pp. 271-2 below.

humiliation was increased by the sending of the same instructions at the same time to Horthy. Teleki had killed himself rather than be pushed into the rending of Yugoslavia immediately after Hungary had made a friendly agreement with her. But without Teleki there was no one strong enough to fight against the whirlwind, and the Magyar troops moved southwards when the German signal came.

The destruction of Yugoslavia during April 1941, and the surrender of Greece to the Germans without reference to the Italians on 23rd April, opened a fresh phase in the history of the Axis. The partition and occupation of the Balkan peninsula was completed and the New Order thus established in Europe apart from Russia as it was to remain with virtually no change until 1944. It led to any number of fresh conflicts between Italy and Germany which came to a head in 1942 and 1943. But the conquest of Yugoslavia and Greece was also the immediate prelude to Hitler's attack upon Russia.

Gradually, during the first half of 1941, Hitler's utterances show that to his obsession with the iniquity of Franco was being added his obsession with the iniquity of Stalin. On every occasion of Axis contact during the winter of 1940-1, and indeed much later, Hitler lamented the lost opportunity of taking Gibraltar, lost thanks to the blind obstinacy of Spain. But as the months passed he worked up his own exasperation against Russia with more and more success. The evolution of his sentiments towards Stalin has been recorded, and it is interesting to see how all along he regards Operation Marita as the overture to Operation Barbarossa. On 27th March he made a statement to his military commanders that " Yugoslavia was an uncertain factor in regard to the coming Marita action and even more in regard to the Barbarossa undertaking later on."[30] In his letter to Mussolini on 5th April he gave as one of the reasons for an immediate attack upon Yugoslavia the pact of friendship which she was in the process of concluding with Russia, though the pact was bound to be as helpless a gesture as the British guarantees to Poland and Roumania had been.

[30] See *Nuremberg Trial Proceedings,* part II, p. 221. Document 1746-PS (G.B. 120).

After asking Mussolini to submit to his orders he explained that he only wished to be certain of an early victory " just because in view of the insecure state of affairs in the east, I shall naturally be glad to be able to free the German formations as soon as possible from their present task."[31]

Part of the preparation of the attack upon Russia involved an implementation of the alliance with Japan, and Ribbentrop had therefore invited his friend Oshima to Fuschl on 23rd February. In March the far from bellicose Japanese Foreign Minister, Matsuoka, made a journey round Europe beginning and ending in Moscow: he saw Ribbentrop on 27th, 28th, and 29th March and again on 4th April[32] and 5th April, the Saturday before the Stukas destroyed Belgrade. The Nazi Minister on each occasion did his utmost to incite the Japanese to attack Singapore and sent Matsuoka back to Moscow to sign a neutrality pact with Molotov on 13th April. This no doubt suited the Japanese, but since Hitler always placed an almost morbid emphasis upon " the element of surprise," it suited him too; it combined with his own pretended renewal of " Sea Lion " preparations with a view to lulling the suspicions of Russia.[33]

The month of May 1941 was a particularly difficult one for the Axis relationship. The war had been won so often and yet it seemed impossible, as Mussolini remarked,[34] to transform it into victory and peace. Renewed commercial negotiations between Germany and Italy proved disastrous; Germany simply could not prepare Operation Barbarossa and a feint Sea Lion without drastically cutting down the coal and oil she sent to Italy. The rapid eviction of the British from Crete by the Germans spelt fresh humiliation for the Duce. The occupation and partition of Yugoslavia and Greece led to every kind of quarrel; developments in

[31] Hitler to Mussolini, 5th Apr. 1941.

[32] With Hitler on 27th March and 4th April.

[33] See Hitler's military conference 3rd Feb. 1961. *Nuremberg Trial Proceedings*, part II, p. 237. " The strategic concentration for ' Barbarossa ' will be camouflaged as a feint for *Seeloewe* and the subsidiary measure ' Marita.' " In June Goebbels went in for calculated indiscretions in the press about the invasion of Britain.

[34] Ciano Diary, 2nd June 1941.

those countries will be examined later. The incorrigible defeatism of the Berliners, which Simoni regarded as incurable once the invasion of Britain had failed, was stimulated in the middle of the month by the flight of Hess to Scotland —Hess, the Deputy of the Führer, who had been officially named with Göring as Hitler's possible successor. The event was never fully exploited by the British; it shook the Nazi régime as effectually as anything before the fall of Mussolini.[35] On 13th May Ribbentrop rushed to Rome to explain away the flight of Hess; the Duce was delighted, after the hints about his own position, to observe how greatly this incident had alarmed the Nazis. On Saturday, 31st May, Hitler demanded to see Mussolini on the Sunday or Monday and they met at the Brenner on 2nd June. According to Mussolini, who was annoyed at being summoned, as he said, like a waiter, Hitler ranted for hours about the sinking of the *Bismarck*, but nothing was seriously analysed or decided; Hitler wept, the Duce said, when he spoke or Hess.[36] The miscreant's place was taken by his assistant, Martin Bormann, who became Party Secretary. The change reinforced the stubborn character of the Nazi régime, for Bormann was a determined, industrious, and ruthless fanatic.

Meanwhile, an ominous silence prevailed with regard to Russia, and when Ribbentrop and Hitler met their Italian colleagues they pooh-poohed Russia as a minor business which could settle nothing one way or the other. On 13th May Mussolini asked whether Germany excluded the possibility of collaboration with Russia, whereupon Ribbentrop was obviously taken aback; after some prevarication he announced that he did not think that Stalin would move against Germany, but if he did Russia would be destroyed in three months. The Führer had been made suspicious by Russian

[35] See Goebbels Diary, 23rd Sept. 1943.

[36] Ciano Diary, 2nd June 1941. Cf Semmler's Diary (1947), entry for 14th May 1941. Goebbels told Semmler, one of his subordinates, " Hitler was in tears and looked ten years older." It seems that the Franco-German protocols (with regard to Axis use of French North African ports) signed five or six days previously were not mentioned on 2nd June, though on 13th May a good deal of time was devoted to France.

behaviour, but had, of course, only strengthened his forces on the Russian frontier *after* the Russians had concentrated theirs.[37] On 2nd June Ribbentrop, in his parrot-like way,[38] appears to have repeated these inspired remarks to Ciano.[39] On the first occasion he replied to a question that the Russians were delivering their goods satisfactorily to Germany, on the second that it would be regrettable if war interrupted the flow of Russian goods. While the Italian Embassy in Berlin was confidentially misinformed by the *Auswärtiges Amt* that Russian deliveries were almost at a standstill,[40] General Thomas correctly stated that they continued satisfactorily until the two countries were at war.[41]

The Hassell and Simoni Diaries give an illuminating account of the atmosphere in Berlin. Anyone with any perspicacity knew that the attack against Russia was being intensively prepared. People were fascinated in a morbid, rather German way by the thought of Napoleon, another of Hitler's obsessions; von Etzdorf openly referred Simoni to the date of Napoleon's passage of the Niemen if he wished to know the date of Hitler's attack upon Russia.[42] Few seem to have been deceived by the Sea Lion feint, but the air was full of rumours about a surrender by Stalin, who was credited with the intention of following Hacha's ex-ample, so that the Russian steppes would have lain open for the realization of the dreams of *Mein Kampf* just as they were dreamt in the Landsberg prison so many years before.

[37] D.G.F.P. series D, vol. XII, no. 511.

[38] See Ciano Diary, 13th May 1941, where he quotes Göring as calling Ribbentrop " the first parrot in Germany."

[39] Ciano Minute, 2nd June 1941, where Ribbentrop is recorded as saying " The rumours of the imminence of operations against Russia are to be considered as unfounded or at least extremely premature. It is the Russians who have begun to concentrate their forces on the German frontier."

[40] Simoni, 15th May 1941.

[41] General Thomas (chief of *Wirtschaftsrüstungsamt*), *Basic Facts for a History of German War and Armoured Economy,* prepared 1944, see *Nuremberg Trial Proceedings,* part II, p. 256.

[42] Simoni, 1st June 1941. Etzdorf quoted Caulaincourt.

The draft plans for Operation Barbarossa had been submitted to the Führer on 30th January 1941, ten days after the Italo-German conversations in January, and much detailed planning work was gone through in the early days of February. The attack upon Russia was originally to have taken place in the middle of May, but the crushing of Yugoslavia delayed it for about five weeks; by the end of April, while Ribbentrop continued to pronounce denials, Hitler had decided upon the date 22nd June.[43] The most horrible thing about this latest and largest conspiracy was the deliberate preparation of the atrocities to be perpetrated in Russia. In a German memorandum of 2nd May 1941,[44] it was stated : " (1) The war can only be continued if all Armed Forces are fed by Russia in the third year of the war. (2) There is no doubt that as a result many millions of people will be starved to death if we take out of the country the things necessary for us." Mr. Alderman said at the Nuremberg Trial (on 25th November 1945) that there was perhaps never a more sinister sentence written than the second of these. At the same time orders were being drawn up for the total disregard of the normal conventions of war—the Russian campaign was to be an S.S. massacre. Men like Hassell easily gathered this from their friends in key positions, and he was horrified at the supine acceptance of such directives by the Wehrmacht as a whole. All through the spring Hitler had felt anxiety as to the extremely independent attitude of Turkey for when it should come to war in the Balkans and Russia; on 18th June a German-Turkish non-aggression pact was suddenly announced and it seemed like the ghost of the German-Russian Pact of 1939. On 15th June, when the farce of Croatia's adherence to the Tripartite Pact was gone through at Venice, Ribbentrop had at last allowed

[43] Report of Conference with Chief of *Landesverteidigung* section of *Wehrmacht Führungsstab*, 30th Apr. 1941. See *Nuremberg Trial Proceedings,* part II, p. 240. On 27th Mar. Hitler had told his commanders that " Barbarossa " would have to be delayed *bis zu vier Wochen*—see 1746-PS.

[44] See *Nuremberg Trial Proceedings,* part I, p. 177. Also *Anatomie des S.S.-Staates* (1965), vol. II, p. 170 on *Kommissarbefehl.*

that, thanks to nothing but the Russian concentrations of troops, a Russo-German crisis " was almost certain."[45] At last, in the night of 21st-22nd June, Hitler communicated to his comrade Mussolini that he had taken " the most serious decision of his life." His letter on this occasion concluded with the words :

" Since taking this decision I feel my spirit to be once more free. In spite of the sincerity of my efforts to achieve a final *détente,* it has often been very painful to me to march at Russia's side, for it always seemed to me that I was denying my past, my ideas, and my previous undertakings. I am happy now to have liberated myself from this torment."[46]

---

[45] Ciano Minute 15th June 1941. In Dec. 1943, in the prison at Verona, Ciano's memory of this day played him false.

[46] Hitler to Mussolini, 21st June 1941.

Chapter XVII

THE NEW ORDER

From the spring of 1941 until the autumn of 1942 there was a strange paradoxical stability in Europe. Victory seemed to have returned to the Axis, even to Italy. The Russian war brought endless German triumph and advance and further occupation of territory; Hitler was always on the verge of total success. When Japan attacked the United States the new battleground was still farther away, and there was a feeling in Europe that Japanese bellicosity and American resources might merely create another distant deadlock. If Ribbentrop at last dropped his formula of ' The war is already won,' he now settled down, in his encounters with Ciano and his lesser vassals, to the slogan ' We cannot lose this war '; it was sometimes suggested by the Germans that a state of war might become permanent.

The Continent, except for the neutral corners which survived to the end, was entirely subjected to the Axis. The German attack upon Russia was the signal for a fresh avalanche of propaganda about the joys of the New Order which the Axis Powers were creating. Every true European must join in the crusade against the Soviets to defend the civilization of the Continent; this heroic struggle would forge a new European Unity. Ciano was ill when Mussolini visited Hitler at his headquarters at the front at the end of August 1941, and the Italian record of the conversation was presumably made by the Duce himself. " The Führer's exposition," he noted helplessly, " was made with order and precision, making the impression of absolute calm and serenity. The Duce judged it opportune to leave the Führer to develop his proposition quite freely ";[1] thus again he failed to stem the tide of Hitler's verbosity and only spoke

---

[1] " Colloquio del Duce col Führer, 25th Aug. 1941 (i)," in *L'Europa verso la catastrofe*. Mussolini saw Hitler at Rastenburg and also visited Kluge and Rundstedt at their respective headquarters. See also D.G.F.P. series D, XIII, no. 242.

at the second meeting that day. Again the Führer broke in,
" repeating what he had already expressed in the earlier
conversation, that he was not fighting for the sake of
destruction or prestige but rather . . . to create the basis
necessary for the construction of a new European order."[2]
In the letters which Führer and Duce exchanged fairly frequently in this year for Hitler to indulge in voluptuous
accounts of the Russian campaign, there is a great deal of
talk of the imminent triumph of " our " or " your " and " my
revolution," or sometimes " the revolution of the Axis." But
what did all this mean? The more one studies the evidence
the clearer it becomes that Mussolini by now had no conception in his mind beyond that contained in the only two
descriptive adjectives one finds that he uses, " nationalistic "
and " dynamic "; to the Führer he did not rant against
the *bourgeoisie*. Hitler, on the other hand, had always
known that it was seldom or never expedient to put it all
kncwn what he wanted, certainly since 1924; he had also
into words and it is unlikely that he ever did so to the
Duce. It is necessary to distinguish between what he
announced that he wanted, which was full of contradictions,[3]
and what in fact he deliberately brought about, which was
not.

On 29th December 1941 he wrote Mussolini a long letter
to wish him a happy New Year. Already, he said, such blows
had been given to Russia that she could never recover, and
the recent entry of Japan into the war was among the most
decisive events in modern history. He hoped for a long
period of peace and reconstruction to follow, which would
give great tasks

" to us in the North and North-East, and to you and
your people, Duce, in those spaces which once were civilized by
Rome.

" Above all, Duce, it often seems to me that human develop-

[2] Ibid. (11).

[3] Apropos the permission for a halfway anti-Nazi speech by Hans
Frank in July 1942 Hassell wrote " Hitler plays this game with
typically subtle duplicity, in order to throw sand into people's
eyes: what is more, he succeeds in doing so." Hassell, op. cit.,
p. 273.

ment has only been interrupted for fifteen hundred years and is now about to resume its former character. That destiny should have given to the two of us so eminent a position in this struggle binds me year by year more closely to you."

It was quite serious. He wished, not to safeguard European civilization, but to undo the evolution of fifteen hundred years. He wished to go back to the time of Attila; the Hun ruler, too, had gloried in "erasing" his enemy's cities. Gibbon likened the Huns of Attila to the Moguls and Tartars.

"The most casual provocation, the slightest motive of caprice or convenience, often provoked them to involve a whole people in an indiscriminate massacre : and the ruin of some flourishing cities was executed with such unrelenting perseverance, that, according to their own expression, horses might run, without stumbling, over the ground where they had once stood."[4]

Sometimes Hitler or his lieutenants would speak of resuming the mission of the Holy Roman Empire in its pristine glory, but while they longed to play with universalism they desired something more barbarous than the régime of a Charlemagne. In 1933 Robert Dell[5] exclaimed in horror to a Nazi acquaintance, "You have gone back to the tenth century!" But Hitler was more accurate in the expression of his dreams when he wrote to Mussolini of a return to the fifths century, when the barbarians of Germany and Scythia were overrunning the decadent Empire of Rome—did Mussolini forget that the period Hitler longed to renew was that of a disintegrating Italy?

The strongest external[5a] influence upon Hitler had been the doctrine of Nietzsche to whom power and the struggle for power—which meant trampling down the weak—provided the ultimate values. Nietzsche had condemned both Christianity and the ideas of the first French Revolution as the triumph of a slave mentality against which he exhorted all master spirits to rebel; they were to create a new code of the strong, the basis of which must be ruthlessness. "A ruling race can only arrive amid terrible and violent conditions.

---

[4] *Decline and Fall of the Roman Empire,* chapter xxxiv.

[5] A famous *Manchester Guardian* correspondent of that day.

[5a] External to Austria.

Problem: where are the barbarians of the twentieth century? Obviously they will only emerge and consolidate themselves after tremendous socialistic upheavals."[6] But Nietzsche's dreams had come to him as professor of classical studies in the humanistic air of Basle; they were Homeric dreams of magnanimous heroes who took risks, and he quarrelled with the monstrous conceptions of Wagner. In the year of Hitler's birth, Nietzsche became permanently mad, and the thought is irresistible that Hitlerism was a form of Nietzsche's madness. In reading Nietzsche, in so far as he ever did so, it is obvious that Hitler had picked out only what he liked and thought he understood. Far from escaping from a lower-middle-class and mechanical age, Hitler's master caste was to be built up without taking risks. Many German writers of the Ludendorff brand had been working up to a doctrine, not of ruthlessness alone, but of total, mechanical ruthlessness; their efforts culminated in the *petit bourgeois* Hitler with his love of machines and his theory of the economy of force.

In order to realize his dreams, Hitler had constructed a human machine. The black-uniformed Schutz Staffeln (S.S.) organized by Himmler since 1929 were to be the nucleus of a master caste which was to stamp out stupid *idées fixes* about social justice and human rights. Those who clung to such notions must either be destroyed completely or become the slaves who were required for several purposes: they must work for the masters and they must provide the masters with material upon which to sharpen the teeth of their brutality. Since Hitler's ideology contained a crude eugenic element which was part of his tendency to equate men with machines and the study of medicine with military science, the slaves could fulfil both these functions and a third at the same time—that of supplying human material for physiological experiment. But the aim of all this could only be revealed to a small *élite* of bold supermen—only a very few even among the masters—partly because only these few were sufficiently 'heroic' or degraded not to flinch, and partly because one of the weapons in the glorious fight of the strong against the weak was to demoralize by the suggestion

[6] Nietzsche, *Der Wille zur Macht.*

of infinitely terrible but undefined possibilities. The Nazi concentration camps[7] were, in fact, an integral and essential part of Hitler's State,[8] for the herding of the slaves at the mercy of the S.S. masters in these places about which no one who had not entered them knew the truth was only too effectual. Those who refused to be good Nazis lived on the threshold of hell with the words " Abandon hope all ye who enter here " in the forefront of their minds. And yet there was little against which one could struggle; it was part of the plan that no outcry could be effectually raised because the Nazis could reply, " But this is just someone's imagination or the propaganda of the Jews—you have no proof." And the nameless terror was complete in the absence of martyrs; in February 1938 Hitler told Schuschnigg contemptuously[9] that the Austrian régime had made the fatal error of creating martyrs, and a month later Schuschnigg himself, who, one may say without cynicism, was cut out for the role, disappeared too completely to discredit Hitler by his sufferings.

The S.S. system was disappointing, however, so long as it could only be applied to Germany, for there was a surfeit of supermen and a shortage of slaves. There were only the German Jews and a relatively small number of very brave Germans to victimize. The year 1938 made available the Austrian and Czech Jews and a good many priests and patriotic Czechs. Then 1939 brought the Poles as victims and 1940 the Norwegians,[10] Dutch, Belgians and Luxembourgeois, and the French and Roumanians, and 1941 the rest of the inhabitants of the Balkan peninsula and the peoples of western Russia and the Baltic States. This was much more consistent with Hitler's aspirations. He had never been a nationalist

[7] The term " concentration camp " is indiscriminately used for internment camps with no ulterior purpose and for the Nazi " KZ " which should be sharply distinguished from all others.

[8] See E. Kogon, *Der S.S.-Staat*, quoted above, which is probably the best book on the subject. The Auschwitz trials in 1964 and 1965 confirmed this picture, see H. Buchheim and others *Anatomie des S.S.-Staates*, (1965).

[9] Schuschnigg, op. cit.

[10] The Danish constitution was not seriously infringed by the Germans until 1942.

in the Mazzinian sense, for that involved a recognition of the equal rights of other nations. Racialism could be interpreted to extol the Germans at the other races' expense and to provide a case for anti-Semitism, but on the other hand it involved one in fearful anthropological complications, and the Nordic brothers in Scandinavia and Holland were sadly unappreciative of the superior caste status which was offered to them. Essentially Hitler was a paranoiac type who cared for nothing but power and the struggle for power and more power; obviously he preferred power over a continent to power merely over his own rather arbitrarily chosen race. Everywhere except in Poland he found a few Quislings as recruits for his master spirits, or in other words for his criminal gangs, and above all he found whole populations to swell the ranks of the slaves. The Führer's faithful apostle, Himmler, declared to his followers : " What happens to a Russian or to a Czech does not interest me in the slightest. What the nations can offer in the way of good blood of our type we shall take, if necessary by kidnapping their children and raising them here with us. Whether nations live in prosperity or starve to death interests me only in so far as we need them as slaves for our Kultur : otherwise it is of no interest to me. . . ."[11] At one time or another Nazi experts wrote endless volumes explaining the legal and economic significance of Hitler's New Order. Quite simply, however, it amounted to the establishment of a very cruel slavery on an unprecedented scale, combined as it was with the concentration of the control of industry and trade in German hands.

Total war embarked upon with inadequate resources vastly increased the demand for labour, and the occupation of Europe made it possible to draft a stream of foreign slaves into the Reich. For that is what not only the prisoners of war, but also the " freely " enrolled foreign workers, became.[12] They were carefully divided into categories, of course : on the lowest plane were the Jews and fairly near

[11] Speech to S.S. Generals at Posen, 4th Oct. 1943, see *Nuremberg Trial Proceedings,* part II, p. 290.

[12] The Nazi leader responsible for all this was Sauckel (*Generalbevollmächtigter für den Arbeitseinsatz*).

them the Slavs and the 'renegades' or 'Communists' of
other races; for a long time the French and the Dutch were
regarded as the super-slaves. Food was distributed accordingly, Jews and Slavs being kept as near to starvation as was
useful. It has been seen that the invasion of the U.S.S.R. had
been planned with the idea of 'liquidating' a considerable
proportion of the population in order that others should
have their food. Consequently the Russian prisoners were
often deliberately starved to death. Occasionally they were
incited to cannibalism in order that propaganda might exploit
their barbarism: Göring seems to have boasted to Ciano
of this when Ciano came to Berlin to sign the renewal of the
Tripartite Pact in November 1941.[13]

In a country which has never been subjected to S.S. rule,
its meaning is difficult to comprehend. It is perhaps worth
repeating that the Axis occupation of Europe, so far as
Hitler and Himmler could shape it, meant the suppression
of every human right and personal freedom. It meant the
suppression of all accurate information. It meant pillage
by the privileged Germans which in turn created dearth
and induced black marketing and inflation. Some of the
French or Belgians were enticed to work in Germany by
golden promises (which were broken), but again many a
chance passer-by in the occupied countries was simply impressed when the S.S. cordoned off a street or a cinema.
If anyone protested or resisted he was liable to find himself
in a Nazi concentration camp or in a Gestapo prison. In
both these places he would be deliberately tortured to
supply information, but also so that his torturers might perfect their own cruelty: further, he might at any moment
be executed as a hostage in reply to alleged insubordination
of which he knew nothing. An act of defiance against some
German soldier in any small centre might lead to the village
being burnt to the ground: often the women and children
were burnt alive in the church while the men went off
into slavery. After Hitler had enrolled the Vlassov Russians
to fight with him against Stalin, the Germans would some-

[13] Ciano Diary, 24-6th Nov. 1941. See also D.G.F.P. series D, vol.
XIII, no. 114.

times bring some of them along: in a French village
which had sheltered Gaullist Partisans near the Swiss
frontier, the German soldiers first arrested the men and took
the supplies they required for themselves, then they let
loose their inebriated Russians to rape and loot as they chose,
the German officer in charge remarking to the French lorry-
drivers who were forced to look on, " You see what the
Russians are like." (One of these French spectators afterwards
reflected that the Germans had nevertheless seemed to him
more wicked than the Russians " parce qu'ils sont plus
conscients.") Thus " horses might run without stumbling "
thanks to the German will to power and organization
of slaves. The supermen and masters had freed themselves
from traditional morality; they lived by cruelty, in which they
gloried, and by its scientific application. But the slaves as a
whole retained their astonishing worship of freedom and right.
Though occasional members of " inferior " races were promoted to S.S. status, very few others accepted the offers
with which they were to have been bribed. Weakened by
suffering, many of them defied their well-fed torturers. They
were not impressed by the mastery of force.

Mussolini often boasted of the Nietzsche he had read,
and when to flatter Hitler he took up anti-Semitism he wrote
the Jews off with Nietzschean phrases about their slave
mentality.[14] But nowhere is there evidence that he thought
out methods by which to put Nietzsche into practice or even
that he contemplated the possibility. Of the Italians who
were sent to Yugoslavia, certain Blackshirt units behaved
with unsystematic savagery in Dalmatia,[15] while the rest
displayed a varying combination of corruption and humanity.
By 1941 the average Italian had had his last hopes of
Fascism destroyed by the German Alliance. His profoundly
humane inheritance through the ages, his fundamental belief
in human rights, made him feel ashamed : Italian soldiers on
leave from Yugoslavia or Greece or, later, back from

[14] Nietzsche himself called anti-Semites *schlechteweggekommen,* or
failures.
[15] There was some deportation to Italy of Slovenes and Croats
from villages on the coast which were to be Italianised.

Russia, constantly said, "We have no right to be there." Italian peasants, especially from southern Italy, felt very close to the Slav peasantry in their understanding of poverty. And then, while Hitler believed in the economy of force in order to be the more forceful, the Italians instinctively looked for ways of avoiding the use of force because they always prefer to win by intelligence, to intrigue, be political, or what you will. Mussolini often despaired of the Italians, Ciano tells us—undoubtedly they had less than no joy in struggle and destruction for their own sake. No one embraces an idea more whole-heartedly than the Italian, but once disillusioned he is easily demoralized. In the Second World War few Italians found any inspiration until it came to resisting the Germans in Italy itself; the Second Italian Army in Yugoslavia was demoralized from the start.

Thus where the Italians had any place at all in the New Order it was always the same thing. Many Germans were in earnest in intending to establish a palpable domination, and their Nazi leaders were in earnest in intending German domination to effect Nietzsche's inversion of morality as interpreted—one might say mechanized—by Hitler. Mussolini, who had originally understood Nietzsche better, was dragged in Hitler's wake now in uncomprehending imitation. The Italians as a people were either not serious about the Axis crusade or utterly opposed to it. Everywhere, in Yugoslavia, in Greece, or in France, they had to contend with stronger initial prejudices against them. Besides this they were poorer—worse equipped and grubby—making less impression, their rations were scarcely half those of the Germans so that they had less to give away. Slowly, nevertheless, it came to be realized that they were humane, that one could put an individual case to them, that they were naturally kind, and, above all, that they detested the systematic cruelty of the Germans as much as did its Serb and French victims. If Italian soldiers heard cries for water from Jews packed suffocatingly into cattle-trucks on their last journey to the East, it was difficult to prevent them from going to the sufferers' help. No wonder the Germans and the Duce in his Germanophile moods despaired of them. Were they not the children, *par excellence,* of that traditional morality which Nietzsche had condemned, the morality of the weak?

After the campaign in April 1941 the division of the spoils in the Balkans caused more than the usual tension between Rome and Berlin. Although the Balkan peninsula had so often been solemnly acclaimed as Italian *Lebensraum,* Hitler dictated the new frontiers here as elsewhere, with the sole exception of those between Italy and Croatia for which it suited him that Italy should be responsible. When Ciano went to Vienna to meet Ribbentrop in the second half of April, he was presented (on 21st April) with orders with regard to cessions to Hungary and 'strong recommendations' with regard to Macedonia.[16] It was curtly conveyed to him on 22nd April that the line Hitler had drawn incorporating Slovenia in Germany to within three kilometres from Ljubljana could not be discussed; Italy might do what she liked with the rest of Slovenia. With regard to Macedonia the Führer had promised all ex-Yugoslav Macedonia to the King of Bulgaria and felt favourable towards his claim to Salonica; he sympathized with Italy's claim to the Kossovo district for Albania, but must keep Mitrovica in German-occupied Serbia owing to the existence of German-owned lead mines there— "the Führer makes a personal appeal to the Duce to recognize his particular interest in this question."[17] In general Ribbentrop insisted on German access to chromium and lead in Macedonia and bauxite in Dalmatia and indeed to everything which the Germans might need.

As for Croatia and Montenegro, Italy was to do exactly what she pleased. Montenegro did not seem politically important. The Queen of Italy[18] eagerly championed her poor relations as candidates for the throne, but they all preferred their poverty, and after various delays and expedients Italy

[16] D.G.F.P. series D, XII, no. 378.

[17] Ciano Minute, 22nd Apr. 1941 and D.G.F.P. series D, XII, no. 385. Arguments over Mitrovica continued for some time. See D.G.F.P. series D, vol. XIII, no. 495 showing the Italians complaining of German intrigues with Albanians against Italy.

[18] Daughter of the last King of Montenegro.

sent a military governor there.[19] His task, however, became one of prime political importance, for the forbidding mountains of Montenegro were a favourite refuge of the Yugoslav Partisans, the first actively military resisters inside Axis Europe. Croatia was a very different matter, for it had constituted for many years a political problem of the greatest delicacy. The Croats had an age-long grievance not unlike the Irish : they felt themselves to be a coherent and civilized community from which national independence had been unjustly withheld for the last thousand years. Before 1914 they had protested against their subjection to Hungary, sometimes demonstrating with considerable success in Vienna that Zagreb merited more confidence from the imperial authorities than Budapest. When the Habsburgs collapsed, Yugoslav[20] impulses, long operative in certain intellectual circles, turned the eyes of Croatia towards Belgrade, but a Yugoslav federation was dreamt of, not a unitary state. Once the latter had been set up by King Alexander Karageorgević, feeling between Croats and Serbs, supposedly fraternal before 1914, became exceedingly bitter; it was this which Mussolini had always sought to exploit. In order to do so it has been seen that he had offered protection to Pavelić and Kvaternik and other Ustaša or anti-Serb terrorists,[21] and it has been seen that Pavelić was waiting in Italy while Yugoslavia was destroyed. The Germans would have preferred Kvaternik to be Leader of Croatia, but Mussolini insisted on Pavelić.[22]

For at least three reasons the Croatian question was more delicate than Mussolini or Ciano seemed to know. In the first place Pavelić was as unpopular in Croatia as any Serb because he was the protégé of Italy. The Croats regarded Dalmatia as purely Croatian and some of them had considered the only good thing in the state of Yugoslavia to be that it had united Croatia-Slavonia with Dalmatia. Italy's Dalmatian claims and her presence at Fiume and Zara were intensely resented, and the Croats joined with the Slovenes in indignation over the Fascist oppression of the Slovene

---

[19] General Pirzio Biroli—see below.

[20] Yugoslav means Southern Slav.

[21] See chapter III, XVI.   [22] See Kordt, op. cit., p. 288.

and Croat minority in post-Versailles Italy. Secondly, Pavelić
represented next to nothing in Croatia. Politically and
socially the Croats were a remarkably homogeneous people;
it was usually estimated that about ninety per cent. of them
supported the Croat Peasant Party, which had been inspired
by the Radić brothers, and, after the death of Stjepan Radić,
led by Maček. The Croat Peasant Party was based upon a
traditional village co-operative organisation, and, being pacifist
in doctrine, rejected Pavelić out of hand. Thirdly, Pavelić
and Kvaternik came from among the pro-Austrian followers
of a certain Dr. Frank who had played some part before
1914; like so many retrograde Balkan politicians who had
had Legitimist connexions at one time or another after 1918,
they accepted Hitler for what he longed to be, heir to the
Habsburgs he had hated so much. They, and especially
Kvaternik, preferred to take orders, therefore, from Hitler
rather than from Mussolini, and they encouraged journalism
intended to show that the Croats were of Gothic, not Slavonic,
descent.

The Axis Powers announced themselves, of course, as the
liberators at long last of Croatia, and the new Croatian State
was given all Bosnia and Hercegovina despite their mixed
Serb and Croat population. At first Italy claimed the whole
of Dalmatia and it is interesting to find that Hitler, for
whom Dalmatia would always be Austrian,[23] instructed Ribbentrop to raise no objection to this in his interview with
Ciano on 22nd April.[24] He was equally content that King
Victor Emmanuel's worthless cousin, the Duke of Spoleto,
should be nominated as King of Croatia. Oddly enough
Pavelić accepted this plan and came to Rome for an *ad hoc*
ceremony on 18th May, but conditions in the new kingdom
were never such as to tempt the Duke to mount his throne.
On 7th May Pavelić had met Mussolini and Ciano at
Monfalcone,[25] and there he persuaded them to allow Croatia
to touch the Adriatic coast at Senj and at Dubrovnik and
to the north of it; there was a tussle over Split (Spalato),

[23] Having been a province of Cisleithania, i.e. Austria, as distinct
from Hungary, before 1914.
[24] Ciano Minute, 22nd Apr. 1941.   [25] See Ciano Diary.

the loss of which, the Poglavnik[26] said, would overthrow his régime, but after the usual giving way to his visitor of the moment, the Duce was persuaded to stand firm.[27]

Meanwhile German troops remained in Croatia. Germans soon gained control of its new army and police. As in every country they occupied, they stripped it neatly and sent all the plunder home. Further, Hitler was determined to control the bauxite mines and the railway lines which ran from Ljubljana and Vienna and Budapest to Zagreb and Belgrade; Ciano observed with his transient lucidity that Croatia " in Ribbentrop's mind is considered as a state very near to, if not directly forming part of, the politico-economic system of the Reich."[28] Marras knew that Germany intended to keep Croatia in her own military control and did what he could to fight Jodl about it.[29] But Hitler understood the intricacy of the Croatian question very well. If it discredited the Italians too much Germany would be " forced " to inter-vene in the Adriatic; if the Duke of Spoleto were involved this might provide a welcome lever against the House of Savoy. Meanwhile the possibilities of intrigue were immense; they might be made to preface any *coup* he fancied, indeed, they might easily lead him in Slovenia's name to Trieste. Fiume had been Hungarian before 1914 and Hitler had fanned the flames of Hungarian revisionism in this direction before now;[30] on 21st April Ribbentrop brought the matter up with Ciano and he certainly let the Magyars know that he was doing so. To crown this edifice of tension and friction Hitler had appointed the Italophobe Austrian General, Glaise-Horstenau, who had once smoothed the Führer's path to Vienna, to be Commander of the German forces in Croatia. To him the Führer explained that Italy must have all her greed satisfied in order to hold her.[31] On 15th June, at

[26] Croatian for leader.
[27] The new Croatia came close up to the south of Split.
[28] Ciano Minute, 21st Apr. 1941.   [29] Simoni, 28th Apr. 1941.
[30] Hassell, op. cit., p. 197.
[31] Ibid., p. 204. Both Glaise-Horstenau and the new German Minister Kasche, were rushed to Zagreb in the middle of April 1941. D.G.F.P. series D, vol. XII, nos. 356, 378.

R.B.A.   L

Venice, Pavelić signed Croatia's adherence to the Tripartite
Pact. " Valore politico dell' evento, eguale a zero," wrote
Ciano in his Diary.[32] It was on this occasion that Ribbentrop
had made clear to Ciano that war with Russia was imminent.

Face to face with an Axis occupation the Balkan peoples
had certain advantages compared with western Europe.
Hitler, in his contempt for them, made few efforts to blind
them by seduction. They were accustomed to tyranny and
oppression though nothing in their history had been so
systematic and therefore so merciless. And then the Slav
peoples, Serbs, Montenegrins, Croats and—in spite of the
Germanophile policy of their rulers at testing times—Bulgars
still felt a filial mysticism towards Russia, retrograde or
revolutionary.[33] Russia, according to their popular traditions,
had ever tried to help them, thwarted though she was by
evil, alien, in fact German, forces—for what did they
know of Disraeli or Salisbury? Now again in 1941 Russia
was their hope. When it became clear that Hitler had
failed to break her in the two or three months he had
said he would require, this hope became something substantial,
no longer a remote dream. And then the fourth Balkan
advantage came into play. It was impossible to subdue
this barren and mountainous country-side with anything like
total effect. Much of the Yugoslav army had melted away

[32] 15th June 1941.
[33] Much of what I had learnt previously about Yugoslavia and
am trying to express here was confirmed to me by a series of letters
written from Bosnia to relatives in Switzerland during the war.
Many of these letters were written by an elderly Serb peasant who
was evidently the scribe for his village; they all date from
1942 or 1943. " We have nothing against Stalin," this old man wrote
on New Year's Day 1943, " rather we should rejoice if the Russian
Army were to approach, for we know that Russia is the mother
of our people. . . . Our Četnici were compelled to join with the
Italians because the Partisans are stronger. The same thing happened in Serbia. . . ." The writer said he was too old to be
either a Četnik or a Partisan; he did not think resistance worth
while, for it only meant that one's village was destroyed by the
Germans. Once he wrote of the Italians that they took Serbs
into their hospitals as well as Croats, for they said the Serbs were
human beings too.

but it had not been destroyed, and now small groups were in hiding wherever there were mountains and especially in Montenegro; there were also indomitable fragments of the Greek Army concealing themselves among the mountains of Greece.

Until the end of 1941, however, a horrible chaos seemed to prevail in what until April had been Yugoslavia, and it was only towards the end of the year that the shadow of a pattern emerged. In the portion which Germany had annexed, the fate of Poland was repeated: the educated classes in particular were condemned to a brutal annihilation since they would be most likely to resist the role of a slave-gang to which the Slovenes were condemned. In Italian Slovenia, things began fairly well; it was a clerical country and the faith which the S.S. were determined to stamp out was readily accepted by the Italian authorities in Ljubljana who were sickened by the news from the immediate north. Serbia, Hitler vowed—strange champion of Francis Ferdinand though he was—should pay for Sarajevo and for the indomitable spirit its people had shown, and only its subjection to the Germans could ensure this. At first, in spite of the terrifying action of the occupying authorities, no Serb or Slovene Quisling could be found, but then in August 1941 General Nedić accepted this dubious role.

Scandalous wholesale massacres of Serbs were carried out by the Hungarians in the Bačka and by Pavelić's Ustaše, especially in Bosnia; many Jews, including refugees from Germany and Italy, were their fellow victims. What seemed like the wholesale destruction of the Serbs and the Slovenes made some of their leaders fear their literal extermination and convinced them that any compromise that saved lives could be justified. The first groups which continued active resistance to the Axis forces had been followers of Serb military chiefs like Mihailović who were Pan-Serb and fiery supporters of the tradition of the last active Tsarist in Europe, Alexander Karageorgević. This king, who had built up a typically corrupt " Balkan " tyranny, had split Serb loyalties, and the sympathy of the bulk of the people had become all the more Russophile now that Moscow was a symbol for social justice in their minds. The attitude of the Croats in April

1941 and subsequent Ustaša atrocities seemed to justify the Serb chauvinists, but then they lost support. They consisted very largely, after all, of Četnici, a Fascist militia *à la serbe*, men who had terrorized their own peasantry and, of course, that of Croatia for years, and using the argument of the danger of extermination Mihailović gradually showed signs of preferring the Axis Powers before Russia and Communism. There were clashes probably before the end of 1941 between his followers and Russophile groups which called themselves Partisans, like the Russian fighters behind the German lines.

Now the followers of Mihailović had had to leave at least their heavy arms behind them at the time of Yugoslavia's defeat. The Italians very soon rescued Italian prisoners from them by giving them arms in exchange; it seemed more reasonable to them to save their fellows rather than to fight an unjustified war at all seriously. The responsible officers also thought it more reasonable to use the Četnici to fight against the more revolutionary Partisans; let these people kill each other in the mountains if they chose rather than that Italians should die. By 1942 the Italians had contrived to reconcile the Četnici and the Ustaše, the Serb and Croat terrorists who had once vowed to exterminate one another; in June 1942 at Doboi, for instance, a pact of alliance was signed by the Italians with representatives of both these groups who thereby undertook to fight with the Italians against the Partisans; this was one of several similar agreements. To many of the best Yugoslav types, Serb, Croat, or Slovene, such pacts were infamous, because Italy was their national enemy and because she was Fascist. It was not very long before groups of the Četnici accepted bribes, often food, from Germans as well,[34] and this hardened the others' determination to resist them; stories from the East made clear that Hitler was the enemy. Maček had been interned by the Ustaše in his home at Kupinec and was entirely cut off from the outside world. But gradually more and more of his followers went off to the mountains and joined the

[34] The village writer quoted on p. 322 (note 33) reported this; letters also came to Switzerland from Četnici themselves, boasting of it, because " one was well fed if one went with the Germans."

Partisans under their at first mysterious leader, Tito, who was a Croat himself. Part of the new Croat Army melted away in the same direction. Thus Tito became something of a Yugoslav national symbol, for he redeemed the Croats in Serb and Montenegrin eyes. The Yugoslavs felt reunited now in fighting for Russia against the Germans and Italians in alliance with their own Fascist renegades.

From the beginning of 1942 it had become clear that the Pavelić régime had nothing but a diminishing number of Ustaša thugs and an increasing number of foreign bayonets behind it. Even the Bosnian Mohammedans, who had originally been among its warmest supporters, began to go over to its enemies. Kvaternik blamed Pavelić for staking too much on the Italian card and listened gladly to German hints to work for a German Protectorate, Bohemian style, in Croatia. Early in October Pavelić reacted sharply; he consulted the Italian Minister and then drove Kvaternik out.

Thereupon more German troops arrived in Croatia, the German S.S. took charge of Maček, and Maček's Party was suppressed. In effect Croatia was now ruled by a young protégé of Ribbentrop's called Kasche, who had been German Minister in Zagreb since the spring of 1941.[35] The Croat peasants were good saboteurs and their harvest had sadly disappointed the Germans. At the end of 1942, therefore, Croat economic affairs were arbitrarily but effectively placed in the hands of Krafft, the leader of the German minority in pre-war days; like all such promoted Fifth-columnists he was strictly obedient to Nazi Party orders. The German troops in Croatia remained under the command of the elderly Austrian General, Glaise-Horstenau, who was on the worst of terms with Kasche and who, as we know, had always regarded Italians with irritation and contempt.

At about this time Glaise-Horstenau grumbled to a personal friend that he had never known anything like the Italian Second Army. " The officers," he said, " live by smuggling Jews, the N.C.O.s smuggle arms, tobacco, and salt, and the soldiers simply steal. They leave the mountains to the Partisans. Ambrosio has on principle done everything he

[35] Kordt, op. cit., p. 305, note 1, says he was expecting to become *Gauleiter* of Moscow.

could to annoy us. . . . An (Italian) colonel had the impertinence to say to me, ' Aspettiamo—we are waiting here. . . .' I reported him, whereupon he was promoted." At the same time Glaise-Horstenau moaned his remorse over his share in bringing the Anschluss about. He added that already a year ago he had reported to Hitler's headquarters that the Italians would barely fight for twenty-four hours, but that his reports never got beyond Keitel unless they were optimistic and seasoned with coarse jokes.

General Ambrosio, who was soon to succeed Cavallero as Italian Chief of Staff, had been in command of the Italian troops in Croatia except while Roatta replaced him between January and October 1942; Glaise-Horstenau had not misinterpreted his attitude. On the other hand, Donosti expressed an equally responsible Italian view when he wrote that Kasche and Glaise-Horstenau " joined in every intrigue . . . and encouraged every incident which shook Italian prestige and consolidated Germany's hold on the country."[36]

The Axis occupation of former Yugoslav territory has seemed to deserve space on account of the illustrative intricacies to which it gave rise. In Greece and in France the position was a little simplified by the greater homogeneity of the inhabitants. It should be noted that the theory of Italy's free hand in the Balkans was honoured by a nominally Italian occupation of Greece except in the area handed over to the Bulgars. From the beginning, however, the Germans had justified Ciano's *mot* when he referred to the occupation of Greece as a *mezzadria,* implying that the Germans were its masters while the Italians received a share of the proceeds for doing the work; in private, the Germans at first missed few opportunities of patting the Greeks on the back for their valorous resistance to Italy. In France again, though the Italians in June 1940 had seemed to be unjustifiably greedy, they had in fact only occupied their fifty-kilometre strip—roughly from Grenoble to Menton—while the German occupation, as ever, overflowed its boundaries into Vichy and Italian territory.

In July 1942, on his way back from Libya (where he had

[36] See Donosti, op cit., p. 271.

arrived a second time to witness an Italian advance degenerate into a standstill), Mussolini stopped at Athens. There he was represented by Pellegrino Ghigi, one of Italy's abler diplomats, who has already appeared in this history of the Axis in Vienna just before the Anschluss.[37] Ghigi was horrified by the folly of German ruthlessness in Greece, for which the Italians were technically responsible, and he arranged that the heads of the collaborating Greek Government should expound their troubles to the Duce. Immediately after his return to Rome Mussolini wrote Hitler a letter carefully pruned of all sentiment but a letter of genuine concern.[38] He stated that the condition of Greece was catastrophic— " last winter 24,000 people died of starvation. . . ." " I prezzi sono saliti alle stelle." In the meantime the food situation had slightly improved, but the financial outlook was becoming worse.

" In my opinion, Führer, there is only one remedy : to reduce the occupation costs. . . . As far as Italy is concerned I told the head of the Greek Government that I am ready to reduce them to the absolutely indispensable minimum. . . . The crisis is apparent in the aspect of the city and the physical condition of the population appears critical.

" I will not remind you of what Greece has meant in the history of the world, I will only state that it is in the interest of the Axis that Greece should be orderly and tranquil, rejecting London's suggestions and giving us no anxiety."

Though this letter from the theoretical master of Greece was obsequious in its tone, it was genuinely insistent, for the Duce emphasized that there was not a moment to be lost.

Hitler's reply written on 4th August was coldly indifferent; stating that he shared Mussolini's worries with regard to Greece he made it clear that he did nothing of the kind. Thanks to Mussolini's competent advisers there a fundamental issue had been raised between Duce and Führer. It has been seen that all along a certain respect for the Czechs or the Poles or for any other nation had survived

[37] See chapter VI, p. 117 above and Donosti, op. cit., p. 272 et seq.
[38] Mussolini to Hitler, 22nd July 1942.

the Fascist corrosion of Italian policy. Rome had expected
Hitler to leave post-Munich Czechoslovakia[39] in peace. In
the autumn of 1939 Rome had wished for the recognition
of a reduced Polish State. Still, after the events of 1941,
the Italians could not overcome a certain regard for other
human beings and the societies they had formed or might wish
to form. The most extraordinary thing of all was that
they could never quite believe that Hitler was determined
to deny all traditional rights and reverse the morality which
induced a regard for them. In the spring of 1942, when
he visited his friends the Bruckmanns, Hitler was thoroughly
pleased with himself and boasted of the S.S. as the bravest
of the brave because they suffered from " no Christian inhibi-
tions. He would see to it that all Germans were cured of
such feelings in the future."[40]

All through the war the question of France provided
the strangest aspect of the relationship between Mussolini
and Hitler. It was the exception which proved the rule,
for in this case the Duce constantly pressed for a more
uncompromising policy. While Mussolini believed that Hitler
was betraying him with France, in this one case Hitler seems
to have kept his word to Italy. " He [the Führer] can
in no circumstances prejudice our relations with Italy by
making concessions to France. He cannot allow our relations
with Italy to deteriorate." This is noted by Raeder after
a secret conference with Hitler at the *Wolfsschanze* headquarters near Rastenburg on 25th July 1941;[41] it is only
one example of many secretly recorded statements to the
same effect.[42] This perplexing fidelity on the part of the
Führer contributed to the débâcle of Axis Mediterranean
strategy for which he continued to blame Franco.[43]

If the Duce was wrong to distrust Hitler with regard to

[39] After Munich Czechoslovakia became Czecho-Slovakia.

[40] Hassell, op. cit., p. 276.

[41] *Führer Conferences on Naval Affairs,* 1941.

[42] See numerous examples in Ciano's Minutes, Hitler's fairly severe
letter to Pétain of 10th Nov. 1941, and especially Hassell, op. cit.,
p. 223.

[43] See Simoni, 9th Nov. 1942, for Hitler's outburst against
Franco that day.

North Africa he was right when he said the French nation was basically hostile to the Axis. It is easy to assume in this and analogous cases that the French only waited to be on the winning side; it is more exact to state that as Germany's military prospect darkened it became possible for essential French elements to assert themselves against the S.S. It has been seen that in 1940 some French leaders showed an abject submissiveness to the conquerors, and it is certain that men like Laval were sincere when they expressed enthusiasm for French participation in the Axis New Order; Laval remained faithful to this hope in spite of perpetual disappointments over occupation costs, French prisoners and workers in Germany, and the many questions at issue with the Germans.

By the end of 1940 there were already anti-German leaflets which were passed from hand to hand in Paris. One of them ended as follows:

"L'aigle allemand marche pompeusement et c'est le pas de l'oie. Partant en guerre contre l'Angleterre, il chante avec ostentation. Et c'est peut-être le chant du cygne. . . .

"Tu grognes parce qu'ils t'obligent à être rentré chez toi a vingt-trois heures précises. Innocent, tu n'as pas compris que c'était pour te permettre d'écouter la radio anglaise.

"Tu en as déja vu de toutes les couleurs. Les verts, les gris, les noirs se sont présentés les premiers. C'était les militaires. Puis sont venus les moutardes avec au bras une bague rouge comme en ont les cigares : c'était les militants.

"Voici venir les sans-couleurs. Ils arrivent par paquets avec leurs petites femmes. A les voir tu jurerais des civils, vêtus de pacifiques vestons, de paisibles jupons, ils logent dans ta maison, écoutent à ta porte, épient tes gestes, dénoncent tes propos.

"Ils sont insonores. Aussi quand ils marchent près de toi, n'entends-tu pas ce fameux bruit de bottes qui, en te faisant dresser l'oreille, te ferme automatiquement la bouche.

"Méfie-toi de tous. Aussi de toutes.

"En prévision des gaz, on t'a fait suer sous un groin de caoutchouc et pleurer dans des chambres d'épreuve. Tu souris maintenant de ces précautions. Tu es satisfait d'avoir sauvé tes poumons. Sauras-tu maintenant préserver ton cœur et ton cerveau?

" Ne vois-tu pas qu'ils ont réussi à vicier l'atmosphère que tu respires, à polluer les sources auxquelles tu crois pouvoir encore te désaltérer, à dénaturer le sens des mots dont tu prétends encore te servir?

" Voici venue l'heure de la véritable *Défense passive*."

Many of the French had surely understood what Hitler wished to do. Inside France, now, they began to resist him with heart and head. For them the idea of the superman was bad because it was stupid—had not Nietzsche himself known that it ended in self-destruction?

In France the Germans were face to face with a paradox of their history. Nietzsche, the German mind unchained, at one moment made efforts to despise French eroticism, at the next bowed down before the lucidity of the French mind. Was Hitler—more logical than Nietzsche in his contempt for the intellect—himself not immune from the Circe-like spells of France? Perhaps he had hoped to out-fascinate the fascinating. On 29th December 1941 he still wrote to Mussolini that he did not wish to go too far lest France might recognize her European obligations after all. But the French were silent—*le silence de la mer*—and the Germans were shaken by the silence of France.[44]

Increasingly the French resisted the Germans and resisted Vichy and Laval. They did not resist the Italians. At first they despised them.[45] But the sympathy of the soldiers of the very Duce who declared that all Frenchmen were Gaullists and demanded that France be taught the lessons of defeat was with the French. When the maquis fighters collected here and there Italian sympathy sometimes extended to them. The French and the Italians were both the children of the old morality; where the French emphasized *cerveau*,

---

[44] Cf. Ciano Diary, 19-20th Dec. 1942, where he marvels at German susceptibility to French *charme*, even Laval's.

[45] The French attitude was illustrated by their attempt to acknowledge only the Germans as their conquerors—see the question of the lorries recorded in the Schmidt Minute of the Duce-Ribbentrop meeting on 13th May 1941.

the Italians perhaps put *cuore* first. Above all the Italians
in France caused particular annoyance to Hitler and Ribbentrop on account of their 'laxity' with regard to the Jews.
A high proportion of Jews of various nationalities had
collected in Vichy France and they sometimes escaped internment and all that it might mean rather through the help
of the Italian, than thanks to the Vichy, authorities. On
24th August 1942 the German police in Paris complained
to the German Embassy there of the unequivocally 'pro-
Jewish' attitude of the Italian Consulate-General. At the
end of the year the Italian Consul-General in Nice refused to
allow any Jews to leave the Italian zone, with the excuse that
they might then disseminate anti-Axis propaganda. Early
in 1943 the Prefect of the Alpes-Maritimes was therefore able
to complain to Laval that he could not organize the transport
of the Jews from south-east France to the concentration
camps to which Hitler and Laval had agreed to send them.
The S.S. chief at Marseille was complaining at the same
time that the Italians protected Jews of every nationality.
They allowed them to live unlabelled and were very friendly
with them, "creating the impression of a big difference
between the German and the Italian point of view."[46]

By about this time a consciousness was creeping into many
minds in the Axis countries of the real significance of
Hitler's New Order. It is false for Germans to claim that
they were not aware of it, unless they add that they were
determined not to be. Many a German soldier on leave from
the Russian front or the other occupied countries had a tale
of horror to tell, though the most terrible details were
supposed to be reserved for the *élite*. When the Germans first
arrived in the Ukraine there was certainly feeling there
against Moscow, and men like Schulenburg, who had been
Ambassador to the U.S.S.R., urged a politic generosity in
the granting of some show of autonomy to Ukrainians,
Georgians, and other separable groups;[47] German propa-

[46] Extracts from this material were published in the *Corriere
d'informazione*, 27-8th July 1946. See also Goebbels Diary, 13th
Dec. 1942. "The Italians are extremely lax in the treatment of the
Jews."

[47] Simoni, 28th Mar. 1942.

ganda had, after all, attacked Russia, as it had formerly fulminated against Czechoslovakia, as a *Nationalitätenstaat*. But Rosenberg, who had had his appointment as Regional Commissar for the *Ostland* drawn up in April 1941,[48] was determined not to be cheated of the exercise of his tyranny, and Koch and Sauckel went to the East to organize the new slavery:[49] all of them became the tools of the S.S. State.

In August 1942 Hassell noted in his Diary:

" Very strained situation in the occupied territories, thanks to the evil Party administration. Particularly in Bohemia after Heydrich's fearful and bloody Reign of Terror. The two obliterated places, where all the men were shot, the women deported and the children taken off to be compulsorily trained, have provided Allied propaganda with glowing symbols. The same thing has now happened in Norway. In France, too, the greatest tension prevails and draconic measures are constantly taken. In Poland terrible things continue; it is like a nightmare and makes one red with shame."[50]

[48] See *Nuremberg Trial Proceedings*, part II, p. 249.

[49] See DeWitt C. Poole, as above. Erich Koch had been Gauleiter of East Prussia and was now appointed as a Reich Commissar in the East. See also A. Dallin *German Rule in Russia 1941-45* (1957).

[50] Hassell, op. cit., pp. 272-3.

Chapter XVIII

ITALY REBELS

From the autumn of 1941 signs multiplied to indicate the transformation of Italy from an Axis Partner into another occupied country of slaves. The Germans by turns suspected and subjected her more completely from this time. When Bottai visited Germany in October 1941, the German Minister of Education, Rust, gave things away badly after a good deal of drink at a banquet at Weimar, for he insisted that when Hitler had done with Stalin he would clear away Mussolini too;[1] even earlier than this Hassell noted that General Milch had said Mussolini no longer had anyone behind him.[2] When Ciano visited the Führer's headquarters at the end of October Hitler, however, talked all doubts away. The gossip-mongers, he declared, were an international gang who spoke ill of anyone. In Germany only such people doubted Italy.[3] And yet when Mussolini wrote to Hitler about ten days later, lamenting the shortage of raw materials in Italy which reduced his industrial production by half, he found it necessary to repeat that if Italy could contribute more, it would be the best answer to the rumours that Italy was seeking to make a separate peace.

As the war went on in Libya it became clear that the question was one of ships and oil to transport the soldiers and their arms. By now Italy was living from hand to mouth for oil, which she could only obtain as German largess, whether it came from Roumania or elsewhere. Her military dependence was advertised, not only by the acceptance of Rommel, but by the special appointment of Rintelen, German Military Attaché in Rome, to the headquarters of the Italian Army,[4] and later by the arrival of Kesselring as 'Commander-in-Chief, South.' Less public but a great deal

---

[1] Simoni, 5th Oct. 1941.   [2] Hassell, op. cit., p. 223.
[3] Ciano Report to Duce, 26th Oct. 1941. D.G.F.P. series D, XIII, no. 424.
[4] Mussolini to Hitler, 24th July 1941.

more sinister was the information Ciano received from the Italian Secret Intelligence people (the S.I.M.) about the German " cells " which were being established in the chief Italian cities.[5] At much the same time the Italian Embassy in Berlin was informed of a plan for the complete occupation of Italy; the S.S. under Dollmann were to ' suppress ' the King and the Prince of Piedmont and hand over such authority as remained to Farinacci.[6] At the time this information seemed too fantastic to be true, but subsequent events and the documents which have come to light since then suggest that it was not misleading.

A disastrous aspect of the Axis relationship may be referred to under the heading of manpower. It has been seen that Mussolini thrust Italian aeroplanes upon Hitler to take part in the bombardments of Britain, but it was Hitler who asked Mussolini, in his letter of 21st June 1941, what he could contribute to the attack upon Russia. As usual the Duce was only too eager that the Italians should ' show up.' In a memorandum for his *Comando Supremo* on 24th July he insisted that a second Italian Army must be added to the one already on its way to Russia. " We cannot be less on the spot than Slovakia and we need to get out of Germany's debt."[7] This was the beginning of a long and tragic story. The Italian Army leaders were nearly all opposed to the project and Marras fought hard to prevent its being carried out. But Mussolini had his way and the wretched Italian soldiers were sent off with most inadequate equipment to face the rigours of the Russian front,[8] when they were soon to be needed much nearer home. They were still trickling back to Italy at the end of 1946 and later.

When the Duce clamoured for raw materials as he was bound increasingly to do, whether in August 1939 or in December 1940 or July 1941, the answer became every time more peremptory : ' We shall send you some of your requirements in return for the sending of Italian labour

---

[5] Ciano Diary, 25th Sept. 1941. Certainly S.S., rather than regular army, activity.

[6] Simoni, 5th Oct. 1941.   [7] *Hitler e Mussolini*, pp. 114-15.

[8] Between late summer 1941 and early 1943 there was an Italian Army in Russia of at least ten divisions plus extras.

to Germany.' Mussolini resented the implication—as he felt—
that Italians could only work but not fight, and he would
always have preferred to send soldiers. In the autumn of
1941 the often scandalous treatment of the Italian working
men in Germany[9] was reported to Rome by an Italian official
who had found that the brother heroes inspired by the
Duce for nearly twenty years were in some cases guarded
by fierce sheep-dogs taught to bite any faltering labourer
This was too much even for Mussolini, and it was on this
account that Ciano visited Hitler and Ribbentrop at the
end of October 1941. Hitler pooh-poohed the whole matter
—one must remember, he repeated, that there were still anti-
Nazi and anti-Fascist elements who had every interest in
creating incidents between the Germans and the Italian workmen in Germany. The Führer, on the other hand, showed
'immediate comprehension' of the Duce's desire to send
more soldiers to Russia—beyond the Caucasus[10] they would
become climatically suitable. It is worth noting that this
was the last occasion upon which Ciano reports the Führer
in good physical form and the first upon which Hitler, convinced though he claimed to be that Russia was beaten,
failed to project any programme of action. There was
much talk about European solidarity, which Ciano dismissed
as the latest German slogan, but no programme; Ribbentrop
assured him that the Führer was shaping Europe for a
thousand years to come,[11] but Ciano, according to the entry
in his Diary, persuaded Ribbentrop to reduce the ten centuries
to one.

In his reports for Mussolini Ciano always beautified the
atmosphere which had prevailed when he met Hitler and
Ribbentrop. He even described their behaviour at the time
of his visit to Berlin in November 1941 as exceptionally
courteous.[12] Simoni gives a different, and probably more

[9] See above, chapters XI and XVI. Also D.G.F.P. series D, vol.
XIII, nos. 281, 397, 410, 444, 446.

[10] A month later "beyond the Caucasus" was stated by Hitler to
be Italian *Lebensraum*. See Ciano Minute, 24-7th Nov. 1941.

[11] Ciano Report to Duce, 26th Oct. 1941, and Diary.

[12] Ciano Minute, 24-7th Nov. 1941. D.G.F.P. series D, XIII, no.
522.

accurate, picture of his visits, of Ciano behaving like a very spoilt boy recklessly distributing rude criticisms of his hosts. In November it was the anti-Comintern Pact which was to be renewed. " Ribbentrop made a long speech intended as an invitation if not a hymn to efficient European collaboration but it seemed more like an order of the day from a despot to his vassals. Ciano is furious. ' I should have liked to answer in the same tone,' he exclaimed, ' everyone would have been with me.' "[13]

After a grim Russian winter Hitler again felt the need to hold forth to Mussolini and a meeting was arranged at Schloss Klessheim near Salzburg at the end of April 1942. Its strategic importance consisted in the planning of an Axis assault upon Malta. The Führer was infinitely verbose, without, it appears, saying anything of importance; it was during this visit that Ciano watched the chiefs of the Reichswehr engaged in ' an epic struggle ' with their desire to sleep through Hitler's post-prandial perorations. On the same visit Edda Ciano, when she visited an Italian labourers' camp, found a workman in hospital whose arms had been injured with a bill-hook; Hitler stormed when she told him. There were several straws which showed a changing wind. Hitler looked tired and for the first time Ciano noted that his hair was going white.[14] From this time on the healthy physical frame in which that extraordinary spirit was contained began to decay; the results, not only of strain, but of Dr. Morell's injections, began to tell, and the morbidity which had been fitful to prevail.[15] Hitler still fascinated Mussolini as he had since September 1937, and, if the Duce's account is to be believed, the Führer threw in a lollipop this time, declaring that the Greek war, by a timely pricking of the Balkan boil, had demonstrated the favour of Providence after all. Nevertheless, the Duce's doubts were growing. Before now he had said that to fight against Russia was to fight

[13] Simoni, 26th Nov. 1941, but in his own Diary Ciano is re-signed.
[14] Ciano Diary, 29th Apr-2nd May 1942. Cf. Goebbels Diary, 27th Apr. 1942, on the danger of Hitler collapsing.
[15] Reports to this effect reached the German Legation in Berne later this year.

endless space, and it seemed that even Hitler could not do
this : the Führer's self-comparison with Napoleon was bound
to nourish Mussolini's jealousy and scepticism, and at the
end of this encounter the Duce remarked to his own entourage that he really did not know why Hitler had wanted
it.

Before the Duce there still lay the last Italian successes
in North Africa which ejected the British from Tobruk on
21st June 1942. But that was the end, and before July
Hitler abandoned the plan against Malta because Italian
morale seemed inadequate. During the second half of 1942
Mussolini's ulcer became a very serious matter,[16] affecting
his judgement and his temper, and it was only because he
was too ill to travel that Ciano took his place at the meetings
with the Führer at the end of the year. It is difficult to
avoid trite reflections at this juncture upon the sorry state
to which the world's two Supermen had been reduced by the
philosophy of force. There were those who said that Mussolini's affair with Clara Petacci, which had now been going
on for about seven years, had contributed to the deterioration
in his health. In the spring of 1942 Ciano complained
to Suñer[17] that there was nothing to be said against a bevy
of mistresses but this concentration upon one had become
a public scandal. The fact is that the talk about " Claretta "
and her intriguing family was chiefly a symptom of rising
discontent.

With the spring of 1942 opposition to the war, to the
Germans, and to the Fascist régime was no longer concealed
in Italy. There was frequently friction where German soldiers
were stationed. In April and May there were many arrests
of anti-Fascists, especially in Rome and Genoa, and in June
in Milan ; in Rome and Milan mostly professional men were
concerned and in Genoa working people. The Sicilians were
very hard hit economically and increasingly indignant, and
in September 1942 several hundred people were arrested
in Naples because the police had found slips of paper stuck
on the walls saying *Vogliamo la Pace*. In Florence the

16 Ivone Kirkpatrick *Mussolini*, 1964, p. 490.
17 See R. Serrano Suñer, *Entre Hendaya y Gibraltar* (Madrid,
1947)

followers of the Rossellis and of the *Giustizia e libertà* movement were stirring. In October, when the R.A.F., in quest
of Ansaldo's, raided Genoa, crowds (mainly women) gathered
to demand peace *and liberty,* and the Socialists, who had
been strong here in the past and were beginning to reorganize,
managed to stick up posters to the same effect. This was
at the time of the celebration of twenty years since the
'March on Rome.' It is interesting to find that when
Mussolini replied to Hitler's letter of congratulation (dated
21st Oct. 1942) he admitted that the R.A.F. had done serious
damage in Genoa, completely destroying a dock where two
air-craft carriers were being made. In Milan the Duce
admitted that the sirens had sounded only after the bombs
were dropping—he blamed Swiss neutrality for making
surprise so easy.

Perhaps the most effective opposition was organized by
the Communists whose stronghold was Turin. Russia's resistance to Hitler had sent up Communist stock and a good many
of the students arrested during the year had been strongly
" red." But the core of Italian Communism was composed of the Fiat workers. In September 1942 they were
denounced by the secretary of the Fascist labour unions of
Turin at an official meeting. " When one is part of a
victorious army," he declared, " when one forms an integral
part of a revolution, one has no right to be weak or sentimental, one has no right to treat the country's enemies other
than as enemies." He complained that even the local Fascists
" failed to regard the democracies with hostility " and that
they seemed to feel concern about " the fierce Fascist repression in the occupied territories." This was the atmosphere in Italy at the beginning of the autumn of 1942.

In addition to the professional and the industrial working
classes, the Italian generals and diplomats were at work.
General Castellano first visited Ciano in April 1942 in order
to make contact between him and Ambrosio, who was
strongly anti-German and wished Italy to make peace.[18] But
the military successes which followed in Africa made further
action inopportune until after Mussolini's visit to Athens

[18] G. Castellano, *Come firmai l'armistizio di Cassibile* (Mondadori,
1945).

in July. Castellano speaks of Ciano's hatred of the Germans as *parossistico* and he believed that the Germans hated him as much. But Ciano, though openly defeatist, was strangely inert; he was blinded by the delusion that when things had gone further the Allies would be ready to make peace with Italy if he took Mussolini's place.

In the night of 7th to 8th November 1942 Allied forces landed in French North Africa. The Axis replied immediately with the German occupation of Vichy France—Operation Attila—and the Italian occupation of Corsica. This was the end of Hitler's ambivalent approach to the question of France. Laval was summoned to meet Hitler and Ciano at Munich on 9th November and to the Führer's headquarters in December. "Laval, qui a toujours eu l'espoir d'être l'égal de Mussolini dans ses rapports avec le Reich, s'est trouvé au quartier général d'Hitler en même temps que le comte Ciano. Mais alors que le Ministre de Mussolini a été bien reçu, Laval a été accueilli avec beaucoup de froideur." He had come full of readiness to help incorporate France in the New Order and even with an offer of French troops, but though Hitler expressed confidence in Laval himself, the Führer subjected him to " de violents reproches sur la duplicité des fonctionnaires et des officiers français qui trahissent la cause européenne dès qu'ils en ont l'occasion pour se tourner vers les ennemis de l'Axe."[19] The subtle distinctions had ended. France was now an occupied[20]—and resisting—country like any other, as the Duce had wished. And yet at the moment when this Axis dispute ended a greater one became acute.

The shock to Hitler of the Allied invasion of North Africa was violent. Simoni accompanied Alfieri to Munich for Ciano's meeting with the Führer on 9th November and he gives a picture of confusion and consternation. The Germans had allowed themselves to be surprised. There was a marvellous moment when, after sybilline antics, Hitler

[19] From the contemporary report of a high French official who was Gaulliste by sentiment.

[20] The vexatious *ligne de démarcation* was retained because the Germans could not spare the troops for a full occupation beyond it. See Schmidt Minute, 25th Feb. 1943.

declared that it was all the fault of Franco (still) and of the *Unsinn* of which he had been guilty.[21] The conclusion Hitler drew was that the Axis must be more remorseless than before. " I belong to those men," he wrote to Mussolini on 20th November, " who, when they receive blows, became more resolute." A stop must be put to the last ambiguities, not only in the matter of France, but from end to end of Europe. But it was Italy's survival which was threatened by Montgomery's offensive from one side and the landing in Algeria from the other. Just when the Duce had got his intransigent way with regard to France, Italian anxiety was sufficiently strong to induce him to follow up his efforts over Greece in 1942 with an attempt to mitigate the New Order as a whole.

On 30th January 1943 Mussolini replaced Cavallero, whose ' servility' to the Germans had so often exasperated Ciano,[22] by Ambrosio as Chief of Staff. At the beginning of February, with the news of the defeat at Stalingrad, he took what appeared to be the contradictory step of dismissing the ' Ciano Cabinet' which he had appointed in the autumn of 1939. Ciano left the Palazzo Chigi to become Ambassador to the Vatican and the Germans were convinced that he had gone there to arrange a separate peace.[23] The ailing Mussolini[24] took over foreign affairs himself, to the tune of a Stefani announcement that politics must now be put back on the same level as the prosecution of war, and the peoples of Europe shown that their sacrifices would bear fruit. The Duce appointed as his Under-Secretary Bastianini, who had been Under-Secretary to Ciano in 1936, then Ambassador in Warsaw and later in London (succeeding Grandi), and Governor of Dalmatia from 1941. He was not a man

[21] On 10th Feb. 1943 the Germans induced Franco to sign a secret agreement promising to resist the Allies should they invade Spanish or Portuguese territory.

[22] Schmidt thought Ciano more servile that Cavallero on 19th Dec. 1942.

[23] Simoni, 8th Feb. 1943.

[24] The eminent German surgeon, Sauerbruch, was called to Rome (see Hassell, op. cit., p. 297, 14th Feb. 1943), but he was then not allowed to see the Duce for fear of what the world might think.

of great worth or distinction, but he had a fixed idea about paying a modicum of respect to the principle of nationality, and had warmly supported Ciano's attempts to help the Poles; he wished at this point to bring together the smaller satellites with Italy on the basis of the rights of each nation, in order to arrive at a compromise peace.[25] If Germany refused to modify the tyranny of the New Order so much the worse for her. For the moment Mussolini had been won over to this policy. The situation in Russia was critical and Hitler refused to consider the proposals of the Duce and others[26] in favour of peace with Stalin. When the Germans threw the blame for the break in Russia and the collapse at Stalingrad upon the Italians the Duce's indignation mingled with that of the rest of Italy. The country was quickly exasperated by the news of how the retreating Germans monopolized the tanks and lorries and left the Italians in the lurch, and in the night of 6th-7th February Mussolini wired to Marras to tell Keitel "that at least a minimum of help is called for if comradeship still has any meaning."[27]

The situation was extraordinarily confused. Germany itself was profoundly shaken by the shock of Stalingrad, and broad if unofficial hints from influential Germans[28] reached the Italian Embassy in Berlin that Mussolini's ancient role of peacemaker should be revived. It was arranged that Ribbentrop should go to Rome "to discuss the military situation," the Italians welcoming the opportunity to press for political changes. The Axis pattern seemed still to be the same. Before he set off Ribbentrop saw Alfieri; while expressing his regret that he would no longer be meeting Ciano he took the opportunity to assert that the present situation allowed of no politics for it could only be fought out. He concluded ominously : " It sometimes appears as

[25] After 8th Nov. the plan mentioned by Simoni for an Italian breakaway was only one of many drawn up by other diplomats along these lines. (See Simoni, 24th Nov. 1942.)

[26] e.g. of Goebbels. [27] Simoni, 7th Feb. 1943.

[28] Simoni, 10th and 17th Feb. 1943. On the second occasion the hints came from the staff of the Press Department of the German Foreign Office.

if the Axis should not trust its own Allies. Still, the Finns and Roumanians must know exactly what would happen if the Russians were to win."[29]

Ribbentrop was in Rome on this visit from 24th to 28th February 1943; he was officially received by the Duce on 25th February. Characteristically enough an unconscionable amount of time must have been spent upon irrelevant digression over a spurious problem like that of the Jews. Ribbentrop told the Duce that he knew that " in Italian military circles—just occasionally among German military people too—the Jewish problem was not sufficiently appreciated. Only thus could he understand an order of the Italian Supreme Command which cancelled measures against the Jews in the Italian occupation zone of France; these measures had been taken by the French authorities acting under German influence. The Duce contested the accuracy of this report and traced it back to the French tactics of causing dissension between Germany and Italy."[30]

Later in the conversation Mussolini indulged in a favourite Axis reflection, that Bolshevism was the revenge of the Jews against Christian civilization; in the same breath he deplored the obstinacy of the Pope in resisting the omnipotence of the Fascist State. He lamented the " proletarian " war the Italians had been compelled to fight armed with the weapons of the war before this one—Ribbentrop might well have asked by whose fault.

Much time was spent on the Yugoslav situation. From the time of the Anglo-American landing in Algeria in November 1942, Hitler had developed a fresh obsession; from now on he was haunted by the fear of an enemy invasion of his *Festung Europa* and he feared it most of all in the Balkan peninsula where Churchill intended it should

[29] Schmidt Minute, 22nd Feb. 1943.

[30] Schmidt Minute, 25th Feb. 1943. At his trial Ribbentrop managed to remember that " a large espionage and sabotage organisation was going at the time in France and that the Führer ordered me in this connection to talk to Mussolini, since the Italians were working against certain measures we had introduced in France." In fact he had declared to Mussolini that 100,000 Jews were the equivalent of 100,000 members *of* the British Secret Service, and that the Italians must be made to take the matter seriously.

come. On 16th December 1942, therefore, he inspired Keitel to sign an order in the following words :

" The enemy employs, in Partisan warfare, Communist-trained fanatics, who do not hesitate to commit any atrocity. It is more than ever a question of life and death. This fight has nothing to do with soldierly gallantry or the principles of the Geneva Convention. If the fight against the Partisans in the East, as well as in the Balkans, is not waged with the most brutal means, we shall shortly reach the point where the available forces are insufficient to control this area.

" It is, therefore, not only justified, but it is the duty of the troops to use all means without restriction, even against women and children, so long as it ensures success. Any consideration for the Partisans is a crime against the German people."[31]

The crisis in the Balkans between the Axis partners was brought to a head at the meeting at the Führer's headquarters in Görlitz forest exactly three days after this. On this occasion Ribbentrop and Keitel received Ciano and Cavallero. According to the German Minute Ribbentrop began with the old story that Croatia was entirely Italy's affair, except, of course, that during the war Germany felt concerned with (1) the suppression of all resistance, (2) the control of the railways and of the whole economic system. Keitel then announced to the Italians that the Führer had decided that the remaining resistance in this area where British influence was so strong must be crushed before the winter was over without fail. " The Führer had declared that the Serb conspirators were to be burnt out and that no gentle methods might be used in doing this. Every village where Partisans were found must be burned down. . . . Roatta had unfortunately believed that he could consolidate the position through political action," but Hitler now absolutely forbade this. Cavallero tried to intervene in favour of the Četnici, but Ribbentrop caught him up sharply and said they were conspirators and must all be liquidated.[32]

[31] See *Nuremberg Trial Proceedings*, part IX, p. 53.
[32] Schmidt Minute signed at Berlin, 23rd Dec. 1942.

In the immensely long letter dated 16th February which Ribbentrop brought to Rome on 24th February Hitler hammered away at this same theme. You counted, he wrote to Mussolini, upon Greek and Albanian support in 1940 with disastrous results. "Whenever and wherever the Balkans are invaded, O Duce, the Communists and Mihailović followers and all the other Comitadji will unite to attack the German and Italian forces immediately, in favour of the invading enemy." On 25th February Ribbentrop went on and on with this argument though the Duce declared that the Četnici had been useful, and—which was true—that the Germans themselves had made use of them. It was a typical Axis situation—the Germans insisting upon the utmost brutality and a purely military ' solution.' An agreement was reached with difficulty and was not very clear. The Četnici were at all events to be disarmed.

As for the projects of Bastianini, they did not get far, either during the discussions or in the statements published after them. Ribbentrop expounded the German slogans of the moment. The Russian flood was to be dammed up behind a great Eastern wall beyond the Ukraine. Simoni had already reported the German attitude of indifference to disasters so long as the war were kept at a distance from Germany and the further breeding of the German race not seriously endangered.[33] But in order to conceal this with adequate bluff, Ribbentrop began secret-weapon hints[34] and told the Italians he hoped the submarine war would soon drive the Western Allies to an invasion of Europe which would certainly end in their destruction. We have seen that Hitler himself was apprehensive about D-day.

It was clear, however, both to Hitler and Ribbentrop, that the Italian fruit was ripe enough to fall and that it might be worth while to make verbal concessions over the New Order and over peace. On 1st March it was indeed broadcast from Berlin that during his visit to Rome Ribbentrop had " repeatedly emphasized the determination of their countries to continue the war with all necessary means until the complete destruction of the enemy forces and the elimination of

[33] Simoni, 16th Nov. 1942.
[34] Already made to Alfieri, see Simoni, 22nd Feb. 1943.

the danger of a Bolshevist Europe. . . . They [the Axis
leaders] once more emphatically asserted the resolute will of
Germany and Italy to set up a new order in Europe after
achieving final victory. . . . The European peoples will be
guaranteed the possibility of productive work and social justice
within the secure frontiers of the great European area . . . an
importance that should not be underestimated is attached
to the discussions in Rome . . . The Italo-German statement
represents the Magna Carta of the Great European area."

At the same time the *Völkischer Beobachter* printed a Stefani
commentary about the Duce's peace-making career and
added that he was fully supported in his humane work by the
enlightened leader of Germany. Further, the Germans suddenly made the most astonishing economic concessions to
the Italians: at a moment when Hitler was proclaiming the
total mobilization of all European labour in the fight against
Bolshevism, he agreed that the Italian workmen in Germany
should return to Italy. The situation is illustrated by the
Führer's remark at a naval conference on 26th February
that it would be best to man with Germans some of the
Italian ships which were to be procured " provided that
this can be done without hurting the feelings of the
Italians."[35]

By March it was too late. On Friday, 5th March 1943, the
week after Ribbentrop's visit, open demonstrations began
at Fiat's.[36] The method, later used in northern Italy against
the German occupier, was adopted of putting forward clearly
justifiable economic demands, in this case the payment of
already promised compensation to bombed-out workmen.
By 1 p.m. on 12 March, 8,000 men of the Mirafiori factory
had gone on strike, and during the day 40,000 to 50,000
workers seem to have become involved. This was the
first big, definite strike in Italy, or for that matter in
New Order Europe, so newly granted its Axis Magna
Carta. On Saturday, 13th March, a manifesto was circulated
among the Fiat employees which ended with the words
Viva la Pace e la Libertà and was signed *Il Comitato*

[35] *Führer Conferences on Naval Affairs,* 1943, p. 11. By this
time Dönitz had succeeded Raeder as Commander-in-Chief, Navy.
[36] G. Vaccarino. *Gli scioperi del marzo 1943.* Turin 1950.

Operai. That day a payment of 300 lire to all workmen who would 'maintain discipline' was conceded, and after the week-end the strike died down. It was a momentous beginning to the anti-Fascist resistance and a number of employers openly expressed sympathy for the strikers against the régime. Rome had ordered ruthless repression but the police authorities of Turin, with troops ready at hand, had been unwilling or unable to obey. There was serious labour trouble in Milan shortly afterwards.[37] Within a few days began the Anglo-American offensive against Tunisia, the possession of which both Führer and Duce had agreed would decide the war in the Mediterranean.

Hitler clamoured to see Mussolini—he wished to inspire him with bellicosity—but he would not travel farther than Salzburg now, and the Duce was so ill that it was the second week in April before they met, once again in the castle of Klessheim. Hitler was fagged and hectic, Mussolini still ill. At Salzburg station, according to one of the Italian diplomats,[38] they greeted one another with emotional warmth. Hitler wished Mussolini to be treated by his notorious quack doctor, " Professor " Morell, but this the Duce obstinately refused. To Alfieri he said : " If you want to know the name of my illness, I can tell you—convoys."[39]

Although Hitler told Goebbels (and he probably believed it) that he had rejuvenated Mussolini,[40] the meeting was a fiasco. One might well say that the Axis broke here. The Italians came determined to urge peace with Russia and the final withdrawal of the Italian armies from abroad to help defend Italy, and on the other hand a fuller working out of some kind of European Charter with a view to peace in the West.[41] Mussolini promised Bastianini and Ambrosio to press for these things. But with the state of his health

[37] See Senise, op. cit.

[38] See article in the *Momento,* 13th May 1945.

[39] Simoni, 11th Apr. 1943.

[40] See Goebbels Diary, 7th May 1943. " The Führer did everything he could, and by putting every ounce of nervous energy into the effort, succeeded in pushing Mussolini back on the rails. . . ."

[41] Hitler talked a great deal at this time about European solidarity against Russia and half hoped to come to terms with Britain on this basis.

as it was he crumpled up even more easily than usual in his talks with Hitler who wished to hear no more sentimental rubbish about small nations.[42]

Meanwhile Ribbentrop thundered out the Führer's views to Bastianini. Russia must be fought—there was nothing else to be done with her. As for Hungarian and Roumanian attempts to reach a separate peace, whoever made efforts of this kind would only hasten his own end.[43] Bastianini, nevertheless, made it perfectly clear that Italy could not continue the war; he referred to the alarming strikes there had been in Turin and Milan. Ribbentrop broke in significantly. He preferred, he said, to speak not of Italy but of the occupied territories. In Norway, in Greece, in France attempts at a compromise had proved a failure and brutal severity the only successful method. "Far be it from Germany," he said, "to wish to oppress any other country," but Churchill's broadcast of 21st March, advocating a Council of Europe after the war, had disturbed the smaller nations and this was not a moment at which to allow oneself to be weak. The Axis could make a declaration more favourable to national autonomy only at a time when the military situation was a hundred per cent. satisfactory. The present was a particularly unfortunate moment because the Führer required radical measures for the mobilization of European labour. If the various countries were allowed governments of their own, "the innate urge against the Axis," say in Holland or France, would consolidate itself, and twice as many occupation troops would be required.[44]

Two or three weeks later Ribbentrop summoned Laval to Klessheim in order to tighten the fetters of France and he sent for Bastianini at the same time. The latter obstinately used this, like every other, opportunity to press for the European Charter he advocated. If his own account[45] is to be trusted he compelled Ribbentrop to listen on 29th April

[42] Goebbels Diary, 8th May, 1943. Mussolini did manage to ask Hitler for aeroplanes.

[43] Ribbentrop knew very well that the Italian Minister in Bucharest was scheming with Mihai Antonescu for an escape from the war.

[44] German Minute signed by Schmidt, 10th Apr. 1943.

[45] G. Bastianini—*Uomini, Rose, Fatti* (1959).

to a disquisition on the necessity for the reconstruction of Europe with France in the place her traditions deserved; it was pointless, he said, to exasperate her national feeling. On 1st May Mussolini went so far as to instruct the Stefani Agency to issue a communiqué in this sense.

With the fall of Tunis on 7th May the shadow of defeat fell darkly across Italy; it was as if in the darkness before dawn the ghost of Mazzini had appeared to his sons and roused them to avenge him, for in one sense the Italians broke with Nazi Germany over the principle of national autonomy. At the same moment their own independence had been lost. While the Duce had contrived to eject Rommel from the command of Italian troops,[46] he had successfully banished the bulk of his own forces to Africa or Russia. When he asked for help from Germany, the Germans insisted upon economizing in the transport of Italian soldiers from the Eastern Front, which meant that only German troops were available. On 13th May Mussolini told Dönitz (who was on a visit to Italy) he would accept only three of the five divisions which Hitler had offered him. At this desperate moment Kesselring observed that this was " an act of political importance inasmuch as it proves that the Italians want to remain masters in their own house."[47] They wished it in vain. It suited Hitler's ends that Italy should be defended, but he made certain that German help meant the German occupation of Italy.

There was a remarkable pendant to Axis relations in the spring of 1943. There had been less haggling over Yugoslavia this April than at any time since the previous November. The Balkan situation had changed very little. The Germans had taken action without the slightest regard for the Italians, who were left in the dark, while the Italians interpreted the " understanding " of February to mean that the Četnici should be disarmed *after* the destruction of the Partisans. All that followed was that the Četnici were demoralized and the Partisans encouraged, and it sometimes occurred that the Axis partners were drawn into fighting against one another. On 19th May Hitler committed one

[46] F. W. Deakin *The Brutal Friendship* (1962), p. 165.
[47] *Führer Conferences on Naval Affairs,* 1943, p. 32.

of his paroxysms of wrath to paper. I am determined, he wrote to Mussolini, to destroy the Yugoslav fighting groups while your General Pirzio Biroli (the governor of Montenegro) is working for their preservation—indeed the Italians have actually created some of the formations. I have tried " with really angelic patience " to arrive at co-operation in the Balkans area, " but my efforts have failed thanks to repeated—I am forced to use this hard word—sabotage and lack of will to restore order." As for any aspersions cast upon Germany's loyalty to Italy, Hitler repudiated them with " the deepest indignation." He knew nothing of Ambrosio and Pirzio Biroli when Italy was fighting Abyssinia, " But it was then that I led Germany on to Italy's side." In order to avoid another North Africa Hitler begged Mussolini to give orders to his High Command to conform, not only in the letter, to the February agreement. " Let me speak to you, Duce, as perhaps your most sincere friend : I know well enough, and so do you, that not all the Italian and German generals have stood solidly behind us. . . . Believe in the sincere attachment of a man who will never abandon the fate of his own Revolution, of yours and of those[48] of Fascism."

The unhappy Duce with his back to the wall tried to defend himself even against Hitler. His letters this spring were more than usually full of petty resentments.[49] When he replied on 22nd May to Hitler's outburst he insisted once more that it was the Italian Army which had broken resistance in Greece.[50] But he accepted Hitler's orders and abandoned Bastianini. At Klessheim, it appears, Himmler had said to him quite simply what was true—that he had no support left in Italy; in that case he had nothing to lose by adopting ruthless coercion, and Hitler advised an Italian S.S.

Fascism had failed to eradicate a certain universalism in the Italian approach, and Mazzini's nationalism, which respected the nationalism of others, had lingered fitfully on. The Italians instinctively felt that Hitler's frightfulness was

[48] Plural used in the text.

[49] See letters to Hitler dated 9th Mar. and 23rd Mar.

[50] Hitler's letter had referred to Germany's " conspicuous contributions " to the conquest of the Balkans in 1941.

bad politics as well as bad morality, and that the two might come to the same thing. Even in Yugoslavia they recognized some kind of national entity in the Četnici. Laval expressed their view when he said to Hitler, " Vous voulez gagner la guerre pour faire l'Europe; faites donc l'Europe pour gagner la guerre." Until the second Klessheim meeting in April 1943 the Duce was balancing precariously between Italy and Hitler. But as his half-hearted attempt to coax concessions from the more resolute Führer broke down, the Italians' desire to free themselves from him could no longer be concealed. If he attempted to liberalize Fascism, it would cease to mean anything; he was forced to choose Hitler as against Italy. When Bastianini met his Berlin colleagues at Klessheim at the end of April he remarked to them that, although Italy's position was desperate,

" Mussolini would never make up his mind to capitulate and that anyway at the first symptoms of surrender the Germans would spring upon us.

" His own talks with Ribbentrop, Bastianini said, had been disconcerting. The Germans suspect Pétain, Kállay, and Mihai Antonescu. They suspect Franco and fear Turkey. And of course they suspect us. All Europe is rising up against the attempt, conducted with so much bestiality, to impose the hegemony of Germany. And Italy, from whom so many peoples had hoped for good sense, has let herself be dragged, like the others, into the vortex of this folly."

" Are we really at the end?" asked Simoni.[51]

[51] Op. cit., 29th Apr. 1943.

Chapter XIX

"MÉSALLIANCE"

"*Saturday, 12th June.* The news of the surrender of Pantelleria has provoked a violent German reaction. They suspect betrayal and demand explanations. . . .

" 9 p.m. Ribbentrop telephones to Alfieri that the Führer has decided to send Marshal von Richthofen to Italy at once with an air unit.

"*Sunday, 13th June.* . . . Richthofen, having arrived in Rome, says he is only on a tour of inspection. . . .

"*Tuesday, 22nd June.* . . . It won't be much : . . a few dozen planes, for which we must put twelve air-fields at their disposal.

"*Saturday, 10th July.* At dawn Allied forces landed in Sicily. . . .

"*Sunday, 11th July.* The news from Sicily is worse. The battle may now be considered lost. Silence from Rome over the most disturbing questions. No instructions at all. . . .

"*Saturday, 17th July* . . . it is now a matter of [German] forces to occupy rather than to help us. . . ."

These are entries in Simoni's Diary in the summer of 1943.

When Dönitz returned from his visit to Rome in the middle of May the Führer expressed doubt as to whether the Duce was "determined to carry on to the end"; as for Ambrosio, Hitler believed that he "would be happy if Italy could become a British dominion to-day."[1] On Saturday, 17th July, Hitler conferred on the Italian crisis with Dönitz, Keitel, Jodl, and others at the Wolfsschanze. Only "barbaric measures," he said, could now save Italy. "Therefore the Führer believes that a sort of directorate, tribunal or court-martial should be set up in Italy to remove undesirable elements. . . . He has already consulted Ambassador von Mackensen, but the latter could suggest no one capable of taking over the leadership." It is curious that on this occasion Farinacci's name was not mentioned, though Goebbels

[1] *Führer Conferences on Naval Affairs*, 1948, p. 38.

351

was still convinced, a week later, that " we can depend upon him blindly."[2]

On the same day Hitler summoned Mussolini to meet him in North Italy on the Monday morning (19th), for their thirteenth encounter Simoni noted.[3] Führer and Duce with their retinues met at the air-port of Treviso and proceeded to Senator Gaggia's villa at Feltre (for the Italians had expected their guests to stay for two or three days): on the way Ambrosio asked Keitel for the reinforcements which the Germans had promised and Keitel replied that, owing to the Russian counter-offensive which had begun during the week-end, he was unable to spare any help at all.

The Feltre meeting was a battle between Hitler and Ambrosio over the tired body of Mussolini. It was Hitler's last chance to reinflate the Italian balloon: it was the last chance for Ambrosio—and indeed the rest of Italy—to induce Mussolini to tell Hitler that he must make peace.

Adolf Hitler held forth for three hours on that Monday morning at the Feltre villa in order to inspire Mussolini with the courage of despair. Everything must be defended, the oil regions, the Ukraine for corn, and Norway, Petsamo, and Serbia for their metals. Work must go on regardless of tremendous air attacks. Above all the Italian air-fields must be properly defended. " It is tragic," he throws in, " that the British are very much on the spot over organization ": this was illustrated by their rapid fitting-up of Pantelleria. Our first task is to weaken the enemy on the Eastern front before the winter. A new weapon against which no protection is known will then be in use against Britain. Italy must be held so that " Sicily may become for the enemy what Stalingrad was for us." There must be total mobilization. Boys of fifteen, the Führer boasts, are manning Germany's A.A. guns. " And if anyone should say our tasks can be left to a future generation I reply that it may not be a generation of giants. The resurrection of Germany took thirty years. Rome never rose again. This is the voice of history." Cold comfort for Italy on the very day of the first bombardment of Rome! And throughout the Führer

[2] Goebbels Diary, 25th July 1943.   [3] op. cit., 19th July 1943.

insists that it is the men—and above all the officers—not the machines, that count. Therefore Germany will give Italy no more machines without Germans to guard them—again she will save Italy only at the cost of occupation.[4]

After a tête-à-tête Superman lunch,[5] Ambrosio and Bastianini, and even Alfieri, urged upon Mussolini his duty to speak out to Hitler before the German party left. All the morning he had opened his mouth exactly twice—once, quite early on, to announce the air attack on Rome and a second time to say something about the population of Corsica. From his reaction to Ambrosio's entreaties it was clear that at lunch it had been very much the same thing.[6] On the way back to Treviso with the Führer he was silent. It was easier to be mesmerized by Hitler. The Germans were strong; it seemed simpler and safer to stick to them. Back in Rome the next evening Mussolini told Ambrosio that he had decided to write a letter to Hitler to say that Italy must make peace, but he never did. Ambrosio asked to resign.

For the last three months Italian anger had been mounting against the Duce. A week after his return from Klessheim in April he had appointed the old terrorist, Scorza, as Secretary of the Fascist Party to follow Himmler's advice. Groups of Fascist thugs reappeared in the streets, but now they themselves were sometimes murdered in the night. A varied clandestine Press reached a good many people and there was a good deal of labour unrest round about 1st May. Representatives of the chief pre-Fascist political parties, together with members of the new Party of Action, began to see more of one another cautiously. They contrived to convey their dismay to the King and to consult with the dissident generals; Mussolini's old enemy, the moderate

[4] This account is taken from the Italian Minutes published in *Hitler e Mussolini* quoted above.

[5] (or possibly before it) This is recorded in an Italian Minute of the Feltre meeting.

[6] Mussolini (*Il tempo del bastone e della carota*) says he asked Hitler for help. Ambrosio and Marras were afraid he had only handed Italy over, bound hand and foot.

R.B.A.   M

Socialist Bonomi, was in touch with Ambrosio before the end of 1942[7] and was received by the King on 22nd June.

Until July 1943 Ambrosio had always hoped to induce Mussolini himself to break with Germany, but from the time of Feltre he agreed with Castellano and other generals that the Duce must be forcibly removed. At the same time the King made up his mind to do what he had always found impossible hitherto, to dismiss Mussolini.

For some weeks the Fascist leaders had been asking that the Fascist Grand Council be summoned to meet (for the first time since December 1939); some of them hoped thus to steady the regime,[8] others to overthrow it. Three days before he went to Feltre Mussolini agreed, and the meeting was fixed for the afternoon of Saturday, 24th July, at 5 p.m.; it lasted, with a short interval at about midnight, until 2.40 a.m. on 25th July. Mussolini admitted that the country was dead against the war, but war was always unpopular, he said; he made a long list of all the help Italy had had from Germany and proposed to fight to the finish. In the end nineteen[9] of the twenty-eight members of the Council voted for an Order of the day proposed by Grandi which invited the King to take over the command of all the armed forces. It was an invitation to Mussolini to quit, but he himself warned the *gerarchi* that they were risking the breakdown of the whole Fascist machine.

The Duce asked to be received by the King at 5 p.m. on the Sunday. The King commented on the Grandi resolution and informed Mussolini that he was placing the government of the country in Badoglio's hands. According to Mussolini's account[10] Victor Emmanuel told the Duce that

---

[7] In 1944 Mussolini claimed to be in possession of Ambrosio's Diary and published an entry from it dated 4th Dec. 1942. "Visita Bonomi—Proposta Badoglio—Abdicazione S.M.—Il Principe—Armi —Cavallero." op. cit., p. 107 *supra*. See also Ivanoe Bonomi, *Diario di un anno* (Garzanti, 1947).

[8] Goebbels and the Nazis in general regarded the Grand Council meeting as an Old Guard Fascist move—see Goebbels, op. cit., 25th July 1943.

[9] Including Alfieri.   [10] op. cit.

he was certainly the most hated man in Italy and had only one friend left, the King himself. On leaving the royal villa Mussolini was gently but firmly arrested and removed in an ambulance by an officer and a force of carabinieri; this had been arranged by the anti-Fascist generals with Acquarone, the Minister of the Royal Household.

Just before 11 p.m. that night the news was broadcast from Rome together with formal proclamations from Badoglio and the King. It was a hot summer night and the streets in all the towns of Italy were thronged with people. When they heard that Mussolini had gone they sang and laughed and wept with joy. It was the end of the long Fascist nightmare, and above all, as Mussolini said to the King as he left him, to the people his fall meant the end of the war.

King Victor Emmanuel's position on 25th July 1943 was certainly not enviable. The House of Savoy had been linked in the popular mind with the Duce, and was felt to have condoned his pro-German policy; the Prince of Piedmont, too, had made himself unpopular by his apparent enthusiasm over war against France. The tardy dismissal of Mussolini gave the King a sudden opportunity; for the moment everything was hoped from him. But he could only satisfy expectation if he showed confidence in his people by quickly appointing a broadly based government and if he made peace.

The King, however, was old and suspicious, and determined, as it seemed, to rule at last. He was afraid of the popular currents of feeling and especially of the leftist parties and the industrial workers in the north. According to Badoglio[11] it was Victor Emmanuel himself who insisted on a Cabinet of technicians which was thoroughly out of touch. Martial law and a stricter censorship than ever were like cold douches to a population which fondly believed it had regained liberty. The other cold douche—this one seemed icy—was the immediate announcement that the war would go on. Now the King and Badoglio probably wanted peace as much as the public, but they knew that the

[11] op. cit.

Germans would try to occupy all Italy in full force if they admitted this wish. The best elements in the country were longing to fight *against* Hitler, but when the political leaders offered mass support in Rome and Milan for immediate resistance, the King and the generals ignored them, and small isolated groups of resisters were shot down when the Germans arrived. In a month or so, after the German occupation, resistance was spontaneously organized, and all the King's manœuvres only saved a portion of southern Italy from the Germans.

There was one member of the Fascist Grand Council who had stood alone. Farinacci, who had been making furious journalistic attacks on the generals since the invasion of Sicily, proposed a motion of his own in favour of the royal command of the armed forces but in favour also of absolute loyalty to the Axis alliance and the Axis *guerre à outrance*.[12] On the Sunday he disappeared from Rome and arrived precipitately (without luggage) at Munich in a German plane with a letter from Mackensen and accompanied by Dollmann;[13] he continued at once to the Führer's headquarters. Although on 17th July Hitler had had no suggestion from Mackensen as to the replacement of Mussolini, it may safely be assumed that Dollmann had been plotting with Farinacci for some time. Mackensen was an astonishingly stupid man and had completely misinformed Berlin;[14] in any case the S.S. had a separate and more powerful organization, in Rome as elsewhere, than that directed by the *Auswärtiges Amt*. Farinacci may have been instructed to follow up his order of the day with armed Fascist pressure which should compel the King to place all the Italian armed forces, as Hitler had so long desired,[15] under German command When, instead of this, Farinacci escaped to Germany alone

[12] For the full English text of the resolutions brought up at the Grand Council meetings see *Mussolini's Memoirs* (Contact, 1949). The third one (Scorza's) is almost meaningless. See also Deakin op. cit., Part I, Book IV, chap. v.

[13] Simoni, 26th July 1943.

[14] See his report to Dönitz, 19th Aug. 1943. *Führer Conferences on Naval Affairs*, 1943, p. 91.

[15] And had demanded in so many words at Feltre.

and found fault with Mussolini, Hitler broke into a good
Austrian rage. "There is simply nothing to be done with
these Wops,"[16] he exclaimed, and "handed him over to
Himmler to look after for the present."[17]

On 26th July the German public was told very coolly
that Mussolini had resigned on account of ill health, but
that this involved no change at all in Italian policy. The
German Press had nothing to say about it all for several days,
but the Berlin public, at least, listened to the B.B.C. as
it had never dared before, and knew all about the demonstrations in Italy and the short work which had been made of
anything like a Fascist Party decoration. The fall of Mussolini coincided not only with the successful Russian counter-
offensive but also with an intensification of the air war—the
British raided Hamburg on quite a new scale on the night
of the Fascist Grand Council, and on 1st August Goebbels
made the sensational announcement that Berlin was to be
evacuated. It all made a tremendous impression, but especially the Duce's fall created an atmosphere of "That's
one of them out: when do we get rid of the other?"[18]
This was typically Berlinese, but not confined to Berlin;
it was interesting that in Bavaria with its odd insularity
a new shock was felt: until then the Bavarian peasants
had very nearly ignored the war, but from this time they
feared Allied air attacks from Italy.[19] When Dönitz went to
Hamburg a little later he reported to Hitler that "the general
feeling of the people is one of depression in spite of their
willingness to work. Everybody sees only the many reverses.
In view of the impressions I gained from my visit in
Hamburg and on the basis of many reports and much intelligence I believe it is very urgent that the Führer speaks to
the people very soon. . . ."[20] It may indeed safely be affirmed
that German morale now touched the lowest level it ever

[16] From a reliable German diplomatic source. "Mit diesen Katzel-
machern ist eben nichts zu machen."
[17] Goebbels, op. cit., 27th July 1943.
[18] Simoni, 25th July 1943, and many German sources.
[19] Information from a neutral visitor to Bavaria at the time.
[20] *Führer Conferences on Naval Affairs*, 1943, p. 88.

reached until 1945.[21] During the last week in July German
diplomats whispered that Himmler was telling Hitler that
the S.S. of the interior could no longer be regarded as
absolutely reliable, and that an S.S. division from the *Ostfront*
had been brought to Berlin;[22] in fact it was transferred to
Italy.[23]

It might be suggested that Hitler and Himmler had
lost their heads, but it is probably more exact to describe
them as greatly excited. Not only were Italy and Germany
vibrating with the shock of Mussolini's fall. The anti-
German parties in Roumania and Hungary and indeed
throughout Axis Europe were stimulated to a degree such
that if the Allies could have followed up their advantage in
Italy, the war might have ended in 1943. And then for Hitler,
whose fantasy had identified Mussolini with himself and
linked the fate of "our revolutions," it was emotionally
a fundamental blow to HIM, greater, perhaps, than the
German defeat at Stalingrad—he probably believed more
profoundly in the Supermen than in the German Army or
the German nation. He dug his feet in, however. When
on 27th July Rommel, Richthofen, and Dönitz expressed
their feeling that Fascism had lost all hold on Italy and
that the only stable influence there with which Germany
could now work was the House of Savoy, Hitler angrily
declared that soldiers did not understand and that Fascism
MUST be restored.[24] Jodl had faith that the Führer could do
this and Göring and Ribbentrop supported him. Four new
operations were to be worked out immediately : (*a*) *Eiche*
for the rescue of Mussolini; (*b*) *Student* for the restoration
of Fascism, with the occupation of Rome; (*c*)*Schwarz* for
the military occupation of a defensible line in Italy; and
(*d*) *Achse* for the capture or destruction of the Italian fleet.

[21] " Some sections of the population are almost in a state of panic."
Goebbels Diary, 27th July 1943. He had noted two days earlier
that " the letters addressed to me are disturbing."

[22] Information received from a particularly good source at the
time.

[23] Deakin, op. cit. p. 493.

[24] *Führer Conferences on Naval Affairs,* 1943, pp. 67-8; cf. Hassell,
op. cit., p. 328.

This had become the meaning of *Achse*. Hitler wished *Eiche* and *Student* to be carried out without delay : he sent for the S.S. man Skorzeny on the same day (27th July) and briefed him over the rescue of the Duce. It may be noted that particular anxiety was shown with regard to the effect of the change in Italy upon the Balkan situation—Hitler was still hypersensitive about this.

On 29th July 1943 Mussolini was sixty. In Germany the birthday—and especially the sixtieth birthday—of any personage was always advertised with fervent eulogy in the papers. This time the Press was unchained in a paean of praise to demonstrate the Führer's fidelity. On 30th July the Deutsches Nachrichten Büro announced that Hitler had sent Mussolini a special edition of the complete works of Nietzsche in twenty-four volumes, with " a cordial personal dedication," and Transocean subsequently referred to Mussolini's belief in living dangerously. At the same time the German Press began to point out that the change of régime in Italy did not seem to have softened the wrath of the enemy.

The action of the Badoglio Government—it was unfortunate but not surprising—was timid and dilatory. On 29th July Marras arrived by air from Rome with a message for Hitler, and proceeded with Simoni to Rastenburg. They were met with an atmosphere of melodramatic suspicion. On 30th July, after being ostentatiously disarmed, they were received by the Führer, covered by Jodl, Schmundt, and Hewel all with their hands on their revolvers. Evidently Hitler had made up a diabolical plot . . . it was another of the familiar symptoms, the attribution of his own intentions to his victims.[25] Marras then invited Hitler to an early meeting with Victor Emmanuel in northern Italy. Hitler refused this for the present but agreed that the Foreign Ministers and Chiefs of Staff should meet instead. He was didactic and reproachful about Communism in Italy, but the hysterical climax which occurred in nearly all his speeches (including

[25] Goebbels (op. cit., p. 324) refers to a plan for parachutists to kidnap the Italian King with his family, and possibly the Pope as well. Gisevius (op. cit.) refers to plans of the kind at Easter 1943, but he is often inaccurate.

those called interviews) was on this occasion induced by
a reference to the British air attacks. History was familiar
with the annihilation of cities. . . . "But the day will
come—it may be in 300 years—when we shall be able
to revenge ourselves."[26] When Hitler spoke of helping
Italy he again made much of the difficulties of transport;
Marras and Simoni had the impression that the Germans were
only really held back from an immediate occupation by the
impoverishment of their resources.

On the day of Marras's theatrical interview it is noted
in the naval minutes that "Operation *Schwarz* is to be de-
ferred, in order to permit pouring as many troops into Italy as
possible while co-operation still continues." On 1st August
—"Movement of German troops into northern Italy continues." At 3 p.m. on 31st July the Italian Consulate at
Innsbruck had reported to the Embassy that German troops
were crossing the Brenner.[27] By now the Germans, except
for Kesselring and possibly Dönitz, felt convinced that Badoglio was negotiating with the Allies. Hitler's 'intuition'
had told him so from the beginning. Characteristically he
missed no opportunity of blaming Italy for his three-year-
old disappointment with regard to Spain which had "decided everything"; one day it was Italian jealousy, another
Italy's attack on Greece, which had made the Spanish hen
broody.

In these peculiar circumstances Ribbentrop and Keitel
met Ambrosio and the new Italian Foreign Minister, Guariglia,
at the unimposing Italian frontier station of Tarvisio on
6th August. The inevitable Dollmann was there to interpret,
together with Paul Schmidt. The Germans were frigid and
menacing, and accompanied by a formidable company of S.S.
guards. Keitel made difficulties when Ambrosio repeated more
forcibly than in the past that the Italian troops must be
brought home from Croatia and France to protect Italy.
He complained that some German troops chivalrously coming
to Italy's help had been held up by Italian frontier authorities at Arnoldstein—Ambrosio said, Yes, the Italians would
prefer to be informed beforehand about German troop move-
ments. In the afternoon Keitel and Ribbentrop disappeared

[26] Simoni, 30th July 1943.   [27] Idem, 31st July 1943.

for two hours without a word, then returned to say that they had just ordered the passage of their soldiers at Arnold-stein. "E un gesto inaudito," Simoni noted.[28]

But Guariglia achieved what he intended and indeed all that he could. He was an exceedingly clever and skilful Neapolitan—*una vecchia volpe,*[29] Dollmann said admiringly—and he teased and puzzled Ribbentrop. When his German colleague asked him whether the Badoglio Government was in touch with the British or Americans, Guariglia lied blandly—No, we are your loyal allies—some irresponsible contact, perhaps, but that he could not know.[30] To Ribbentrop's "And how do you propose to fight now?" Guariglia came back quickly with "And you? You will have to make peace with Russia, if you can." Ribbentrop in revenge shook menacing fingers at him over the unleashing of Italian Communism. Guariglia brushed that aside—Italian Communists were different—and followed Bastianini in stressing the importance of respecting the rights of nations,[31] at one point he even remarked to Ribbentrop that if the Germans were to occupy Italy, all Italians would regard it as an act of hostility. By lunch-time Ribbentrop had thawed a little and consented to lunch in Guariglia's train. To his enticing proposition that the King of Italy, the Prince of Piedmont, and the chief Italian generals should soon visit Hitler in Germany Guariglia was all smiles. Ribbentrop added that the Duce's resignation had been a great blow to the Führer, "from a personal point of view as well."[32]

Simoni's account of the meeting at Tarvisio begins with a reference to shooting between soldiers and partisans in the neighbourhood a full month before the Armistice.[33] It ends with Dörnberg's warning given to a friend of Ciano's that

[28] Simoni, 6th Aug. 1943. [29] Ibid. (=an old fox).

[30] He did know that a colleague of his had begun to sound the Allies in Lisbon on 4th August.

[31] This account is based mainly upon a conversation with the Italian protagonist. It should be noted that Ribbentrop was particularly suspicious of Guariglia, since he had only just returned from the Italian Embassy in the neutral town of Ankara. cf. Goebbels Diary, 27th July 1943.

[32] See Italian Minute given in *Hitler e Mussolini* quoted above.

[33] The district is mixed Italian-Slovene in character.

Galeazzo should beware of falling into German hands, for
" they will kill him."

The Allies were perhaps excessively cautious in their attitude to the new Italian Government and in their plans for
the future conduct of the war. Anti-Fascist Italy hoped they
would quickly have landed near Genoa and elsewhere in
the north. At last on 3rd September the unconditional surrender of Italy was secretly accepted; on 8th September
it was announced and the Allied forces landed on the main-
land at Salerno. Italy north of that was quickly in German
hands. But if operation *Schwarz* was successful, operation
Achse was not, for a number of Italian ships joined the
Allied navies and the battleship *Roma* was sunk.

The hysterical contradictions in Goebbels' Diary for 10th
September reflect the scene at Rastenburg to which, upon
news of the Italian armistice, he had been summoned to meet
the Führer. " The Führer anticipated Italian treason as
something absolutely certain. . . . And yet when it actually
happened it upset him pretty badly. He hadn't thought
it possible that this treachery would be committed in such
a dishonourable manner." Both Dönitz and Goebbels thought
that Hitler had been marvellous about the whole thing,
and yet Goebbels said it was all the fault of German policy.
In spite of the fatigue he had manifested for months, the
Führer appeared after a night of two hours' sleep inspired
so as to look " as though he had just come from a holiday."
Pavolini,[34] Renato Ricci,[35] and the Duce's son, Vittorio, were
already at the Führer's headquarters drafting a Neo-Fascist
appeal to the Italian people, and Farinacci was to be allowed
to join them. Philip of Hesse, on the other hand, was
arrested and handed over to Himmler. " The Duce will
enter history as the last Roman," Goebbels reflected, " but
behind his massive figure a gypsy people has gone to rot."

The Duce seemed more likely to disappear from history
as a broken man. To a formally polite note from Badoglio
he replied on 26th July with an almost servile letter; though
Mussolini quotes it in his book, Hitler was convinced that
it was forged. The Italians knew that Hitler intended the
Duce's rescue and they soon learnt that the Allies would

[34] See chapter XIV.   [35] See Chapter XIII.

require him to be handed over to them. It was expedient, therefore, to move him from place to place cautiously. The naval officer, Admiral Maugeri, who conducted Mussolini from Gaeta to the island of Ponza and from Ponza to La Maddalena has recorded their conversations on board.[36] He describes him, not as sulky, but depressed and indignant, and more than anything torn in two directions about Germany; on the first voyage he was full of the necessity for Italy to make peace and on the second he had veered away from defeatism. Exile to islands off the west coast of Italy was agreeably stimulating to Mussolini's Napoleonic vanity. He himself notes with pride that he spent the days in translating Carducci's *Odi barbare* into German and in reading a Life of Jesus by Ricciotti; the latter book was found marked to indicate that Mussolini, too, had been betrayed. Badoglio allowed him the twenty-four volumes of Nietzsche with considerable delay; " Una vera meraviglia dell' editoria tedesca," Mussolini remarked in his own account, and adds that he had time to read the first four volumes containing Nietzsche's early poems. He was taken, finally, to a small hotel at the Gran Sasso, high up in the mountains of the Abruzzi, the higher the better, it was thought.

On 10th September the Führer broadcast from his headquarters the speech to which Dönitz and Goebbels had been urging him. According to this latest version Germany had had to face war in 1939 " alone and forsaken." But Mussolini was not to blame—he was " the greatest son of the Italian land since the downfall of the ancient Roman Empire." And henceforth Germany could continue the struggle freed from all burdensome restrictions.

On Sunday, 12th September, Mussolini was rescued by Nazi glider formations; Otto Skorzeny was in command of the Operation. The Germans who had just occupied Rome had impressed a senior officer of the Italian military police, General Soleti, to come with them in order to order Mussolini's guards not to shoot. The rescue of the Duce, together with the rapid occupation of nearly all Italy, was the token

[36] See *Politica Estera*, August-September and October numbers, 1944. Also *From the Ashes of Disgrace* (1948).

of Hitler's recovery. The rescue had all the right heroic colouring that Hitler had wished. The democracies had been fooled again, and still more fooled were all those who had faith in them. The Gran Sasso incident, together with Hitler's fierce speech a couple of days earlier, re-invigorated German morale, while the German papers were let loose to shout their threats to the satellite Finns, Hungarians, and Roumanians, who had hoped to follow Italy's example. Mark well how treachery is rewarded, they shrieked. And on 15th September, the day after his arrival at the Führer's headquarters, Benito Mussolini was proclaimed to have resumed the supreme direction of Fascism in Italy with the publication of six Orders of the Day. On 18th September the Duce broadcast from Munich and the Italian Social Republic was born. " Hitler and Mussolini embraced after their long separation,"[37] Goebbels noted (on hearsay, for he was in Berlin on 14th September); " it was a deeply moving example of loyalty between men and comrades."

It was nothing of the kind, though until he went to the Führer's headquarters on 22nd September it appears that Goebbels did not suspect the truth. It was a listless Mussolini who had left the Gran Sasso on 12th September. When his S.S. rescuers asked him where he wished to go, he merely said, " My political life is over—where should I go but to Rocca delle Caminate?"[38] But when Soleti pointed out that they were heading for Austria he did not protest, and in a short time he found himself in Vienna. From there on 13th September he travelled to Munich whither his wife and younger children had been brought to meet him. Early on 22nd September Goebbels arrived at Hitler's headquarters, and, accompanying the Führer on his morning walk, had the Führer's soul poured out to him. Without accepting Goebbels as a disinterested reporter, since he feared too great friendship between Führer and Duce, his Diary makes

[37] It was less than two months since Feltre.
[38] In his *Storia di un Anno* Mussolini makes no complaint about Badoglio's treatment of him except that from Badoglio, too, he had asked to go to his home at the Rocca. His health appears to have been shaky but not desperate. People said he looked large-eyed and emaciated.

plain that the arrival of Mussolini had added to the Führer's griefs.

" We may consider him absolutely disillusioned concerning the Duce's personality. . . . He [the Duce] is not a revolutionary like the Führer or Stalin. He is so bound to his own Italian people that he lacks the broad qualities of a world-wide revolutionary and insurrectionist. . . . There was, of course, no actual quarrel between the Führer and the Duce."

Hitler seems to have been exasperated because, while on the one hand Mussolini was only really angry with the King, on the other, as soon as he reached Munich he had allowed Edda to reconcile him with Ciano, who had mysteriously been removed from Rome on 27th August on Himmler's instructions.[39]

" That means this poisonous mushroom is again planted in the midst of the new Fascist Republican Party. . . . Ciano intends to write his memoirs. The Führer rightly suspects that such memoirs can only be written in a manner derogatory to us, for otherwise he could not dispose of them in the international market. There is therefore no thought of authorizing Ciano to leave the Reich; he will remain in our custody, at least for the present."[40]

Goebbels was delighted with Hitler's disappointment in Mussolini; he only feared it might not be complete. Steps were rapidly taken to annex Trieste with Istria to Germany as *Gau Küstenland*,[41] under the Gauleiter of Styria, and on 5th October the South Tyrol (that is the Italian provinces of Bolzano, Trento, and Belluno) was incorporated in Germany as the *Alpenvorland* under the administration of the Gauleiter of *Tirol-Vorarlberg*. Further, the Führer was prepared, now, to consider his Minister's appetite for Venetia; it might, he thought, be included in the Reich " in a sort of loose federation."[42] Why Lombardy, which had been Austrian only

[39] Cf. Deakin op. cit., pp. 543, 554.

[40] Goebbels Diary, 23rd Sept. 1943.

[41] The *Küstenland* was a province of pre-1914 Austria, though not an administrative district.

[42] Goebbels Diary, 23rd Sept. 1943; cf. Pfitzner's programme mentioned in chapter XI.

seven years' less time, was not coveted as well is harder
to explain; it must have been forgotten in the excitement
of the moment, though on 10th September Goebbels had
remarked that the Austrian Gauleiters " excel at making territorial claims."

It is clear from the entries made by Goebbels in his
Diary for 23rd September that Hitler had received a very
great blow. Belief in Fascist Italy as a pillar of the Nietzschean
paradise had been part of his psychological structure. He
was now forced to admit that a major pretence of his
life had been nonsense, that Italy had been no better in
this war than in the last, and that Mussolini was excessively
Italian. His Mentor, his twin-Superman for twenty-one years,
was a perfectly ordinary man, who, he now believed, had
even been willing to "betray" him.[43] Hitler was so shaken
that he forgot the Balkan danger which had obsessed him
for months and was now magnified tenfold; Goebbels himself, a little earlier,[44] noted that in Dalmatia and Slovenia,
Italians and Slovenes were joining the Partisans. Of course
Hitler would "never forget" all that Mussolini had done
to help him with regard to rearmament, the Anschluss, and
"to integrate the Protectorate into the Reich." But it had
become clear that all the King's horses and all the King's
men could not really put Mussolini together again. Searching furiously for a scapegoat, the Führer satisfied himself
that the Duce had been corrupted by Ciano.[45] Ciano could
perhaps be made to pay for the greatest disillusionment of
Hitler's life.

[43] Goebbels says that Badoglio's speech to his officers in this effect
also persuaded Hitler of this. See Diary, 23rd Sept. 1943.

[44] 20th Sept. 1943. On 10th Sept. 1943 he referred to the danger
in Hungary and Bulgaria. Hitler seems still to have trusted old
Antonescu in spite of his justified suspicions of Mihai.

[45] Goebbels Diary, 23rd Sept. 1943.

Chapter XX

NAZIS AND NEO-FASCISTS

Mussolini had no illusions left to be destroyed when he arrived at Hitler's headquarters on 14th September 1943. He had feared and admired and envied the Führer for many years; these emotions in relation to the paranoiac Austrian had woven themselves into a feeling of fascination, garnished with hatred, never with sympathy. Sometimes he believed that Hitler had wished to bring about his fall in order to tighten the German hold on Italy. Mussolini knew, as he had said at the Gran Sasso, that his political life was finished—there was no future for him except as Hitler's pawn, and he had no German taste for the tragic joys of self-destruction. He was unwell and tired and had longed to go home to the Romagna, not to Rastenburg.

The Führer, however, had made up his mind. He had looked at Farinacci and Pavolini and the other Fascists who had taken refuge in Germany, and he had decided that they would not do. As Goebbels said, Mussolini's name was the oldest Fascist password, and Hitler, who had felt the effect upon the Germans of Mussolini's fall, was determined not to be deprived of so precious a symbol.

As Hitler had confided in Goebbels so Mussolini at a later stage entrusted different versions of his meetings with Hitler in September 1943 at one moment to Anfuso whom he sent to succeed Alfieri in Berlin, and later, at the beginning of 1945, to his neo-Fascist Minister of Propaganda, Mezzasoma. Anfuso was told that Hitler had been politely puzzled over the collapse of Fascism, that he had taken it for granted that Mussolini was prepared to reconstruct his régime but had made no threats nor conditions: even over the 'traitors' of July he had merely expressed appreciation of Mussolini's family feelings.[1] Accord-

[1] Anfuso, op. cit., pp. 326, 328. Oddly enough Mussolini seems often to have said to Anfuso that he did not wish to be a Quisling.

ing, however, to Mezzasoma[2] Hitler began his interview with Mussolini on 14th September by 'recalling him to realities' —just as the King had, Mussolini commented crossly. Mussolini expressed his intention of retiring into private life in order to avoid civil war in Italy. Hitler then faced him with a number of disagreeable threats towards his own person and against Italy. On the next day he had acquiesced in his own come-back and was then informed of the new conditions in which he was to act. The Führer, liberated from 'burdensome restrictions' now required 'territorial security to prevent any further crisis'.[3] Goebbels need not have been afraid; South Tyrol and Trieste were already marked down, and Italy was to give up Dalmatia. It was also plainly indicated that Italy had forfeited her claims upon France. Hitler seems to have gone on from this to suggest what was to be the economic structure of his coming world; there was to be a great deal of 'internationalization' of ports and of communications in general, but in each case internationalization was to mean co-ordination under strict German control, the liquidation of any other authority.[4]

At this point Mussolini's memory may well have been as elastic as his decisions and his sympathies, and it is not uninteresting that he painted Hitler blacker at the later date. Perhaps he invented, perhaps he misunderstood, the threats; at any rate he had felt them. In some ways his surrender to Hitler seemed the most abject of all the surrenders of those who had been devoured by that monstrous spirit; it was symptomatic that Mussolini now submitted to an examination by Morell. Thus the last chapter of the history of Duce and Führer is macabre and ghostly. The spine of their relationship had been Hitler's belief in Mussolini and the spine was broken and the relationship dead.

[2] See *Il Momento* Rome, 1 to 8 November 1945 where the story was put together from notes left by Mezzasoma and by other neo-Fascist *gerarchi* such as Tassinari. Although Anfuso seems the best source, we shall never know which version is the more reliable.

[3] Goebbels Diary 23 September 1943.

[4] This programme was endorsed by Hitler on other occasions.

In addition to Farinacci, Pavolini, Ricci and Vittorio Mussolini, several other Fascist fanatics had fled from Badoglio's Italy to take refuge in Germany, among them Giovanni Preziosi[5] and another anti-Semitic journalist called Evola. The irony of the situation was that they were nearly all disloyal to their Duce and rather hoped to take his place. Especially the Jew-baiters, Farinacci and Preziosi, complained that Mussolini's anti-Semitism had never been serious, and in general that he had been intolerably tolerant and was to blame for the recrudescence of Freemasonry in the shape of the Badoglio régime.[6] Mussolini told Mezzasoma later on that it was the attitude of some of these people, faithfully reported to him by Vittorio, which helped to make up his mind that he would not retire. It is significant that Hitler approved of Farinacci and particularly of Preziosi[7] as the only intransigent and genuine pro-Germans, yet he would not accept their proposals for the dethronement of the Duce. He had had a Neo-Fascist Government proclaimed three days before the Duce was " freed "; it had been proclaimed in the name of Mussolini, and Mussolini's ' weakness ' was not to change that.

For the moment these men who were to breathe new life into Fascism agreed on one point alone, and that was the condemnation of the Monarchy in Italy; their broadcasts consisted almost entirely of abuse of the House of Savoy. This gave the Neo-Fascists an unexpected advantage, for the precipitate flight of the royal family before the Germans had increased national feeling against the Monarchy from end to end of Italy.

In the Orders of the Day which were pronounced from Rastenburg on 15th September it is interesting that, apart from Mussolini, only two other Fascist leaders were felt to be worth naming. Pavolini was proclaimed Secretary of the reconstructed *Partito Fascista Repubblicano* and Renato Ricci

[5] See chapter VII.

[6] It was true that Badoglio belonged to Masonic circles.

[7] According to E. Amicucci, *I 600 giorgi di Mussolini* (Faro, Rome 1948), Preziosi arrived in Germany on the same day as, though independently of, Farinacci, and, unlike the latter, was immediately received by Hitler.

chief of the Fascist Militia.[8] A week later a new Fascist
Government was appointed whose weight was increased
by the presence in it of Buffarini-Guidi[9] as Minister of
the Interior and of Graziani as Minister of Defence. The
enlistment of Graziani was the only small Neo-Fascist
triumph, though the Marshal's action was probably motivated
by very little but his notorious detestation of Badoglio.
Graziani made a fairly successful speech at the Teatro
Adriano in Rome on 26th September, and there were those
who would have preferred him to head a purely military
Neo-Fascist régime. Clearly Hitler would never have consented to this, but Graziani was not, apparently, on bad
terms with the Führer, whom he visited very soon after,
describing him as looking like a monk who had put on
civilian clothes.[10] Mussolini himself once more took over
the direction of Foreign Affiairs with Mazzolini[11] in Bastianini's place. Farinacci, still indignant, and declaring that
Mussolini was far too ill to rule, refused to hold office and
went home to Cremona to pour all his venom into his newspaper, the *Regime Fascista*. On the day of the announcement
of Mussolini's new Cabinet, Goebbels noted that Pavolini had
so far recruited exactly fifteen men in all Rome for the
resurgent Fascist Militia.[12]

In the next few months Neo-Fascism, helped by the slow
progress the Allies made in Italy, was able to gain at least
a foothold. A National Assembly met at Verona on 14th
November at which Fascism was defined afresh; in several
ways it went back to its abortive revolutionary programme

[8] Until then the Germans would not publish even their names,
" as they are too unimportant." See Goebbels Diary, 10-11th Sept.
1943.

[9] See chapter XIII.

[10] See R. Graziani, *Ho difeso la Partia* (Garzanti, 1948). Graziani
claims to have been impelled by nothing but the purest patriotism in
his every action.

[11] Count Mazzolini had been Italian Minister in Egypt until
June 1940 and later Civil Governor of Montenegro.

[12] Goebbels Diary, 23rd Sept. 1943. The first meeting of the
revived Milan *Fascio* took place at the Piazza San Sepolcro on 17th
Sept.

of 1919.[13] There was to be one Republican Chamber, which, owing to "the partially negative experience of a method of appointment too rigidly hierarchic," was to be to some extent genuinely elected. Further, there was to be workers' control in industry—the employers were not mentioned—and considerable nationalization of the land. All this, at so desperate a stage in the war, was peculiarly academic, but it reflected, not only the Duce who had now been more than ever exasperated by the *bourgeoisie,* but also the young pre-1922 Mussolini; if his role during the autumn and winter was not an active one, it is impossible not to feel his participation in this part of the Neo-Fascist programme. Its seventh point stated, "Members of the Jewish race are foreigners. For the duration of the war they belong to enemy nationality."

Another issue had divided Mussolini from Hitler from the moment he arrived in Germany. The fallen Duce desired no more feuds and no revenge against the *gerarchi* who had voted for Grandi's motion at the Grand Council meeting; he even wished to assume responsibility for them.[14] As for his family circle, he had always had a weakness for his stormy daughter, Edda, and, apart from the inevitable friction between the women,[15] he was yearning for a little private life at home in Italy. To Hitler this humanity was an outrage, the mark of a slave mentality; far from being 'a world-wide revolutionary and insurrectionist,' Mussolini turned out to be hoping in his undecided way for an end to strife. But Hitler required a ferocious punishment of the nineteen, for there is no way but *Furchtbarkeit.* They had criticized : they had rebelled. They had rebelled, not in order to struggle more furiously, but in order to abandon the struggle. It was essential to make an example of them in order to terrify all those in other countries who might be tempted to behave in the same way. And of all the nineteen, Hitler was most incensed against Ciano. Ciano knew too

[13] See Muriel Grindrod, *Then New Italy* (R.I.I.A.), Appendix I, and chapter I above.

[14] Goebbels Diary, 23rd Sept. 1943.

[15] Donna Rachele reproached Ciano furiously as the " new Brutus," see Amicucci, op. cit.

much. Ciano's insolent jokes against the Germans had re-echoed round the world. His cynical impishness was corrosive of the atmosphere necessary to New Order Europe.[16] And then a superman should know how to be severe above all with those personally close to him. Had Hitler hesitated to strike at his closest friend, Röhm, when the moment came? Finally, if the Führer was less sure now than he had been that Ribbentrop was greater than Bismarck,[17] he would be glad enough to concur in giving him Ciano's scalp.

One can imagine the feeling of relief with which Mussolini left Rastenburg on 17th September to join his various relations in Munich; at first he was lodged in the Prinz Karl Palais there, just as he had been in the days of his glory. Then he was moved to a castle in Upper Bavaria.[18] One can feel how, in spite of the sharp things they had said about one another, Mussolini and Ciano were relieved, nevertheless, by the familiarity of being together in the nightmare Germany in which they now met: the Duce even mentioned to Rahn the possibility of re-instating his son-in-law. Mussolini had always found Ciano good company and Ciano had a lingeringly filial affection for his Duce. At first it seems impossible to explain Ciano's acquiescence when the Germans offered to bring him to Germany. It seems likely that Dörnberg's message at Tarvisio was far from being the only one sent or received to warn him to avoid falling into German hands. Naturally he wished to go to Spain, to the protection of his good friend Serrano Suñer, but Badoglio had made difficulties. It was Dollmann and Kappler who thereupon offered to help him; the offer was probably mixed up with some velvet threat about his children. He was spoilt and charming and vain and sure that the worst things would only happen to other people; and besides, Edda could always manage her father and there was nothing else to fear. So on 27th August Galeazzo Ciano had walked straight into the S.S. trap.

[16] "Ciano is the Satan of the Fascist movement and the curse of Italy," wrote Goebbels, obediently echoing his Satanic master (Diary, 23rd Sept. 1943).

[17] Ribbentrop lost influence with Hitler during 1943.

[18] Deakin, op. cit., p. 561.

Quem Deus vult perdere. . . . Instead of behaving with
a little care both Edda and Ciano seem to have lost their
heads in the villa in Upper Bavaria, next-door to the Nazi
writer, Johst.[19] Impatient, perhaps, and scared to find the
Duce powerless, they began to threaten him with the revela-
tions in Galeazzo's Diary. Hitler was quickly informed about
this, and naturally incensed and provoked; according to
Goebbels he now felt convinced that Edda's mother had been
Jewish. " The Führer would like the Duce to hand Ciano over
to him. He would stand him up against a wall immediately. . . ."[20]

It was impossible for Mussolini to resist German pressure
for any length of time. In the middle of October, Edda
having been dispatched with a nervous breakdown to a
sanatorium near Parma, Ciano was sent back to Italy; he
was arrested on reaching Verona on 19th October 1943.
Early in November Mussolini sent for Clara Petacci, of whom
the Cianos ' disapproved.' Quarrels over ' Claretta ' perhaps
contributed to the Cianos' fall.

" The personal conduct of the Duce with his mistress whom
Sepp Dietrich had to bring to him," Goebbels noted on 9th
November in pious indignation, " is a cause for much
misgiving. One can see from it that he has no clear understanding of the seriousness of his situation, and that, accordingly, the reconstruction of the Fascist party is more a
matter of theory than of practice. While he has had
his son-in-law arrested, all those in the know understand
clearly that he won't have him condemned to death. It
is assumed that the absent Count Grandi will be condemned
to death only because he is missing, whereas the rest will
get off with terms of imprisonment or perhaps life sentences,
which will then be commuted after a few weeks. One
certainly can't begin reconstructing a great revolutionary
movement in that way! It is tragic to think how far the
Duce has drifted away from his original ideals."[21]

It was, however, soon made grimly clear to Mussolini
that his new republic would only pass Hitler's test, if there
were death sentences to include Ciano. It was made so

[19] Goebbels Diary, 23rd Sept. 1943.　　　[20] Ibid.
[21] Ibid., 9th Nov. 1943.

clear that Hitler could go through the farce of saying that he was not concerned and would not dream of interfering.[22] The Special Tribunal for the Defence of the Italian State was revived, but at Christmas Mussolini still seemed hesitant and undecided. He must have known by now that he could not escape from the murder of Ciano, and Rahn claimed that his " decision " was made on 30th December.[23] At last early in January 1944 all the 19 members of the Fascist Grand Council who had voted for Grandi's motion were arraigned and condemned for treason. By now Mussolini seems to have shut himself in with his mistress, refusing to receive Edda grown desperate. If Edda and Galeazzo had lived wild, dissolute lives, they had a certain rough affection for one another, and they were genuinely bound by their children. In his cell Ciano wrote that prostitutes and pimps—by which he meant the Petacci family—were responsible for his fate, but he was also struck by a grisly joke : he had made a bet with Ribbentrop in August 1939 that France and Britain would fight if Germany attacked Poland, and Ribbentrop still owed him *una collezione di armi antiche*—was this how the debt would be paid?

At the last moment it seems that Ciano was nearly saved by no other than the German woman then called Frau Beetz whom the S.S. had put in charge of him and who developed a great weakness for him. Himmler, it is thought, was willing to be bought with Ciano's Diary after all, and, using Frau Beetz, to stage a rescue operation on 7th January in return for it.[24] If this is true Hitler took care to block this little conspiracy, and the trial opened on 8th January 1944. Of the six accused who could be brought into court, five were condemned to death, one to thirty years. The executions took place on 11th January 1944, at dawn. The five victims were tied to chairs in which they were made to sit, and shot in the back : the neo-Fascist execution squad was totally incompetent and could not shoot dead —" it was like the slaughtering of pigs."[25] Ciano tried to face the fire ; he died as bravely as one could. A journalist

[22] Deakin, op. cit., pp. 636-7.   [23] Deakin, op. cit., pp. 637.
[24] D. Susmel *Vita Shagliata di Galeazzo Ciano* 1963.
[25] From an account by a German diplomat at the time.

who claims to have seen him on 5th April 1945 declare that she heard Mussolini say that he had been dying since that January morning and the time seemed atrociously long.[26] Only Edda could escape and taste a moderate revenge. Earlier she had sent the children to Switzerland in charge of a priest, and soon after this she conveyed the Diary[27] into the safety of neutrality. It is certain that the Germans would have wished to destroy it. As it is, it is incomplete, and notably shorn of references to Edda Ciano herself.

Periodically Mussolini was treated to lectures by German experts on the invincibility of Germany because of her new arms, but between the lectures he knew perfectly well that Germany was beaten. His life was the life of a privileged prisoner. He had returned to Italy on 23rd September and held his first Cabinet meeting at Rocca delle Caminate in the 27th. But on 10th October he had moved to Gargnano on Lake Garda. There he was lodged in the Villa-Feltrin-elli with his wife and younger children, with Vittorio as chief secretary, and a horde of relatives including his nephew, Vito, close by. The German Embassy was at Fasano next door, and S.S. headquarters at Gardone a little farther down the road. Hitler had long wished to provide him with an S.S. bodyguard:[28] now he was watched by S.S. men, the German Staff doctor, Zachariae, who was with him every day, and a kind of social and political nursemaid, or *Betreuer* as he was called, a certain Nazi princeling, Fürst Urach, who seems to have lived in Mussolini's villa for some time. In January 1944 Urach himself gave the following account to some colleagues in Switzerland:[29]

" I always sing or whistle when I cross the garden as there is a German S.S. man with a pistol behind nearly every tree. He [Mussolini] is fantastically guarded. There

[26] *Il Tempo* (Rome edition), 3rd Sept. 1947.

[27] With the help of her lover, the devoted Marchese Pucci. On 10th Jan. she made a last attempt to save Ciano by writing a last blackmailing letter to her father (Photostat published in *Unità*, 28th June 1945).

[28] See Goebbels Diary, various references.

[29] He happened to be travelling through.

are a few Italian Black Shirts thrown in in order to keep up appearances.

" Mussolini," Urach continued, " tends to withdraw himself from all practical questions of Government. If a German General comes to him with some request, he says, ' Oh, do talk to Graziani.' If Leyers[30] or some economic expert comes he says, ' Oh, do see my Economics Minister, won't you?' He wishes to be enthroned above the clouds like a Patriarch, while we, of course, are concerned to exploit all the authority he still has with the Italian Fascists."

On the day after the publication of the Italian Armistice the German wireless had announced the re-establishment of a Fascist régime. In the next few days the German Army was rushed into Italy with all speed. A local armistice was made with Marshal Caviglia according to which the German soldiers would remain outside Rome : the same thing was promised to General Ruggero at Milan, but both undertakings were practically ignored. On the day of Mussolini's rescue Kesselring proclaimed all Italian territory under his jurisdiction a war zone in which German martial law was valid and the organization of strikes and sabotage punishable by death.[31] Most of the Italian Army at home, in France in Greece, or in Croatia was easily disarmed. The Badoglio Government, having done nothing to prepare the men, took hastily to flight, and the battered army, like the civilian population, felt stunned. The Nazis thought there would not be much resistance trouble with this rotten people, provided it were thoroughly terrified. It was particularly easy for the S.S. to pounce upon innumerable anti-Fascist victims; they had exposed themselves heedlessly during the forty-five days, as the period between Mussolini's fall and the Armistice was called. Not only was an example made of these people, but also the persecution of the Jews began in earnest. The S.S. amused itself—no, trained itself to heroism—by forcing Jewish children of ten and eleven to crawl up and down stone steps on their bleeding knees in the San Vittore prison in

[30] The German General in charge of the economic organization of Italy, see below.

[31] See Enzo Collotti: *L'amministrazione tedesca dell'Italia occupata* 1943-1945, (1963) p. 95.

Milan : an Italian jailer who had to witness these things broke down completely.

As for the Neo-Fascist Government, it did not get very far. Farinacci and Preziosi poured out their hatred in print, and distributed leaflets explaining that the Allies meant to take, not only the colonies and the islands, but also southern Italy.[32] Fascist officials arrived in northern Italy from the south and the centre, and, after various moves, the Ministries were set up in the vicinity of the Duce at Maderno and Salò on Lake Garda. It was for this reason that his new republic was called the Little Republic[33] of Salò. Ricci found it difficult to enrol anything but half-criminal adolescent riff-raff in his Militia. For this reason all members of the Party were later forced to serve in the new *Brigate Nere*. At first all Italian military personnel were ordered to report to the Germans, but then Graziani was given a chance to do some recruiting of his own at good rates of pay; those who reported were mostly sent to Germany to be trained. Urach remarked how strange it was to see some Italians running about in Germany in uniform and fully armed and others in a state of the most abject servitude.[34]

For all those Italians—quite apart from active anti-Fascists —who would not positively support Neo-Fascism were now treated as belonging to the lowest category of subhuman enemy. Ordinary Germans felt bitterly towards them for their second " betrayal " after they had been supplied and bolstered up by their ally; most Germans, probably, accepted Goebbels' propaganda, and fell in with Hitler's policy. Goebbels had long ago pronounced that he judged a nation by the positive nature of its response to anti-Semitism, and events were now confirming that the Italian response was feeble. The dissolution of the Axis was expressed by the German treatment of General Marras. He, with his Naval colleague, and Göring's old friend the Air Attaché, Teucci,

[32] One of these leaflets brought out in the middle of Sept. 1943 is reproduced on pp. 378-9.

[33] It was usually referred to by Italians as the *repubblichetta di Salò* and its supporters as *repubblichini*.

[34] On the same occasion in Jan. 1944, when he went to Germany for a few days and returned to Gargnano via Berne.

Propaganda leaflet of the Neo-Fascist Government circulating in September 1943

Italiani!

Valorosi soldati dell'Esercito, della Marina, dell'Aeronautica e della Milizia!

Pietro Badoglio ha completato il suo tradimento. Colui che, Capo di Stato Maggiore all'entrata di guerra dell'Italia è responsabile della sua impreparazione bellica, si propone ora di consegnare la patria ai nemici.

Pietoso è il suo tentativo di addormentare la coscienza insorgente del popolo italiano con frasi insulse. La verità è, che se il tradimento si consuma, non soltanto l'Italia perderà irremediabilmente il rango di grande potenza, ma perderà altresì tutti i frutti di risorgimento della prima guerra mondiale e della rivoluzione fascista, di un intero secolo di battaglie e di sacrifici.

L'uomo che ha per anni ingannato il DUCE e che ha pertinacemente puntato al potere attraverso la disfatta, intende ora di attuare il monstruoso piano per cui la patria verrebe mutilata per sempre.

La patria senza Sicilia, senza Sardegna, senza possedimenti d'oltremare, probabilmente senza la stessa Italia meridionale, e colla prospettiva sinistra, verso cui si vorebbe storgere il destino del paese.

E a questo scopo non si tratta già di uscire della guerra. Badoglio non si è impegnato soltanto a cessare le ostilità contro i nemici, si è impegnato a iniziarle contro la potenza alleata ed amica, contro le agguerriti forze germaniche venute alla difesa d'Italia, al cui fianco i nostri combattenti si sono fin qui battuti in fedele cameratismo. Le nostre forze armate dovrebbero, con un voltafaccia inaudito negli annali dell'onore militare, passare agli ordini di un generale straniero, il cui nome è Wilson, dovrebbero andare incontro alla morte senza più gloria, trasformando, ben più che per il passato, il territorio nazionale in campo di battaglia.

Italiani! Combattenti! Il tradimento non si compirà!

Si è costituito un governo d'Italia nazionale e fascista. Esso sorge ed opera nel nome di Mussolini. Il governo nazionale fascista pugnerà inflessibilmente i traditori, i responsabili veri ed unici delle nostre sconfitte, ed agirà con ogni mezzo per trarre l'Italia dalla guerra col suo onore intatto e con le possibilità della sua vita a venire.

È terminata la triste farsa di una sedicente libertà, imposta con lo stato d'assedio, col coprifuoco e con la censura. Il sangue purissimo degli squadristi e dei combattenti uccisi nei giorni dell'ignominia ricaderà sul capo degli assassini in basso e sopratutto in alto.

Basta con lo slittamento al bolscevismo, basta colla reviviscenza dei vecchi uomini, in un'Italia che vuol aprire le porte alla gioventù combattente e onorare i titoli conseguiti col sacrificio e col valore guerriero. Si stringono intorno alla nostra bandiera, insieme coi combattenti e coi giovani le forze del lavoro, la cui marcia nel terreno sociale, incominciata col Fascismo, nel Fascismo raggiungerà le sue mète.

Combattenti! Non obbedite ai falsi comandi del tradimento! Rifiutate di consegnarvi al nemico! Rifiutate di rivolgervi contro i vostri comilitoni germanici! Tutti, ai quali riesca possibile, continuino le operazioni al loro fianco. Gli altri raggiungano le loro case, nei paesi e nelle città, in attesa degli ordini che verranno prontamente impartiti.

Dalla sofferenza e dalla vergogna noi vogliamo risorga un'Italia pura e potente.

Il Governo Nazionale Fascista.

all of them entitled to diplomatic privilege, correctly left
Berlin for Italy at the time of the Armistice. At Munich
they were arrested, sent back to be kept forty days in
solitary confinement at Gestapo headquarters in Berlin, and
then sent as 'political delinquents' to the concentration
camp at Oranienburg for five months; since Italians, unless
they re-attached themselves to Mussolini, were to be treated
as traitors they were allowed no extra food-parcels at all,
though these were customarily received by the otherwise
starving inhabitants of Oranienburg.

Simoni had heard shooting in the mountains near Tarvisio
early in August, and, if demoralization was widespread at
the time of the Armistice, it was by no means complete.
In France and Croatia and Slovenia some Italians joined the
local resistance. In Italy some of the Alpini kept their arms
and established themselves in the mountains above Bergamo
or in Piedmont. Instead of reporting to the Germans or
Graziani, men of military age disappeared to join such nuclei
or to form fresh ones themselves. Certain industrialists
came to the rescue in the difficult matter of supplies. When
in September 1943 some Alpini Partisans came down to the
village of Boves in Piedmont to look for provisions, they
overpowered a few German soldiers they found there and
took four of them away as prisoners. German troops from
Turin very soon appeared, and the priest of Boves was
told that unless the four prisoners were brought back within
two hours, the village would be burnt to the ground. So
the village was obliterated and most of the villagers who
survived were taken off by the Germans to be beaten up :
none of those captured survived.

Italian resistance did not break; it was fortified. Allied
strategy was difficult to understand and Allied air-raids seemed
merciless. Ordinary life was very hard, with scarce supplies
and soaring prices. Yet Neo-Fascist propaganda, with its
generous offers of revolutionary social reform, made little
impression. The Italians turned out to be very artists of
resistance. After the hateful Axis years the best elements
threw their souls into this fight against the Germans, while
the common humanity of the ordinary people drew them in,

too, on the patriots' side. Immediately after the armistice the O.K.W. had offered 1,800 lire or £20 sterling [sic] for any Allied prisoner handed over to the Germans. Though the rewards increased and the punishments for failure to comply were terrible, it was the rarest thing for a prisoner to be betrayed; rather he was fed and clothed and helped on his way. Secret all-party committees of national liberation[35] sprang up everywhere. Clandestine newspapers multiplied. The Partisan or Patriot groups increased. Germans were sometimes struck down in the streets. Then ten times as many Italian hostages would be shot.

The German Reign of Terror in Italy was associated in the public mind with Himmler's agent, the indispensable Dollmann, who had been attached to the German Embassy in Rome since 1939 and whose fluent Italian had explained his presence at the most important Axis interviews; on such occasions the Führer had been wont to offer him special marks of favour. The career of S.S. *Standartenführer* Dollmann is characteristic of successful German candidates for the master class. His mother was the daughter of a well-known Munich doctor; of his father nothing seems to have been known. Before Hitler came to power Frau Dollmann kept a *pensione* in a palace near the Pincio, and Eugen, her good-looking son, studied *Kunstgeschichte* and flirted with the pretty ladies he guided around Rome. He was genuinely *cultivé,* but believed in the philosophy of force and naturally became an enthusiastic Nazi. This and his perfect Italian led to his enrolment as interpreter when Himmler went to Libya and to his appointment to the German Embassy in Rome as a Cultural Attaché. With the outbreak of war Dollmann went into S.S. uniform and tore around Rome in a giant Mercedes car. In the spring of 1940 a Swiss diplomat spoke of him as " complètement transformé physiquement; d'un joli garçon blond et un peu mou," he had become a fiend of forcefulness with tightly pressed lips and chin thrust forward. General Maeltzer was the Reichswehr officer in command in Rome in 1943, but it was Dollmann who, as Himmler's representative, was felt to be ultimately responsible for the

[35] Co-ordinated by the central *Comitato di Liberazione Nazionale* (C.L.N.) of Upper Italy in Milan.

torture-houses in the via Tasso and at the Pensione Jaccarino; he was considered responsible for the orders carried out in detail at S.S. headquarters at the Hotel Regina in Milan and for certain Neo-Fascist criminals, like Koch and Carità, who were thus indirectly his instruments. In March 1944, in the via Rasella, near the tunnel in the centre of Rome, a bomb was thrown and killed thirty-two German soldiers. Though Kesselring was technically in command it was the S.S. who bore the responsibility for the gruesome machine-gunning of 320 hostages in the Fosse Ardeatine in revenge.

The *Resistenza* was stiffened, not weakened, by these things, and very little information was elicited from the victims of the S.S. No doubt Dollmann nurtured S.S. ferocity with so large an increase of obstinate slaves to maltreat, but he was short of German personnel; the existence of the Neo-Fascists, who were like the Germans' jackals, suited him also because they diverted some popular hatred from the Germans themselves. But in Reichswehr eyes the urgent practical need in 1943 was industrial output—labour, therefore, and industrial plant. Northern Italy was rich in both and was therefore an area of paramount importance. The Germans were primarily interested in transferring Italian labour to Germany. The S.S. found reason to deport large numbers of people punitively. In addition, an appeal to the Italians had been published in Kesselring's name before the end of September 1943; they were invited to join the free workers who were founding the New Europe in Germany; applicants, it was stated, would not need an Italian passport for the journey. From that time on the Neo-Fascist papers were full of the most seductive offers from leading German firms such as Siemens; the response, however, was negligible.

Though all the key economic positions were now in direct German control, the attempt to stimulate production in the north Italian factories was disappointing. The workers found every imaginable reason to go slow, to be ill, to indulge in short sit-down strikes (based on some technical complaint) which were difficult to punish. Many employers conspired with them to keep production down. One of the basic principles of the New Europe which Hitler wished to create was the concentration of industry in the hands of the class of masters with its centre in Germany; territory which was not so dominated by the supermen was to be de-industrialized. Since, in addition, it was impossible to make the Milanese and Torinese workmen work hard in Italy, and since the north Italian factories were most inadequately defended from air attack,[36] the German economic authorities aimed at the transference of Italy's industrial plant to Germany. There were large-scale strikes in Turin in November and in December 1943 and March 1944 on various pretexts. These sharpened the intentions of the Germans, but when in June 1944 the Fiat workers found the occupation authorities preparing to remove their plant from the suburbs of Turin they staged a fresh series of strikes.[37]

While the S.S., which represented the thought of Hitler, believed that Neo-Fascism had its uses, the Reichswehr and especially General Leyers, who was in economic command in Italy, complained that one could have worked far better without the Mussolini shadow-Government. Indeed, the Germans occupying Italy were soon on the very worst of terms with the Neo-Fascists. Both S.S. and Reichswehr disliked the socialistic slogans emanating from Salò, slogans which in their view encouraged the subversive tendencies in the Italian factories. Normal German contempt for Italians was naturally increased tenfold by the half-criminal, half-frivolous personnel which was almost all that the Neo-Fascist leaders could enrol. Any better elements which had joined them tended more and more to desert to the patriots. Some youths joined the Republican Guard (the Militia was incorporated in this) in order not to be sent to Germany and in order to procure arms with which to desert. German sources claimed that the major part of the Neo-Fascist Monte Rosa and San Marco divisions, trained in Germany, deserted to the Partisans when they were brought back to Italy : this was an exaggeration, however. The rest of the story of General Marras is typical. He and his colleagues were returned to Italy in the spring of 1944, but the Neo-Fascist soldiers in whose charge they were went over to the Patriots and Marras

[36] The Germans deliberately neglected the air defence of Italy.
[37] Collotti, op. cit.

became a Partisan chief. At about this time—on 18th April—a decree was issued in Mussolini's name which threatened every Partisan with summary execution if he failed to surrender by 25th May; the effect, however, was trivial.

The friction between Germans and Neo-Fascists was so great that ordinary citizens lived by it. If the Neo-Fascist authorities threatened to confiscate one's house, the best thing to do was to appeal to the Germans for protection, and if one was in difficulties with the Germans there was a chance, though a very much smaller one, that the Neo-Fascists would help one out. The patriots were very early aware of this, and it became one of the trump cards in the C.L.N. hand.

The war dragged on disappointingly for everyone through the winter of 1943-4. On the one side people became desperately tired of waiting for the " Second Front," on the other they wearied of the hints about new weapons of victory. In March Hitler had, as he thought, cleared away the last anomaly he had left in Axis Europe, which was the semi-autonomous Hungary of Horthy and Kállay. When Horthy was summoned to Klessheim in the previous year to be rapped over the knuckles for his unheroic attitude to the Jews the uncomprehending old man had asked, " But what am I supposed to do? Shall I beat them to death, perhaps?" The answer came back: Yes,[38] and the Germans marched into Hungary to see that it was done. Yet if Budapest was conquered, there was insurrection in Zagreb. Pavelić, the doyen of the Quislings, had congratulated the Führer upon the elimination of Italy from her long-promised *Lebensraum* in the Balkan peninsula. He thereupon started negotiations by which he hoped to induce the suppressed Croat Peasant Party to collaborate with him. This was defection to the enemy and Kasche forbade it. Pavelić was defeated, however, not by the German veto, but by persistent refusal from the followers of Maček.[39] In 1944 the

[38] See *Nuremberg Trial Proceedings,* part X, p. 141; *Nazi Conspiracy and Aggression,* vol. VII, pp. 190-1.

[39] A sharp refusal was sent by Maček's deputy, Kosutic (who had married the daughter of Stjepan Radić), to Pavelič on 30th Sept. 1943.

German hold on the Balkans was like that of a rotting, dead hand, which the Russian armies would soon strike away.

Every imaginable rumour circulated with regard to Mussolini. Some said he was dead or bedridden, others that he had gone back to Rocca delle Caminate, and others again that he had gone to live with the Führer. Occasionally he was brought out for some anniversary celebration,[40] but he looked so old that no member of the public was allowed to see much of him. From time to time it was found necessary for a special correspondent of the *Völkischer Beobachter* to assure the world that there was still the old fire in his eyes. In February 1944 Hassell noted with disgust that the Germans had photographed Mussolini triumphant at chess, a game which he never played.[41]

There were endless rumours, also, about Mussolini's state of mind. According to Neo-Fascist diaries posthumously found,[42] he desired at one point to denounce the Lateran Pacts and favoured Farinacci's furious campaign against the Vatican. It is even claimed that he would have begged Hitler to use V-weapons against Rome had not his mistress protested. Apart from outbursts of boasting and strutting, and apart from the fact that he must have known very little about the outside world, it is difficult to believe that Mussolini had re-acquired many illusions. No doubt he changed his mind at least as frequently as in the days when Ciano recorded his vacillations. But in his heart he knew the truth—that he would not have long to wait for retribution and that there was nothing he could do to save himself. He was not very active. What with the doctor, the masseur, his children, and his mistress who lived near by with her family, there was not much time left in the day. In the old days he had prided himself as an equestrian, but now the only exercise he could manage was to ride a bicycle round the garden. The old journalist read and

[40] Such as that of the death of D'Annunzio on 1st March each year.

[41] Hassell, op. cit., p. 350.

[42] That of Tassinari, for instance. See *Il Momento* (Rome), 9th and 13th Nov. 1945.

marked[43] as many newspapers as he could get, and later on he wrote the apologia which was published that summer as a series of articles in the Neo-Fascist *Corriere della Sera.* According to the Editor of that paper[44] the German censorship interfered several times, on one occasion on Farinacci's behalf. On another Mussolini described Hitler as having told him at Munich in 1938 that on returning to Germany from Italy in the previous May he had doubled the pensions of the Socialist ex-Ministers, since it was they who had rid Germany of the Hohenzollern monarchy. This revelation was too much for the German Embassy, and we are told that Mussolini dropped the whole story rather than ask Hitler's leave. His articles then appeared as the book to which reference has been made.[45] The last sentence of the Duce's preface to this publication was exquisitely ambiguous : " Italy is crucified to-day," he wrote, " but already the dawn of the Resurrection can be seen on the horizon."

After Mackensen's disgrace[46] Rahn had been appointed German Ambassador to Italy; he withdrew at an early stage from Rome to Fasano. He was a relatively mild Nazi who succeeded in taking his job seriously. He occasionally protested to Sauckel about the drain of Italian labour to Germany and he occasionally protested over German looting of Italian works of art. But he was not much more effectual than Mackensen and he could not stem the tide of the New Order which had lashed across Italy. Mussolini probably had more contact with Rahn at this time than with his own Ministers.

Towards the end of April 1944, Mussolini made a brief demonstration of energy. He undertook an expedition to Germany with Graziani and Mazzolini and Rahn and the inevitable S.S. comrades, Karl Wolff and Dollmann; Anfuso, Ciano's former *chef de cabinet,* who was Neo-Fascist Ambassador to Germany, left Berlin to join them. Hitler received the party in the later Axis tradition at Schloss

[43] According to Rahn's friend quoted below (p. 390).
[44] See Amicucci, op. cit.   [45] *Il tempo del bastone e della carota.*
[46] Simoni noted at Tarvisio that Mackensen was suddenly ordered to Berlin, and though he returned to Rome once again it was only to take leave.

Klessheim on 22nd and 23rd April. It was like a phantom play, except for one novelty: the German records of the conversations[47] reveal the astonishing fact that Mussolini and Graziani were allowed time to speak. While Mussolini felt compelled to refer more than once to his profound belief in the victory of Germany, he managed to indicate some Neo-Fascist weaknesses: he found courage, moreover, to protest very cautiously against the German seizure of South Tyrol and Trieste and to complain that the treatment of Italian 'internees' in Germany depressed the morale of their relatives in Italy. Hitler replied with a variety of strange and significant statements showing, *inter alia*, an odd conflict in his mind between the occasional recrudescence of his attitude towards the Duce before September 1943 and his new condition of disbelief. He complained that the Italian workers in Germany were lazy and Communist and that " the Italian troops at the [Russian] front had sung the ' Internationale' and had made insulting remarks about the Duce and himself." He also stated that among the Italians " only Fascist units and certain anti-German elements had had real military value." Finally he made it plain that it was still essential to his plans that Mussolini should be kept alive, and in connexion with the Duce's health Hitler intimated that mistrust of Morell[48] was as absurd as mistrust of Galileo had once been. All this was recorded in the German Minute. Graziani noted that Hitler argued against capitulation on the grounds that coalitions never last for more than five years.[49]

At last in June great events crowded upon one another's heels. On 4th June the Allied armies entered Rome, and on the night of 5-6th June Allied troops landing in Normandy began the invasion of France. A week later the first V1 was fired from Northern France at Britain.

[47] *See Department of State Bulletin,* vol. xi, nos. 381 and 388.

[48] A German diplomat who frequented the Führer's headquarters told his colleagues in Switzerland in Dec. 1942, that Hitler called for Morell to give him injections at all hours of the day. Only Jodl seems to have escaped from treatment by Morell.

[49] See Graziani, op. cit., p. 461. Mussolini, he says went from Klessheim to inspect the San Marco Division and returned to Italy on 25th April.

The Axis was broken when Mussolini fell, but the expulsion of the Germans from Rome, eleven months later, revealed its utter disintegration. Although Florence was not to be liberated until 11th August, Italy vibrated with the fall of Axis Rome.[50] The Neo-Fascist generals met at Bergamo on 15th June to review the situation together with representatives of the *Wehrmacht*; the Minute of the meeting was dated 22nd June. It was a frank confession of defeat. " After the fall of Rome a greater depression of a spiritual character . . . and a big increase in the number of Partisans must be noted." General Montagna reported that " the rebels already control nearly all Piedmont " and referred to the National Guard as scarcely resisting them even when it did not " actually connive." General Jalla reported a serious situation in Liguria, while General Diamanti feared that 1,000 rebels had just entered Milan in the night (14-15th June). To oppose the Partisans the Neo-Fascists could barely muster 1,100 in all Milan, 500 of whom belonged to the now dubious Muti battalion.[51] The 300,000 industrial workers of the city, solidly anti-Fascist, were expected to occupy the factories at any moment. As for the Veneto, that was reported to be in a state of great disturbance. It was characteristic of the whole situation that the Neo-Fascist commanders, whose inadequate forces were inadequately armed, begged the participating German General, Lungershausen, to allow them at least the arms which were taken from captured 'rebels.' Lungershausen answered politely but he promised nothing; he emphasized that various Neo-Fascist battalions had disappeared since the fall of Rome, and he ordered steps to be taken to concentrate their men at Bologna in order that the severest punishment be inflicted upon them.[52]

[50] On 22nd Apr. Mussolini had urged upon Hitler that this would be so.

[51] See *Verbale del 4° Gran Rapporto tenuto dal Capo di Stato Maggiore dell' Esercito a Bergamo il 15 giugno 1944 XXII.*

[52] In addition to the Republican Guards and the *Brigate Nere,* Neo-Fascism had several other ' para-military ' groups of supporters, the chief ones being the Muti battalion named after Ettore Muti (killed in Rome in July 1943), and the 10th M.A.S. (*Motoscafi anti-sommergibili.*)

Two days later Kesselring himself issued an Order to the following effect :

" The Partisan situation in the Italian theatre, particularly Central Italy, has recently deteriorated to such an extent that it constitutes a serious danger to the fighting troops and their supply lines as well as to the war industry and economic potential. The fight against the Partisans must be carried on with all the means at our disposal and with the utmost severity. I will protect any commander who exceeds our usual restraint in the choice of severity of the methods he adopts against Partisans. In this connexion the old principle holds good that a mistake in the choice of methods in executing one's orders is better than failure or neglect to act."

And on 20th June this Order was reinforced by a second which emphasized that the first one

" does not represent an empty threat. . . . Wherever there is evidence of considerable numbers of Partisan groups a proportion of the male population of the area will be arrested, and in the event of an act of violence being committed these men will be shot."[53]

This expressed the relative restraint of the Reichswehr chief in Italy, of whom the S.S. and Hermann-Göring Division were semi-independent.

On 18th June

" two German soldiers were killed and a third wounded in a fight with Partisans in the village of Civitella. Fearing reprisals, the inhabitants evacuated the village, but when the Germans discovered this, punitive action was postponed. On 29th June when the local inhabitants had returned and were feeling secure once more, the Germans carried out a well-organized reprisal, combing the neighbourhood. Innocent inhabitants were often shot on sight. During that day, two hundred and twelve men, women and children in the immediate district were killed. Some of the dead women were found completely naked. . . . Ages of the dead ranged from one to eighty-four years. Approximately one

[53] *Nuremberg Trial Proceedings,* part IX, p. 53 et seq. While Kesselring emphasized the gravity of the situation in central Italy, the Neo-Fascist generals had been reporting mainly on the north.

hundred houses were destroyed by fire. Some of the victims were burned alive in their homes."[54]

This was only one of innumerable incidents of the kind. The Bozen S.S., young Germans from the South Tyrol, who mostly spoke Italian, were notoriously cruel. A Swiss friend of the new German Ambassador in Italy came back horrified from a visit to him[55]—the Hermann Göring Division and Karl Wolff's S.S. troops were behaving in Italy as if it were Russia, he said. And, what was more, they now often introduced so-called Cossacks or Vlassov troops to finish off their atrocities for them, as we know had happened in France.[56] The friendship of Italy and Germany consummated in the Steel Pact and the New Order amounted to this.

The Neo-Fascist Ministers, as Mussolini knew, were intriguing more than ever against one another and against him. Sometimes they courted the Germans, sometimes they sought contact with the patriots. Mussolini himself did much the same. After the Allied capture of Rome he decided that he must see the Führer again, but it was not until 20th July that, together with Graziani and Dollmann, he arrived at Rastenburg. Mussolini's train was met by a shaken Hitler with burnt hair and a graze on his right hand. For it was the very day upon which Stauffenberg's bomb had exploded at the Führer's midday conference, killing Schmundt and three others, slightly injuring Hitler's right arm and leg and damaging his eardrums. But he told Mussolini that he had just had the greatest good fortune of his life: Providence had snatched him from peril once again, in order that he should "finally" triumph over his enemies. At 5 p.m. the Führer-Duce Conference began, with Ribbentrop, Göring, Keitel, as well as Graziani and Dollmann. Hitler was restless, not to say distracted, and was constantly on the telephone. All the German leaders had become physical and psychological wrecks. For two years now Hitler had ordered them to be injected by Morell. On this fearful summer afternoon with the Allies advancing easily in France and the Russians not far away from the gates

[54] *Report of United Nations War Crimes Commission*, quoted at Nuremberg Trial, 13th Mar. 1946.

[55] Apr. 1944.   [56] See above, chapter XVII, p. 288.

of Warsaw, these German heroes began to quarrel pettishly over the tea as to why the war was not won yet; Ribbentrop, angry that someone had neglected his *von* by adoption,[57] cursed the generals, and Göring shook his marshal's baton at him. Mussolini was horrified. These northern savages were worse than his Neo-Fascist intriguers.[58] Long ago, in Hitler's heyday, he had asked Starhemberg whether Hitler was mad—now he must have known he had harnessed himself and his country to a chronic paranoiac. It was significant that on this occasion Keitel asked Graziani for Italian air units to come to the Germans' help against the advancing Russians. Above all the Italians had the satisfaction of finding that Germany had its 'traitors' too.

When Hitler broadcast towards midnight that night he declared that the group which had perpetrated the assassination plot against him "believed it could thrust a dagger into our back as it did in 1918." At the same time the Führer himself likened the abortive attempt of 20th July 1944 to what he chose to call Badoglio's *coup* against Mussolini almost a year earlier. It is worth noting that the Italian collapse had made so great an impression in Germany that Kluge, who was in command of the German troops in France, thought it opportune to announce on that same day that "For us there will be no repetition of 1918, nor of the example set by Italy." Kluge had flirted with the Stauffenberg conspirators and his statement was an attempt to save himself with the Führer.

Above all Hitler was resolved to show no humanity; if Mussolini, when put to the test, had proved to be a mere human weakling, he, Adolf Hitler, would show that he was strong and inexorable, a master not a slave. For over two years now he had been unhealthy, and more often than not in an insane condition; for the next nine months he became even more disagreeably abnormal. The story of his end has been told with such dangerous wit as to obscure the importance and the strength of Hitler's rule

[57] The *von* was due to his adoption by an aunt in 1925.

[58] One account of this meeting came from Dollmann later, when he was in Allied captivity. It was quoted in Allen W. Dulles, *Germany's Underground*. See also Anfuso op. cit. pp. 449-50.

until 1942; however disloyal his underlings were to one
another, they were held in his grip. But it is incontestable
that after July 1944 the story degenerated into nothing but
a ghastly farce.

There was discontent and opposition and despair in Germany, but after summer 1943 an obstinate resignation kept
the Germans fighting. At no time was there any popular
mass movement against the Nazis—no serious strikes—although people worked badly from morose fatigue. By this
time the majority of factory workers were terrorized foreigners. Berlin jokes were always as important as anything
in indicating the *Stimmung* at least of the capital : in
March 1944 Hassell noted the saying, " I prefer to believe
in victory than to go about with no head on my shoulders."[59]
On 20th July and after that Hitler himself ordered the S.S.
to be—if that were possible—even more ruthless, and the
punishment meted out to all those who could be in any
way implicated with Stauffenberg was indescribably terrible.
But while this was so, and while, as Kogon has said,[60]
the task that the S.S. had set themselves became so enormous
as to defy fulfilment, Hitler and the faithful voice of
Hitler, Goebbels, somehow kept their hold on a considerable portion of the German people. The so-called officers'
clique of conspirators had ramifications which reached to
certain labour leaders, but not to mass opinion or sentiment. On the contrary mass feeling probably accepted the
party and S.S. version that the attempt on Hitler's life had
been made by " reactionaries " in their own class interest.

The attempt of 20th July had nourished Hitler's fantastic
superstitiousness, for it was true that his life had again
been saved by the chance of the position he had taken up; he
was only obliged to take to his bed for a few days in the
next few weeks. While S.S. stalwarts like Himmler and
Kaltenbrunner and Karl Wolff put out all the peace-feelers
they could to West and to East, Hitler convinced himself
that the Allies and Russia were sure to fall apart in time
to save him if he only held out. After six years of war,
Frederick the Great had been saved from destruction by
the defection of Russia from the hostile alliance when the

[59] Hassell, op. cit.   [60] op. cit.

Empress Elizabeth died in 1762. One of Hitler's favourite pastimes in this period was to have Carlyle's account of this miracle read aloud to him; when Roosevelt died on 12th April he once more believed that Providence had " finally " pronounced in his favour.

While Hitler lost himself in an insane intransigence which he mistook for greatness, Mussolini was pursuing the opposite course. There were moments, of course, when all Neo-Fascists were to die fighting to the last on Italian territory, scorning to take refuge in Germany. Mussolini has been said to have wished at one point for the last stand to be made at Trieste (which was out of his control) but Pavolini decided that the Valtellina was to be Italy's Redoubt. At the time of the German offensive in the Ardennes in December 1944 Mussolini made his last descent on Milan before the journey which ended with his death. Rahn had urged the desirability of a public speech from the Duce, but when on 16th December 1944 Mussolini appeared at the Teatro Lirico the whole performance seemed to be a gesture in favour of the autonomy of the Neo-Fascist Republic; it included the implication that its administration would in future be based on Milan out of reach of the German authorities on the shores of Lake Garda. For the moment, but only temporarily, Mussolini's speech, which was unusually sensible, earned applause. He coupled it with an attempt to renew his ministerial team so that it, too, should seem more autonomous and more socialistic. The Duce's offensive, like that of the Germans, petered out. The chief ministerial change he made was to dismiss his most experienced Minister, Buffarini-Guidi. Possibly this enabled Karl Wolff to forestall him, Mussolini, in putting out feelers to the Allies.[61] In March 1945 Mussolini made his last real effort by bringing Anfuso from Berlin to Salò to be the new Neo-Fascist Foreign Undersecretary.[62]

Soon the Duce seemed to be searching, like many disillusioned Axis supporters in that last war winter, for any compromise at all. At the time of the Duce's last speech Graziani seems to have expressed strange confidence. He had almost consistently desired peace with Russia, and there

[61] Deakin, pp. 751, 775.　　　　[62] Deakin, p. 782.

R.B.A.　　　　　　　　　　　　　　　　　　　N2

are indications that he would have welcomed negotiations with the Western Allies had they concerned themselves with him. The correspondence between Hitler and Mussolini had continued across the yawning gulf of disaster, and on 27th December 1944 the Führer wrote his last New Year letter to the Duce. He was glad to hear from Mussolini that Fascism was slowly re-consolidating. " One thing is certain," he said, " and that is that neither Fascism nor National Socialism will ever be replaced in Europe by democracy." He was convinced that 1944 had been the nadir, and that fortune would renew her favour now. The chief object of the letter, however, seemed to be to refer again to the " lack of perfect harmony" which had at one time become evident between Germany and Italy with regard to Greece and Spain. In other words, the Führer implied very broadly in this letter that if Italy had not attacked Greece—how both of them were haunted by this " if "!—Spain would have joined them, Gibraltar would have been conquered, and the war would have been won. It was always said that when Mussolini was captured by the Italian Partisans he was found to be treasuring this letter to prove with it that he had made his contribution to the Allied victory, but there is no evidence to prove this.

Early in 1945 Mussolini began to offer amnesties to the Partisans. He also encouraged a renegade Liberal called Cione, in conjunction with the journalist Concetto Pettinato, of the Turin *Stampa*, to start a ' democratic ' Neo-Fascist wing which favoured greater freedom of criticism. Farinacci was indignant to the last, but the leader of one of the chief Neo-Fascist fighting groups, Prince Borghese of the 10th M.A.S., supported the Cione attempt at conciliation and gave orders to his followers accordingly. The Duce's search for a compromise was as futile as Hitler's determination to triumph implacably. By the end of 1944 the Italian Patriots felt confident. They had a collection of German uniforms by now which helped them to carry out all kinds of dare-devil feats. On New Year's Eve groups of them sprang on to the stage in three cabaret-cinemas near the Porta Venezia in Milan and forced the actors to read out Resistance manifestoes; then they withdrew with impunity.

Since nothing else could influence or eliminate Hitler, the war had to be fought out. The end of the Axis dictators has been only too favourite a journalistic theme. In each case it was characteristic. Mussolini see-sawed between the hope that the Germans would save him and the knowledge that they would not. He himself began to toy with the idea of fleeing to Switzerland, and it is interesting that Buffarini-Guidi had applied to the Swiss authorities several times for permission to cross the frontier but was always refused. Remembering that he had once been a Socialist himself Mussolini thought wildly of saving himself by joining up with the clandestine Socialist Party, which was not represented in the Government of Rome at the time, though its representatives sat on the Committee of National Liberation.[63] When at last on 25th April, the day the Patriots were to liberate northern Italy, Mussolini met the Archbishop of Milan, Cardinal Schuster, in order to negotiate with the C.L.N., he found that Karl Wolff had agreed to unconditional surrender to the Allies in Italy without any reference to the Neo-Fascist Government. Mussolini took to flight then, thinly disguised as a German soldier with some German troops, only to be discovered by two Partisan officers. His last friends and his mistress also fell into Patriot hands that day, and, when Claretta Petacci asked to be allowed to join Mussolini, her captors agreed. He and she were separated from the rest, he faltering to the end between despair and the hope that the Partisans would be indulgent; the two were not maltreated but were shot together at Mezzagra near Tremezzo on the western shore of Lake Como on 28th April by Communist command. Paviolini, Farinacci, and the others were shot too, and the corpses of all of them were taken to Milan[64] and hung upside down in the Piazzale Loreto, where there had been a horrible massacre of patriot hostages in the summer of 1944.

[63] See *Mussolini's Memoirs* (Contact, 1948), Introduction by C. J. S. Sprigge.
[64] Starace was among these people, though he had been in disgrace with Mussolini since 1941 and played no part in the Republic of Salò.

It is not certain how fully Hitler was informed about Mussolini's death and its aftermath : it is therefore a matter of conjecture how the news may have affected him. On 30th April, ten days after his fifty-sixth birthday, he stage-managed his own exit to Valhalla, dragging for her only conjugal consolation his photographer's assistant, the wretched Eva Braun, along with him.[65] In his last will and testament he bequeathed to the German nation the barbarous heritage of persecuting the Jews, concealing to the end the forms which Nazi persecution had taken.

[65] The details have been made familiar by H. Trevor-Roper in *The last days of Hitler* (1956). A new story was launched in 1965 that two children of Hitler and Eva Braun survive.

Chapter XXI

EPILOGUE

At Christmas 1888, in Turin, Nietzsche wrote the preface to his main fulmination against Wagner[1] which he called —as well he might—" an essay for psychologists, not for Germans." Crispi was Premier of Italy at the time and was leading the country into quarrels with France and closer friendship with Germany. It was four months before Hitler's birth. " I would have a word to whisper in the ears of the Italians, whom I love . . . an intelligent people will never make anything but a *mésalliance* with the Reich." We have seen how the Axis which Hitler created and to which Mussolini gave its name fulfilled Nietzsche's warning.

Each of these dictators was like a malicious caricature of his own people. Mussolini was theatrical, vain, hypersensitive, and sceptical; he never really stepped outside traditional continuity. Hitler was hysterical, fanatical, romantic, and cruel. In their satisfaction in inflicting pain on other human creatures the cruelty and romanticism of Germans like Hitler and Himmler met; in sadism their split personalities were integrated. They were barbaric without the excuse of being primitive.

For many years Mussolini had rolled his eyes and brandished his chin, he had shouted cruel phrases with Romagnol violence, but his goal had never become clear to him : after years of delay, he had committed certain vague aspirations to paper, but without ever thinking out a method by which as a Sorel ' myth ' or as the stimulus to the political specu- they might be realized. The aspirations in fact served chiefly lation so dear to Italians. In practice Mussolini was an opportunist, and, far from destroying the ideas and institutions which he found in existence, he generally sought a compromise with them. Hitler made himself President as well as Chancellor of Germany and immediately started a preliminary campaign against the Christian Churches, but Mussolini came

[1] *Nietzsche contra Wagner* (Vorwort).

397

to terms with both the King and the Pope and he preserved the Senate. The fact that the Fascist Grand Council, which the Duce created, could instigate his downfall, was a piece of "conservatism" which seemed ludicrous to Hitler: it helped to convinced him that Mussolini was no "world revolutionary." By and large Mussolini remained an ordinary human being in doubt. Perhaps it is doubt which distinguishes the sane and the civilized from the mad and the barbarous.

Mussolini, partly owing to physical weaknesses, doubted excessively. This fact explains what Gafencu[2] has analysed so brilliantly, "le phénomène Ciano." "La fonction de Ciano était d'entretenir le doute." His relation to the Duce —again it is Gafencu who was inspired to grasp this— was like that of a court fool—"dont les plaisanteries provoquaient un malaise salutaire"—to his king. Lear's fool comments, as no one else could, on the old man's folly in placing his destiny in the hands of Goneril and Regan. Ciano was cheap and dissipated and sometimes servile, and one flinches a little from the parallel, but his role was the same. "La voix du jeune ministre ne pouvait pas s'élever bien haut, puisqu'elle correspondait à une voix intérieure dans le chef du Gouvernement." Mussolini and Ciano "forment une unité contradictoire, un couple dis proportionné et pourtant indissoluble." Sometimes he liked to play the hero enthroned in solitude, above all he had been potent —except in Germany—as an orator addressing the masses; but Mussolini was dependent upon personal relationships. How different from Hitler who was never in doubt and who was never amused!

The metal with which the Rome-Berlin Axis was forged, so that it seems to have been warped from being a straight line into becoming a vicious circle, was Nietzsche, inspirer of Mussolini's words and of Hitler's deeds. Nietzsche was a German who longed to be a Pole; he admired France and he loved Italy. The medical records of his madness[3] show that he identified himself either with God or with

[2] op. cit.
[3] See E. F. Podach, *The Madness of Nietzsche* (1931).

the first King of modern Italy. He feared the Germans as Mussolini did, and he despised them as Hitler despised them when he found them unappreciative. Out of his fear of the commonplaceness of the German middle class and of the mentality of anti-Semitism, Nietzsche formulated the doctrines which then nourished Hitler; "Rien en lui ne semblait sortir de l'ordinaire," Gafencu noted as his first impression of the Führer.

"When to-day we see German youth marching under the sign of the swastika, our minds go back to Nietzsche's *Thoughts out of Season,* in which this youth was invoked for the first time. . . . And when we call out to this youth *Heil Hitler,* we greet at the same time, with the same cry, Friedrich Nietzsche." This was written by Bäumler in 1937.[4] Nietzsche's was far from being the only thought which influenced Hitler; it has been seen that there were strong currents of the old Pan-German Austrian state of mind in him and of Wagnerian mythology which intermingled with them and with *Geopolitik.* The influence of Nietzsche, however, remained predominant, of Nietzsche who was shocked by the 'vulgarity' of John Stuart Mill.[5] It is almost incredible to find how exactly Nietzsche formulated Hitler's egocentric obsession. "I teach that there are higher and lower men," he wrote, "and that a single individual may in certain circumstances justify whole millennia of existence—that is to say, a wealthier, more gifted, greater and more complete man, as compared with innumerable imperfect and fragmentary men . . ."; ". . . . the 'higher nature' of the great man manifests itself precisely in being different, in being unable to communicate with others . . ."; and, again, he defines mighty men as those with a passion for dominion and a love of change and deception. Nor does Nietzsche fail to insist upon the forcible prevention of the reproduction of lower beings. All this is to be found in *Der Wille zur Macht.* As for *Zarathustra,* it echoes through the events of Hitler's life; one has only

[4] *Nietzsche und der Nationalsozialismus,* by A. Bämuler (Berlin 1937).

[5] This because Mill could claim that "what is right for one man is right for another."

to think of the threat to Schuschnigg to overwhelm him
" like a storm in the spring."

It has been said that Hitler's ascendancy over the Germans
has never been explained. The Communist formula which
equates National Socialism with Fascism as a camouflaged
" come-back " of the propertied classes at the price of bread
and circuses is misleading. It is true that the most powerful
industrialists in Italy used Fascism as their instrument.
In Germany the majority of the big employers and land-
owners, after they lost faith in Hugenberg, favoured Hitler's
rise to power. Rearmament and the policy of Schacht suited
them very well, and the *Führerprinzip* in the organization
of industry satisfied their most conservative dreams. On the
other hand, it is certain that Hitler went to war against their
wishes, and it is probable that they would have liked to be
rid of him long before material destruction in Germany
reached the point at which it had arrived in April 1945.
Hitler was the ally, while it suited him, of the German industrialists, but never their tool. Like Mussolini, they were
forced to be part of the dream of this unbalanced adolescent
who, with all his consistency in action, might well have
ended in a humbler madhouse than the Berlin bunker of the
Führer.

It seems monotonous to refer to Nietzsche again, but it is
he who illuminates most brightly the irrational nature of
the power of Adolf Hitler. In one of his outbursts against
Wagner[6] Nietzsche speaks of that hysterical and erotic quality
which so much pleased Wagner in women. " Only look at
our women when they are ' wagnetisiert ' : *welche ' Unfreiheit
des Willens '*! . . . *Welches Geschehen-lassen, Uber-sich-
ergehen-lassen.*[7] Perhaps they guess that they are more
attractive to some men in this state . . . reason the more
to worship their Cagliostro and magician!" Anyone who
has lived in Germany will recognize what Nietzsche meant
—Shirer described it in his *Berlin Diary* when he spoke of
the audience at Hitler's *Winterhilfe* meeting on 4th Sep-

[6] *Aufzeichnungen zu einer Schrift über Wagner* (*Werke*, Bd. VII,
Leipzig, 1931).

[7] Impossible to render in English—it indicates an hysterical passiv-
ity.

tember 1940.[8] Hitler expressed and integrated something which then became monstrously powerful, the hysteria of Germany.

"Lorsque, à la suite d'une formule ou d'une idée, il s'échauffait assez pour livrer un peu de soi-meme, le son de sa voix, et plus encore le sens de ses paroles, le choix de ses arguments, l'enchaînement de ses pensées semblaient se trouver en une étrange harmonie avec une force invisible qui l'entourait. Il devenait alors un démagogue dans le sense antique du mot: l'homme qui prête sa voix à la foule et à travers lequel la foule parle . . . derrière lui, on le sentait, il y avait son double—un double collectif: 'la masse,' la foule innombrable, le peuple—et le discours avait l'allure d'une grande armée en marche."[9]

With the madman's knowledge of how to excite, Hitler combined the madman's—or the superman's—inability to communicate normally with others as individuals: he either mesmerized or frightened them or perhaps did both these things. The women of Germany, it has been seen, were peculiarly susceptible to his approach, nor were the men very different. Though Hitler, like Nietzsche, was thought to be impotent and not a pervert, the masculine homage he received was often passionate, whether it came from members of the Stefan George circle or from groups of *Wandervögel*. Negatively it was of importance that " he had the gift of inspiring in those who resisted him a feeling of isolation,'"[10] a gift which had helped him to conceive the system of the Nazi concentration camp.

Another factor in Hitler's success was his skill in concealing his true objectives except from an inner *élite*. The majority of professing National Socialists held only authoritarian views; they were willing to sacrifice liberty to efficiency and they were racially arrogant, but they did not wish for the destruction of 1,500 years of civilization nor for the inversion of accepted morality. By the time that they began to feel that Hitlerism spelt the end of Christianity and humanism in favour of biological mechanism, there was very little they could do by way of protest. The scepticism and gloom in Germany, and especially in Berlin, during much of

[8] See chapter XIV.   [9] Gafencu, op. cit.   [10] Gafencu, op. cit.

the Axis period, may be attributed to the hysterical and the esoteric nature of Hitlerism. Between the injections of hysteria, enthusiasm flagged, and doubt grew as to what it was to which one was committed.

Mussolini was neither perverse nor hysterical. To charm Italian crowds he had had to be theatrical. It was by stimulating his lust for power and the fear of isolation that Hitler had subjugated Mussolini; from May 1936 when he felt cut off from France and afraid of Spain he had been won by the Führer. There was never any personal intimacy between Hitler and Mussolini, quite apart from the formal second person plural to which their sense of their importance kept the dictators. When Hitler wrote to Mussolini in 1942 that he perhaps better than any other human being could share the Duce's feelings at the Acropolis[11] he was writing in terms of "greatness," not in terms of friendship. While Mussolini was perplexed by Hitler, for Hitler Mussolini was simply a symbolic figure in Hitler's world of fantasy until September 1943.[12] Mussolini was always devoured with doubt and anxiety with regard to Hitler and he pounced on Gafencu in the spring of 1939 to know what the Führer had said about the Axis. Neither to Lloyd George in 1936 nor to Gafencu in 1939 nor to Sumner Welles in 1940 did Hitler speak of his friendship with Italy, for he was sure of it. (Instead he excited himself about Britain.) It was part of his madman's logic to wish to destroy Ciano who was Mussolini's doubt.

It has been seen that the New Order can be partly explained as Hitler's interpretation of the aspirations of Nietzsche, and it has been seen that the Italians had sabotaged this New Order with growing effect, both before Mussolini's dismissal in July 1943 and after his supposed rehabilitation in the north of Italy. Between the collapse of Fascism and the end of the war, the biggest shock to Hitler's New Europe came in August 1944 with the liberation of France and the defection of Roumania. When de Gaulle arrived in Paris

[11] Hitler to Mussolini, 4th Aug. 1942.

[12] Except, perhaps, on the occasion when Mussolini insisted on piloting their aeroplane and Hitler was scared.

to witness the damaged Fif.h Column of the colonnade of
the Hotel Crillon it was felt that Europe was freed. But
this was a dangerous anticipation. Though the Russians
joined up with the Partisans and freed Belgrade in October
1944, and the British were in Athens by the end of the
month, it was May 1945 before the Germans in Croatia
surrendered. Between summer 1944 and spring 1945 Hitler
worked much evil, an enormous amount of pointless destruction, until suddenly the Germans collapsed and the concentration camps gave up their living and their dead. One
of the finest performances of this time was the prevention
by the Italian Partisans of the destruction of their factories
as Hitler had planned it; by their skilful preparation they
saved the major part of Italian industrial plant from the fate
of the factories in many other parts of Europe.[12a]

With masochistic German method the *Götterdämmerung*
was prepared. Since 1941 plans for the case of defeat had
been begun, and it is suggested that Hitler communicated
some of this programme to Mussolini at Rastenburg on 14th
September 1943.[13] The earth was to be scorched so that the
Allies should be blamed for famine and unemployment.
One must go on fighting a hopeless struggle partly because
the Allies and Russia might fall apart before they had won,
but for other reasons too. The fighting must go on in
order to gain every possible hour for the preparation of the
Nazi Redoubt in the mountains of Bavaria, the Tyrol or in
Styria. There it might be possible to resist actively for some
time, Hitler thought, and this would not only give scope
for the nihilistic joys of self-destruction after the will
to power had been temporarily satiated, but would have
great importance for the Nazi 'myth'. For two or three
years now the Nazi leaders had been willing to admit that
Germany might lose the second great war in the Nazi century, only to triumph more tremendously in the third.
And she would never have been beaten. In 1918, as the
legend ran, she was 'stabbed in the back by the civilians,'

[12a] Some credit for this must go also to Karl Wolff and the other
Germans who contributed to the German surrender in Italy.

[13] See *Il Momento* (Rome), 3rd Nov. 1945, and other (earlier)
sources.

but now she would fight till she could fight no more, only to rise again. Sometimes there was talk of an Italian sector in the ' Redoubt ' to which the Neo-Fascists should retire, but it has been seen that they and Mussolini were without persistent enthusiasm for such plans.

When on 20th July 1944, at the Hitler-Mussolini tea-party at the Führer's headquarters, someone mentioned the massacre of 30th June 1934, Hitler is said to have leapt to his feet with foam on his lips; he ranted about the revenge he would take against women and children after Stauffenberg's attempt upon his life.[14] But the intensified S.S. terror which closed in upon Germany after this was not merely a matter of revenge, for it was more deliberate. Mass arrests of all possibly oppositional personalities were intended also to prevent any group from negotiating with the Allies to accept surrender.

Preparations were made to provision and fortify the ' Redoubt ' and Hitler was to go to Bavaria on his last birthday, 20th April 1945, to direct the fighting from there. He decided, however, that events had overtaken that part of his plan. The rest of it held good. The Führer himself was to leave no trace behind him so that some kind of Barbarossa legend should arise—he would not have feared refutations by witty Oxford dons. The tenacious Martin Bormann, in whose hands the organization of clandestine Nazi activity for the future was concentrated, was to disappear; of the major War Criminals he was the only one who could not be found. Lastly, the initiated were to become Communists in the Russian area of occupation and whatever facilitated their work in the Allied zones, in order to foment discord between the U.S.S.R. and the English-speaking Powers. The " Redoubt " was to be a basis for clandestine Nazi work which would exploit the aftermath of the South Tyrolese dispute; the post-war Italian offer of repatriation to the German-speaking South Tyrolese, who had opted for Germany in December 1940, provided an opportunity for the return of good Nazis to intensify friction.

It is a terrifying reflection that a sick man like Nietzsche,

[14] See A. Dulles *Germany's Underground* (1947), p. 10, quoting account by Dollmann to the Allied authorities.

who knew that he would lose his reason and who was written off years ago as a *fin de siècle* failure, should have projected and facilitated the agony of Europe forty years after his death. The fact is not altered by dismissing Nietzsche as an early symptom of decay. Where Nietzsche gloried in the cruelty of nature, half a century later Hitler gloried also in the cruelty of machines. It seems strange that Nietzsche has been classified with the philosophers; his place is perhaps with the poets and certainly with the prophets. At the beginning of January 1889, hovering between sanity and madness, Nietzsche wrote: " I myself, I, who with my own hands have created this tragedy—I who have tied the knot of morality into existence—I myself have killed all the gods in the fourth act—because of morality! What is to become now of the fifth? Where is the tragic solution to be found?" And then, as if he foresaw the funeral pyre of Hitler and the suspended corpse of Mussolini: " A satyr's game, a farcical epilogue, the continued proof that the long essential tragedy is over. . . ."[15]

Europe revolted against Axis rule, human decency rose up against *Furchtbarkeit*. But both the New Order and the struggle against it were so costly that we scarcely know yet whether the price paid was not civilization itself. That would be the fulfilment of Hitler's suicidal dream.

[15] Quoted in Podach, op. cit.

BIBLIOGRAPHY

It will be obvious that many of the books in the following list present special pleading; as such they have their own interest.

E.W.

ALFIERI, D.—*Due dittatori di fronte* (1948).
ALOISI, P.—*Journal, juillet 1932—juin 1936* (1957).
AMICUCCI, E. I.—*600 Giorni di Mussolini* (1948).
ANFUSO, F.—*Da Palazzo Venezia al Lago di Garda* (1957).
AVON—*Facing the Dictators* (1962).
    The Reckoning (1965).

BADOGLIO, P.—*Italia nella Seconda Guerra mondiale* (1946).
BASTIANINI, G.—*Uomini, Cose, Fatti* (1959).
BATTAGLIA, R.—*Storia della Resistenza Italiana* (1953).
BONOMI, I.—*Diario di un amno* (1947).
BRACHER, K. D.—*Die Auflösung der Weimarer Republik* (1955).
BRACHER, K. D. & others—*Die Nationalsozialistische Machtergreifung* (1960).
BRAUNTHAL, J.—*The Tragedy of Austria* (1948).
BROOK-SHEPHERD, G.—*Dollfuss* (1961).
    Anschluss, the Rape of Austria (1963).
BULLOCK, ALAN—*Hitler* (1964).

CASTELLANO, G.—*Come firmai l'armistizio di Cassibile* (1946).
CATALANO, F.—*Storia del C.L.N.A.L.* (1956).
ČELOVSKY, B.—*Das Münchener Abkommen 1938* (1958).
CHABOD, F.—*A History of Italian Fascism* (1963).
CIANFERRA, C.—*The Vatican and the War* (1945).
CIANO, G.—*Diario* (1946).
    L'Europe verso la catastrofe (1948).
    Diario 1937-38 (1948).
COLLOTTI, E.—*L'ammistrazione tedesca dell' Italia occupata 1943-1945* (1963).
CRAIG, G. AND GILBERT, F—*The Diplomats* (1953).

DAHLERUS, B.—*The Last Attempt* (1948).
DALLIN, A.—*German Rule in Russia 1941-45* (1957).
DEAKIN, F. W.—*The Brutal Friendship* (1962).

DE FELICE, R.—*Mussolini il Rivoluzionario* (1965).
DEUERLEIN, E.—*Der Hitler Putsch* (1962).

DOMARUS, M.—*Hitler: Reden und Proklamationen 1932-45* (1962-63).
DONOSTI, M.—*Mussolini e l'Europa* (1945).
DULLES, A. W.—*Germany's Underground* (1947).

FAVAGROSSA, C.—*Perchè perdemmo la guerra* (1947).
FERMI, L.—*Mussolini* (1961).
FISCHER, F.—*Griff nach der Weltmacht* (1961).
FRANCOIS-PONCET, A.—*Souvenirs d'une Ambassade à Berlin* (1946).
    Au Palais Farnse. Souvenirs d'une Ambassade à Rome (1961).
FUCHS, M.—*A Pact with Hitler* (1939).
FUNDER, F.—*Als Oesterreich den Sturm bestand* (1957).

GAFENCU, G.—*Derniers jours de l'Europe* (1946).
GAMELIN, M. G.—*Servir—les Armées français de 1940* (1946).
GEHL, J.—*Austria, Germany and the Anschluss* (1963).
GISEVIUS, H. B.—*Bis zum bittern Ende* (1946).
The Goebbels Diaries (1948).
GRAZIANI, R.—*Ho difeso la patria* (1948).
GRAZZI, E.—*le principio della fine* (1946).
GUARIGLIA, R.—*Ricordi 1922-46* (1950).

HASSELL, U. VON—*Vom andern Deutschland* (1946).
HAUSHOFER, K.—*Grenzen in ihrer geographischen und politischen
    Bedeutung 1927, Weltpolitik von Heute 1934, Weltmeere und
    Weltmächte* (1937).
HEIDEN, K.—*Adolf Hitler—eine Biographie* (1936-37).
HITLER—*Mein Kampf* (1933)=last unexpurgated edition.
    Hitler's Table Talk 1941-44 (1953).
    Hitlers Zweites Buch (1961).
    The Testament of Adolf Hitler (1961).
    Hitler's War Directives 1939-45 (1964).
HITLER E MUSSOLINI—*Lettere e documenti* (1946).
HOSSBACH—*Zwischen Wehrmacht und Hitler* (1949).

JETZINGER, F.—*Hitlers Jugend* (1956).

KIRKPATRICK, I.—*Mussolini* (1964).
KOGON, E.—*Der S.S. Staat* (1946).
KORDT, E.—*Wahn und Wirklichkeit* (1947).
    Nicht aus den Akten (1950).
KRAUSNICK, H. and others—*Anatomie des S.S.-Staates*—1965.

LANGER, W. L.—*Our Vichy Gamble* (1947).
LATOUR, C.—*Süd Tirol und die Achse Berlin-Rom* (1962).
LEMKIN, R.—*Axis Rule in Occupied Europe* (1944).
LÜDECKE, K.—*I Knew Hitler* (1938).

MAGISTRATI, M.—*L'Italia a Berlino 1937-39* (1956).
MALAPARTE, C.—*Technique du coup d'état* (1931).
MAUGERI, F.—*From the Ashes of Disgrace* (1948).

MONELLI, P.—*Roma 1943* (1946).
MUSSOLINI, B.—*Opera Omnia* ed. by E. & D. Susmel (1951-61).
La mia vita (1947).
Memoirs 1942-3 (1949).

NAMIER, L. B.—*Diplomatic Prelude* (1948).
Europe in Decay (1950).
In the Nazi Era (1952).
NIETZSHE, F.—*Der Wille Zur Macht, Also Spracht Zarathustra,*
Title of second Nietzsche book mentioned is *Also Spracht
Zarathustra,* etc.
PECHEL, R.—*Deutscher Widerstand* (1947).
PODACH, E. F.—*The Madness of Nietzsche* (1931).
Procès du Maréchal Pétain (1945).

RAHN, R.—*Ruheloses Leben* (1949).
RAUSCHNING, H.—*Die Revolution des Nihilismus* (1936).
Hitler speaks (1939).
REITLINGER, G.—*The Final Solution* (1953).
S.S. Alibi of a Nation (1956).
ROBERTSON, E. M.—*Hitler's pre-war policy and military plans 1933-39*
(1963).
ROSENBERG, A.—*Das politische Aagebuch* Alfred Rosenbergs (1956).
SALVATORELLI, L. and MIRA, G.—*Storia d'italia nel periodo fascista*
(1964).
SALVEMINI, G.—*Mussolini Diplomatico* (1952).
Prelude to World War II (1953).
SCHLABRENDORFF—*Offiziere gegen Hitler* (1946).
SCHMIDT, P.—*Statist auf diplomatischer Bühne* (1949).
SCHUSCHNIGG, K. VON—*Requiem in Rot-Weiss-Rot* (1946).
SENISE, C.—*Quando Ero Capo della polizia* (1946).
SHIRER, W.—*A Berlin Diary* (1941).
SIEBERT, F.—*Italiens Weg in den Zweiten Weltkreig* (1962).
SIMONI, L.—*Berlino—Ambasciata d'Italia 1939-43* (1946).
SOREL, G.—*Réflexions sur la violence* (1908).
SPRIGGE, C. J. S.—*The Development of Modern Italy* (1943).
STARHEMBERG, E. R. VON—*Between Hitler and Mussolini* (1942).
SUÑER, R. SERRANO—*Entre Hendaya y Gibraltar* (1947).
SYLVESTER, A. J.—*The Real Lloyd George* (1947).

TEMPLEWOOD—*Ambassador on Special Mission* (1946).
Nine Troubled Years 1931-40 (1954).

TOSCANO, M.—*Le Origini del Patto d'Acciao* (1956).
TREVOR-ROPER, H.—*The Last Days of Hitler* (1956).

WEIZSÄCKER, E. VON—*Erinnerungen* (1950).
WELLES, SUMNER—*A Time for Decision* (1944).
WHEELER-BENNETT, J. W.—*Munich* (1948).
  The Nemesis of Power (1953).

ZERNATTO, G.—*Die Wahrheit über Oesterreich* (1938).

OFFICIAL DOCUMENTS

Nazi Conspiracy and Aggression (1946-8).
Nuremberg Trial Proceedings (Major War Criminals).
    One series published in London from 1946. Another series
    published Nuremberg from 1947.
Documents on British Foreign Policy (D.B.F.P.). Published from
    1947.
Documents on German Foreign Policy (D.G.F.P.). Published from
    1949.
Documenti Diplomatici Italiani (D.D.I.) series VI to IX covering
    some of the years 1918 to 1940 published from 1952.

Documents Diplomatique François (D.D.F.). Published from 1964.

The Films of a number of unpublished papers of the German Foreign
Ministry are available in the Foreign Office Library at Cornwall
House.

ARTICLES

Some of the most useful have appeared in the *Vierteljahlshefte für
Zeitgeschichte* published in Munich.

e.g. in 1955 (April) by Pese, W. W.—Hitler und Italien 1920-
        1926.
    in 1957 (January) Rosen, E. R.—Mussolini und Deutschland
        1922-1923.
    in 1962 (April) by Robertson, E. M. Zur wiederbesetzung des
        Rheinlandes 1936.
    (Among the documents attached to this article is a hitherto
    unpublished piece of Hassell's Diary for 1936.)

See also Vaccarino, G. *Gli Scioperi del Marzo 1943 in Aspetti della Resistenza in Piemonte,* Milan, April 1950.
International Affairs, London, April 1957.
Watt, D. C.—An earlier model for the Pact of Steel.

Appendix

THE STEEL PACT

THE PUBLISHED TEXT[1]

German-Italian Pact of Steel, 22 May 1939

The following are the terms of the military pact between Germany and Italy signed in Berlin yesterday. The preamble runs:

" The German Reich Chancellor and His Majesty the King of Italy and Albania, Emperor of Ethiopia, consider that the moment has come when the close relations of friendship and affinity which exist between National-Socialist Germany and Fascist Italy should be strengthened through a solemn pact.

" Since a safe bridge for mutual help and support has been created by the common frontier between Germany and Italy, which has been fixed for all time, the two Governments acknowledge once again a policy which in its bases and objects has already previously been agreed upon by them and which has proved itself successful, both for the promoting of the interests of the two countries and also for the securing of peace in Europe.

" Closely bound together through internal relationships of ideologies and through comprehensive solidarity of interests, the German and Italian peoples have decided in the future also side by side and with united strength to stand up for the securing of their Lebensraum and for the maintenance of peace.

" In this way, which has been prescribed to them by history, Germany and Italy, in the midst of world unrest and disintegration, desire to devote themselves to the task of securing the foundations of European culture."

The pact consists of seven articles:

I

" The high contracting parties will remain permanently in contact with one another in order to agree on all questions affecting their own interests or the European situation as a whole.

I I

" Should the common interests of the high contracting parties be endangered through international events of any sort they will

[1] *Völkischer Beobachter,* 23rd May 1939.

immediately enter into consultations with one another in order to take measures to protect those interests.

III

" Should the security or other vital interests of one of the contracting parties be threatened from outside the other contracting party will afford the threatened party its full political and diplomatic support in order to remove this threat. If it should happen, against the wishes and hopes of the contracting parties, that one of them becomes involved in warlike complications with another Power or with other Powers the other contracting party will come to its aid as an ally and will support it with all its military forces on land, on sea, and in the air.

IV

" In order to secure in specific cases the rapid execution of the obligations undertaken in Article III, the Governments of the two contracting parties will further intensify their co-operation in the military sphere and in the sphere of war economics.

" Similarly the two Governments will also keep each other permanently informed about the measures necessary for the practical execution of the provisions of this pact.

" For the purposes laid down in paragraphs 1 and 2 of this article the two Governments will set up a Permanent Commission which will be subject to the direction of the two Foreign Ministers.

V

" The high contracting parties bind themselves in the case of a jointly waged war to conclude an armistice and peace only in full concord with one another.

VI

" The two contracting parties are conscious of the importance which must be attached to their joint relation with the Powers with which they are friends [Hungary, Japan, and Manchukuo]. They are determined in the future to maintain and develop such relations in common and in accordance with the unanimous interests by which they are united with those Powers.

VII

" The pact comes into force immediately upon being signed. The two contracting parties agree to fix the first period of its validity at ten years. They will come to an agreement about the prolongation of the validity of the pact in good time before this period has elapsed."

THE SECRET PROTOCOL[2]

" On signing the friendship and alliance pact agreement has been established by both parties on the following points:

" 1. The two Foreign Ministers will as quickly as possible come to an agreement on the organization, the seat, and the methods of work on the pact of the commissions on military questions and questions of war economy as stipulated in Article IV of the pact.

" 2. For the execution of Article IV, par. 2, the two Foreign Ministers will as quickly as possible arrange the necessary measures, guaranteeing a constant co-operation, conforming to the spirit and aims of the pact, in matters of the Press, the news service and propaganda. For this purpose in particular, each of the two Foreign Ministers will assign to the embassy of his country in the respective capital one or several especially experienced specialists, for constant discussion in direct close co-operation with the respective Ministry of Foreign Affairs, of the suitable steps to be taken in matters of the Press, the news service and propaganda for the promotion of the policy of the Axis, and as a counter measure against the policy of the enemy powers.
Berlin 22nd May 1939 XVII."

[2] *Nazi Conspiracy and Aggression,* vol. v, p. 453 (part of Document 2818-PS. as there translated; the remainder of this Document contains other matter not part of the Steel Pact, i.e. this is the complete text of the Secret Protocol).

PERSONS
(with biographical notes)

Attolico, [cont'd.]
Hitler's seizure of Prague 170;
and Steel Pact 179; meetings
with Ribbentrop July and
August 1939, 190-1; tells
Ribbentrop Italy requires supplies before hostilities 206;
and League of Neutrals 217;
delivers Mussolini's letter to
Hitler January 1940, 231;
anxiety of February 1940, 232;
recalled from Berlin 247-8

Badoglio, Marshal Pietro, Chief
of Italian General Staff to
December 1940, Italian Premier
after dismissal of Mussolini
July 1943; 80, 199; occupies
Addis Ababa 5 May 1936, 78;
sees Mussolini 26 May 1940,
254; at staff meeting 29 May
1940, 254-5; replaced by
Cavallero 287; appointed Prime
Minister 354-61.

Balbo, Italo, Fascist Quadrumvir
1922, Air-Marshal 1933,
Governor of Libya, killed June
1940; 171, 254.

Barrère, Camille, French Ambassador to Quirinal 1897-1924;
14

Barthou, Louis, French statesman,
murder of, 60, 61.

Bastianini, Giuseppe, Fascist Party
official and member of Fascist
Grand Council, Under-Secretary
for Foreign Affairs to 1936,
Ambassador in London 1939-
40, Governor of Dalmatia
1941, again Under-Secretary
for Foreign Affairs February
1943; 290, 340, 346, 348.

efforts to achieve a "political"
solution, 341, 344, tells Ribbentrop Italy cannot continue
war 347; at Klessheim, late
April 1943, 347, 350; at Feltre
19 July 1943, 353

Battisti, Cesare, Italian Socialist
leader in Trent, executed by
Austrian authorities, 19

Beetz, Frau, Nazi agent 374

Beneš, Edvard, Czechoslovak
Foreign Minister 1918-35,
President of Czechoslovak
Republic 1935-8 and again
1945-8; 26, 60, 113, 265;
condemned by Mussolini September 1938, 158

Bethlen, Count István, Hungarian
Premier, 47

Bismarck, Prince Otto von, grand-
son of "Iron Chancellor"
German Minister in Rome 276

Blomberg, Field-Marshal Werner
von, German Minister of War
1933-8; and Four-Power Pact,
50; impressed by Coronation
of George VI, 102; visit to
Naples, 103; at meeting 5
November 1937, 109, 113;
loses War Ministry 113-4

Blum, Léon, becomes French
Premier, 78, 80

Bocchini, Arturo, Fascist Police
Chief 1925-40, 95, 209

Bodenschatz, General Karl, personal adjutant to Göring; 187;
goes to Italy 2 May 1938,
135

Bohle, Ernst Wilhelm, Gauleiter
of the *Auslandsorganisation* of
N.S.D.A.P., then head of this
in German F.O.; 148, 183;

Foreign Minister, travels round
Europe, March-April 1941, 304

Maugeri, Admiral Franco, 363

Mayr, Captain Karl, engaged
Hitler's services for Reichswehr,
became Socialist and died in
concentration camp, 29

Mazzini, Giuseppe, 348, 349

Mazzolini, Count Serafino, Italian
Viceroy of Montenegro 1941,
Neo-Fascist Under-Secretary for
Foreign Affairs, 370, 386

Metaxas, General, Prime Minister
of Greece, 268, 269, 275

Mezzasoma, Fernando, Neo-
Fascist Minister of Propaganda,
367-8, 369

Mihailović, General Draža, Yugoslav Monarchist resistance
leader 323-4, 344

Miklas, Wilhelm, President of
Austria, 63, 64

Milch, Field-Marshal Erhard, 187,
333; visit to Italy December
1940, 287

Moeller van den Bruck, 23

Molotov, Viacheslav Mihailovich,
succeeded Litvinov as Russian
Foreign Minister 1939, 294,
304; visit to Berlin November
1940, 285, 292, dines with
Rosso 13 December 1940, 293

Montagna, General Renzo, 388

Morell, Professor Theodor,
Hitler's doctor, 336, 346, 368,
387, 390

Morgagni, Manlio, of Stefani
news agency, 103

Morreale, Eugenio, Italian Press
Attaché in Vienna, 56, 57,
64; recalled 84

Mussolini, Benito, passim, agitates

against Libyan War 1911, 17;
editor of *Avanti* 17; youth in
Switzerland 18; dispute with
C. Treves, goes to Trent 1909,
19; foundation of Fascist Party
20; and Monarchy and Church,
21; "March on Rome"
October 1922, 21; establishes
One-Party State, Fascist Grand
council, 22; play performed at
Weimar, 37; and South Tyrol,
30, 39; pays Heimwehr 41,
47; discussions with Starhemberg, 42-3; and German
politics 1932-3, 43-4; differences with Hitler over Jews,
44-5; and Austrian Socialists,
51; and Dollfuss, 51-2; first
meeting with Hitler June 1934,
52-3; and murder of Dollfuss,
56-7; decides on conquest of
Abyssinia 57-8; and France,
59; at Stresa, 61-2; and
Schuschnigg, 80-2, 100-2;
attacks Abyssinia 68; and
Hoare-Laval Plan, 71; and remilitarization of Rhineland, 74;
and intervention in Spain, 78;
surrenders over Austria, 79-81;
receives Hans Frank 23 September 1936, 87-8; speech at
Milan 1 November 1936, 92;
receives Göring 23 January
1937, 97-8; accepts invitation
to Germany 1937, 104; entertained at Munich, visits
Krupp's, 105; speech at *Maifeld*, 105-7; impressed by
Germany, 108; receives Ribbentrop October and November
1937, 112; plans Hitler's visit
to Italy, 125; acceptance of

Soleti, General Fernando, **Italian** police chief 363-4

Sorel, Georges, 18, 22, 397

Sperrle, General Hugo, 119

Spoleto, Aimone, Duke of, first cousin once removed to King Victor Emmanuel III, 320, 321

Stalin, Joseph Vissarionovich, 214, 262, 341. Hitler's views on, autumn 1939, 214; March 1940, 236, 238; winter 1940-1, 297, 305

Starace, Achille, Secretary-General of the Fascist Party 1928-39, then Chief of Staff of Fascist Militia, 55, 103, 199, 395n; accompanies Mussolini to Germany 1937, 104; on anti-Semitism 143

Starhemberg, Prince Ernst Rüdiger, Heimwehr leader in Austria 53, 56, 57, 64, 65, 68, 263.

And Hitler 34, 42; and Mussolini 42, 46-7, 49-50, 73, 77, 79; Mussolini decides against 79-81, 82

Stauffenberg, Count Claus Schenk von, 390, 392, 404

Stoyadinović, Milan, Yugoslav Prime Minister, 151, 152, 264; fall of February 1939, 169

Strasser, Gregor, Nazi leader murdered 30 June 1934, 31, 47; Mussolini's interest in, 43; dismissed by Hitler 44

Streicher, Julius, Nazi "specialist" in anti-Semitism, 31

Stresemann, Gustav, German Chancellor 1924, then Foreign Minister till his death in 1929, 31, 39

Suñer, Rámon Serrano, Spanish politician, brother-in-law to Franco, Minister of Interior 1938-40, Foreign Minister 1940-2, 279, 280, 283, 337, 372; talk with Ciano and Ribbentrop November 1940, 285

Suvich, Fulvio, Italian Under-Secretary for Foreign Affairs 1932-6, 51, 53, 74, 86

Tabouis, Mme Geneviève, French journalist 71n, 236

Tavs, Dr. Leopold, Austrian Nazi, 116

Tedaldi, Adolfo, member of Inter-Allied Delegation in Germany, 30

Teleki, Pál, Hungarian Prime Minister, visit to Germany April 1939, 174, 251; and National Socialism 264; suicide 303

Templewood, Viscount, see Hoare

Teucci, Col. Giuseppe, Italian Air Attaché in Berlin 1933-8 and 1939-43, 220, 377

Thomas, General Georg, chief of *Wirtschaftsrustungsamt* 306

Thomsen, Hans, German diplomat 139

Tito, Marshal, 325

Tolomei, Ettore, Fascist Senator, intransigent italianiser of South Tyrol 40

Tower, Reginald, British Consul-General in Munich 1906, 26, **46**

INDEX B

SUBJECTS AND PLACES